D0772124

BISON
BOOKS

Yupiit Qanruyutait

Transcriptions and translations from the Yup'ik
by *Alice Rearden* with *Marie Meade*

University of Nebraska Press

Yup'ik Words of Wisdom

New Edition
Edited by *Ann Fienup-Riordan*

With a new introduction by the editor and translator

Lincoln and London

This project is supported in part by a grant from
the Alaska Humanities Forum and the National
Endowment for the Humanities, a federal agency.

Library of Congress Control Number: 2017962957

Set in Minion and Cronos by Michael Travis.
Designed by Michael Travis.

Introduction to the New Bison Books Edition

We are happy to introduce this second printing of *Yupiit Qanruyutait*. The original text has not been altered. Although we have continued to learn new things over the last ten years, everything between the covers of this book has stood the test of time. Moreover, elders continue to share these *qanruyutet* (oral instructions). Sharing knowledge is a central part of what it means to be a Yup'ik person. One well-known adage declares, "Those who share are given another day," meaning long life. Conversely, they say don't be stingy with your knowledge or it will rot your mind. We should recognize the wisdom of this attitude toward knowledge—sharing *qanruyutet*, giving them away, enables us to keep them. Although this view is not unique to Yup'ik people, they stand out in the degree to which they have been willing to share what they know, both within their own communities and beyond.

In the last ten years, most of the elders quoted in this book have passed away, including Frank Andrew, John Phillip, Theresa Moses, and David Martin. As described in the original introduction that follows, these men and women were born into a world much like that of their forbearers. All were raised in small settlements, where men were educated in the communal men's house (*qasgi*) and women in homes where people spoke the Yup'ik language. This is no longer true for today's elders. Many received a formal education (either in a village classroom or boarding school away from home), speak English as well as Yup'ik, and have lived alongside non-Natives most of their lives. Although the Yup'ik region continues to retain many social patterns and traditions that have been lost in other parts of Alaska, times are changing. We are grateful to have had the opportunity to have known and worked with this generation of elders—men and women who have left a legacy of knowledge and wisdom for those who come after them.

As we had hoped, this book has been of great interest to Yup'ik readers. We have heard young people refer to it as their "Yup'ik Bible," which is high praise. It has also been of use to those who want to know not just what Yup'ik men and women have to say but how they say it and why they believe their words are so important to remember.

Over the last decade, the same team that produced *Yupiit Qanruyutait* has continued to work with elders in southwest Alaska and to share what we learn in bilingual books. These include three regional studies (Rearden and Fienup-Riordan 2011, 2013, 2014), two life-histories (Andrew 2008, Rearden and Fienup-Riordan 2016), and three topical volumes—one on *qanruyutet* pertaining to the environment (Fienup-Riordan and Rearden 2012), one on narratives surrounding bow-and-arrow warfare (Fienup-Riordan and Rearden 2016), and one on traditional tales (Fienup-Riordan and Rearden 2017). Like *Yupiit Qanruyutait*, all of our bilingual books are first-person accounts in which readers are invited to learn from the elders themselves. An introduction sets the stage, followed by statements and stories by individual elders shared at length.

In 2012 our bilingual book *Qaluyaarmiuni Nunamtenek Qanemciput/ Our Nelson Island Stories* won an American Book Award, a literary award recognizing both the eloquence of the elders' oratory and the power of the translations. Ann Fienup-Riordan's role as editor and what in many places is the new, challenging, and extremely important work of anthropology were well described in a review of the book appearing in *Arctic*, in which Elizabeth Marino wrote:

> This book likewise represents an operational paradigm of anthropological research that is new, though it has often received lip service: that is, a serious effort at the co-creation of knowledge by academic researchers and Alaska Native research participants and communities. The research methods, presentation of content, and authorship, and publication itself (by the Calista Elders Council), all speak to this partnership. In this way, this book provides an important example of how Alaska Native communities can take the lead in research projects and how academic researchers can act as important facilitators for these projects. A great compliment to Fienup-Riordan throughout this book is her ability to do what must have been significant amounts of work and then get out of the way.

This was our intent in *Yupiit Qanruyutait*, and we hope we have succeeded.

Ann Fienup-Riordan and Alice Rearden

References

Andrew, Frank. 2008. *Paitarkiutenka/My Legacy to You*. Transcriptions and translations by Alice Rearden and Marie Meade. Edited by Ann Fienup-Riordan. Seattle: University of Washington Press.

Fienup-Riordan, Ann, and Alice Rearden. 2012. *Ellavut/Our Yup'ik World and Weather: Continuity and Change on the Bering Sea Coast*. Seattle: University of Washington Press.

——. 2016. *Anguyiim Nalliini/Time of Warring: The History of Bow-and-Arrow Warfare in Southwest Alaska*. Fairbanks: University of Alaska Press and Alaska Native Language Center.

——. 2017. *Qanemcit Amllertut/Many Stories to Tell: Tales of Humans and Animals from Southwest Alaska*. Fairbanks: University of Alaska Press and Alaska Native Language Center.

Marino, Elizabeth. 2012. "Review of *Qaluyaarmiuni Nunamtenek Qanemciput/Our Nelson Island Stories: Meanings of Place on the Bering Sea Coast*." *Arctic* 65:239–40.

Rearden, Alice, and Ann Fienup-Riordan. 2011. *Qaluyaarmiuni Nunamtenek Qanemciput/Our Nelson Island Stories: Meanings of Place on the Bering Sea Coast*. Seattle: University of Washington Press.

——. 2013. *Erinaput Unguvaniartut/So Our Voices Will Live: Quinhagak History and Oral Traditions*. Fairbanks: Alaska Native Language Center.

——. 2014. *Nunamta Ellamta-llu Ayuqucia/What Our Land and World Are Like: Lower Yukon History and Oral Traditions*. Fairbanks: Alaska Native Language Center.

——. 2016. *Ciulirnerunak Yuuyaqunak/Do Not Live Without an Elder: The Subsistence Way of Life in Southwest Alaska*. Fairbanks: University of Alaska Press.

Contents

Acknowledgments

First and foremost we wish to thank the many Yup'ik men and women who shared these *qanruyutet* (words of wisdom) in hopes that they might benefit those who came after them. We are especially grateful to elders Frank Andrew, Theresa Moses, Paul and Martina John, John Phillip, David Martin, and Peter Jacobs, who attended small gatherings to work with younger Yup'ik men and women, answering their questions concerning *nutemllaat* (traditional ways). These younger "EITS" ("Elders in Training") also deserve recognition for their thoughtful questions and good listening, which encouraged elders to share so much. They include Noah Andrew, Freda Jimmie, Mark John, Elsie Mather, Marie Meade, Dennis Sheldon, Sophie Shield, Lucy Sparck, and Walter Therchik.

The following pages are based on conversations during conventions and gatherings organized by the Calista Elders Council (CEC), with offices in Bethel and Anchorage. Convention and gathering topics were chosen by the CEC board of elders, including Nick Andrew, Winifred Beans, Irvin Brink, Peter Jacobs, Paul John, Paul Kiunya, Joseph Lomack, and John Phillip, with help from their director, Mark John. Their choices were instrumental, not academic. They focused on what they believed younger Yupiit today need to know to survive, both physically and mentally.

Even with the elders' strong desire to be heard, neither their public conversations nor the conversations' publication in written form would have been possible without the ongoing support the CEC received from the National Science Foundation's Office of Polar Programs (Grant Number 9909945), the Administration for Native Americans, the Alaska Humanities Forum, Calista Corporation, and the Rasmuson Foundation.

While we are extremely grateful for their support, we acknowledge that any opinions and recommendations expressed here are ours and do not necessarily reflect the views of these organizations.

In transcription and translation of the words shared during these conventions and gatherings, Alice had the able assistance of Veronica Kaganak, Freda Jimmie, and Monica Sheldon. The editing and polishing of the finished translations was done in collaboration with our friend and associate Marie Meade, a translator with twenty years of experience. Her dedication to accuracy and clarity shine through these pages. We are also grateful to Elsie Mather for reading earlier drafts and providing invaluable corrections and suggestions. The clarity of the English text has benefited from the sharp eyes and light touch of University of Nebraska Press freelance editor Sarah Nestor. Finally, special thanks to Matt O'Leary for locating place-names and to Patrick Jankanish for preparing the map.

We are also deeply indebted to the Smithsonian National Museum of the American Indian (NMAI) in Washington DC for permission to publish as illustrations the wonderful photographs taken by dental surgeon Dr. Leuman M. Waugh during his travels in southwest Alaska in 1935 and 1937. The Waugh collection, including more than 1,100 historical images from Alaska and some 1,500 images from Canada, was first brought to our attention by Igor Krupnik of the National Museum of Natural History Arctic Studies Center. He and his colleague Stephen Loring, along with NMAI staff members Donna Rose, Lou Stancari, and Lars Krutak, have been involved in researching and cataloging the Waugh collection since 2001. During a research visit to the museum's research branch in 2002, NMAI photo archivist Donna Rose provided CEC staff and elders with color copies of the 300 tinted lantern slides Waugh made during three trips to southwest Alaska. The NMAI also generously provided the CEC with a CD of the photos, which we subsequently shared with the local newspaper, *The Tundra Drums,* so that people throughout the region could enjoy these vivid images of life along the Kuskokwim River and lower Bering Sea coast. Many called the CEC office, identifying the elders pictured and requesting copies of the unique photos of their parents and grandparents. These wonderful images are the first color photographs known for the region. Moreover, they depict years when the majority of elders quoted in these pages were growing up themselves, listening to their own elders. Although not in need of dental work, Frank Andrew vividly remembers visiting Waugh's tent camp on the lower Kuskokwim when he was a teenager.

Finally, we wish to thank our parents and spouses for supporting us in our work and our children, who are the reason it is so important these *qanruyutet* not be forgotten.

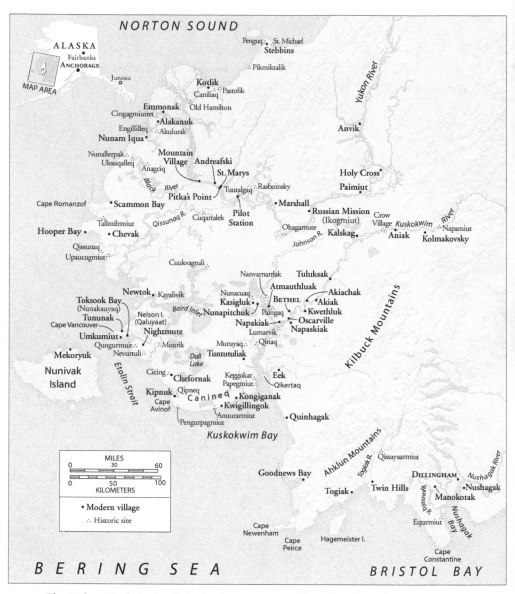

The Yukon-Kuskokwim Delta Region, 2004. Patrick Jankanish and Matt O'Leary.

Introduction

Qanruyutet: Words of Wisdom

The following pages comprise the bilingual companion to *Wise Words of the Yup'ik People: We Talk to You because We Love You. Yup'ik Words of Wisdom: Yupiit Qanruyutait* is not a supplement to that book—it is an equal partner. As in a good marriage, the two books work together in different ways toward a common goal, providing a generation divorced from Yup'ik oral tradition with a deeper understanding of the life lessons that tradition continues to provide. *Wise Words* weaves together hundreds of statements by dozens of Yup'ik men and women from throughout southwestern Alaska on the values that guide human relationships, both past and present. *Yup'ik Words of Wisdom* also presents different elders' personal perspectives on the moral underpinnings of Yup'ik social relations. Unlike *Wise Words,* however, this book highlights the words of expert orators and focuses on key conversations that took place among elders and younger community members in the process of documenting their view of the world.

Wise Words includes statements made by elders and younger Yup'ik men and women during gatherings large and small between 1995 and 2002. These ranged in size from annual conferences of several hundred held in small villages, to meetings in Bethel of one to two dozen participants, to still smaller get-togethers involving three to six people in Bethel or Anchorage. All were sponsored by the Calista Elders Council (CEC), representing the thirteen hundred Yup'ik men and women sixty-five years of age and older. Its board of elders initiated the gatherings and chose the topics to be discussed. *Wise Words* also includes recordings I

made with Paul John in 1991 and 1994, conversations Marie Meade and
I had with elders in 1993 and 1994 in preparation for the Yup'ik mask exhibit, *Agayuliyararput,* and information shared during a teacher-training
workshop sponsored by the Lower Kuskokwim School District in June
1995.

Yup'ik Words of Wisdom focuses on a handful of expert orators, especially Frank Andrew from Kwigillingok, Nelson Island elders Paul John
and Theresa Moses, and David Martin of Kipnuk. All four were raised in
isolated coastal communities where Western influence was slow to arrive and were educated in traditional *qanruyutet* much like their parents
and grandparents before them. More important, all are willing and able
to share that knowledge, including detailed explanations of the principles
underlying their views of how the world works.

Frank Andrew (Miisaq) was born in Kwigillingok in February 1917.
His father was originally from Qinaq and his mother from Kwigillingok.
The family moved to fish camp on the Kuskokwim every June and July,
where they lived near relatives in Tuntutuliak. Frank recalled that from
late summer to freeze-up in November they were constantly moving and
fishing until they returned to Kwigillingok for the winter. There Frank
spent many hours in the *qasgi* (communal men's house) listening to his
father and other village elders, and he has never forgotten what he
learned. Frank married in the 1940s, and together he and his wife raised
six children, all of whom live in Kwigillingok with families of their own.

Paul John (Kangrilnguq) was born in Cevv'arneq, the original site of
the modern village of Chefornak, fifteen miles south of Qaluyaat (Nelson
Island) in 1928. The much-loved only child of John Kungurkaq and Anna
Angayiq, Paul lived with his mother and aunts in a sod house until age
five. Later he joined his father and uncles in the *qasgi,* where he spent
countless hours listening to their stories and advice. Schools had not yet
been established in most coastal communities, and the first resident mis-
sionary settled on Nelson Island after Paul was born. Paul recalled:

When I became aware, people I saw survived only through hunting and
gathering. And I personally never ate Kass'aq [non-Native] food besides
a little bit of flour and sugar. . . . That was the way I saw it, even though
I am not very old. These Kass'at didn't come to the coast right away. A

school was not built in my village for many years. That is why I saw that way of life, the way our ancestors lived. . . . And when I was seven years old, the priest [Father Deschout] finally arrived. I became aware of my surroundings before the ways of the authentic Yup'ik people changed.

Paul grew to manhood following the seasonal round of his forebears, moving between spring and fall camping places and their permanent winter settlement in Chefornak. In April 1953 he married Martina Usugan and moved to Nightmute to live with her family. The young couple continued to move seasonally until 1960, when they settled in Nightmute so that their eldest son, Mark, could attend the new school.

In 1964 Paul led a number of families to found the village of Toksook Bay to avoid the arduous annual move between the winter village of Nightmute and spring camp at Umkumiut. In this and many other endeavors Paul has been a leader among his people, both locally and regionally, and to this day he is active on numerous corporation boards and commissions. He has also been a leader in the sharing and documenting of traditional knowledge, convinced that Yup'ik young people will be better prepared for the future if they understand their past.

Theresa Moses (Ilanaq) was born in 1926 and, like Paul, was raised in Cevv'arneq. She moved to Nightmute as a young woman after her father arranged for her to marry Teddy Moses. Unlike Paul, however, Theresa lost her mother, who died when she was young. She describes the loneliness she felt and how hard she and her sister worked to care for their younger siblings and teach themselves the skills they would need in their adult lives. Teddy Moses's family was large and prosperous, including three capable sons and two daughters, and Theresa took her place among them as a daughter-in-law without the support of immediate family. She and her husband lived together until his death in the 1980s, raising six children together. Her moving descriptions of the personal restraint and compassion that marriage, parenting, and family life required are based on personal experience.

David Martin (Negaryaq) was born in Kipnuk in 1913. Like Theresa, he was orphaned at a young age and had a difficult childhood. In gatherings he eloquently described how his desire to better himself caused him to listen well and remember the life lessons elders shared with him when he was young — lessons that he continues to share with young people today. When it came time for David to marry, he chose an orphan like himself, and together they raised seven children.

In our work with these men and women over the years, two extended conversations stand out, providing the heart and soul of this book. First are Frank Andrew's conversations with Alice Rearden and me in September and June 2000 and in October 2002, when Frank and his family spent close to a month in Anchorage while his wife received medical treatment. Frank, his son Noah, Alice, and I met day after day, talking and learning together. We are deeply indebted to Frank's patient and eloquent answers to our endless questions.

The second set of conversations took place in Bethel in April and November 2001, when Paul John, David Martin, and Theresa Moses attended small CEC gatherings during which Alice Rearden, Marie Meade, other younger Yup'ik men and women, and I listened to their explanations of key concepts, including *tuqluutet* (relational terms), parenting skills, and the important roles and responsibilities of marriage.

Elders addressed a variety of topics during their gatherings, including traditional child-rearing practices, methods of discipline, and family values. The common threads in this rich tapestry were the *qanruyutet* (words of wisdom, teachings, or oral instructions, from *qaner-*, "to speak") that surrounded these activities. Elders explained each topic with reference to these "rules for right living," which they referred to in a variety of ways, including: *ayuqucirtuutet* (instructions and directions, from *ayuquciq*, "way of being"); *qaneryarat* (words of advice, sayings, literally, "that which is spoken"); *aarcirtuutet* (warnings); *inerquutet* (admonishments or prohibitions, from *inerqur-*, "to admonish, to tell or warn not to do something"); *alerquutet* (laws or instructions, prescriptions, from *alerqur-*, "to tell to do something, to advise, to regulate"); *elucirtuutet* (directions or instructions, from *elucirtur-*, "to give direction, to instruct"); *piciryarat* (manners, customs, traditions); *pisqumatet* (sayings, ways of doing things, from *pi-*, "to say, to do"); and *eyagyarat* (traditional abstinence practices). These concepts are related but not interchangeable, and the term used depends both on the speaker and the topic addressed. Elders used *qanruyun* or *qanruyutet* (word or words of wisdom) most often when speaking of the instructions that they had learned as children and that continue to guide their lives today.

During the last three years all of these discussions have been transcribed and translated by CEC staff, supported by a grant from the National Science Foundation. Alice Rearden did the lion's share of the work, with the able assistance of Freda Jimmie, Veronica Kaganak, and Monica Sheldon. I also work with CEC as part of their National Science Foundation project to document traditional knowledge, and on a daily basis Alice Rearden and I exchange ideas on what we have learned and questions that still need answering. In 2002 I used Alice's transcripts as the basis for *Wise Words*, incorporating main conference topics with additional information previously recorded by my friend and colleague Marie Meade. I edited and organized the transcribed texts, adding my observations about what elders meant by what they said and about how their discussions involve larger questions in anthropology where I thought it would aid understanding. Primarily, I tried to portray these Yup'ik elders' advice about what younger Yup'ik men and women should know and why they should know it.

While working on *Wise Words*, I kept a running file in Yup'ik and English of all statements quoted from the original transcripts.[1] I knew that the long Yup'ik passages would need to be shortened to make them more accessible to English readers, and I wanted to retain a complete, uncut record of the most important points elders had made. I made initial selections from the transcripts, creating a bilingual text mirroring the organization of *Wise Words*. Alice then reviewed these selections line by line with Marie to insure accuracy and eloquence in the final translations. Discussions were long and fruitful, and without Marie's expertise and Alice's dedication the elders' wisdom would still be hidden from view. The result of these efforts is a bilingual book of first-person accounts by Yup'ik elders instead of anthropological analysis. Beyond this introduction, readers will learn what they learn from the elders themselves.

Interested readers can consult *Wise Words* for further explanation. The order of elders' statements as well as the chapters in the two books parallel one another. The wording of individual translations, however, varies in many cases. The translations in *Wise Words* reflect Alice's more literal style, with clauses closely following Yup'ik word order. Working together to refine translations for this book, Marie and Alice chose a freer translation style, with word order more nearly approximating written English. Neither style is more correct than the other, and both are expertly done.

In fact the differences are instructive, underlining the complexities of the apparently transparent translation process discussed in detail below.

Chapter 1 introduces traditional Yup'ik oral instruction and what it was expected to communicate — the moral code surrounding interpersonal relations. Elders admonished young people to adhere to the *qanruyutet* (words of wisdom) rather than invite disaster by "following their own minds." John Phillip (March 2000:16) of Kongiganak told them, "Do not live without guides." Paul Kiunya (November 2000:193) of Kipnuk added: "Refrain from acting on your thoughts and desires, because Ellam Yua [the Person of the Universe] is watching." These *qanruyutet* were numerous and required years to fully understand. Some have noted that learning among arctic peoples was primarily through observation and practice, with oral instruction restricted to the transmission of a moral code. This moral code, however, was both complicated and nuanced. Only constant verbal instruction and careful listening enabled one generation to pass values on to another. As contexts for such conversations diminish, elders rightly fear that their view of the world will die with them.

Chapter 2 addresses what it means to be a Yup'ik person, including how people experience the world around them; how they learn, think, and feel; and the subsequent requirement to treat both human and non-human others with compassion and restraint. Elders describe a view of the world in which thought and feeling are closely tied. Both must be subordinated to *qanruyutet* that a person learns while young and comes to value while living life.

Chapter 3 explores the relatively small number of memorable adages elders used to communicate the basic tenets of Yup'ik moral instruction. In their daily acts of speaking, elders taught young people how to use their body as a whole organ to perceive knowledge. They "thingafied" knowledge for their young listeners, presenting it as something that one could put in one's pocket, take out, shake, even steal for use later in life. Elders used formal adages and metaphors — boys are like puppies, women are death — to objectify complex and essential life lessons.

Chapter 4 describes the Yup'ik understanding of how the fundamental relationship of parents and children shaped lives. Children differed from their parents in both their ignorance of the rules and their sponge-like ability to learn. Their relationship was structured to take advantage of children's strength — memory — to teach them the rules they needed to know to survive. Parents were advised to talk to children even before they were born, giving them instruction in a loving way. This potent combination, words and love, ideally permeated Yup'ik education. Parents admonished children to carefully control their senses, restricting food intake, sleep, movement, even their breathing when passing a member of the opposite sex. Children were not expected to understand these lessons right away but were told that later in life, when they experienced what had been described, they would remember what they had heard and it would guide their actions.

Chapters 5 and 6 detail the moral code guiding interpersonal relations between men and women, extended family members, one's community, and strangers. Elders described the essential characteristics and actions of a "real person" in the contexts of home, community, surrounding villages, and the world at large. Compassion and restraint continue to be important values in all these personal interactions.

Chapter 7 includes discussions of the system of *tuqluutet* (relational terms) used to refer to and address one's relatives. A detailed list of these terms appears at the end of the book, along with a glossary of other essential Yup'ik terms used in the English text.

Chapter 8 discusses traditional restrictions following major life events. Elders rarely failed to mention this special class of rules, known collectively as *eyagyarat*, when describing the continued relevance of *qanruyutet*. *Eyagyarat* are often discussed separately in reference to such diverse topics as the relationship between men and women, illness and wellness, and death and dying. Elders understand these abstinence practices as connected by the common purpose of keeping people in a vulnerable condition safe in a knowing and responsive world.

Chapter 8 of *Wise Words*, "Yup'ik Views of Self and Other," describes the contemporary relevance of past practices, based on elders' belief in the essential unity of humankind and respect for cultural difference. Although CEC gatherings contributed to this discussion, the chapter draws heavily on conversations between Paul John and me, published in *Stories for Future Generations* (Shield and Fienup-Riordan 2003) and consequently omitted from this volume. Extended quotations from Chapters 9 and 11 of *Wise Words* are also omitted here, as elders' most salient observations on these topics have been folded into earlier chapters.

Elders' statements are not casual observations, but self-conscious and carefully crafted public presentations. Their words have been recorded, translated, edited, and organized for a larger audience, with all the attendant pitfalls. Yet reaching out to others was what motivated the elders to share words and feelings, so that younger generations would better understand their lives and live more thoughtful lives themselves.

As a companion to *Wise Words* this book makes an essential point: We base what we know on the elders' narratives. The bilingual presentation allows for long, lightly edited passages from the original transcripts, providing a safe harbor for the information jettisoned in the interests of communication to a wider audience. Certainly the extended accounts will interest Yup'ik readers, especially younger men and women who have never heard these stories. Like *Wise Words,* however, the book also serves a larger audience, including linguists, folklorists, anthropologists, historians, and others interested in Native American oral tradition. *Yup'ik Words of Wisdom* is for those who want not only to know what the elders have to say, but also how they say it.

Creating a bilingual companion for *Wise Words* also provides an opportunity to confront the texts outside an interpretative framework. I have heard many Yup'ik men and women discuss the question of how much interpretation should be included with the translations. All agree that understanding the context of a story is essential to grasping its meaning and that many non-Native readers as well as younger Native community members required some background information to fully appreciate the texts. Many of my Yup'ik colleagues, however, are reluctant to designate the "moral" of a story. When asked if there were questions that were appropriate in a storytelling context, many said no, stories were "just told" and asking questions destroyed them. We lose something when stories are explained, they reminded me. Successive hearings or readings reveal different meanings, depending on the experience the listener brings to them. This depth of meaning, many point out, is the mark of great literature worldwide. Yup'ik scholar Elsie Mather compared analysis of oral literature to "opening up stories with a can opener," causing listeners to lose their sense of awe. Another compared analysis to rotten meat, warning us, "Be very careful of analysis, as it can poison you." While agreeing that some contextualization is important for readers unfamiliar with Native oral literature, Elsie and others feel strongly that much more is lost than gained by the scholarly tendency to overanalyze and explain.

Nor are titles a traditional feature of Yup'ik oral literature, although narrators sometimes refer to a story according to the action that takes place. In written form we have used key phrases as titles for the different texts. These key phrases are followed by the speaker's name and the gathering or interview date and transcript page number, preceded by a number in parenthesis corresponding with the abbreviated passage in *Wise Words*. A list of contributors at the beginning of the book includes the elders' dates and places of birth as well as their current residences.

Why Elders Spoke

Julie Cruikshank points out in her *Social Life of Stories* that even after we understand what a story says, we will understand very little about it if we do not know why it was told.[2] The elders in this book spoke for a variety of reasons. Most, like Paul John and Frank Andrew, believe firmly that Native young people need to understand the rules to guide their future lives. Paul John compares the healing quality of such "speaking out" to medicine: "This usual method of speaking, the method of giving guidance to someone, apparently is like medicine which can heal a person's body and mind. . . . This method of giving advice and guidance is unquestionably the right way."[3] Paul John and others know that writing their words, both in Yup'ik and in English, extends their reach. They recognize that Native young people, especially, are hungry for their history, and they are concerned that they be fed.

Richard and Nora Dauenhauer note that no matter how careful, translation transforms oral text to stone.[4] Yet once written down, storytelling continues. In one gathering Paul John insisted that we record, transcribe, and translate what he said so it would be remembered. He sees himself as an educator, as do many elders. Talking into a tape recorder is just one of many ways he exercises that role. Paul John, Frank Andrew, and other elders emphasized the strength of their language; even in an English-first world, its power must still be retained. This book is an expression of Yup'ik pride, a gift to both Native and non-Native readers. Their ancestors lived according to these oral instructions, their elders explained them, and the book makes these gifts available to readers interested in their uniquely Yup'ik form.

When elders share words with listeners and readers, these are undeniable acts of compassion. Elsie Mather noted that she grew up listening to stories that she really did not understand. The value of the stories, she said, was in hearing them. The fact that her parents and other village elders cared enough to tell her stories was more important than any particular moral or meaning the story might possess. In sharing their words, both the elders and their translators insist that we not cease listening to wise words that can allow us to be real people. Ironically, sharing the *qanruyutet*, giving them away, enables us to keep them. This has always been true of oral traditions, and in *Yup'ik Words of Wisdom* both elders and translators see the sharing continuing in new ways.

Elders ask that we present what they have taught with dignity and respect, as accurately as we can, so that their words can not only be passed on but seen on a level with other great literary traditions. The elders' statements are not mere texts but loving and healing acts. The potency of such acts recalls the power of words in Yup'ik oral tradition, where words have the ability to constitute that which they signify. The elders' words have come across language and time, from oral to written form, from people living off the land to those living in urban centers. The fact that such meanings survive is testament to their power.

This collection offers readers a gesture of compassion and respect. Both elders and translators are providing entertainment, advice, and knowledge, some also seeking to correct false images of Native peoples as those without literature. Among the Yupiit, elders correct only those whom they care about, giving them advice that they hope will help them later in life. Readers should take this as a high compliment and cherish the gift they have been given. If they read these pages, someday, as they experience life, these wise words may come into their minds, guiding them and allowing them to make wise choices and live well.

Southwestern Alaska

Alaska's Yukon-Kuskokwim and Nushagak region, a lowland delta the size of Kansas, is the traditional homeland of the Yup'ik Eskimos. The region's current population of more than thirty thousand (the largest Native population in Alaska) lives scattered in seventy villages, ranging between two hundred and one thousand persons each, with larger regional centers in Bethel and Dillingham. Today this huge region is crosscut by historical and administrative differences, including two dialect groups, three major Christian denominations, six school districts, two census areas, and three regional Native corporations.

The Bering Sea coast supports abundant resources, including sea and land mammals, waterfowl, and fish. Beginning in March or early April, men hunt for bearded seals, spotted seals, ringed seals, and walrus from the shore-fast ice. By May geese and ducks crowd the flyways, returning to their summer nesting grounds. In June families move to fish camps, where men set nets for herring, salmon, and flounder that women dry for winter use. Children fill baskets with herring eggs laden with kelp and the tiny capelin that wash up during high tides. Women gather greens close to home or camp for days at a time with their families on the tundra to gather eggs and berries. Fishing and trapping continue into the late fall until people once again return to their winter villages, where harvesting activities are more circumscribed. Prehistorically this abundance supported the development and spread of Inuit culture, and some scholars have called the Bering Sea coast the "cradle of Eskimo civilization."

Although it is rich in subsistence resources, the lack of commercial resources — whales, furbearers, mineral deposits — historically made the region less attractive to a resident non-Native population than other parts of Alaska. The most dramatic result of initial contact in the 1840s was the rapid decline of the Native population due to epidemic diseases. The first non-Natives to settle in significant numbers were Christian missionaries in the late 1800s. Elders living in the region today were born into a world very much like that of their forebears, especially seen in their reliance on the harvest of fish and game. All were raised in small settlements residentially divided between a communal men's house (*qasgi*) and separate sod houses for women and children — places where people spoke the Yup'ik language and engaged in traditional harvesting activities.

Rapid change has since come to coastal communities. Social reforms of the 1960s, passage of the Alaska Native Claims Settlement Act (ANCSA) in 1971, and the Alaska oil boom of the 1980s supported the establishment of modern villages, each with its own high school, corporation store, daily air service to the regional center of Bethel, electricity, television and telephone service, and, in some cases, running water. Despite these changes, both late contact and lack of commercial resources have meant that the Yup'ik region has retained many social patterns that have been lost in other parts of Alaska, and many traditions — especially dancing and elaborate community gift giving — remain living links to the past.

The Yup'ik language is the second most commonly spoken Native language in the United States and the third most common in North America north of Mexico, following Navajo and Inuktitut. More than half the Native residents of southwestern Alaska speak Yup'ik as their first language. Yup'ik is the first language of everyone from the eldest to the youngest in a quarter of the villages. This continued cultural and linguistic vitality has helped to place the Yupiit among the most traditional Native American groups, actively working both to retain the best of their past and to carry values and traditions forward into the future.

Notes

1. This is the third bilingual companion volume I have assembled in this manner. The first, *Agayuliyararput: Kegginagut, Kangiit-llu (Our Way of Making Prayer: Yup'ik Masks and the Stories They Tell)* (Meade and Fienup-Riordan 1996), accompanied the Yup'ik mask exhibit catalog, *The Living Tradition of Yup'ik Masks: Agayuliyararput (Our Way of Making Prayer* (Fienup-Riordan 1996). The second, *Ciuliamta Akluit: Things of Our Ancestors* (Meade and Fienup-Riordan 2005) accompanies *Yup'ik Elders at the Ethnologisches Museum Berlin: Fieldwork Turned on Its Head* (Fienup-Riordan 2005).
2. Cruikshank 1995:71.
3. Shield and Fienup-Riordan 2003:325.
4. Dauenhauer and Dauenhauer 1999.

Yup'ik Transcription and Translation

The Yup'ik people of southwestern Alaska speak the Central Alaskan Yup'ik language, as distinguished from the Inuit/Iñupiaq language of the Arctic coast of northern Alaska, Canada, Labrador, and Greenland. Although structurally similar, Inuit/Iñupiaq and Yupik are not mutually intelligible. In the nineteenth century the Central Alaskan Yup'ik language was one of five Yupik languages. The other four of historic times were three Siberian Yupik languages and Pacific Yup'ik (Alutiiq), which was spoken around Prince William Sound, the tip of the Kenai Peninsula, Kodiak Island, and part of the Alaska Peninsula. These two language groups — Inuit/Iñupiaq and Yupik — constitute the Eskimo branch of the Eskimo-Aleut family of languages.[1]

The Central Yup'ik language, of which there are four dialects (Norton Sound, Hooper Bay / Chevak, Nunivak, and General Central Yup'ik), is spoken by Yup'ik people living on the Bering Sea coast from Norton Sound to the Alaska Peninsula as well as along the Yukon, Kuskokwim, and Nushagak rivers. Most elders cited in this book speak General Central Yup'ik, while the remainder speak the Cup'ig dialects of Chevak, Hooper Bay, and Nunivak Island. All four dialects of the Central Yup'ik language are mutually intelligible with some phonological and vocabulary differences.[2]

The Central Yup'ik language remained unwritten until the end of the nineteenth century, when both missionaries and Native converts began developing a variety of orthographies. The orthography used consistently throughout this book is the standard one developed by linguists in the 1960s and detailed in *Yup'ik Eskimo Grammar* by Irene Reed, Osahito

Miyaoka, Steven Jacobson, Pascal Afcan, and Michael Krauss; *Yup'ik Eskimo Orthography* by Osahito Miyaoka and Elsie Mather; and *A Practical Grammar of the Central Yup'ik Eskimo Language* by Steven Jacobson.

The standard orthography for Central Yup'ik represents the language with letters and letter combinations, each corresponding to a distinct sound. The Yup'ik alphabet consists of: vowels a, e, i, u; stop consonants p, t, c, k, q; fricatives v, l, s, g, r; vv, ll, ss, gg, rr; y, w, ug, ur; and nasals m, n, ng. Included in the standard orthography are three symbols: apostrophe ('), hyphen (-), and ligature or arch connecting two letters (uĝ). The standard orthography never represents the same sound with different spellings, nor is the same spelling ever pronounced in two different ways.

The following comparison in the new and old writing system will help those familiar with the old system understand the new one. The example is a Bible translation of John 3:16-21 by the first Yup'ik converts and early Moravian missionaries taken from *Kanerearakgtar* (The New Testament, literally, "the wonderful instructions"):

> 16Toiten Agaiutim tlamiut kinikkapigtshamíke kēngan Kitunrani tsikiutika, kina imna itlēnun ukfalra tamaskifkinako taugam nangiyuílingoramik unguvankriskluko. 17Toi Agaiutim Kitunrak kanerstāriyagtorstinrita tlamiunik, taugam anertōmaskluke itlēkun. 18Kina imna itlēnun ukfakuni kanerstarumangaitok, kinadlo itlēnun ukfanrílkune kanerstarumauk áka, toi Aagaiutim kēngan Kituranun ukfánrilan. 19Whanewhadlo una kanerstaarun, toi tankik nunamun tutngeran yut tanigak kinkinruamigto tankigeme, tshaliating ashilata. 20Ashilingortulrim tamarame nasivaganayukluke. 21Taugam pitsiuulramik atulrim tankik utlālára tshaliane nasivaganalúke toi Agaiutim piskute atuamigtgo.

Here is the same passage written in the new orthography:

> 16Tuaten Agayutem ellamiut kenkaqapigcamiki kiingan Qetunrani cikiutekaa kina imna elliinun ukvelria tamaasqevkenaku taũgaam nangyuilngurmek unguvangqerresqelluku. 17Tua-i Agayutem Qetunraq qanercetaariyarturcetenritaa ellamiunek, taũgaam anirtuumasqelluki elliikun. 18Kina imna elliinun ukvequni qanercetaarumangaituq, kina-llu elliinun ukvenrilkuni qanercetaarumauq ak'a, tua-i Agayutem kiingan Qetunraanun ukvenrilan. 19Waniwa-llu una qanercetaarun tua-i tanqik nunamun tut'engraan yuut tan'geq kenkenruamegteggu tanqigmi caliateng assiilata. 20Assiilngurtulriim tamarmi tanqik uumik'laraa ullag-

yugpek'naku-llu caliani nasvagnayukluku. 21Taũgaam piciulriamek atul-
riim tanqik ullallaraa caliani nasvagnaluku tua-i Agayutem pisqutii
atuamegteggu.

Translation

"Much of great importance is lost and added in translation," A. L. Becker
reminds us.[3] The truth of his words captures both this book's weaknesses
and its strengths. Each translated text is at once less than the original telling — devoid of the shapes and sounds of the speaker's voice — and more.
Through the double process of translation from Yup'ik to English and
from oral to written form, readers gain access to a body of Yup'ik literature just as compelling as the classics of Western and Eastern civilization.

Linguist Gregory Shreve aptly describes the paradox of translation.
Languages themselves can never be translated, only the "sociocultural
containers of social meaning and communicative value" called texts. He
concludes:

> One could claim that all of translation is patently impossible, but be-
> cause we so much desire to read, in our own language, what others have
> written in theirs, about their experiences, . . . we do it anyway. We must
> accept translation's inherent faults, or rather faulting . . . in the geologi-
> cal sense. The translation . . . slips away from the source along the fault
> line of sociocultural difference. . . . The translation is like the Phoenix, it
> rises from the ashes of the old text, its parent, but it is a new being, alive
> in its own right, alive in its own writing.[4]

In their roles as translators, Alice Rearden and Marie Meade confronted
the enormous challenges Becker, Shreve, and others describe, and they
offer distinctive strategies for bridging differences between Yup'ik and
English without erasing them. Their goal throughout has been a "natural-
sounding," free translation, as opposed to either literal translation (at one
extreme) or paraphrasing (at the other). Paraphrasing may communicate some of the sense of the original, but such interpretive translations
modify the original to the point that the speaker's voice is either erased
or transformed. Literal, word-for-word translation is also inadequate. At
best it is awkward, and at worst it makes no sense. Alice's and Marie's
translations employ a free style in which the elders' choice of words is

respected, while word order and sentence structure are modified where necessary to communicate their original meaning.

Like all Eskimo languages, Central Yup'ik is a "suffixing language" made up of noun and verb bases to which one or more postbases and a final ending are added to denote such features as number, case, person, and position. For example, the word *Yup'ik* is derived from the noun base *yug-* (person), to which the postbase *-pik* (real or genuine) has been added, literally, "a real person." Similarly, the word *yua*, "its/his/her person" is the same noun base *yug-* with the third-person possessive ending.

Because of the Yup'ik language's reliance on the process of suffixing in the creation of words, Yup'ik and English often appear as mirror images of each other. For example, the English phrase "my little boat" would be written *angyacuarqa*, literally, "boat little my" from *angyaq* boat, plus *-cuar(ar)* small, plus *-qa* first-person possessive. The English sentence "I want to make him a big box" would translate *"Yaassiigpaliyugaqa,"* from *yaassiik* box, plus *-pag-* big, *-li-* make, *-yug-* want, *-aqa* I-to-him, literally, "Box big make want I-to-him." Translation is thus a continuous process of reordering.

As these examples indicate, Yup'ik words generally show a clear division between bases, postbases, and endings, which are "glued" rather than "fused" together, making them easy to identify. Yup'ik is also generally characterized by a one-to-one correspondence between the meaning and the sound shape of a base or postbase, albeit with regular sound changes. As a result, linguists designate Yup'ik an *agglutinative* language, a term derived from a word meaning "to glue."[5]

Several grammatical features make for potential problems in the translation of the elders' statements. First, relatively free word order characterizes the Yup'ik language. For example, the meaning of the English sentence "The man lost the dog" can only be conveyed by placing the words *man, lost,* and *dog* in this order. A Yup'ik speaker, however, can arrange the three words *angutem* (man), *tamallrua* (s/he lost it), and *qimugta* (dog) in any of six possible word orders with no significant change in meaning. Nevertheless, word order is not totally irrelevant to interpreting Yup'ik sentences; it may be the sole key to appropriate interpretation where the ending alone would give two different interpretations. For example, the sentence *Arnam atra nallua* (literally, "woman//his/her name//s/he not knowing it") can mean either "The woman does not know his name" or

"He does not know the woman's name." The same three words in a different word order, however, are less ambiguous. *Arnam nallua atra* is commonly taken to mean "The woman does not know his name." Contrasted with languages that have a freer word order, the relative position of postbases inside Yup'ik words is very rigid. Consequently, a word may have internally syntactic problems like those a sentence has in other languages.

In their translations Alice and Marie consistently rendered accounts according to English word order. Like many contemporary translators, they aimed for a fluid English translation that communicates both the literal meaning of the words and the dynamic flow of the original narrative. Although a more convoluted translation might be closer to the Yup'ik original, they strove for natural-sounding translations accessible to contemporary English readers. Other "exuberances" in the Yup'ik originals, however, have been carefully retained. For example, redundancies and repetitions were commonly edited out of translated texts in the past, while Alice and Marie have retained them as integral to both the structure and the meaning of elders' accounts. Use of repetition gives these texts a denser texture than that in typical English phrasings.

Elders included frequent repetitions in their oratory. They also often framed a statement with repeated phrases to mark its beginning and ending and to set it apart. Structured repetitions and framing are characteristic features of Yup'ik narrative and vital to its structural integrity. To smooth them over or omit them would impoverish the translations. Repetition, common to all oral literature, was used to enhance memory as well as to add emphasis and depth. This was important as, until recently, the minds of elders were the stories' sole repositories. As Paul John reminded his listeners, "These Yupiit don't write things down on a piece of paper so that they can look at it. Starting from way back, the paper they had was in their heads. When they say something to us, their young, they would say it without making a mistake." In 1977 Paul said of himself, "I used to learn them and apparently not forget again after hearing them just one time."

Translation from Yup'ik is further complicated by the fact that the Yup'ik language does not specify gender in third-person endings, so the listener is left to deduce it from the context of the account. When describing women's tasks, we have translated the pronominal ending as "she," as that is the way a reader can best understand the narrator's intent. Conversely, pronominal endings are translated as "he" when a speaker is describing a hunter's activities. In general discussions we have used either "it" or "he," depending on the context. Readers should also be aware that Yup'ik orators sometimes mix singular and plural endings in a single oral "sentence," and we have retained some of these grammatical variations to reflect the complexity of the Yup'ik original.

Another common source of confusion is the Yup'ik preference for pronominal endings over nouns. This can cause difficulties for the uninitiated, especially in statements involving several unspecified persons. For clarity, then, some pronominal endings have been replaced by nouns — often enough to make the meaning clear yet not so often as to burden the text.

Yup'ik verb tenses also differ from those in English. Although some postbases place an action clearly in the future and others place it definitely in the past, a verb without one of these time-specifying postbases may refer to an action that is happening either in the past or the present.[6] Accounts of events or customs that are no longer practiced in southwestern Alaska have been translated in the past tense. Where tense is specified, it is translated accordingly; for example, "In the past people celebrated the Bladder Festival." Readers should also note that tense may vary within a paragraph, especially in discussions of *qanruyutet* marked by the enclitic "-gguq," which can be translated "they said," "they say," or "it is said" depending on the context. Traditional *qanruyutet* that elders indicate still apply are therefore translated using the present tense.[7]

As we ponder both the limitations and the power of translation to communicate meaning across cultural and linguistic boundaries, it is useful to return to Becker and his recognition that translation is not the end point of understanding but the beginning.[8] Similarly, the reader is invited to engage Alice and Marie's translations and use them as starting points for understanding and respecting the profound differences between literary traditions, which, in turn, make it possible for us to recognize our own exuberant selves.

Yup'ik oral tradition values close attention to detail and consistent retellings, and Alice and Marie continue to work in this tradition. Although elders may express and explain *qanruyutet* differently, the *qanruyutet* themselves remain the same.[9] As Elsie Mather noted, "The most respected conveyers of Yup'ik knowledge are those who express things that listeners already know in artful or different ways, offering new expressions of the same."[10]

Good translation is much more than a technical process — it is a moral act involving responsibility and respect. A Malay friend once told Becker that he hoped he would not translate a Malay classic into English, because then no one would read the original. All indigenous people face the same dilemma. Alice's and Marie's efforts to understand and provide access to the *qanruyutet* are not neutral acts but are "necessarily full of politics and semi-intended errors." Becker concludes: "Translation fidelity itself demands reciprocity, a sorting out of exuberances and deficiencies, a confession of failures and sleights of hand. It is the only way I know of by which to make restitution to those who, in old Malay, 'wrought the words and in that sense own them.'"[11]

Transcription and Annotation

As if translation from one language to another were not challenging enough, this book also involves the movement from oral to written language. The starting point for the book is the verbal artistry of individual elders, but critical to understanding each performance is the transformation of the orator's voice onto the page.[12] Through the 1970s little attention was given to reflecting the dynamics and dramatic techniques of the performance, including the speakers' shifts in tone and rhythm. The oral origins of texts were all but hidden from view. Texts were routinely transcribed in paragraph form, as if the paragraph were the natural form of all speech.[13]

Beginning in the 1980s, when so many basic tenets of anthropology were being reconsidered, the ubiquitous paragraph came under attack, especially in the work of Dell Hymes and fellow linguist Dennis Tedlock. Rather than assume a prose format in their transcriptions of Native American material, both men experimented with verse forms in an effort to more accurately reflect both the structure and the dynamics of the original performances. Hymes focused primarily on the structure of Native American texts, and his concerns were fundamentally formal. Tedlock, on the other hand, worked with recent recordings of narrative performances to develop a transcription style that reflected the dynamics of oral performance. Both used broken lines, spacing, and small and large type to reflect voice quality, pause length, and other speech patterns. The length of the pause in a speaker's delivery was the determining factor for where lines and stanzas should end. As Tedlock pointed out, oral storytelling is a kind of measured poetry.[14]

Together, Tedlock and Hymes inspired a generation of linguists and anthropologists who have since adopted and adapted their insights in a variety of ethnopoetic transcription styles, igniting a veritable renaissance in the translation of Native American literature.[15] Although Alice and Marie have not chosen to employ the "short line" verse format favored by many translators, they use the prose format with a new sensitivity. In their work paragraphs are no longer arbitrary groupings disconnected from the speaker's original oral performance but are distinguished by prominent line-initial particles such as *tua-i-llu* ("so then"), by cohesion between contiguous lines, and by pauses between units.[16]

Along with paying close attention to the written form, Alice and Marie have worked together to ensure that readers understand the elders' meanings and intentions. For Yup'ik readers and other "cultural insiders" familiar with indigenous narrative tradition, little explanation may be necessary. Yet regardless of how knowledgeable the listener and skillful the translator might be, written texts do not unambiguously speak for themselves.[17] As Dick and Nora Dauenhauer point out, oral performances tend to be highly contextualized, which in translation creates a "laconic and confusing text."[18]

In these introductory remarks I have tried to provide readers with a better understanding of the speakers' background and intentions without explaining their words away or tying them down to a single interpretation. Speakers assumed their listeners possessed basic linguistic and cultural information, and this, rather than elaborate interpretation, is what the introduction provides.

Some judge the written text as no better than a chunk of ice in comparison with the ever-changing rivers and streams of oral tradition. Translation and transcription, they say, transform the dynamic storytelling process into a static, objectified text. Others contend that the so-called frozen text still gets read and retold in myriad ways. Actually a different dynamic occurs in written texts, which can be introduced to younger generations, recirculated, and retold in new and previously unimagined ways. Alice's and Marie's transcriptions and translations of the elders' instructions do not just represent past interaction, but also occasion interaction in the future.[19]

Notes

1. Following the Alaska Native Language Center standard orthography, I have dropped the apostrophe when speaking of the Yupik family of languages and retained it when speaking of dialects within Yupik, including Cup'ig and General Central Yup'ik (Yup'ik).

2. Jacobson 1984:28–37; Woodbury 1984:49–63.

3. Becker 2000:90.

4. Shreve 2002:7.

5. Miyaoka, Mather, and Meade 1991:13–14.

6. Jacobson 1984:22.

7. Detailed discussions of Yup'ik grammar can be found in Reed et al. 1977, Miyaoka, Mather, and Meade 1991, and Jacobson 1995.

8. Becker 2000:18.

9. See Morrow 1995:32.

10. Mather 1995:32.

11. Becker 2000:19.

12. Dauenhauer and Dauenhauer 1999.

13. Hymes 2002.

14. Hymes 1981; Tedlock 1983.

15. Swann 1994:xxviii.

16. Orr and Orr 1995:xv.

17. Cruikshank 1990:ix.

18. Dauenhauer and Dauenhauer 1999:21.

19. Sarris 1993:4.

References

Becker, A. L. 2000. *Beyond Translation: Essays toward a Modern Philology.* Ann Arbor: University of Michigan Press.

Cruikshank, Julie. 1990. *Life Lived Like a Story.* Lincoln: University of Nebraska Press.

———. 1995. "'Pete's Song': Establishing Meanings through Story and Song." In *When Our Words Return: Writing, Hearing, and Remembering Oral Traditions of Alaska and the Yukon,* ed. Phyllis Morrow and William Schneider, 53–75. Logan: Utah State University Press.

Dauenhauer, Nora Marks, and Richard Dauenhauer. 1999. "The Paradox of Talking on the Page: Some Aspects of the Tlingit and Haida Experience." In *Talking on the Page: Editing Aboriginal Oral Texts,* ed. Laura Murray and Keren Rice, 3–42. Toronto: University of Toronto Press.

Fienup-Riordan, Ann. 1996. *The Living Tradition of Yup'ik Masks: Agayuliyararput (Our Way of Making Prayer).* Seattle: University of Washington Press.

———. 2005. *Wise Words of the Yup'ik People: We Talk to You because We Love You.* Lincoln: University of Nebraska Press.

———. 2005. *Yup'ik Elders at the Ethnologisches Museum Berlin: Fieldwork Turned on Its Head.* Seattle: University of Washington Press.

Hymes, Dell. 1981. *"In Vain I Tried to Tell You": Essays in Native American Ethnopoetics.* Studies in Native American Literature 1. Philadelphia: University of Pennsylvania Press.

———. 2002. "Translation of Oral Narratives." *Anthropology News* 43 (5): 2.

Jacobson, Steven A. 1984. *Yup'ik Eskimo Dictionary.* Fairbanks: Alaska Native Language Center, University of Alaska.

———. 1995. *A Practical Grammar of the Central Alaskan Yup'ik Eskimo Language.* Fairbanks: Alaska Native Language Center, University of Alaska.

Mather, Elsie P. 1995. "With a Vision beyond Our Immediate Needs: Oral Traditions in an Age of Literacy." In *When Our Words Return: Writing, Hearing, and Remembering Oral Traditions of Alaska and the Yukon,* ed. Phyllis Morrow and William Schneider, 13–26. Logan: Utah State University Press.

Meade, Marie, and Ann Fienup-Riordan. 1996. *Agayuliyararput, Kegginaqut, Kangiit-llu: Our Way of Making Prayer, Yup'ik Masks and the Stories They Tell.* Seattle: University of Washington Press.

———. 2005. *Ciuliamta Akluit: Things of Our Ancestors.* Seattle: University of Washington Press.

Miyaoka, Osahito, and Elsie Mather. 1979. *Yup'ik Eskimo Orthography*. Bethel AK: Kuskokwim Community College.

Miyaoka, Osahito, Elsie Mather, and Marie Meade. 1991. *Survey of Yup'ik Grammar*. Anchorage: University of Alaska Anchorage.

Morrow, Phyllis. 1995. "On Shaky Ground: Folklore, Collaboration, and Problematic Outcomes." In *When Our Words Return: Writing, Hearing, and Remembering Oral Traditions of Alaska and the Yukon*, ed. Phyllis Morrow and William Schneider, 27–51. Logan: Utah State University Press.

Orr, Eliza Cingarkaq, and Ben Orr. 1995. *Qanemcikarluni Tekitnarqelartuq (One Must Arrive with a Story to Tell): Traditional Narratives by the Elders of Tununak, Alaska*. Fairbanks: Alaska Native Language Center.

Reed, Irene, Osahito Miyaoka, Steven Jacobson, Paschal Afcan, and Michael Krauss. 1977. *Yup'ik Eskimo Grammar*. Fairbanks: Alaska Native Language Center, University of Alaska.

Sarris, Greg. 1993. *Keeping Slug Woman Alive: A Holistic Approach to American Indian Texts*. Berkeley: University of California Press.

Shield, Sophie, and Ann Fienup-Riordan. 2003. *Qulirat Qanemcit-llu Kinguvarcimalriit (Stories for Future Generations): The Oratory of Yup'ik Eskimo Elder Paul John*. Seattle: University of Washington Press.

Shreve, Gregory. 2002. "Translation, Fidelity, and Other Mythical Beasts I have Sited." *Anthropology News* 43 (7): 7.

Swann, Brian. 1994. *Coming to Light: Contemporary Translations of the Native Literatures of North America*. New York: Random House.

Tedlock, Dennis. 1983. *The Spoken Word and the Work of Interpretation*. Philadelphia: University of Pennsylvania Press.

Woodbury, Anthony C. 1984. "Eskimo and Aleut Languages." In *Arctic*, Vol. 5 of *Handbook of North American Indians*, ed. David Damas, 49–63. Washington DC: Smithsonian Institution Press.

Yup'ik Contributors

This list reflects Yup'ik protocol. Names are ordered by community, running north to south along the Bering Sea coast and upriver to Bethel. Within each community, individuals are listed by age (eldest to youngest).

	Residence	Birthplace	Birth Year
Nastasia Andrew	Marshall	Pilot Station	1935
Cecelia Foxie	Stebbins	Penguq	1912
Bennedict Tucker	Emmonak	Cingigmiutret	1918
Mike Utteryuk	Scammon Bay	Scammon Bay	1926
Louise Tall	Chevak	Upaucugmiut	1902
David Simon Sr.	Hooper Bay	Hooper Bay	1929
Edward Shavings Sr.	Mekoryuk	Nunivak	1928
Phillip Moses	Toksook Bay	Nightmute	1925
Theresa Moses	Toksook Bay	Cevv'arneq	1926
Sophie Agimuk	Toksook Bay	Cevv'arneq	1928
Paul John	Toksook Bay	Cevv'arneq	1928
Martina Chugluak	Toksook Bay	Nightmute	1932
Martina John	Toksook Bay	Nightmute	1936
Dick Anthony	Nightmute	Cevv'arneq	1922
Simion Agnus	Nightmute	Nightmute	1930
Hilary Kairaiuak	Chefornak	Kipnuk	1922
Agnes Alexie	Chefornak	Cicing	1934
David Martin	Kipnuk	Kipnuk	1913
Frank Paul	Kipnuk	Anuurarmiut	1921

Frank Andrew	Kwigillingok	Kwigillingok	1917
Noah Andrew Sr.	Kwigillingok	Kwigillingok	1951
John Phillip Sr.	Kongiganak	Anuurarmiut	1925
Charlie Evans	Quinhagak	Quinhagak	1934
Wassilie Berlin	Kasigluk	Tuntutuliak	1916
Sophie Nicholas	Kasigluk	Qipneq	1933
Elena Martin	Kasigluk	Nunacuaq	1943
Nicholai Berlin	Nunapitchuk	Qikertaq (Iik Island)	1912
Evan Alexie	Nunapitchuk	Nanvarnarrlak	1927
Peter Jacobs Sr.	Bethel	Cuukvagtuliq	1923
Elsie Mather	Bethel	Keggukar	1936
Lucy Sparck	Bethel	Chevak	1940
Wassilie Evan	Akiak	Napaskiak	1930

Yup'ik Words of Wisdom

Tegganret Qalartellruut Ayagyuat-llu Niicugniluteng

Ayuqucirtuutiit atauciuguq

(1) Hilary Kiaraiuak, November 2000:126

Allanun-llu nunanun ayangermi qanrutkelaraat atauciuvakaan, nunanun taukunun tekilluni ayuqucirtualriamek niiskuni, kingunermini-llu
cali ayuqucirtuun niitellni elitaqluku atauciullinian. Tua-i allamek pitai-
lami, uum taugaam paircilriim navguumalalliniani.

Aarnarqelria tamarmi picurlautekaq inerquutetangqertuq

(2) Frank Andrew, June 5, 1995:70

Man'a tua-i ciulirnertaq qanruyun, yull'aq augna, nepaitellruuq atulua-
qerluku atullratni augkut. Cat tamarmeng inerquuterluteng. Tang makut
inerquukaraat amllepialriit. Tua-i aanarqelriit inerquutetangqetuut. Aarnarqelria tamarmi picurlautekaq inerquutetangqertuq. Aarnailnguq taugken kiikirtuuterluni, ellimertuutmek aiparluni.

Caunrilngalngermi tua-i inerquutmek pilek, anglanaqngalngermi, te-
gulayunaunaku. Piluaqautekaunrilnguq taugaam inerquutngulliniuq.
Avaken ak'a tamaaken ayagluni inerquun cimiyuunani yuum elluarrluni
pitkaqenrilkii. Assilria taugken ellimertuutmek taugaam pitarluni.

Elders Spoke and Young People Listened

Their instructions are the same

(1) Hilary Kairaiuak, November 2000:126

And when you go to other villages, they speak of similar lessons because they are the same. When one arrives in a particular village and hears a person giving instruction to others, he will recognize those teachings he heard in his hometown because they are the same. There are no other [rules that people live by], and rules are only broken by those who go against them.

There are rules against every peril

(2) Frank Andrew, June 5, 1995:70

People lived in harmony and peace when instructions were thoroughly followed by people back in those days. There were *inerquutet* [admonishments] for everything we did. There are so many warnings in our everyday life. There are admonitions we have to know for every hazardous situation. Every bad situation that could annihilate a person usually has an admonition attached to it. But you try to steer and encourage people toward security and success.

If something has an admonition attached to it, it's best to stay away from it even though it appears to be trivial and fun. There are admonitions for everything that can set you back. There are admonitions that have been passed down from generation to generation for everything that can negatively affect a person. But there is encouragement toward things that can bring good to people.

Ayaruq una yuum tegumiaqekuniu
qanruyun elitellni aturluku picurlagngaituq
(3) Frank Andrew, June 7, 1995:17

Nunavut-wa tua-i man'a ayuqucimitun tua-i ayuqenrilnguq. Yuvriu-mavkenani ca man'a, aarnarqelria nallukvut amllelria. Taugken ayarum aperturyugngaluku aarnarqelria yuum picurlautekaa. Arnat-llu aturluku tua-i ciunerteng man'a, qeraqata'arqameng-llu assilria yuarluku ayagaqlu-teng. Tuaten ayuqluni ayaruq.

Imkut taumek ayaruicuitellrulriit. Uksuarmi-llu waten arcaqerluteng, kiagungraan-llu ayaruicuunateng tangvallrenka. Tua-i aaqekseng yuvri-qerrlainarluku.

Tuamtell' qenuqami cali cat aarnarqelriit cali nallunarqetuluteng. Ciku-llu qaillun mamtutacia uunguciitnaqluni. Ayarum taugaam tugermek iqulgem apertuatuluku yuum temiin ayagvigkaa cikum qaingakun aar-narqenrilngurkun.

Ayaruq tua-i una calilriaruluni yuum tegumiaqekani, ciuliqagtengu-luni tua-i tumkaanun. Assilriakun tua-i pekcecugngaluku, aarnarqelria apertuagurluku. Tuaten ayuqluni.

Tuamtell' imarpigmi qamigaqtaangaqameng qayatgun negcik una aler-quutngulria; aipaqerrlainarluku tua-i. Qayaq-llu amllinernek qavcinek uniarteqatang'ermiu teguqerrlainarluku pisqelluku. Tua-i aipaqerrlainar-luku pisqelluta. Cali tua-i negcik tuaten ayuqluni. Ikayuriyugngaluni uu-mek tegumiaqesteminek. Atraqataquni-llu negciim tugran assinrilnguq nalluvkenaku; kitugqaarluku nutaan atrarcecugngaluku qayani.

Tuamtellu urugyungkan mayuqataquni, tamaaggun cali kitugqaarluku mayuryugngaluni. Atraqataquni-llu kitugtellrung'ermiu mayuqataller-mini yuvriqerrlainarluku, urugyuum nalliini. Nutaan cikumi cali, qainga man'a assingraan, imarpigmi, ciuneni yuvrirrlainarluku tumtangqeng-raan. Camaggun atam nangtuani cikua, qainga-am man'a cukaillruluni, camaggun taugaam aciakun.

One who walks with the walking stick following
the teachings they learned will not get into trouble

(3) Frank Andrew, June 7, 1995:17

Today our environment is indeed different from the way it was before. There are many unknown hazards in our environment. However, the *ayaruq* [walking stick] can point out the dangerous spots along our way and keep us safe. Women also used walking sticks to find firm ground before crossing the land. That is the nature of the walking stick.

That was the reason why people carried the walking stick at all times back in those days. Especially in the fall and even in the summer, those people I observed always carried the walking stick. They would always check a potentially dangerous spot with their walking stick as they traveled.

During the time the rivers, lakes, and ground begin to freeze, it's difficult to see dangerous spots. And the thickness of the ice is usually difficult to determine by looking at it. But a walking stick with a sharp point will show the person where it is safe to walk on ice.

If a walking stick is properly used by a person, it will work for the person and will lead him in the right path. It will allow the person to travel on a safe path by pointing to the hazards along the way. That's how the walking stick works.

And also when seal hunters began to go out to the ocean, they were instructed to always keep the *negcik* [hooked gaff] by their side. He was told to always hold the gaff, even if he was only to take a few steps away from his kayak. They told us to always hold it by our side. That's also the nature of the gaff. It could also help one who is holding it. And as he proceeded down to the ocean to launch his kayak, the gaff showed the bad spots on the edge of the shore ice. He could then launch his kayak after checking the bad spot.

And again in the spring thaw, when a hunter was ready to go back up on land, he was told to always use his gaff to check the ice and make sure it was safe before going up. And when he came back down again, he was to use his gaff again, even though he had already checked the way when he was going up. You always did this during the spring thaw. And again on the ocean ice, a hunter was told to always use his gaff, even though the ice appeared safe and there were trails and footprints there already. Ice underneath normally gets eaten away faster than on the surface.

Tua-i ayaruq calilriaruluni. Tua-i yuum picurlanritlerkaa pucurlau-tekaa-llu nalluvkenaku. Taugaam uum tegumiaqestemi ayarum pisqutiin pillrakun, qanruyun nallunritellrakun tegumiaqestemi. Elitnaurtaunani ayaruq, camun atuugarkaucia nalluluku, ayarum ikayurciigataa, aarnar-qelriamek-llu apertuutesciiganaku. Tua-i piyaraa uum tegumiaqestemi elisnganrilaku.

Man'a qanruyun ayarutun ayuquq. Tua-i niiteqainalriim tegumiaqeqai-naraa qaillun-llu alerquatiikun kangallerkani nalluluku. Tauna tua-i nii-teqainalriamek aterpagingatuuq, umyuangcartevkenani. Taumek aler-quutengqellrulriakut qalartellria qanra uniurteksaunaku qalareskan, caungraan, niicugniuraasqelluku qalartellra taqvianun.

Man'a-am qanruyun ayarutun ayuqellinilria. Yuum eliskuniu niicug-niurallermikun wall' tangvaurallermikun, tamana ayaruqelriatun qan-ruyun yuuciqluni. Uuggun tegumiamikun qanruyutekun, cauciak ukuk malruk tumkak nallrunritarkauluku.

Qanruciuratulit

(4) David Martin and Theresa Moses, April 2001:218–19

David Martin: Tua-i-gguq taugaam imna, yuum mat'um ayagturallrani piurallerkaanek yuullrani qanengssagturalria, tua-i tauna nutaan ayuqu-cirturilriaruuq, tua-i aug'umek tekitarkamek qanengssagturalria.

Theresa Moses: Ilii-gguq taugken cingumainrilnguq qanruciyuunani, elliin-gguq taugaam cani qanrutaqluki. Tua-i-gguq taum cingumainril-nguum taukut tutgarani, cani tua-i qanrutaqluki, allanun-gguq taugken qanqayuunani. Tua-i-gguq tauna cingumainrilnguq. Ilaminun taugaam ayuqucirtuutmek qanraqluni, makut-llu tua-i tangengermiki ilangcivke-naki. Allat cingumavkenaki tua-i, taukut taugaam elliin cingumak'ngani qanrulluki. Illii-gguq taugken tua-i, tamarmi-gguq tuar alaunani, ta-ngellni tamalkuan ayuqucirturluku, tua-i-gguq tangellni tamalkuan taum cingumaluki, assillerkaanek yuullerkaanek qanruqu'urluku. Nutaan-llu-gguq tangeng'ermiu assillerkaanek taugaam qanruqu'urluku. Tua-i-gguq tauna cingumailria.

The walking stick was vital. It showed the safe and dangerous spots on a person's path. But the walking stick would only work if the owner used it according to traditional teachings. A person would not be helped by the walking stick if he didn't know how to use it properly. If he didn't know how to use it, it wouldn't show him where the dangerous spots were located on his path. This would be the case if the person didn't know the proper use of the walking stick.

The *qanruyutet* [words of wisdom] work like the walking stick. A person who merely hears the teachings and does not live by them is only holding them and has no idea how to use them properly on his path. Such a person was referred to as one who merely heard superficially and one who didn't think over advice given. It was for this reason we were told to be attentive to speakers as they talked and to look at their mouths until they stopped speaking.

Words of knowledge apparently work just like the walking stick. When a person masters the teachings of elders by listening and observing and applies them to his life, they will work like the walking stick for him. By holding on to the *qanruyutet* he will know the two paths he can travel on.

Those who continually speak to others
(4) David Martin and Theresa Moses, April 2001:218–19

David Martin: They say one who continually speaks to others about living properly is one who truly gives direction and guidance to others about what is to come in the future.

Theresa Moses: But they say some people who do not want others to lead a good life do not give instruction to them but instruct only their own relatives. That person who does not encourage others only speaks to their grandchildren or relatives, but they do not give instruction to others whatsoever. They call that person *cingumainrilnguq* [one who doesn't encourage others to do well in life]. They give advice only to their relatives but ignore others around him. They don't encourage others but only those they want to see succeed in life. But they say it is like some people have nothing to hide and advise and encourage everyone they see, always speaking to them about how to live a good life even though they see them for the first time. They call that person *cingumailria* [one who gives others encouragement].

David Martin: Irniaqenrilngermiki qanruqu'urluki yuullerkaatnek mat'umek, ciutmun ayallratni piurallerkaatnek. Augna-am cali cingumainrilnguum ayuqucirtuutii matuuguq. Murilkelriaruameng augkut ciuliaput, una-gguq cingumainrilnguq apqanguarunruuq ilaminun. Apqanguarunruuq canek tua-i. Akusrarutnun makunun, cali yuum picurlautekainun tamakunun, apcuunani, anglaninerkaitnun-gguq taugaam apqanguarunruuq tauna cingumainrilnguq.

Yuut ayuqenrilameng-am tuaten ayuqellinilriit tua-i. Ilait apqangualteng tamakut ilaqtuurluki canek tua-i qanemcisnguaraqluki. Tua-i-gguq tauna cingumainrilnguuguq makunek kinguverkanek.

Kenekngamceci qanrutamceci

(5) Paul John, November 2000:119

Augkut tang waten elluarrluki yukegcinamek ayagyuani qanruqaarluta una qanrutkerrlainalallrukiit, "Kenkenrilkumci qanrucanritamci." Yuum tang taugaam kenkicini umyuaminek qamaken aturluku waten ayagyuamek qalarucilalria. Una wani kenka avanirpak aturluku ciuliaput calillruciat pug'arrnaluku qancuaqeryugtua.

Avanirpak tang waten qanrutetukaitkut qanruqaarluta, "Kenekngamci qanrutamci. Kenkenrilkumci qanrucanritamci."

Tua-ll' una kenkem tua-i kayua tangerqalriatun tutgara'urluma iliitgun pillruaqa cat iliitni. Tuaten-am call' tutgara'urluma qanrutellma kinguani, pircirtuq cakneq, tua-i pircirluni qakemna. Piinanermini itertuq tua-i qainga qanikcillerkani anaggluku qanikcaam nevluku. Piaqa, "Qaill' pilriaten anagulluten qanikcissiyaagpakarta qain tamana?" Imna niicugninricukelqa qanertuq, "Imna qanruyutellren ellami qerrucaram ayuqucianek, yuilqumi qaillun anangnaqsaraq qanruyutellren atullruaqa patucukiini qanikcaam. Nanluciinani ellminek anangnaqlerkaq naspallruaqa." Cunaw' tang tauna tutgaraurluqa imna niicugninricukelqa niicugnillrullinilria. Waten arenqialluggluni yuilqumi ellminek anangnaqsaramek ellarayagmi qanruyutni tua-i ukveqluku atungnaqluku tuani qanikcirluni itlinilria. Tua-llu piaqa, "Tua-llu-qaa tua-i?" Tua-i-gguq assirluni ellminek ikayungnaqkuni piyuumaciqsugnarquq.

David Martin: Though they are not his children, he would constantly teach them about proper living, about the right path they should follow as they progressed in life. The advice given regarding those who don't encourage others to do well is this. Since our ancestors were keenly aware of the behavior of others, they said a person who does not encourage others only asks superficial and unimportant questions. He does not speak about dangerous situations that a person can encounter, but one who does not encourage others to live a good life only asks questions about having a good time.

That is how people are, because they are all different. Some of them add their own comments to things they ask and recount stories filled with falsehoods. They say that person does not encourage the younger generation.

We talk to you because we love you

(5) Paul John, November 2000:119

After giving us young people instruction on living proper lives, our elders always told us, "If we did not love you, we would not speak to you." One only gives advice and guidance to a young person by using love from inside one's heart. I would like to speak a little about the fact that our elders used love as a means of discipline.

They always told us this after they spoke to us: "I am telling you this because I love you. If I did not love you, I would not say anything to you."

Now, I witnessed the power of love through one of my grandsons one time. After I had given my dear grandchild words of advice, one time during a storm he came inside completely covered in snow. I asked him, "Why are you covered with snow?" The one who I thought hadn't listened said, "Those instructions you gave me about cold weather and how to survive outdoors, I tested your teaching about how one should try to survive in a snowstorm where a lot of snow is piling rapidly." Apparently my grandchild, who I thought was not listening, had been listening to my advice about surviving in the wilderness alone during bad weather. He had come inside covered with snow after testing his lesson. Then I said, "So what happened?" He said that he could probably survive if he tried to help himself in that situation.

Cali waten kenkem aturyaraa ayuqluni wiinga tua-i cuqequrallemni.
Ava-i qancurlagacaraunritellra ayuqucirtungnaqikumta niiquraraput.
Una tang cali waniwa qancurlagatenrilkurcaram ilakmingatellinikii. Qan-
rucunailngurmek aprumangraan yuk uluruaravkenaku qanenrilnguarutevkenaku piurqumteggu qancurlaganricaram taum ilakmingatellinikii.
Aterpagtaqluku *hi*-aaqerluku uluruaravkenaku, caungraan qanrucunail-
ngurmek ap'langraatgu.

Cali una taringvallakarngatellruamku tuatnayaraq qanrucunailngur-
mek ikayuringnaqluni pilriani. Ilurangqertua tua-i taangangnaqu'urrlai-
nalriamek kesianek. Arcaqallruluta-llu wangkuta taangaq atungnaqen-
ringvailemteggu akaurcan wii avavet Bristol Bay-mun ayagyaurtelqa.
Tua-i avavet ayagaqamta taangaq imutun tua-i camek nagutaunaku atu-
llerkamtenun ayatuluta.

Tua-i wiinga tamaani atunringnaqellma kinguani, tauna-am tua-i
ilu'urqa cakaniucuunaku tua-i piuratukeka. Imumek kuvyanaiteqerluku,
Yaquleyagaat umgusngallrata nalliini kuvyallerkamtenek, quyurngaluta
uitaluta amllerrluta piinanemni, tua-i-am tekiteurluraakut taum ilu'urma
tua-i ayuqucini kaumavkenaku. Tua-i tekicamia alla cauvkenaku iluqaa-
raanga, "Iluq, tua-i tang wii ikasvaumalaqevnga angtuamek cakneq." Camek neq'angcallagyaaqua tungiinun ikayuutellemnek neq'erpek'nii ika-
yuqaqsailamku tauna. Tua-ll' iqlukluku tua-i umyuarteqngama piaqa,
"Wiinga-wa camek ikayuutemnek tungevnun neq'ak'ngailngua." Tua-llu
tuaten iqlukluku umyuarteqlua piama ikayuqaqsaitniamni pianga. "Ikas-
valararpenga angtuamek. Imutun yuut upucuirullua, tangyuirullua, tua-i
caniqliqngermegtenga. Tuaten piaqatnga umyuarteq'lartua, 'Ilama ken-
kenriraatnga tamaqapiarmeng. Kenkestengssagairutua. Aciatni-llu ilama
tamalkuita umyuaqa ellirluni, tua-i kitumek kenkestengssagairullua.' Tuaten piinanemni yaatemnek nepelkitellriamek niiskuma takuyarciqua elpet." Tua-i yaaqsingraan upuartengnaq'laamku yaavet qayagaurlua, ta-
llini elucirararaa, "Camaken yuut aciatnek mayurtelararpenga yaaviarlua
erinavkun piaqavnga, yugnun manigtatekliullua." Tang ilumun qaill' qan-
rucunaitetaluku niitelangramteggu yuk uluruarayunaitellinikvut, kenkakun maaggun *hello*-qerluku, waqaaqerluku, tuqluqerluku piurqumteggu
tua-i kenekmek tauna cikiryugngallinikvut ilavut qaillun qanrucunail-
ngurmek pitangraan.

Tua-i augkunek ava-i, uumek iquliqalaamku, tutgara'urluunka qan-
ruqurainarqamki, kenkekni taugaam yuum qanrut'laqii, augkut ciuliat qa-
neryaraat aturluku. Tua-i tauna tutgara'urluqa kenkucini taringamiu tuat-

This is the way I understand love, as I have been figuring things out through experience. We have heard that we should not speak abusively when we are trying to teach a person. This seems to be related to the instruction not to speak rashly toward others. Ignoring and not speaking to one who they say has a bad reputation seems to be related to not speaking abusively to others. One should say their name and say "Hi" and not ignore them, even though they say he has a bad reputation.

I came to understand how to treat those with a bad reputation when trying to help them. I have a cousin who was always trying to drink alcohol. We were heavy drinkers like him before we tried to quit drinking since I've started traveling to Bristol Bay [for commercial fishing] a long time ago. When we got there, nothing held us back from drinking.

After I had quit drinking, I was always friendly to my cousin [who continued to drink]. During a time when the [Alaska State] Fish and Game officials closed the fishing period, while many of us were gathered together waiting to fish, my poor intoxicated cousin came upon us. When he came up to me, without looking at anyone else, he called me and said, "*Iluq* [cousin], you help me tremendously." At the end of what he said, I tried to think of an instance and did not remember the time I had helped him. I said to him, "I do not recall a time when I helped you." Then he replied, "You have helped me tremendously. People have actually stopped acknowledging me, and they don't even look at me, even though they are right next to me. When they treat me that way, I think to myself, 'Everyone around me doesn't love me anymore. No one loves me any longer. And I feel as though I am beneath everyone. No one loves me any longer.' As I am feeling that way, when I hear a voice from nearby, I look, and it is you." Because I am always trying to acknowledge [my cousin] even though he is far away, he made a gesture with his arm. "You bring me up from down under people when you call me, treating me equal to other people." Indeed, even though we hear that one has a bad reputation, we should not ignore him, and we can show that we care for a person by constantly saying "Hello" and calling him by name, even though others have labeled him a bad person.

When I speak to my grandchildren, I always end with our ancestors' teaching that a person only gives instructions to those he loves. When my grandson understood that I loved him, he tested the validity of my instructions. Also, my cousin said that I brought him up to the level of other

nallinilria alerquatni tauna naspaaluku. Tauna-w' cali iluurqa wangnun kenkucini taringumiimiu mayurtelakluni yugtun pugtatariluni tuani call' qanellruluni. Augkuk ava-i taringcetaarukaraak *example*-aak qanllemnun ap'qengagka kenkamun taikaniqautngunayuklukek qanqautek'luugtagka.

Cali una umyuaqela'arqa ayagnirraanemtenek-am, waniwa kiingan pinrilamku avani-ll' ciungani umyuaqutkelaamku. Una waniwa manumteni *Calista Elders Council* unayaqiuq wangkutnek. Aturluku ayagyuamtenek ikayuringnaqnaurtukut. Man'a maa-i taringumakvut, pinerrluangellrat ikayungnaqsugluku, arenqigillerkaatnun eguaqungnaqsugluki. Tuatenam taugaam una waniwa qanengraan estuulum qacarnerani, wangkutnek aturtailkuni imutun piniilngurtun, egilranrilngurtun-llu ayuqeciquq. Wangkuta taugaam ayauskumteni waten quyurteqainarmi pivkenaku, ayagyuamtenun makunun, ellalirangnaqluki, maryartengnaqluki, una waniwa caliyugngauq igaq manumteni. Wangkutnun taugaam atauq.

Ayuqucirtuutet elluarrluta yuuvkallruakut

(6) Frank Paul, November 2000:96

Ayuqucirtuumalliniukut ayagmek mik'nata ayagluta elluarrluta taugaam pillerkarput pitekluku, qanernaunata, nangrunaunanta tuaten ayuqellerkarput pitekluku. Ayuqucirtuun man'a wangkutnun waten ayagmek atuusqumalliniuq.

Ciutemta-gguq inglua umegluku niicugniarkaugukut

(7) Mike Uttereyuk, November 2000:60–61

Maa-i elpeci ayagyuani waten wani qanrucilriamek niiskuvci niicugniarkaugarci. Waten qanrucetullrukaitkut augkut ciuliamta; una-gguq ciutemta inglua umegluku yugmek qanrucilria niicugniarkaugarput, ciutemta inglua umegluku. Niicugniarkaugarput yuum qanellra wavet uuggun itercelluku. Una ciutemta-gguq inglua umegluku niicugninrilkumta imum yuum qankegtaarallra, una niitarkarput, uuggun-gguq itquni tauna yuum imum qanruyutii niicugninrilkumteni akiakun anciquq tayima. Imna tauna yuum qanellra tayima wavet nagtevkenani [nasqumtenun], akiakun ciutemta anluni. Augkutun tuaten niicugnikumteggu una ciutemta inglua umegluku, nutaan tuavet wavet arulairciquq nasqumtenun. Tua-i piciuluni qanruyun tamana.

people when he understood that I loved him. I have spoken about those examples because I thought they would help us understand the principle of love more clearly.

I have also thought about this since we started, and not just now, but I have thought about this for a long time. The sign that says "Calista Elders Council," which is in front of us here on the table, is asking for people to become involved. Through this forum we must try to help our young people. The situation we are in today, the problems we have with young people that we are fully aware of, we want to address the issues and try to guide them in the right direction. But even though the sign is saying that, if we don't participate and get involved the process will have no strength and will not progress. But if we all move forward with it, and not just talk about it in a meeting like this, we will work together and find solutions to problems our young people are facing, giving our young people guidance, trying to lead them. It is up to us.

The instructions allowed us to live proper lives

(6) Frank Paul, November 2000:96

We were given *ayuqucirtuutet* [instructions] from the beginning, from the time we were children, for the purpose of living proper lives so that we would not offend others. We are obliged to follow this teaching from the beginning.

They say we must listen by closing our other ear

(7) Mike Utteryuk, November 2000:60–61

This is how you young people must listen to someone who is teaching. Our elders told us that we must close our other ear while listening to a person who is instructing, close the other side of our ear. We are to listen to what the person is saying by letting his words enter our ear. They say if we do not close our other ear while listening, the wonderful instructions that we hear will come out the other side. What that person says will not stay in our heads. It will come out of our other ear. However, if we listen to them by closing our other ear, it will then stop here inside our heads. That lesson is true.

Tauna wani qanrucunailnguq-gguq tuaten ayuquq. Ciutiin ingluakun antuuq man'a qaneryarakegtaar aturarkaa. Qanrucunarqellriim tauna tua-i ciutmi ingluakun itqan anevkarpek'naku qelkeciqaa. Man'a taugaam Yupiit piciryaraat aturturluku, atungnaqu'urluku eglereskumta nutaan elluarrluta eglertarkaugukut, assirluta eglertarkaugukut. Tuaten kiingan Yupiit piciryaraat elpekellruamku tamaasqumavkenaku yugnun ilamnun uitalartua.

Ca tamarmi elicugngauq

(8) Frank Andrew, September 2000:133

Ayagyuanun wangkutnun arcaqalria waniwa. Niisngayaraq, takaqiyaraq ayagyuamun atuusqumauq arcaqerluni. Takaqiluni, niisngaluni-llu, yuum-llu aklua tamalkuan takaqluku. Una takaqiyaraq niisngayaraq-llu assirluni yuum, tan'gaurluum, atuquniu elluarrluni nangerngaciquq nunami, ilaminek-llu cangakuurtaunani, qanemyuugautnguyuunani-llu, canun-llu itercivignun-llu itqetaarpek'nani. Arcaqalriaruuq una. Arcaqalriaruluku tan'gaurluullemteni qanrutkumatullruuq niisngayaraq, maligngalluni-llu piyaraq.

Maa-i ca tamarmi qanyuilengermi-llu elitnaurumaaqami niisngarilartuq keneknariluni-llu yuunrilngermi. Qimugta-llu keneknariluni malignaluki ukut pikesteni, qang'a-llu ungungssiq. Ca tamarmi elicugngaluni. Tua-i-llu wangkuta ayagyuani tuaten ayuqesqelluta arcaqerluta pitullruitkut, niisngaluta, takartarluta.

Man'a yuum niicugnituyaaqengermiu tamalkiringanrilnguq tuaten ayuquq, catkevkenaku niitetuyaaqengermiu. Imna taugken qanrucunarqelria tan'gaurluq nasaurluq-llu, niitepig`gluni niitetuli taringluni-llu, tuaten ayuqenrituq. Imna taugken niicugnitungermi taringcanrilnguq tua-i picurlallerkamikun ayalartuq tekicamiu-llu piunrirluni ayagyuarluni. Tuaten ayuquq. Ukuk malruk, niisngayaraq takaqiyaraq-llu atuluaqerlukek atuusqumalukek pitullruitkut. Tua-i tan'gaurluum nasaurluum-llu tamana atuquniu piluaqeryugngaluni, atunrilkuniu-llu picurlagluni nasaurluuli, tan'gaurluuli-llu.

It is said a rebellious person is like that. The wonderful *qaneryaraq* [advice] that he is supposed to follow comes out his other ear. If it goes inside the ear of one who listens and is willing to follow instructions, he will hold onto it and not let it come out. We will be healthy and lead good lives if we follow the traditional ways. I encourage people not to lose our traditional ways, because I lived by them.

Every living thing can learn

(8) Frank Andrew, September 2000:133

This [advice] was especially important to us young people. Young people are especially asked to be obedient and respectful of others and their belongings. If a boy lives respectfully and obediently, he will stand on earth contentedly and those around him will not criticize him, and he will not be the source of arguments and will not go in and out of jail. Being obedient and mindful were our most important lessons as boys.

These days every living thing becomes obedient when taught even if it doesn't speak, and it becomes lovable even if it isn't human. And a dog or other animal becomes lovable when it obeys its owner. Every living thing can learn. They especially asked us young people to be like that, to be obedient and respectful.

Even though a person listens, a person who doesn't listen wholeheartedly is like that. He doesn't care about what he hears. However, a boy or girl who is easy to give instruction to and genuinely listens and understands is not like that. However, one who does not try to understand [what he is told], even though he listens, heads toward peril and dies young when he arrives. That is what happens. They wanted us to listen obediently and be respectful. A young man or woman living by that can be fortunate, but if they do not live by it, they get into a life-threatening situation.

Ikiulrianek qanerturalriit ilangcivkenaki
assilrianek-llu qanerturalriit niicugniluki
(9) Theresa Moses, April 2001:144

Wiinga alerqutullruatnga, ellami-gguq kangarlua ukuk wani caumallu-tek tekiciiqagka qanerturalriik. Maaten-gguq niicugniqerciqagka yuliur-lutek taugaam, yuum taum nalluani callranek ikiullranek qanaalriik. Ilangcivkenakek-gguq kiturlukek ayakilii. Ingkuk-gguq cali caumatellriik tekiciiqagka, niicugniqerciqagka assilriamek ayuqucimek qanerturalriik. Tua-i-llu-gguq tuani nutaan arulairlua niicugniurlukek qanerturallrak.

Ciutek-gguq iinguuk
(10) David Martin, April 2001:148

Qipnermiungulua camek pugcikuma taukuni nunani, qanernarqutmek pugcikuma, nunat amlleret qanemcitgun niiciiqaatnga. Qipnermiuni-gguq tauna-am tamatumek pugcilliniuq. *Meaning*-aaq cali tauna, "Ciu-tek iinguuk." Tangvanrilngermiu qanemcilriatgun tua-i tauna taukuni nu-nani qanemcikluku tuaten piniluku.

Tegelkassaagalriatun ayuqlelalrianga umyuamnek aug'anritaqan
(11) Charlie Evans, November 2000:52

Tumatellu cali qanrutnauraanga, "Cam iliini tarripakarluten yuukuvet angutmek calilriamek nall'arkengkuvet tauna murilkekiu, caliara ayuqe-liluku nalluvkenaku caliaqniaran. Palayilriamek tangerrluten palayiara murilkekiu qaillun calillrucia. Wall'u ikamrilriamek nall'arkengkuvet cali tua-i murilkelluku. Wall'u kuvyamek qemilriamek, wall'u ilaarturilria-mek." Angucetaryarat makut caliat yugmek tangerquma tauna murilkes-qelluku. Maa-i tua-i wangkuta waten ayuqerkauyaaqukut, aug'um iliita qanrutkellruciatun, teglegaqluki tuaten. Wiinga-llu tua-i qanrucimaa-qama qalarucilriamek nall'arkengaqama imutun tua-i tegelkassaagalria-tun ayuqlelalrianga umyuamnek aug'anritaqan.

**Ignore those who are speaking of bad things
and listen to those who are speaking of good things**

(9) Theresa Moses, April 2001:144

They told me that someday while walking outside I would come upon two people speaking. I would listen and hear that they were only gossiping about people's misdeeds behind their backs. They said that I should ignore them and walk away. I would also come upon two other people and listen awhile and hear them speaking of good things. They said I should stop and listen to what they said.

They say ears are eyes

(10) David Martin, April 2001:148

If I cause trouble in the village of Kipnuk, something controversial, a lot of villages will hear about me through stories. They will say that person from Kipnuk is responsible for that problem. That is also the meaning of "*Ciutek iinguuk* [Ears are eyes]." Even though he hadn't seen him, he hears through others what that person did.

I am like a thief trying to steal knowledge when I don't forget it

(11) Charlie Evans, November 2000:52

He also told me, "One day while walking outside, if you come across a man working, observe him so you will know how to copy his work. When you see a person building a wooden boat, observe how his boat is built, or observe if you come across a person building a sled or someone hanging, tying, or mending a fishnet." They told me to observe those working on men's tasks. That is how we are supposed to be, like what that previous speaker said, stealing knowledge. When I come across someone giving instruction, I am like a thief trying to steal knowledge if I don't forget it.

Avani aavsegutnek pitaitellruuq

(12) Theresa Moses, April 2001:143

Avani-w' allanek pitaitellruan, carugarnek tangerrnaitellruan, apqiitnek aavsegutnek pitaitellruan, kiimi taugaam ciulirneq-llu takarnaqluni callerkaa. Catailami qasgiq-wa kiingan quyurrviat yuut angutet; cataunani. Maa-i mat'um nalliini nek'artuluteng *office-a*anek qanraqluteng. Tamaa-i tamakut umyugaita aavuqutait. Elitnaurluteng cayarat amllerrluteng umyuangqesciiganani avanicetun. Uumek umyuami arcaqakek'ngaanek umyuarteqaqluni pilria una, qanernginakun niitengermiu umyugaanun iterpek'nani. Tauna taugaam caliani arcaqakek'ngani, umyugaa tuanlluni. Niitengermiu cavkenani, alingnarqevkenani-llu. Tuatenllu aperluku alingnaqtullruningermiu. Alingnaqtullruniluku qanelria qan'ngermi, umyugaa-ll' taum pektevkenani, taumun taugaam caminun umyuarteqluni. Qanerpakarluni qanelriim ayuquciq taugaam nall'areskaku ellangarrluni.

Taumun taugaam caliaminun, caminun, *school*-aminun; tamaa-i tamakut aavuqutet. Kiingan tua-i talluryutullruukut wangkuta catailan allamek-llu carpaulriamek tangerrnaitellruan. Maa-i mat'um nalliini carugaat amllerrluteng. Kina qanngermi avani yuullminek alingnaqniluku, umyuaq-llu pektevkenani. Taumun taugaam tua-i qanerpakarluni qanelriim iliini tayima yuulci lekuk'arluku qanlalriit, qanerluni nall'ara'arrluku yuulerpeci iliit, elitaqluku-llu elpeci.

Qanruyutminek saagilria

(13) David Martin, April 2001:149

Waten qanrutkaat tamana qanruyutmek saagilria. Iciw' ava-i unuaq ayagnillemteni qanemciskemken umyuamta malruk atuqengamta ellimertuutiikun pituniluta. Taum-gguq tua-i umuyuani imutun ellminek tangrruarluni angelriarurrluni, tuarpiaq ilamini angenrurrluni. Qanruyutellni makut alerquatellni cakaarluki umyuarrani aturluku, ilani makut caunrilleksagulluki yuulria tauna taunguciquq. Qanruyutminek-gguq maligtaquinrilnguq tua-i taunguciquq. Ellminek taugaam piliani man'a angelriaruluku tangvagluku. Ellminek taugaam angeksagutellria tuaten pitulliniluni.

There weren't distractions back then

(12) Theresa Moses, April 2001:143

Since there weren't a lot of distractions back then, the only thing that was important in our lives was respect and care of elders. There was no other place to congregate, but the *qasgi* was a gathering place for men. These days there are many places to gather, and they speak of offices. People become distracted in those places. They are getting formal education and jobs these days, and one can't think and do things they did in the past because of these distractions. A person whose mind is preoccupied with things they consider more important will not soak in the traditional teachings he hears by word of mouth. Their minds are only preoccupied with the job they value more. [Instructions they hear] do not frighten them, even though the speaker notes that it was frightening. They aren't startled but only think of their own affairs. They come to their senses only when one of the speakers finally says something that concerns their own behavior.

They are distracted by their jobs and schooling. We were never distracted, but we were shy because we weren't distracted by big objects and things. There are many distractions today. Even though a person brings up a significant life experience from the past, it doesn't concern us. But sometimes when a speaker touches upon your life and brings up some of your own experiences, you recognize them.

One who scatters his teachings

(13) David Martin, April 2001:149

This is what they say about *qanruyutminek saagilria* [one who scatters his teachings, not adhering to them]. You know how I told you when we started this morning that we go along with the decisions made by the two minds that we possess. They say that person is egotistical, like he is better than others. He does as he pleases and uses his own will, disregarding his instructions, and he is disrespectful toward others. They say a person who is not following instructions is like that. They value their own views. One who develops a large ego is like that.

Piniqerkauluku qanruyun

(14) Frank Paul, November 2000:98

Camun tekitaqamta imna qanruyutellerput ayuqucirtuun wanteqaaq-
luni, umyuaqeqaaqluku. Tua-i-llu taum imum wani neq'aqallemta ayuqu-
cirtuutem taumun imumun pivkarpek'nata, cirlakevkarpek'nata. Tauna piniqerkauluku, man'a qanruyun niitellerput piniutekarkauluku wangkuta.

Yuk naugg'un kitugiyuitelliniuq qanruyutekun taugaam

(15) Frank Andrew and Alice Rearden, October 2001:135–37

Frank Andrew: Pitqevkenaku umyugaa. Tauna pisteni eq'ukevkenaku,
taquutekellriatun-gguq taugaam elliluku tua-i ayuqiinek calingaunani
ellii. Tauna-llu pisteni akinaurngaunaku. Piluaqamek-gguq iqungqenri-
tuq nekayugyaraq. Ilii maa-i yuum, angutnguli, arnaq-llu, mik'aqameng-
llu tua-i pinriqerrluteng, umyugaat naveglluni. Tamaa-i nekayugyaraq
assilriamek caliarunani. Una taugaam waniwa pulengtaq atuusqelaraat
cangayuyuunata-gguq, akinauyuunata, ilalciuluta-gguq. Una ilalciurya-
raq waniwa atuusqekii ciuliamta-llu augkut. Yuullgutemta tuaten pingraakut elliitun akiksaunaku. Nekatalleq assinrituq, calinrituq-gguq tememek
assilriamek.

Alice Rearden: Qaillun-mi pisqetullruitki, iciw' kia wani nekayugceska-
ten, wall'u-q ingluliuqaten kia, qanruyutetangqertuq-qaa, alerquumall-
ruuci-qaa qaillun, kiingan-qaa uitacesqelluku. Kina augna qanellruan kel-
gesqelluku ilaliurluku-llu pilaasqelluku tuaten yuk ayuqellria.

Frank Andrew: Tamana tamaa-i tamiin niicugnilallruarput. Ilamta-llu
waten tan'gaurlurni akusrarrnginanemteni nakukluta pikakut egmianun-
gguq uniskilaput. Wall'u-gguq tan'gaurluullgutvut nangelrakuakatgu ilain,
ilalirpek'naki-gguq teguluku ayauskilaut. Tamana-gguq tukninruuq.

Alice Rearden: *Adult*-aukuvci-mi, taqneruluci-mi kia wani inglukekaci.
Qaillun piarkauceci, tuaten-qaa cali wall'u-q'?

Frank Andrew: Ilalcilleq-gguq pininruuq ingluliuryarami. Matuullini-
luni nakukesten ingluliuyuilkuvgu aug'ariciquq pivakarluni. Assiriluni
tungevnun tua-i, camek assiilngurmek piirulluni. Wangkuta tua-i yugni

That instruction will be the source of strength

(14) Frank Paul, November 2000:98

When we come upon certain situations, our *ayuqucirtuun* [instruction] comes to mind, and we remember it. And that teaching we remembered will not let the situation defeat us. That instruction we heard will be our source of strength.

A person cannot be fixed by another means, only through instructions

(15) Frank Andrew and Alice Rearden, October 2001:135–37

Frank Andrew: They told him not to succumb to the situation. He was told not to hate the person who hurt him, but to let it go, as if he was braiding it into strands of hair, not reacting the same way he was treated and not retaliating against the person who hurt him. They say resentment and anger do not result in good. These days some people, be they male or female, even children, their feelings get hurt, and they react negatively. Anger does not result in good. But they constantly told us not to be offended, not to retaliate against others but to be restrained. Our ancestors told us to be restrained and not respond, not to retaliate against our peers even though they treated us badly. Being easy to anger is not good for our bodies.

Alice Rearden: What did they tell them to do then? Is there an instruction or were there rules to follow if someone hurt you or was picking on you, or were you just to leave them alone? Someone said that they were supposed to invite them over and be friendly toward those who are like that.

Frank Andrew: We always heard that. And they told us to leave immediately if one of our young male peers picked on us while we were playing. Or they told us not to get involved but to take one of our male peers away if others were beating on him. They say that is more powerful.

Alice Rearden: What if someone was fighting with you as an adult or elder? What were you supposed to do? Were you supposed to react that way as well?

Frank Andrew: They say not retaliating and having self-restraint is more powerful than retaliating. It appears to mean the following. If you do not counter those who picked on you, they will forget about it some-

alerquutekarput tuaten assinrilan. Ilaminek-gguq waten tussuciluni piya-raq iquggliquq, pininruyugglainarluni, angenruyugglainarluni ilamini, ilami makut umyugaat cakevkenaki. Tuaten ayuqesqelluta pinritaitkut. Iquggliquq-gguq. Yuum-gguq umyugaa tukniuq.

Makut maa-i kinguqliput mikcuaraat arcaqerluki inerquutekaput, nasaurlucuayaaq, tan'gaurluq-llu nangelrakqaasqevkenaki. Ilii-gguq angliaqami akinautuuq. Arnassagaureskuvet tuatnallrukuvet ilii nangel-rakluku pillerpet pinialikuvet akinauryugngaluten. Wiinga-llu ayagyua-llemni tuatnallrukuma, angutet iliita, tan'gaurluum, cirlaureskuma aki-nauryugngalua. Neq'anarrlillret-gguq, picurlallret elliraat arcaqerluki nalluyaguciyuitut tuaten pimallermeggnek. Alingnarquq-gguq tamana.

Nunivaami ak'a avani ciuqvani Kass'at pilangeqarraallratni, Kass'aq tauna kiputellria. Ciuqlirmek avani yaaqvani tan'gaurlucuarmek malig-luni kipussaagyaaqellrani, Kass'am taum tegliullruyukluku melqulgutmi-nek, atii tauna tuqutelliniluku, qetunrayagiinun tangvagtelluni. Qetun-rayagii tauna taum kingurpiini, piunriumariamiu tauna atami pistellra, akinaurulluku atani, qanemcillrulliniuq mik'nani tuani tuqutellrani um-yuarteqlerminek tuani, "Kaaka waniwa pinirillerkaqa tekilluku una Kass'aq tangvagngaitaqa." Yuratuameng, yuratullruameng tamatum yu-ram nalliini tuqutellrullinia caskukun pivkenaku, atani akinaurulluku. Nayumiqaluku teguluku nerevkarluku tua-i anertevkarviirucami-llu tu-quluni. Caskukun pivkenaku. Tamaa-i-gguq kingum yuan alingnarqutii tangellruat tuani Nunivaarmiut. Iliit tua-i tuatnayugngauq tayima. Ilu-mun alingnarquq una *young*-alria.

Alice Rearden: Augkut-llu cali Kass'at-wa piciryaraatni mikelnguut ilait tangvagluki piuralalriit, "Una tang puqilria, una puqissiyaagpek'nani." Tuaten-qaa pitullruut-llu tamaani.

Frank Andrew: Pitullruitkut waten: "Una tang waniw' avaurtaitellinilria elpeceni, avaurtaillruluni." Aug'um ayuqsaaqaa puqigniluku, nalluyagu-taitniluku-llu. Yugni tuaten aterpagtetullruat, avaurtaitniluku. Nalluyagu-ciyuunani. Tuaten tauna pimauq. Tamana tua-i cali tuaten niirqevkalaraa wangkutnun. Pinauraitkut, "Tua-i waniwa kinguqliqsaaqeksi-llu elpeci-llu avaurtailucimikun ciuqliurtellria waniwa elisngaamikun." Aptaqluta-

day. They will begin treating you well and no longer have hard feelings toward you. That is a teaching for us, because [retaliating] doesn't have a good consequence. They say there is a bad consequence for stepping on others, always trying to be stronger than others, trying to be superior, not taking others' feelings into consideration. They tell us not to behave that way. They say that has a bad consequence. They say a person's mind is powerful.

We were especially admonished about those younger than us, not to mistreat little girls and boys whatsoever. They say some retaliate when older. If you mistreat someone, he can repay you when you become an old woman, when you are weaker. And if I did that to a boy while he was young, he can repay me when I become weak. They say those who remember wrongdoings committed toward them, especially orphans, never forget how they were treated. They say that is extremely dangerous.

A long time ago on Nunivak Island, when white people first came to this area, a white man was trading goods. When [a man] accompanied by a boy was trading, that white man thought [the man] was stealing his furs and killed [the boy's] father while his young son watched. After seeking revenge on his father's murderer many years later, [the boy] recalled what he thought as a young boy about his father's death, "I will not see this white man alive when I get strong." Because they still practiced dance customs [involving feasting], he sought revenge for his father's death during the time they were having a festival and killed him, but not with a weapon. He held onto him and fed him, and the man died when he could no longer breathe. He didn't kill him with a weapon. They say the people of Nunivak Island witnessed how dangerous the younger generation can be. That can happen to anyone. Indeed, mistreatment of a young person can be dangerous.

Alice Rearden: Also, white people will observe a child and say, "This person is intelligent, this one is not as intelligent." Did they do that back then?

Frank Andrew: This is what they said about us: "This person here does not forget things as easily as you." It is like saying that one is intelligent and not forgetful. They say some people don't forget things. They do not forget. That is how that is stated. They let us hear the following. They told us, "This person here is actually younger than you, but because he does not forget things he has surpassed you through his intelligence." And they

llu pitullruamegtekut qanruyutnek test-aqaaqluta. Tamaaggun pitullruit-kut tuaten. Neq'angcaryaaqnaurput iliini wangkuta kinguqlimta-llu tua-i tan'gaurluunrulriim ciullegggluta iliini aperturnauraa. Yuungermeng ta-mana, man'a yuvriqeryaraat elisngaciatnek atutullruat, Kass'ani maa-i qai-llun *test*-arluki pilalliit.

Waniwa irnianka wii alerquuteka aturluku qanruyutemnek ayaglua caliaqanka. Assirluki yuullerkaat nepaunaki-llu ilakulluki pillerkait, qi-nucetaarutevkenaki, yagirateksaunaki-llu wall'u qenqerruteksaunaki, tua-ten ayuqesqelluki. Qanruyun man'a tua-i calilriaruuq. Yuk naugg'un kitu-giyuitelliniuq qanruyutekun taugaam. Qanruyutem-llu tua-i elluarrluku ayagacugngaluku elitellran elliin. Taugken qalarucimayaaqengermi nii-cugniyuilnguq niicugnipiggluni carrluuluni yuugarkauguq, qanernarqaq-luni. Waten piniluku niitnaugaqluni. Assirpek'nani tua-i ilami-llu akluit-nek tegulaucugluni. Tuaten-am qalarutketuat tamana.

Niipakarluku-gguq piinanemteni taringurainangciqaput

(16) Elsie Mather and Theresa Moses, April 2001:147

Elsie Mather: Augna-wa, ilait amlleret maa-i ayagyuaqsilriit waten as-gurakluku-llu pilalriit imkut niiqurallrit. Waten taringevlaangramteki pu-lengqurluki ayuqeqapiaraatnek pinrilengraata, taugaam allauciquq tauna qanruyun atauciungermi taikuni. Tua-i-ll' waten tuartang alerqullrukait-kut tamakut wani niitellrungramteki ciungani iciw, piuraasqelluki, tari-ngekanirciqniluki atata. Umyuamtenun ek'artelangeciqut-gguq atata tua-i-ll' taringekanirluki.

Theresa Moses: Piinanemteni-llu taringurainangciqaput. Wall'u picurla-karluta pikumta tua-i nutaan tauna taringluku. Waten-gguq niitengram-teggu wangkutnun cauvkenani, tua-i-gguq niipakarluku-gguq taugaam taringurainarciqaput. Tuaten pitullruatnga-ll' wiinga. Niipakarluku-gguq taugaam taringurainarciqaqa.

tested our knowledge of *qanruyutet* [instructions]. We tried to think of the answer sometimes, but a much younger boy might answer before us. They practiced that method of testing their intelligence even though they were Yupiit, like white people probably do these days.

I've raised my children following the instructions I was taught. I wanted them to live properly and peacefully and not to intentionally provoke or abuse one another or get angry at each other. Instructions work when you apply them to your life. A person cannot be fixed through another means but only through instructions. And the rules he learned can allow him to lead a good life. However, one who does not listen attentively while given instruction will be a bad person. He will be the source of gossip, and stories about his bad conduct and behavior will be told. He will not be a good person and will like to steal others' belongings. That is what they say about them.

Having heard it repeatedly, later in our life we would eventually understand it
(16) Elsie Mather and Theresa Moses, April 2001:147

Elsie Mather: It seems as though many young people do not believe what they hear these days. You should always bring up instructions repeatedly, even though we do not understand them fully. And those teachings will be different and not stated in the same way when retold to us. And it seems they told us to continually speak of them, that even if we heard them before, we would understand them more clearly [when they were repeated]. They said we would remember them later on and understand them more clearly.

Theresa Moses: They said we would begin to understand them as we were living. Or we would understand the principle behind that teaching if we got into a bad situation. They said it would not mean anything to us at first, but we would begin to understand it after hearing it numerous times. That is what they said to me as well. They said I would start to understand it after hearing it repeatedly.

Qaneryaraq-gguq wavet cingillemtenun
qillrulluku waten aug'arrngairutelluku

(17) Frank Andrew, October 2001:134–35

Tan'gaurluq-gguq nasaurluq-llu qanruyutminek angayuqaagminek-llu caliyaraagnek elitnaurumatuuq. Tua-i-llu elluarrluni pikuni nasaurluq aanamitun pitariluni elilluni, cangallrunrirluni caliara. Tuamtellu tan'gaurluq atamitun pitariluni.

Tua-i-llu qanrut'laraitkut waten. Atam-gguq nasaurluulriani, aanavut tuqukan qaill' calisciigalkumta unguvangramta tuquniartukut. Elisngavkenaku aanamta caliyaraa, camek calisciiganata cumigutellrunrilamteggu. Akluirulluta-llu. Tan'gaurluq-llu ayuqlutek.

Taugken-gguq elitnaurutvut murilkelluku cakneq calituluta angayuqamcetun pikumta, aatavut tuqukan, tan'gaurlurni caliara caliaqetukumteggu, caliara aatamta unguvavkarluku, calivkarluku. Nasaurluq-llu tuaten ayuqluni cali. Maa-i-llu mat'umi qaneryarami, New Testament-aami qanrut'laraitkut qaneryaraq-gguq niitellerput ukvekluku, caliara caliaqesqutii caliaqenrilkumteggu tuqumaciquq.

Waniwa elpet camek caliyugngangerpet, mingeqsugngangerpet, keniryugngangerpet, camek caliyugngangerpet, iqairiyugngangerpet, qessanayullren aturluku piyuilkuvet, amtall' piyugngaluten, tua-i caliarkat tuqumaluteng. Wiinga tuamtellu tuaten ayuqlua, piyugngayaaqlua taugken tua-i, calikuma tuaten ayuqelriamek ayuqeliluku caliyugngayaaqlua, tua-i tuqumavkarluku caliaqenrilamni. Uitayulleq una tua-i qessayaraq amllernek apaatengqertuq: Aningyaaryukuma, qessayukuma, uitayunqegkuma caliyugngangerma.

Tua-i tuaten ayuquq qanruyun. Taumek pitullrukaitkut qaneryaraqgguq alerquateput wavet cingillemtenun, cingitun imutun sap'akit cingiicetun qillrulluku katagngairutelluku, waten aug'arrngairutelluku. Cingillrutekluku-gguq, tua-i *loose*-arngairutelluku wavet, katagngairutelluku. Cunawa uum iluanun ekluku qamiqumun. Yugni ciuqliit augkut *elder*-aat wavet elliluku, cingillermun qillrucesqelluku qanruyun pitullruitkut. Cunawa wavet wani umyuam uitayaraanun.

They used to tell us that we should tie our instructions to our ankles with our shoelaces so that they would not become untied
(17) Frank Andrew, October 2001:134–35

They say boys and girls are taught how to work by their parents. And if a girl learned well, she learned just as much as her mother and worked no differently than her mother. And a boy became like his father also.

They then told us the following. They told us girls that we would die even though we were still alive, if we didn't know how to work when our mother died. We would not be competent in our mothers' way of working, because we were not attentive and eager to learn. And we would eventually run out of possessions. It's the same for a boy.

But they said if we paid attention to our teachings and worked like our parents, when our father dies, if we young men continue to do his work, we would allow our father's work to live on after he died. It is the same for a girl. And according to the Bible, the New Testament tells us that if we didn't live according to the teaching and truly believe in it, our faith would be dead.

Now, even though you are able to work on tasks, though you are able to sew, cook, wash clothes, if you do not do so and follow your laziness though you are capable, those tasks that are to be worked on are dead. If I was like that, though I was capable of working on something, though I was capable of doing the same work, I am causing it to be dead if I don't work on it. There are many words to describe sloth and laziness: *Aningyaaryukuma, qessayukuma, uitayunqegkuma.*

That is how the *qanruyun* works in our life. That is why they told us that we should tie our instructions, our teachings, to our ankles with our shoelaces so that we would not lose them, so that they would not become untied. They said that we should tie them so that they would not become untied, so that we would not lose [our instructions]. They actually meant putting it into our minds. Those first Yup'ik elders said to tie the teachings onto our shoelaces. They actually meant to put them in our minds.

Elitnaurvigmi elitnaurilqa

(18) Frank Andrew, June 5, 1995:6–7

Wii elitnaurvigmi ayagniqarraarcetellratni, imkunek tua-i mikcuayaarnek. Taukut mat'umek angayuqritnun, angayuqaqenrilengraitki-llu, niisngallerkaatnek, maligtaquuraulluki, takaqluki aanait maligngangnaqluki pillerkaitnek piqarraallrukenka. Augkunek-llu tua-i angenritnek pivkaatnga, mat'umek kevgartuayaramek, piyugngariluki angayuqritnun ikayuutellerkaatnek, ikayualluki. Wall'u makut kevgaitulriit tangrrinarpek'naki pillerkaatnek. Tamatumek tamaa-i arcaqerluku pilallrukenka.

Makut-llu tua-i augkut angenrit cali man'a pingnaq'ngellerkaat kanarluku cali, aulukestengurtellerkaat, aipangllerkaat-llu tekilluku qaillun yuungnaq'ngellerkaatnek. Tamakunek tamaa-i angtaciit tangerrluki qalarut'lallruanka, qalarut'laranka-w' tua-i.

Ellangyuallemni murilkessagullua qanruyutek'lallemnek augkut mikcuayagaat qalarut'lallruanka takaqillerkaatnek aanaitnek. Aanait-llu maligtaquurluki inerquraqatki-llu inerciryarluki pillerkaatnek.

Ilumun una yuk taugaam ellminek pikuni piyugngauq

(19) Paul John, November 2000:198

Tua-llu akwaugaq qanelriit iliit qanellruuq wangkutnek taugaam pikumta piyugnganiluta. Ilumun una yuk taugaam ellminek pikuni piyugngauq. Wiinga tamana tua-i niipailemku, aug'um-llu, ataatakellrukeka, angutem ataucim qayacuallerramni inangqainanemni uyangllua qanrutaanga, "Kia kituggngaitaaten, kia picisngaitaaten, kia ikayurngaitaaten aug'umek ciunerkarpenek elluarrluku atungnaqerkarpenek, elpenek taugaam piciqan tekitarkan augna." Tuani tua-i taringqapigtenricaaqekeka qayacuallerramni inangqalua uyangllua qanellrani. Maaten tang yuvrirqa augkut ava-i aarcirtuutet qularpek'nateng ciuliamta ayagyuameggnun qanaatek'lallrit, assiitnik'ngait ilait atunrilkurrluki, assirluki pinaqnikait maligtaqungngnaqluki; tuatnakuma wangnek taugaam tua-i ilumun pipigciiqellinilrianga. Augna ava-i ellminek taugaam ilumun yuk pikuni piyugngallinicia ikayuqautekluku piaqa.

The time I taught at school

(18) Frank Andrew, June 5, 1995:6–7

When they first had me come to the school to talk to little children, I began speaking to them about the importance of listening to, heeding, and respecting their parents and other adults. I talked about the significance of following the advice of parents. And when they asked me to talk to the bigger children, I talked to them about the importance of helping their parents and the support and assistance they should provide for their caregivers and others in need of help. Those were the main things I talked to them about.

And I talked to older children about becoming responsible community members and providers themselves. My talks to them included the responsibilities of becoming a spouse and having families of their own. Those were some of the things I talked about, depending on the age group.

I talked to the little ones in the school about the importance of respecting parents, the same lesson I was given when I was their age. I talked to them about the importance of following the advice of parents and the significance of adhering to the direction and guidance they give.

Indeed, one can succeed only if he desires to do so

(19) Paul John, November 2000:198

And yesterday one of the speakers said that we could only accomplish things ourselves. Indeed, one can succeed only if he desires to do so. Before I heard this, my *ataata* [father's brother] peeked in while I was lying in my small kayak and said to me, "No one will change you, no one will do things for you, no one will help you live a proper life in your future, but you can only accomplish what is in your future yourself." I did not fully understand what he meant when he peeked in and said that to me while I was lying in that small kayak. When I thought about it, I realized that our ancestors instructed their young people about dangerous situations without holding anything back. I would lead a good life if I tried to avoid the things they warned me about and followed their good advice and guidance. I just wanted to say that if a person wants to accomplish things, he can surely do so on his own.

Paniguam elitnaullra

(20) Peter Jacobs, September 1998:28–31

Tua-llu wiinga tan'gurra'urluulua, aanaitellruukut. Nangteqluta. Ukut taugken akiqliput elliraat cali aanangqerrluteng, mingqesterluteng. Wangkurlumta taugken mingqestaunata atangqerrssaaqluta, kaigyugnaunatallu. Taugken taukut akiqliput, elliraat, aanangqerrssaaqluteng qaqimaluteng angayuqertuumalriacetun qaqimalriacetun ayuqluteng. Imkut yuut naklegtartut tangrrinaqengyuilameng.

Tua-llu waniwa wii aquilrianun ilagautenga'arcama imkut nasaurluut, tan'gaurluut-llu amllellrunritut Cuukvagtulimi. Arnartangqellruuq Arnangyiaraq, taum pilu'ugturnauraakut. Pilu'ugturraarluta . . . waniwa ayagyuani murilkurkiciu. *School*-aumalqa qanrutkeqatarqa ciuliamtenek. Taqe'rtaqamikut anqata'arqamta qanruarrnauraakut, "Kitek-at' ilaten unuamek kenkurluki piurqina. Eq'ukengkatgen-llu nayungnaqevkenaki uniqurqiki." Una piciuguq. Nallunritaat ukut yuut tamarmeng. Elitnaurani murilkurkiciu qaillun wangkuta ciuliamta elitnaurilallrat wangkutnek.

Tua-i tuaten qanrutelnguamia, mikerrlainarngailama, tangerrluki makut ilanka ciuqliit qanikciulriit, qanikciurun tegulanga'arcamku, angukarnaat iliit, uum-gguq Anirtuutem Atiin tangrramia quyuarluni pianga, "Qasgim elaturraa carriran. Enekenrilngerpeki-llu qakemkut, cariquvki yuut quyaciqut." Tuaten qanrucanga, nutaan *first grade*-aurraarlua, taum angukarnallraam uum-gguq, Anirtuutem Atiin *second grade*-aurtaanga. Nutaan aipirilua *second grade*-aurtaanga. Aling cakneq-lli imkuni piciatun pillrunritlinivaa. Angliqataarallratnek ayagluki qanruqu'urluki piniriinallrat maliggluku.

Pivakarlua nutek cali tegumiaqengaarcamku, ayaganga'arcama, imkurluut qangqiiret pitaqetullruamteki, talliman cipluku picama, Ata'urluqa qasgimi nallunrilamku aqvaqurlua ullagluku piaqa, "Tang qangqiirtellrianga amllernek!" Pianga, "Kitek Arnangiar imna malrugnek payugesgu." Tang imkut piciatun pivkenateng elitnaururaturatullrukaitkut wangkuta. Tuaten agucamni, itrucamni Arnangiar qanertuq, "Aling quyanarpiitli ilangcinrilgu ukut pitaten amllenerpameggnek cimingeciqut." Wiilkuk-am alartellinilua waniwa watua waniwa amllenritnek cikiqataryuklua utaqalgiarluku. Kiituan tang uitalnguunga. Pingairucanga angniinii anlua qanrulluku tang umyuaqa, "Iqlungarpaa-ll'."

How Peter was educated

(20) Peter Jacobs, September 1998:28–31

When I was a young boy, we had no mother. We suffered. But our neighbors, who were also without a parent, had a mother. They had someone to sew for them, but we had no one to sew for us, but we had a father, and we were far from going hungry. But our neighbors, without a parent, seemed like they had everything and had both parents because they had a mother. Those people had a lot of compassion, because they did not look the other way after seeing [someone's] need for help.

When I started to play with other children, there weren't many young girls and boys in Cuukvagtuli. There was an elderly woman who helped put our *piluguut* [skin boots] on. After putting our boots on . . . Now listen closely, you young people. I am going to talk about my schooling from our ancestors. When she was done, she would simply tell us before we ran outside, "Be kind to others today. If they pick on you, do not stay with them but leave them." This is true. All of these people here know this. You schoolchildren, be aware of what our ancestors have taught us.

When she got tired of telling me this, because I was not always going to be a young boy, I observed the older boys who were shoveling doorways. When I started to shovel them myself, one of the old men, Anirtuuq's father, saw me, he smiled and said, "You are clearing the porch of the *qasgi*. Though it is not your house, if you clear their porches, the people will be happy." When he told me this, I was in first grade, but Anirtuuq's father promoted me to second grade. Gee, those ancestors certainly didn't say or do things carelessly or pointlessly. They constantly gave advice to children from when they were little until they were grown adults.

When I started to handle guns and to go out hunting, because we used to catch poor ptarmigans, when I caught about five, I ran to my father, who I knew was in the *qasgi*, and told him, "Look, I caught a lot of ptarmigan." He said, "You should give Arnangiar two of them." You see, our ancestors did not teach us without a good purpose. When I brought it over to her and brought it in, she said, "Why thank you very much. Your catch here will be replaced by more than you gave me." I mistakenly thought she was going to give me something in return immediately and waited. Gee, I waited for a long time and got tired. When she didn't give me anything, I went out disappointed, thinking, "What a liar."

Ata'urlumnun aglua qanrutaqa. Itrama quuyuarall'erluni pianga, "Tuallu-qaa augna payugtellren qaill' pia." Piaqa, "Iqlukiinga tang. Amllenerpiinek cimiryuguarraarluku cikinrilkiinga." Nutaan Atallerama quyuarluni pianga, "Tauna tuaten pinrituq. Yuilqumelngurmek piaten. Tua-i tua-inguuq." Tuaten qanrucanga umyuama, maa-i matum nalliini elitnaurat imkut nauwa, *third grade*-aurtaatnga taukut nutaan.

Aling imkuni-lli picirrluatun pinripaa angliriurallrat maliggluki. Pinariama mikerrlainarngailama nulirtullerkaq una canimellian, ataurluma piqaraanga, "Aipangqesqumayaaqamken wii tangvauraqallerkamnek." Tua-i taugaam tuaten qanrullua. Niugtarmiunun-llu qamigarlua, tekicarturlua nell'eramtenun itertua, ukut qasperet *room*-amni agalriit. Umyuaqa nall'artenrilan alqerput piaqa. "Kia makut aturai?" Kiugaanga, "Nulirpet." Nallumni nulirturcetlinikiitnga. Aren, nasaurlungqerrlua-llu Cuqartalegmiumek. Nallunritaat ukut angutet iliita aipaquratullruamnuk.

Pivakarluni tuaten nutaan pinarilliama atama qanrutaanga, "Tua-i nulirturtuten. Yuut qakemkut qanrit elpenun pitgaqutarkaugut. Qungyarnarqellriit umyuamek navgurinarqellriit ciutegpeggun niiteng'erpeki, angu ukveqsaqunaki tamakut." Tauna atullerallrulliamiu qanrutkekii. Taugaam qanrucaaqlua waten, "Iigpegun taugaam tangerquvgu nutaan ukveqina." Waniwa man'a augkut ciuliamta nallunrilamegteggu pitgaqucaqaat wangkutnun navguutnguniluku. Ilumun navguutnguuq. Inerqullrungraanga wii kanaksutullruaqa aipaqa allanun pisqumavkenaku. Kasngukevkenaku qanrutkaqa man'a. Tang imkut piciatun pillrunritlinilriit.

Tuamtellu irniangamegnuk irniangqerrsaram ayuqucianek qanruqu'urlunuk cali pillruyaaqlunuk. Tang imkut piciatun pivkenateng. Maa-i mat'um nalliini tuar qanruciaqameng pukukaqluku una, una amaken aqvaluku qanqautekaqluku, taringnaunani. Taugaam ilumuuguq una kanaken ayangyaarluku qanrutkurqumteggu irniamtenun, tutgaramtenun-llu nutaan neq'aqerciqaat. Wii neq'aqalarqa ilanka kenkurluta aquisqelallratni. Atuqataryaaqluku, neq'aqaarqamku taq'aqluku. Waten taugken caperrnariluki, tan'gaurluq una; qanrucaaqaqamki-llu qetunraanka wa-

I went to my father and told him. As I walked in, he smiled and asked, "So how did that person you gave the gift to react?" I said, "She lied to me. She said that she was going to replace it with more and didn't give me anything." Then my father smiled and said, "No, you got it wrong. She is replacing it with animals in the wilderness. That is what she meant." When he told me that, like kids who are in school these days, when that knowledge was given to me by those people I entered third grade.

Those people certainly knew and understood proper child rearing. When I was getting older and reaching the age to marry, my father said to me, "I want you to have a wife so I can watch you." When I arrived home from seal hunting in Newtok, I walked inside our small house and saw *qasperet* [hooded garments] hanging in my room. I didn't know why, so I asked our oldest sister, "Whose clothes are these?" She answered, "Your wife's." They obtained a wife for me without my knowledge. Gee, and I had a girlfriend in Cuqartalek. One of the men here knows who she is, because he and I were good friends.

Then one day, perhaps when I was ready to hear this, my father said, "Well, you have a wife now. People's mouths will be directed at you like arrows being shot at you. Do not believe the things that you hear with your ears that can cause jealousy and injure the mind." He told me this because he probably experienced it. But actually he was telling me, "Believe it only if you see it with your own eyes." Because our ancestors knew this, they were trying to tell us that it could break a relationship. It certainly can cause hardship and pain in relationships. Even though he warned me, I was jealous and suspicious of my wife and didn't want her to be with others, telling her not to mind other men. I'm telling you this without embarrassment or remorse. Our ancestors certainly didn't do or say things without a purpose.

And again, when we had children, they also gave us advice and guidance on raising children. You see they did not do things without a good purpose. And it seems like when they talk to people these days, they talk a little bit about something here and then they take something from over there and talk briefly about it, to the point where it is not understood by anyone. But it is really true that our children and grandchildren will remember their instructions later on in their lives if we keep lecturing them from the time they are little. From time to time I remembered my instruc-

ten kiularaatnga, *"You not graduate. I graduate."* Qetunrama tuaten qan-rut'laraatnga. Akekatak aknirrlua-llu.

Tang man'a-llu *college*-aallerteng, *graduate*-allerteng-llu ilaita puqig-liurcukluteng umyuarteq'lartut. Man'a nallunritniarput, irninrilngaitut makut kinguliaput. Kitaki aanaulriani maurluulriani-llu irniangekuvci aug'utun qanqautaqluki, "Ilaten ata unuamek kenkurluki pikiki." Augkut ciuliamta piciryaraat maligqurluki. Waten pukuktaarpek'naki pivkenaci, taugaam tungmiquurauciicetun uingekan-llu uingyaram ayuqucia, nulir-turyaram-llu ayuqucia qanrutekluku, irniangyaram-llu ayuqucia qanru-tekluku. Quyanarpait-lli caknerpak.

tion to be kind when playing with other children. And when I was on the verge of going against that advice, I would stop when I remembered their words. But when they are older and set in their ways, when I attempt to instruct my sons, they'd answer me, "You did not graduate. I graduated." My own sons tell me that. When they do, it's very painful.

Some people who went to college and graduated think they have become wiser. We should all keep in mind that the younger generation will not cease to have children. I encourage mothers and grandmothers who have children to tell them, "Now, be kind to others today." May we follow our ancestors' *piciryarat* [customs and traditions]. Do not take fragments of our teachings when teaching our children but teach them everything about marriage and child rearing. Thank you very, very much.

Umyuaq Tuknilria

Elliraat-gguq arnassagaat-llu angukara'urluut-llu umyugaat tuknirituuq quyatmek

(21) Frank Andrew, September 2000:94

Tua-llu una tuvqakiyaraq, takumcukiyaraq. Taukut tua-i elliraat, aipainret, angukara'urluut wall'u arenqiallugingalriit piyugngangermeng, temseng akngiringaluku-llu tamakutgun-gguq tamaa-i, unangkengatgun neqkakun kevgiuryarakun-llu caliarkaugukut. Waten-llu inerquumaaqluta, "Nunuliryungraaten, akiliryungraaten arnassagaam ciuniuryaqunaku tuaten pingraan." Inerquutellerput tamaa-i. Camek cikiqumteni arnassagaam camek elliin piyungraakut pisqevkenaku. Wall'u elliraat augkut carrarmek piyungraakut pisqevkenata.

Maaten man'a *New Testament* qaneryaraq *Jesus*-aam qanrutkaa cikiqengyaraq-gguq atawaunruuq akurtunermi. Tamatuullinilria inerquutaq'lallerput ciulirnernek. Waniwa arnassagaq cikiumaaqami angnilartuq cakneq, angukara'urluq-llu ikayuumaaqami, quyatmek cakneq tua-i quyaq'apiarluni, quyanaqvaaraluni tua-i arenqianani. Tuaten-gguq qanngermi tauna cikirteni atu'urkaanek cikitua yuunginanrani elluarrluni, umyuani nall'arrluni camek pikani, angniutekaanek nutaan, elluamek, elluarrluni pillerkaanek. Tuamtellu iliit cikiumaaqami waten qanernaurtuq, "Anirtaqulluk." Iqulirpek'naku tangrrumanrilngurmek-gguq alaitenrilngurmek-gguq cikirluku, elluarrluni pillerkaanek taugaam.

Elliraat-gguq arnassagaat-llu angukara'urluut-llu umyugaat tuknirituuq quyatmek. Taumek tamakut tamaa-i arcaqerluki murilkesqelluki aulukestairutellriit, neqkarrlainaq-llu pivkenaku tangerrluki atu'urkaitnek piyugngastaitnun cikilaasqelluki atu'urkaitnek, aturarkaitnek, neqkarrlai-

A Powerful Mind

**They say orphans' and elders'
feelings of gratitude become powerful in time**
(21) Frank Andrew, September 2000:94

And now about generosity and compassion. They said we should help orphans, widows, elder men, or those who are disabled through sharing food and doing chores. They admonished us and said, "Even though an old woman wants to pay you, do not accept it." That was our admonishment. They told us not to accept it when an old woman gave us something in return after we gave them something or not to accept it if orphans wanted to give us something little.

When I read the New Testament after that, Jesus said giving is better than receiving. That was actually the teaching that came from our elders. An elderly woman is extremely happy when given something, and an elderly man is extremely grateful when helped, and they express their gratitude by repeatedly thanking you with great conviction. Even though he is merely thanking him, he actually gives the gift giver something that is useful in the future. He is giving him something to be thankful for as he is living his life, a good thing, something that will help him positively in his life. And when one is given something, they say, "*Anirtaqulluk* ["It is no wonder" or "It serves him right," an expression used to declare a good or bad outcome to someone's actions]." They would say just that and nothing else, but it is said that by doing that, they are giving them an unseen blessing, only a positive thing.

They say orphans' and elders' feelings of gratitude become powerful in time. That is why they asked us to take special care of those with no pro-

narnek pivkenaki. Tamaa-i tamakut aulukesqelluki arcaqerluki pissuryug-
ngalrianun arnanun-llu pitullruit.

Yuum-gguq umyugaa tuknipialliniuq
(22) Frank Andrew, September 2000:96

Up'nerkitullruut, up'nerkilartukut unani cenamun elkarrluta imar-
pigmiutarnek pissungaqamta. Nunamiut piciryaraqenrilkiitnek unani
taugaam Bering Sea-mi pissutuukut, imarpiim ceniinun *move*-arluta. Waken *village*-aanek *camp*-anun ayagaluta avani pitullruukut, *seal hunting*-
aaryaranun up'nerkami.

Uani Kusquqviim paingani up'nerkilriit taukut ilangqelalliniut nukal-
piamek taumek piculriamek maklagculuni. Arnat makut uqicetaaryaraq
apqiit piyuumiutekaat cenarmiut. Tengruluteng cakneq uqicetaatuut, uqi-
qutuata-llu uqunek kemegnek tapirluki, arnarrlainaat angutmek ilauna-
teng. Tan'gaurluut-llu mikelnguut ilagaucuunateng inerquumatuameng.

Maa-i piciryaralput allaurtuq. Tauna-am atralliniuq pissurluni pina-
riani. Taggliniuq maklaggluni. Keluirturluku tua-i arnat-am tengruluteng
tua-i tekicartullrani assigtateng piluki. Piinanratni un'um elpekngamiki
nunullinii, uqicetaangraata maa-i uqumek cikircesngaitniluki. Angniur-
luryaaqellret imkut umyugaat igtelliniuq. Kingutmun caululuteng uterte-
lliniluteng angnirpek'nateng tengruyaaqellret imkut. Ilait qanlalliniut,
"Anirtaqulluk. Kiingan up'nerkarpak pitaqeciqvakii." Piculria tauna qunuluni [pilleq] up'nerkarpak kiingan pitaqelliniluku.

Allamian qamigaami pill'uni-am tagngami erinami uum engelqayagu-
caki qayagpagalliniuq uqicetaaresqelluki. Taum-gguq tan'gaurluut pissu-
tulit inerqualallrui elliin ayuqucillni maniluku, angu qunuqaasqevkenaki
mat'umek pitaatnek, arnat piyaraatnek. Yuum-gguq umyugaa tuknipia-
lliniuq.

Pikangqeng'ermi tengruluni pirraartelluku umyugaa navegluku pillerkaa — ava-i augna egmianun qanravet wanteqertuq-am augna qunuluni
umyuaqegtaariitnek tamatumek navgilleq, assinrilngurkun umyugaat navegluku, akiliutii-gguq ava-i navkengyaram.

viders, and not to give them just food, but for those who are able to give them clothing and things to use. They told hunters and women to especially care for those people.

They say a person's mind is indeed very powerful
(22) Frank Andrew, September 2000:96

We used to move to our spring camps on the coast when we started hunting for sea mammals. We moved down to the coast and hunted in the Bering Sea, a custom not practiced by the inland people.

Down near the mouth of the Kuskokwim River, those who were living in spring camp had a *nukalpiaq* [successful hunter] among them who was a great seal hunter. The women of the coast were always looking forward to the sharing of freshly caught seal meat and blubber, *uqicetaaryaraq*. Only the women and not the men were extremely eager to participate in this distribution of freshly caught seal meat and blubber. And the boys did not participate either, because they were taught not to.

Our traditions have changed today. When it was time, a hunter went down to hunt and came back up with a bearded seal. The women came down to the shore to meet him when he was approaching, holding their containers with excitement. When the hunter saw them, he scolded them. He told them that he would not give them seal blubber this time, even though they asked for it. The women who were excited became unhappy. They turned their backs and returned home sad after their anticipation. Some of them said, "*Anirtaqulluk*, let him try and hunt and see if he catches anything else all spring." That was the only [seal] the man, the great hunter caught that season.

So the next year when he went seal hunting and came home with a catch, when he got close enough so the women could hear him, he yelled and called them to come and get fresh meat and blubber. They said that man used to caution younger hunters, revealing his past experience and telling them never to be stingy with their catch. They say a person's mind indeed is very powerful.

To disappoint someone who had been eager to receive something, although they had something to give—when you spoke, the story of how that person's stinginess disappointed and hurt others came to mind immediately, and the consequences of such an action.

Qutegngalria

(23) Frank Andrew, June 2001:12

Waniwa wii tua-i tuaten ayuqekuma ciullegcessngaitua elpenun. Umyuarpet-llu tuaten pisqumangraanga, catkevkenaku, wii taugaam umyuamkun wii pivkararkauluten. Allam umyugaakun pingaunii wii, wii taugaam umyuamkun tua-i. Tua-i-gguq qutegngaluni. Ilani catkevkenaki picirkiqayunaunani-llu. Angenruluni ilamini ukuni. Qutegngaluni-gguq tua-i. Tamaa-inguuq tamana, arnauli angutnguli-llu ayuqlutek, tua-i tuaten ayuqellriik piyugngalutek.

Makut picirkiutet atuusqumalriit tamalkuita navgurluki pivakaqumta-gguq atam Ellam Yuan ellangcarniaraakut

(24) Frank Andrew, September 2000:96, 136

Tauna tua-i alingcirtuutekluku cali pitullruitkut. Makut picirkiutet atuusqumalriit tamalkuita navgurluki pivakaqumta-gguq atam Ellam Yuan ellangcarniaraakut. Arenqiallugtelluta cakneq tua-i. Tamaa-i tamatumek cali pitullruitkut. Alerquutnguuq augna ava-i aulukestailngurnun wall'u aulukestengqengraata arnassagaat angutessagaat-llu camek cikiqaqu'urluki pilaasqelluki. Quyatiit-gguq una cauluni tut'etuuq, utertetuuq ellaitnun yuunginanratni assilriaruluni tua-i assiilnguuvkenani.

Tuaten-llu qalarutaqamegtekut, tauna tuatnallerkarput qanrutkelaraat. Ellam-gguq Yuan tangvagaakut, taumun piciqniluta umyugiurpakaqumta. Una umyugiuryaraq pisqutni aturpek'naku piyarauguq, taugaam ellmi piliani elliin aturluku, inerquuteksaaqengermiu. Cirliqelriim niitenrilnguum akusrarutet ciumurut'larai, neqnikluki, anglakluki-llu. Ilamitun-llu ayuqevkenani nunam qaingani yuutulliniluni. Nuqlilluni ilamini, ilamitun pisciiganani. Imna taugken qanrucunarqelria, niisngalria, takaqilria-llu qacigtellriatun ayuqluni, mat'um nerangnaqellran paivngalulluku.

One who is arrogant
(23) Frank Andrew, June 2001:12

If I am like that, I will not let you surpass me. I will ignore your wishes, but I will make you do what I want. I will not follow the direction of others but will only follow my own mind. That kind of person is referred to as *qutegngalria.* They do not care about what others want, and it is not easy to tell them what to do. He thinks he is more important than those around him. They say he is arrogant. Either a woman or a man can be like that.

If we keep breaking the rules, they say Ellam Yua will do something so we come to our senses
(24) Frank Andrew, September 2000:96, 136

They warned us about [Ellam Yua, the Person of the Universe]. If we keep breaking all of these rules to live by, Ellam Yua will allow us to experience something that will cause us to come to our senses. He would allow us to go through hardship. That is what they told us as well. It's a traditional value to give aid to those without providers and old men and women even though they have families to take care of them. They say the gratitude is returned to the givers as they are living in some way or another, as a positive thing and not negative.

When they spoke to us, they told us that Ellam Yua was always watching us and that we would be reprimanded if we did as we pleased and continually lived according to our own will and desire. *Umyugiuryaraq* means that someone is not living by what is expected of him but is using his own will. They use their own will even though it is against their *inerquun.* A person who has no strong convictions, one who does not adhere to instructions, favors indulgent and fun things and becomes addicted to those behaviors. And his life would be different from others. He would not be as prosperous as others and would not be able to accomplish what others do. But one who listens and lives by what he is taught and is respectful and humble has an easy life. Food is readily available to him.

Qanruyutem taugaam mat'um niicugniurluku elitellrakun yuk menuirucugngaluni

(25) Theresa Moses, June 5, 1995:67

Cali-llu man'a menuunani piyaraq yuucimikun; qanruyutem taugaam mat'um niicugniurluku elitellrakun yuk menuirucugngaluni. Taumek irnialegni qanci ikingqayunarqaci nallunrita'arqevcenek qanruyutnek piniutekaitnek. Ellangyugallratni-llu canun iqlutun aakulagnarqelrianun ullagatevkenaki. Pinircautekaqenritait tamakut, menuunateng-llu nanger-ngatkaqevkenaki. Anglikuneng tayima ilulliqutekarpecenek iluvaucugngariciqut elpecenun, carrlugnek qiatekarpecenek akngirutekarpecenek-llu. Maa-i atungaat amlleret.

Umyuiqelria

(26) David Martin, April 2001:178–79

Tamana-am tamaa-i umyuiqsaraq cali nalqigtellermeggni nalqigutekaat umyuiqsiyaalria-gguq taugaam umyugaan-llu mat'um unaketua, callerkairutetua. Ilaminek waten irniaminek wall'u tungelquminek nangelrianek tuquluteng umyuiqsiyaalria, umyugaan unaketua tamakut qivrukluki, qunuksaaqluki tuququllret tamakut.

Qanrutkekuniu-llu assiriqerrluni

(27) Theresa Moses, April 2001:179–80

Apervikuayaraq. Qanrutkenrilkurrluku augna tuaten pilria qanrutkekuniu-llu assiriqerrluni. Tamana aassaqutekluku camek pillni qemangqakuniu, qanrutkenrilkuniu, uum qanellratun ellirluni, umyugaan ilii cimirluni. Usviilrianek-am tamakut acitungatait. Qanrutkenrilkurrluku camek pikeggnerunrilengraan-ll' ayagnirluni, tamaa-i qanrutkenrilkurrluku qemangqaluku, tuaten pikuni assiirutarkauluni-gguq. Taugken-gguq egmian qanrutkekuniu tamarluni.

Piciatun tua-i piyuk'ngaminun tauna tuaten pillni tunluku, qanrutekluku qanyunakek'minun. Nutaan-llu tangengermiu qanyunakekuniu qanrulluku, qanemcilluku.

A person can only become clean and pure by listening and learning *qanruyutet*

(25) Theresa Moses, June 5, 1995:67

How does a person stay clean and pure? A person can become clean by listening, learning, and living by instructions he was taught. Therefore those of you who have children must continue to teach your children the instructions you learned, which will give them strength. When they are small and just becoming aware of their surroundings, avoid bringing them to confusing settings that might muddle their minds. That kind of influence does not strengthen them, and it will not help them to stand clean and pure. As they get older they may learn to bring home things that might make you cry, deceitful and hurtful things. Many children and parents are in that situation today.

One who is depressed

(26) David Martin, April 2001:178–79

When they explained *umyuiqsaraq* [being depressed or distraught], they said the mind and emotions of one who is distraught prevail over him and cripple him. One who is too saddened or troubled over the death of his child or relative will experience a mental breakdown.

Speaking about it makes one feel better

(27) Theresa Moses, April 2001:179–80

Apervikuayaraq [The way of confessing or confiding in someone about what is troubling them]. One who keeps secrets will heal only if he speaks of them. He will end up like what he said if he keeps his misdeeds inside. They would become despondent. I think they call those people *usviilriit* [ones with no reasoning, who lose their ability to function normally]. Even though it isn't something serious to begin with, if he decides not to speak of it and keeps it inside, his health and well-being will deteriorate. However, he will forget it if he speaks of it right away.

They can tell anyone about what is troubling them, speaking to those they find easy to talk to or telling a stranger if they find it easier to confide in him.

Yuum-gguq quyallra nekayullra-llu tukniuq

(28) Theresa Moses, June 5, 1995:63

Cali-llu man'a inerquutalput, yuum-gguq quyallra tukniuq, cali-llu-gguq nekayullra tukniluni. Maa-i tang makut alerquutektulput wangkuta. Yuullemteni yuullgutvut nekalinritengnaqu'urluki piuraasqelluki qanemtenek, taugaam quyalingnaqu'urluki yuullgutput. Yuum-gguq quyallra tukniuq, cali-llu-gguq nekayullra tukniluni.

Tang maa-i makut wangkuta inerquutaqelput avani. Makut maa-i cakneq aarcirtuutnguluki niitetulput. Ilumun-llu piciuluni yuum quyallra nekayullra-llu [tukniuq]. Piciulliniluni. Wiinga quyassiyaagaqama iluteqlua-llu cacirkaitaqama agayuaqama tua-i agayutetuanka tuaten; iliini qialua iliini-llu qiavkenii. Ilumun tua-i yuum umyugaa quyallra tuknilliniami, nekayullra-llu cali tuknilliniluni. Cat tua-i avani wangkutnun qanrutkumallruuq, ikiullra assillra-llu.

Umyuarput cangraan angliriqertevkenata ilamtenun qanerteresqevkenata. Tua-i maa-i inerquutalput wangkuta. Cali tua-i piyugngaurallemteni cauraasqelluta: "Atam pisciigalikuvci pisciigalillininiartuci." Iqluquyugnaunateng. Piyugngaurallrani yuk cauraasqelluku, taugaam man'a kemgan akngirtellerkaa murilkurluku. Iqulirluku-llu, "Atam piyungerpeci pisciigalikuvci pisciigalillininiartuci." Ilumun piciuluni. Apqucim wangkuta tut'aqakut cayungramta casciigalilriatun ayuqelartukut. Imutun pitullemtun piyugyaaqlua-ll' wii iluteqtuyaaqua.

Ciuliaput kusgurtallruut

(29) Wassilie Evan, July 2000:28

Augkut kusgurtallruut. Mana-llu cali kusgurtaryaraq takumcukiyaraq ak'a avaken ayagluni piuguq. Ilaput-gguq augkut tuaten pilallrulliniut. Waten-llu qanraqluteng, "Angukaraurluut ikayuangnaqu'urluki, kusgualuki, canek-llu piaqata, qerrutnek-llu ciqiciaqata allurrluki."

They say a person's feelings of gratitude and humiliation are powerful

(28) Theresa Moses, June 5, 1995:63

We were also admonished about the following. They say a person's feelings of gratitude and feelings of humiliation are powerful. These were our teachings. They taught us how to use discretion among our fellows and not to say things that might hurt their feelings. *Yuum-gguq quyallra nekayullra-llu tukniuq* [They said a person's feelings of gratitude and humiliation are very strong].

These were some of our *inerquutet* [admonitions]. These were some of the warnings we heard. And there's truth in the axiom, "*Yuum quyallra nekayullra-llu tukniuq* [A person's feelings of gratitude and humiliation are very strong]." When someone does something that makes me very grateful, sometimes the only thing I can do is to pray for his well-being. And sometimes my feelings would be so strong I would weep. There's truly strength in a person's feelings when he is happy or when he is wounded emotionally. Back in those days everything was taught to us, both the good and the bad side.

When we were offended, we were taught to have self-control instead of becoming haughty. These were some of our admonitions. We were also taught not to be lazy while we were able, and this was said to us: "You see, when you are disabled you will discover that you definitely cannot do anything at all." They were telling the truth. A person was continually told to work while he was able but to be careful not to injure his body. They talked to people about this and added, "You see, when your body is not able to function anymore, that's when you'll discover that you couldn't do anything at all." It is true. When illness falls on us, we do become helpless. Sometimes I cry, wishing I was still quick and agile like I was when I was younger.

Our ancestors were compassionate people

(29) Wassilie Evan, July 2000:28

Our ancestors were compassionate people. Being compassionate and having pity was always the custom of our people. They said our ancestors were like that. And they said to us, "Always help the old men, take pity on them, and when they're doing chores, and emptying their urine buckets, take it away from them and empty it."

Man'a tang maani qanruyun imutun
iinruullinilria tememun uumun yuucimun

(30) Paul John, June 7, 1995:67–68

Man'a tang maani qanruyun imutun iinruullinilria tememun uumun yuucimun. Cali-llu maa-i umyuiqelrianek qanlalriit, umyualiurtenek-llu qanraqluteng. Tua-i yuut avanirpak tuatnatuyaaqelliniut ilait, umyua-meggnek piluteng. Taugaam augkut ciuliamta, kenka aturluku, tuatnalriit qanrucugngastaita, tua-i kenkakun qanenqegcaarauqurluki taringevkar-luki auluktullrulliniit. Augkut umyuiqelrianek aplerkaat nalluamegteggu usvikayalrianek taugaam aptullruit ellangeqarraallemni. Usvikayalrianek piaqluki. Cunawa umyuameggnek makut pilriit tamaa-i kenkakun qanen-qegcaarauqurluk' pillratgun assiriaqluteng tamaa-i pilallrullinilriit.

Ilii maa-i qanyunakek'minun qanaagaqluni ayuqucia uqeglilartuq. Cali maa-i aturtengqertuq avani piciryarallrat ciuliat.

Taumek man'a qanruyun iinruuluku wii tangvala'arqa umyuamkun wangkutnun, kitugutkellruatgu-llu ciuliamta ayagyuameggnun. Ayagyua-teng uitatevkenaki qalaruqu'urluki. Tua-i ayagyuameggnun kitugutek-luku.

Cali-llu tamaani, mat'umek itukutaitellrani, allanemta makut qatellriit cayaraatnek, atrarrniluteng ciulirnemeggnun qanyuitellruut ayagyuat. Caluteng nunurnganateng-llu, wagg'uq umyuameng qamum tenguqli-rutekvaka'arqaku una qanrutarkani, tutgarani, usruni, cani pini tunga-yani, umyuami apqiitnek tenguqlirutekvaka'arqaku tua-i qanrutaqluku nunurnganaku. Elpeurluurluku, ingyuurluurluku, ayuqucirkaanek qan-rulluku, "Wateurluq tang ayuqellerpeggun tuaten ayuqeqataurlulriaten." Nakleguurluku.

Apertuagaqamegteggu waten qanrutpigainalalliniluku: "Piicagturqina-at' ernerpak." Aling, agayumapiallinivakar ciuliamteni!

Watua taugken ellimerturilriartairulluni, "Tuaten-at' ernerpak ayuqe-kina." Piicaasqurilriartaunani. Agayuvik-wa kiingan tua-i pinariaqan ullagyugtain ullagluku piicagyarturviat.

Words of wisdom are like medicine to body and life

(30) Paul John, June 7, 1995:67–68

Apparently *qanruyutet* were like medicine to the body and the spirit. And today we hear about people who become dispirited and depressed, and they also talk about mental-health therapists. Mental disorders did exist in our people for years. But our people in the past only used *qanruyutet* that were enriched with kindness and compassion when they tried to help people. And a person was carefully chosen to approach the person in need of loving words of wisdom. They'd pick an experienced person who might be able to alter the patient's outlook. Consequently this method was practical and helped people to find peace in themselves.

This method is still used by our people today. When a person continues to confide in someone about his difficulties, he begins to feel better, and his oppressed spirit begins to be lifted up again.

I believe that words of wisdom are truly medicine for our minds. They were also used by our ancestors to improve the lives of their young people. Instead of sitting back, they continually spoke to their youth about good things and bad things in life, improving the lives of negligent youths.

And in the past, before this new way of life became attached to our ways, the ways of the white people, our guests, the young people were never critical of their elders or said that they were belittled by them. When elders corrected the behavior of their grandchildren, nephews, or close relatives, they lectured to them earnestly and sounded like they were chiding them. They candidly talked to their youth about their faults and said, "You pitiful one, someday you will be a crestfallen person if you continue to behave using your own mind." They expressed their disappointment and sorrow openly to them.

When they spoke to someone about proper living, they would finally say this to him: "Throughout the day make sure you have continual communication with the Creator." Our ancestors certainly were extremely faithful people.

And today there's no one telling others, "You should behave all day today." People aren't being told to have constant contact with God anymore. The church is the only place where at certain times some people go to pray these days.

Quyallagallermegteggun-gguq cikirteteng elluarrluteng pillerkaatnun cingqaqutuit umyuamegteggun

(31) Frank Andrew, September 2000:150

Tua-i taugken tangerrluki ilateng nangutellriit neqnek cikiraqluki piyugtaita. Tua-i murilkelluki, augkut-llu imkut aulukestairutellriit, elliraat arcaqerluki. Tamakut pitullruit angutmek pingnaqestailnguut elliraat piyugngariksailnguut. Angukaralleraat arnassagaat-llu cali tua-i pinricesciiganaki camek unangaqameng. Augna pitekluku pitulliniluki qanrutkellrukeka iciw' akwaugaq, quyallrat. Quyallagallermegteggun-gguq cikirteteng elluarrluteng pillerkaatnun cingqaqutuit umyuamegteggun. Tamana tamaa-i pisqutngullruuq cali wangkutnun qanrutaarullemteni. Qunuyugpek'nata ikayuutekluki taugaam pisqelluki ikayurnarqelrianek.

Yuullerpeni qutkauyaqunang

(32) David Simon Sr., November 2000:207

Akwaugaq aparrluamneng qanelrianga wani. Ukut civuqliit qanqautellri qanqauteqerlaki. Waten pilqaanga civuqliiuluku: "Yuullerpeni qutkauyaqunang. Wii kinguneqa naklegnarquq. Kankut imkut ikayurnarqelriit ikayuumakiki pinerturarpetun. Naken-llu tekitengraata nunaneng allaneng qaingatgun tangerrsaqunaki, aturaitgun tangerrsaqunaki, tangerrluksaqunaki. Tamakuneng ikayuritukuvet, ilavneng, nunuliutiit ang'uq."

Qaruyutekun kiingan

(33) Dick Anthony, November 2000:86–87

Waten-am qanellruuq aug'umek qanruyutmek, angliyugallrani mikelnguq auluklerkaanek. Ilaita qanqautek'laryaaqaat ilii taugaam elluarrluku qanrutkeksaitaat. Tua-i mikelnguum man'a caacuurtellerkaa taugaam uluryanarquq, arcaqalriaruuq. Aipaqutellriik caliarkaqngamegnegu una wani mikelnguum anglicarallra, anglicarluku-w' tua-i qanrutenrilkurrluku piyunaitaa, taugaam qanqautaqluku amllerinrilengraan piurquni, mikelnguq, nasaurluq, wall'u angun, tan'gurraq. Waten ilumun pileryagaluni mikelnguq qanrucunaitaa. Waten ilii pilartuq qaruyutekun taugaam elluarrluni niicugniyunruciquq mikelnguq. Uuggun qanpagakun, yag-

They say they push their givers toward good fortune with their minds when grateful

(31) Frank Andrew, September 2000:150

Those who wanted to gave food to those who ran out after seeing their need. They watched over those who did not have caretakers, especially orphans. They gave to those who did not have a male provider and orphans who were not yet capable. And they always gave to elderly men and women when they caught something. [They gave them food] because they say they push their givers toward good fortune when grateful. That was one of the values they wanted us to follow when we were instructed. They told us to help those who needed assistance without being stingy.

Do not be arrogant while you are living

(32) David Simon Sr., November 2000:207

Yesterday I spoke about my grandfather. Let me mention the first lessons he taught me. This is what he told me first: "Do not be arrogant while you live. I come from a very poor and humble background. Help those who need assistance as best you can. And do not judge others who arrived from other villages based on how they look and the clothes they wear. Do not judge them by how they look. The reciprocity of those you helped will be great."

Only through encouragement

(33) Dick Anthony, November 2000:86–87

He mentioned an instruction concerning raising a child. Some people have spoken about part of it, but they have not covered it thoroughly. The possibility of a child becoming a bad person is very serious and reprehensible. Because it's the responsibility of a couple to raise a child, they must not withhold instructions from him, but give a female or male child instruction even though it is not a lot. Indeed, one must not discipline a child inappropriately. Some say that a child will become obedient only if taught rules and instructions. One will not help a young child who is starting to listen by yelling and hitting with hands. They said if one treats

taakun unatetgun ikayurngaitaa yuum ayagyuaq mikelnguq waten ciu-
tengelria. Tuaten-gguq ayuqekuni qanrutkelallrukiit-am, nunurluku
qatpagalluku, qanpagalluku piaqami, umyugaa-llu naivterrlainarluku,
caunrilkelluku irniaqenrilengramteggu, caacuurtetuuq. Qaruyutkun
taugaam piarkaulliniarput, piarkaulriaruyaaqerput.

Una wani mikelngumek navgurillerkaq atawaunritqapiaralriaruuq,
assirpek'nani-llu iqua. Waten-gguq ayagyuaq qanpagaqurluni, unatet-
gun-llu yagteraaqluni teguleraluku piyunaituq. Tuaten-gguq tamana aturluku anglicariyaaqekunek irniarak tauna caacuurciiquq teglengarluni, iq-
lungarluni, ca tua-i aturyugluku ellminek pingkuni. Qanqautengermi-llu
qanrem ciuqliim unaksuunaku, unakesciigaliluku. Wagg'uq asemrurr-
luku, pamairulluku.

Waten wani taunarrlainaq-llu pivkenaku navgutullinia yuum wall'u
angayuqaqenrilngermiu, irniani-gguq yuum. Qanruqu'urararkaugaa
imutun kenkeqapiaralriatun. Qaruqurluku piurquni-gguq taugaam mikelnguq elluarrluni-gguq angliciquq.

Tua-i tamana tamaa-i aarnarqelriarulliniuq makunun mikelngurnun
irnianun, tan'gurrarmun arcaqerluni arnamun-llu ping'ermi tua-i utu-
manruluni. Tuaten-gguq pileryagaluku, qanpagalluku piyaaqekumteggu
pamaircarciqerput, pamaunani qanqauteng'ermi-llu maligarucuunani.
Waten qanqaulluku pikumteggu inerqurluku tua-llu niitenrilkan anglir-
ikanirluku qanrulluku, erina tegg'ikanirluku. Tua-i tauna mikelnguq nav-
gurciqliniarput tuaggun. Yuum navguriciqlinia tuaggun ulumikun, ke-
gginamikun. Tamaa-i wagg'uq asmururrluku, pamairulluku, qanqam
ngelqaqenrirluku.

Ilii yuum tangvallra tataitelartuq. Iliit tua-i uitacurlagluni tauna qanrutkellra qasgimi pitullrukiit ilaita. Tua-i cunawa tuaten ayuqelliniuq. Ilii
taugken qanelriamek niiteng'ermi, tua-i camek niitenrilngurtun ayuqluni.
Tuaten ayuqelliniuq tamana mikelngurmek anglicariyaraq. Cali-llu anga-
yuqaarulriani mikelnguq tauna takurquraluku piyunaunani, atunem qan-
pallagallutek piyunaunatek taukuk.

a child that way, scolds him, yells at him using a loud tone of voice, and always pours his emotions out on the child, putting him down even though he is not his child, he will become a bad person. We should only use encouragement to discipline a child.

Abusing a child is very harmful and has a bad consequence. They say it is not necessary to constantly yell at and abuse a child with our hands, grabbing him. If one uses that means of discipline to raise a child, *caacuurciiquq* [that child will become a bad person], a thief, a liar, and will be abusive when he becomes independent. And he will no longer listen the first time we tell him to do something. He will become stubborn and unresponsive.

Even adults who are not the parents can destroy a child through this means. One must constantly speak to them with unconditional love. If one constantly encourages a child, he will grow up healthy.

That kind of abusive treatment is very dangerous for children, especially boys, but not as serious for girls. They say they will become stubborn and uncooperative if we abuse and yell at them, and they will not obey even when asked to do something in a normal voice. We will ruin a child by admonishing him by raising our voice after speaking to him in a normal tone. They will ruin that child with their tongue and facial expressions. He will become stubborn and will no longer be receptive to a regular tone of voice.

By looking at a person you can tell that he is stubborn by his behavior. The men in the *qasgi* could recognize the demeanor of a person and would mention it and talk among themselves about his behavior and personality. However, there are others who sit back and take in information as if they are not listening. That is what raising children is like. Also, parents should not fight and argue in front of their children.

Nekani taquulluku angiararucetenrilkurrluku

(34) Theresa Moses, April 2001:65–66

Tua-llu cali augna ukurrilluni pilria. Aug'um ilurairutma Tununermium maurlullran kelegcellua kassuucimarinemkun qanrutaanga tuqlurlua. Kitaki-gguq waniwa qanrutqataraanga umyuamnek aug'arngailngurmek. Kitaki-gguq waniwa uituumakilii nekaka taquulluku angiararucetenrilkurrluku. Cunawa tua-i tauna umyuamnek aug'ararkaunrilnguq.

Kassuutellriit tamarmeng akqitullilriit atunem aulukutarkauluteng. Uini cirlaukan auluku'urluku pinerrlugceteksaunaku akqillruukut ayuqluta. Nauwa iliini arivut'lartukut-llu uiput-llu, wagg'uq tua-i kiutaagulluta, arivulluta, quyinrungnaqluta. Tuaten ayuqelleq neptunarquq. Tauna angun qanngengraan, aciqcangraani-llu, cangraani, pingraani, kiuqaqsaunaku kiutekani amllengraata. Anssaagluteng kiutekat piyuitut, puvulluteng. Tamaa-i wii qanruyutektullrenka. Qaneryaraq-gguq anssaayuituq ikiuluni kitngiarulluni puvucuunani-llu. Qemangqaurallra-gguq assinruuq. Taugaam-gguq una assinra paivngavkarluku.

Tauna-gguq tuaten ayuqelria yuk'egtaarmek aprumauq. "Tang ingna yuk assirtuq, nekani qemaggluku yuulria aipaa manimaluku assinra, ik'inra qemangqaluku qamani." Tuaten ayuqukut yugni. Nekayutuukut. Qaneryugngatuyaaqukut nekanangnaqluta, tua-i taugaam tuacetun aipaakun qemaggluku nekanarqerkaq tauna. Anssaagluni-gguq puvucuituq. Qemagtellra-gguq assinruuq taum nekanarqelriim. Tauna-gguq tuaten ayuqelria yuk'egtaarmek aprumauq. Maa-i tang wangkuta makut qanruyutektulput.

Tauna-llu tua-i uimta arivqaqengraakut, cangraakut, picilirturluta pingraakut, uitaurqumta-gguq uimta tenglugngaitaakut. Tuaten qanrraarluteng, arnaq-gguq kitugciyugngauq, cali-llu ikiurciyugngaluni. Qanqerqan egmian kiugurluku. Pinritengnaqsaaqvigminek-gguq angun tauna assirraarluni ikiurrluni, kiituani-gguq nuliani tenglugyaurtaa.

Maa-i makut wii nangyaqellrenka. Nekayutuyaaqukut ayuqluta taugaam qemaggluku ing'umun qanrutkenrilengramteggu tauna nekayulput cavkenani assinruluni, cagtevkenani-llu. Qemangqallra assinruluni.

Braid one's anger into one's hair so it won't come loose

(34) Theresa Moses, April 2001:65–66

Now, in regards to being a daughter-in-law. After I got married the late grandmother of my late cousin from Tununak invited me over and talked to me. She said that she was going to tell me something that was not going to leave my mind. She said that I should be a wife to my husband by braiding my anger and hurt feelings into my hair so that they would not become loose. It turned out that I would never forget what she said.

Perhaps every married couple vows to take care of each other. We all made vows to take good care of our husbands, spouses, even when they become handicapped. You know sometimes we argue and call each other names, trying to outdo each other. Having that kind of relationship is noisy. It is better to be quiet and not answer back even if your spouse keeps talking and calling you names, even though you have a lot of words in your mind. The words we want to express don't come out of our mouths by themselves. These are some of the things that I was taught. They said that our words don't try to come out, they do not kick. They said that keeping it inside is better. They said that we should mostly speak of positive things.

They say a person who has that trait is referred to as a wonderful person. "That person over there is good, one who is trying to keep his hurt feelings inside, displaying positive behavior, keeping the negative inside." That is how we people are. We all get hurt. We are all capable of speaking with anger, but we should choose to be the other way, keeping our hurt feelings inside. They say [hurt feelings] do not try to come out by themselves. They say keeping anger inside is better. They say a person who does that is referred to as a wonderful person. Those were our instructions.

And they said our husbands would not hit us if we did not respond when they called us names, doing something to us, making accusations. After saying that they told us that a woman is capable of improving her husband's nature or making it worse. Talking back when he speaks [makes it worse]. They said after he had a good disposition and was composed, he could develop a bad nature and eventually hit his wife.

These [words] were what frightened me. We all get hurt, but we should keep it inside. It is better if we do not express our hurt feelings and let them spread. It is better to keep it inside.

Takartarluni yuuyaraq qigcikiyarauguq

(35) Frank Andrew, September 2000: 2–3, 18–22, 32

Maa-i taugaam mat'um nalliini makut ellalinqigtellriatun ayuqut. Allaurrluteng. Tua-i-llu cali makut nunani waten pingnatuungengamta yuum aklui qigcikluki cakneq. Wall'u yuilqumi uitalria yuum aklua qig-cikluku. Arcaqerluki makut ciulirneret, angayuqaak-llu, arnat, arnassa-gaat qigcignarqellruut cakneq takarnaqluteng.

Enenun-llu allanun kevgarturpek'nata cenirtaarciiganata, taugaam angayuqamta, wall'u qasgimi ellimerraqatkut eniitnun ayatuluta, kevgiur-luta. Kevgiurpek'nata inerquutaqellruaput taugaam kevgiurluta. Tamaa-i tang tuaten ayuqulluta anglivkallrullinikaitkut keneknamegtekut. Muril-kelluta cakneq, naucurlagcetevkenata. Assilriamek tuarpiaq naucetaatun imutun, angliluaqallemtenek tangniqluta merqurluta qanruyutmek.

Tua-i-llu ilumun piciuguq yuk, mikelnguq angayuqaagken tegumiar-kaqaak avvnatkaanun, murilkelluku cakneq makuni aklumini murilkenru-luku. Tuaten ayuqutellruitkut wangkuta, unitaarpek'nata, ayagatevkenata enenun. Ilakengramteki-llu ullagatsiyaagpek'nata anelgutkengramteki, ellangyuallemteni. . . .

Inerquagura'aqluta tamaani enemi, aanama-llu taum ellami qagaani pi-kuma ayuqucirkamnek ernerpak unuakumi pilu'uglua piaqamia. Pilu'ug-luta-ll' tua-i carangllugnek-llu piiniraqluta, makunek-llu cataunani, im-kunek taugaam *rabbit*-aanek maqaruanek-llu muruterluta. Tuaten tua-i ayuqluta.

Ayuqucirkamnek ernerpak qalaruqu'urnauraanga ilamnek-llu eq'uki-lua pisqevkenii, ilalkiksauni-llu, nangelrakiksauni-llu. Kenkurluki erner-pak ilanka ilakesqelluki. Tuaten tua-i inerquagurnauraanga. Tua-i tuaten ayuqngamta nepaunata tua-i mikelngurni pinaurtukut ellami, ilalkucuu-nata qenqerrucuunata-llu. Makut-llu nasaurluut assirluki call' ilakluki, avukluki tua-i ellami akusrartaqluta.

Tua-i taugken waten cali pituluta neryartuqataqumta tan'gaurluullgut-vut unayaqluki neryartuusqelluta. Tua-i taugken cali nerqataamta aqu-mevkarluta qantaput-llu ciuqamtenun elliluki. Ellirraarluki pinauraitkut, "Kitaki ata qantan murilkelluku nerkina. Takuyaqtaarpek'nak, ilaten-llu qanruteksaunaki, qantan murilkelluku nerkina." Neru'urluta taugken tua-i ayuqluta tua-i nepengssagaunata, qantaput imait nerluki. Kenira-

Being respectful is like honoring others

(35) Frank Andrew, September 2000: 2–3, 18–22, 32

It is like these people are living in a whole different world these days. Things have changed. When we started to provide for ourselves, we were extremely respectful of other people's belongings in the villages and even in the wilderness. Elders, parents, and elderly women were especially respectable and extremely intimidating.

And we could not go in and out of other houses without doing chores. But we went into their houses and served them when our parents or those in the *qasgi* asked us to complete tasks. We were admonished not to go in and out of houses without doing chores for others. They had us grow up behaving that way because they loved us. They kept a very close eye on us, not letting us grow up in the wrong way. Like a plant, they watered us with the *qanruyun* so that we would grow older beautifully.

Also, it is true that the parents' responsibility is to hold onto a child until they part, watching over him, and keeping a closer eye on him than their own belongings. That is how they raised us. They did not leave us constantly. They did not take us to other houses. And they did not bring us visiting with others, our relatives and even our siblings, while we were becoming aware of our surroundings. . . .

They admonished us all the time at home. My mother also told me how to behave all day outside when she was putting on my boots in the morning. And we would put on boots with grass insoles, and we did not have modern clothing, but we had rabbit-fur insoles. That is how we lived.

[My mother] constantly spoke to me about how to behave all day and not to pick on, mistreat, or fight with others. They told me to always treat my peers with kindness and compassion all day. That was her constant advice to me. Because we were raised in that way, we kids quietly played outside and did not fight or become angry at one another. And we played amiably with girls outside.

They also asked us to invite our friends to eat. And before we ate, they would let us sit and put our bowls in front of us. After putting them down they would say to us, "Watch your bowl and eat. Do not look around, and do not speak to your friends. Watch your bowl and eat." We all behaved the same, not making sounds, eating the contents of our bowls. And if we were eating soup, we would lick the inside of our bowls clean. And when

nek-llu pillruaqamta iluit pairturluki, painqegcaarluki. Tuamtell' enernek unkumiutarnek nerngamta pukunqegcaarluki tua-i cakneq, pisqutvut aturluku. Nerevlacagpek'naki, uqlarpek'nata-llu, uqlanrilkurrluta, kencikluku tua-i neqa sagcesqumavkenaku. Taqngamta-llu tua-i nernermek taqluta tua-i. Meqsungaarcaaqeng'erma-llu, meqsuglua qanerciiganii nernerraama.

Arcaqerluku takaqellruaqa ataka. Aanaka taugaam takaqengramku qanrutaqluku. Piyaaqngama waten meqsugyaaqnilua kiunauraanga, "Nernerrartuten, mernariksaitaaten." Tua-i-llu taqlua tua-i. Tuaten tua-i ayuqutellruitkut. Meliurcetevkenata tua-i. Pinauraitkut meq-gguq unaqserrnarquq. Tua-i taugken nutaan kinguqliliriamta uitamarraarluta nutaan mertelluta. Ellaita cikirluta meq amllertacirkaatnek ikgetnilukullu elaravkenata. Mer'et-llu paivngangraata wangkutnek pisciiganata inerquumalaitkut. Nalluatni-llu pisciiganata. Tuaten tua-i ayuqluta pilallrullikaitkut.

Qanruqu'urlua tua-i assirluta pillerkamtenek. Waten-llu quyungqaaqamta atakumi anelgutenka-llu ukut qalaruqu'urnauraakut aanamta taum ilakluta pillerkamtenek. Pinrilmiamta-llu atamta taum qalarulluta cali assirluta pillerkamtenek. Taumek tua-i takarnarqellrulriit. Nallunguanrilamegtekut tua-i caqallerkarput ancurtunaqluni cakneq, camek piyugyaaqengramta atamtenun pimallerkaput wall'u aanamtenun. Ilaputllu makut piyaaqaqata wangkuta inerquagaqluki. Inerquumalaamteki tua-i anelgutvut nepaunata, nepaunata tua-i.

Kenkuyulluta taugaam tua-i pisqumaluta. Taumek enet nepaitellrulriit qanpagalriamek-llu niicuunata. Waniwa aanamta taum qancurlagalluta piyuitellruakut, atamta-llu cali qancurlagalluta piyuunata qalaruquraraqamikut. Tua-i tuaten kiimta pivkenata. Tuaten ayuqellrata takarnarqevkarluki qigcignaqluteng tua-i. Nek'engramteggu tua-i qigcignaqluni angayuqaput catailengraata, camek piyungramta pisciiganata qanruqaarpek'naki. Pinayuku'urluta taugaam, waten-llu pilaitkut, "Nallumegni atam camek pilaquvci umyuarpuk assiilkan nunularniamegceci." Tamana alikluku tua-i nunuumallerkarput. Taumek qigcikellrukput tua-i, takaqluki tua-i nek'engramteggu, tuaten pimallerkarput assikevkenaku, nunuumallerkarput. Tuaten tua-i ayuqluta anglivkallruitkut. Wiinga kiima pivkenii — tua-i allat-llu qakemkut tuaten pimatullrullilriit. Kenkuyulluta tua-i umyuarput piyaaqengraan piyuunata tua-i, ancuunaku inerquumalaamta.

we ate sea-mammal bones, we would eat the bones completely clean of meat, doing what was expected of us. We did not eat carelessly and tried not to make a mess. We were careful with food. When we were done eating, that was it. And though I suddenly got thirsty, I couldn't ask for water because I had just eaten.

I was especially respectful of my father. Even though I respected my mother, I told her things. When I said that I was thirsty, she would answer, "You have just eaten. It isn't time for you to drink." I would not ask again. That is how they raised us. They did not let us drink water whenever we wanted. They told us that water causes the body to be weak and flimsy. They allowed us to drink when we asked a second time, but only after some time passed. They gave us a certain amount of water, and we would not complain that it wasn't enough. And we could not serve ourselves, even though water was sitting out, because they admonished us. We could not [drink] behind their backs. That is how they raised us.

They constantly told us to behave properly. And when my siblings and I gathered together during the evenings, our mother constantly spoke to us about how we should treat one another. And if she didn't, our father instructed us about good behavior. That is why they were so respectable. Because they did not ignore us, we were cautious and reserved and afraid of being scolded by our father or mother. And when our siblings misbehaved, we admonished them. We were peaceful and harmonious, because we admonished our other siblings.

They expected us to treat one another with love and kindness. That is why homes were quiet, and we did not hear people raising their voices. My mother never spoke to us abusively, and our father never spoke to us abusively when he gave us advice. And we weren't the only ones [who were raised that way]. Their behavior made them respectable, very honorable. And even our home was respectable when our parents were gone. We could not take what we wanted without asking them. We thought they would scold us because they told us, "We will scold you if we become upset when you take things without our knowledge." We were afraid of being scolded. That is why we respected things in our own home. We did not want to be scolded. That is how they raised us. I wasn't the only one who was raised that way—others were probably raised that way as well. We loved one another and did not express our [hard feelings], because we were admonished.

Alqairutemta-llu imum angliamta tua-i egmiulluku cali aanami ta-mana pilallra, inerquagaqluta kinguqlirmini. Tua-i-llu wangkuta tua-i tuatnalangluta, kinguqliinka-llu wii inerquraqluki tuaten pisqevkenaki. Tua-i ellimertuutekngamteggu-am call' tua-i tuaten pilallerkaput anelgutemtenun wall'u anelgutkenrilengramteggu inerqurilallerkarput. Tamaa-i tamana yuum atuquniu takartarluni yuuciqliniuq. Una ancurturyaraq takaryugyarauguq.

Waniwa yuk, yuum ilii tangrraqavgu ciungani-llu tangeqsaunaku kegginaa-llu waten qukarturluku tangerciigat'laran. Imutun alikelriatun ayuqluku tua-i, takaqluku tua-i, qanrucesciiganaku. Tuaten-am ayuqengramta ellimertuuterluta-am cali takarnarqengraan ciulirneq camek kangiiyukumta apcesqelluta camek kangingqerrucianek augna. Tamana pisquteluku-am cali, apyutekluku, kangiiturluku. Maa-i apyutengqerrucimtenek pilaqaitkut kangiitullerkarput pitekluku caucianek. Quyatekelriatun tua-i ayuqnaurait tuaten ciulirnerem nallunritellranek tamana apyutkaqamteggu, egmian maniilluta ayuqucianek assirluni pillerkaanek assiinaku-llu pillerkaanek. Una apqauqaqluni pilleq ikayuuqapiartuq, pisqutnguuq cali. . . .

Augna ava-i una takartaryaraq qigcikiyarauguq, takaryulleq. Yugmek iqlutun ayagcecingaituq aturteminek. Takartarluni yuuyaraq qigcikiyarauguq. Picurlagcecingaituq takartaryaraq. Una waniwa niisngayaraq malingnacarauguq, maligtaquluni, piyullermikun pivkenani, taugaam pisqutmikun piluni. Tua-i piluaqeryugngaluni maligtaqu'uraulluni pisqutminun navguivkenani, qigcikluku tamana.

Tangelten tamalkuita ilaliurluki

(36) David Martin, April 2001:54

Avani apa'urluma — maligcaurpailegma-llu piunrillruan tauna atalqa — apa'urlullrama taugaam aug'um yuum yuuyaramek mat'umek qanemcitaqamia pilaraanga, "Ellirauguten. Naklekestaicukekuvet, naklekestaunak umyuarteqkuvet, ellirauguten, tua-i aanaunak ataunak-llu; Waten yuucingqerkuvet, tangelten tamalkuita ilaliurluki, ayagyuarli, ak'allaurrli, wall'u arnaukan maurluuli, allauli tayima." Takarnarqengnaqevkeniigguq ilaliurturluki qanrramkun imutun, qanenrilkurtellria-gguq una takarnarquq. Maaten tua-i tamana qanellra yuvriamku piyaurtengama piamku piaqa, tuaten imum qanellra ilumun nall'arrluku ak'allaurtellria

My late older sister carried on my mother's teachings when she grew older, and she admonished us, her younger siblings. We eventually did the same, and I would tell my younger siblings [not to misbehave]. We were told to admonish our siblings and others. One who is raised like that will be respectful. *Ancurturyaraq* [being cautious and reserved] is a way of being respectful.

When you see some people whom you have never seen before, you cannot look directly into their faces. It is like you are afraid and respect-fully shy and unable to speak to them. We were told to ask elders if we wanted to know about something, even though we were shy. They wanted us to ask questions, to have them explain the meaning. Today [people] ask us [elders] if they have any questions so that they can understand the meaning behind something. Elders were grateful when we asked questions and immediately explained both sides, both the right and the wrong ways to approach it. Asking questions here and there is good and is encouraged. . . .

Takartaryaraq [being respectful] is like *qigcikiyaraq* [honoring others]. It will not lead a person who lives by that value astray. Being respectful is like honoring others. *Takartaryaraq* will not cause a person to get into a bad situation. *Niisngayaraq* [listening obediently] is a way of adhering and not doing as one pleases but doing what's expected. One can be for-tunate if he follows what is expected of him, not dishonoring but honor-ing and respecting what he is told.

Be friendly toward everyone you meet
(36) David Martin, April 2001:54

Back then my grandfather — because my father died before I was able to follow him — when my grandfather talked to me about the proper way of living, he said, "You are an orphan. If you feel that no one can take pity on you [because] you are an orphan who has no mother or father, be friendly toward everyone you meet, be they young or old, a female, a grandmother, or another." He said I should not be inhibited and shy, but I should always try to be sociable by just speaking to them, that one who refuses to speak is uncomfortable to be around. When I tested what he said when I started living independently, when I asked elders questions

qanenritaqan wiinga piqa'arqamni ciumek tuarpiaq ung'aqertellriatun pilaraanga, "Aa-a, elpet-am tua-i apcugngalliniarpenga mat'um yuum yuuyaraanek." Tuaten tua-i imutun tua-i nallunairtellriatun cali takarnarqellra imna tamaqerluni tayima. Makut taugaam nutarat apcunaitaput, kinguqliput. Ciulirnerem taugaam waten qanemciyugngaaci augkut ciuliat ayuqucillrat tamalkuan apyutkekuvceni nalqigucugngaaci taugaam ciulirnerem. Eskimo-ryarakun maaggun ciuliat augkut piciryarallritnek nalqigucugngaaci, nallunrilkengameggnek. Augna tuaten cali ik'um qanemcia ilaqerlaku.

Tua-i wangnun takaqevkenii tua-i qanengssagtuten umyuan tuar maniluku, ayuqucin maniluku, takaqevkenii tua-i qanengssaullua. Wangnun kenkucin, elpet-llu kenkucin wangnun nallunairteqsiyaagluni tua-i. Ii-i, meaning-aara-am tamana nallunairteqsiyaagyaram ayuqucia. Takaqevkenii tua-i qanengssautelaqevnga wanirpak, engelarnariaqluni akuliini.

Kenka

(37) Frank Paul, November 2001:98

Una taugaam waniwa aturarkarput ayuqucirtuutvut, ayuqucirtuutemta angenqurraat kenka, kenka una. Tauna-gguq una wani kenka atuqumteggu, makut wani wangkuta ayuqucirtuutemta angenrat, atuqumteggu-gguq tauna waten iquani qanertuq, "Elluarrluci piciquci." Qaneryararluni waten. Una-gguq ayuqucirtuutet angenrat atuqumteggu, aturluku pikumteggu, elluarrluta-gguq piciqukut.

Elpet alungutevkun qanaateksaqunaku cikiqengkuvet

(38) Peter Jacobs, November 2001:198–99

Wiinga-llu qaneryugtua ciuliamta anglicarilallratnek pek'ngartaqamta, arcaqerturnganani una piuq. Pek'ngarcamta kenkuqu'uraasqelluta ayagnillruakut kanaken ayagluta. Una waniwa kenka nalluvkanritengnaqnaqsaaqerput irniamtenun. Cali-llu cikiqengyaraq, ikayuqengyaraq-llu tauna cali arcaqerluku wangrramni nalluvkanritengnaqnaqsaaqerput.

Una arcaqerluku kenka nalluvkanritengnaqnarqerput cikiqengyaraqllu una. Qanruyutmek niitetuunga cikiqengeng'erma alungutemkun wang'ulua qanaatekesqenritaa ata'urluma. Arnaaraam-gguq angutem-llu quyassiyaallni niilluku, uumun cikiqaqu'urallni qanrutkekuniu, tauna-

when I didn't understand something and approached them first, they responded affectionately, "Yes, you can ask about how a person is supposed to live." The inhibitions one felt for a person seemed to disappear. But we should not ask younger people, the younger generation. Only an elder can tell you about how our ancestors lived if you ask. They can answer your question using their knowledge of the customs and traditions of our Eskimo ancestors. I only wanted to add to what that person said.

You are speaking to me openly without being shy, like you are revealing what you are thinking, revealing your personality, speaking to me without inhibitions. You have revealed your affection for me. That is the meaning of *nallunairteqsiyaagyaraq* [being uninhibited]. You speak to me without any inhibitions, and our conversation becomes humorous at times.

Love
(37) Frank Paul, November 2001:98

However, one principle that we must live by, the most important among our *ayuqucirtuutet* [teachings], is love. If we live by loving others, the most important of our teachings, there is a saying, "*Elluarrluci piciquci* [You will do well in life]." That is a saying. If we live by our most important teaching, we will be fortunate.

Do not tell anyone with your own tongue if you give to someone
(38) Peter Jacobs, November 2001:198–99

I also want to say that it seems the following was the most important value our ancestors expressed to us. When we started to move about, they told us to always love one another from the time we were very small. We should not fail to teach our children about love. And we especially should not fail to let them know about giving and helping.

We should especially teach them about loving and giving. I heard my father say not to tell anyone with my own tongue if I gave to someone. He said that the only thing that does not have an admonition is hearing the gratitude of a woman or man when given something by a particular per-

gguq taugaam inerquucetaituq. Tuaten wiinga qanrut'lallruanga ata'ur-luma. Alungutemkun qutgutekluku cikiqengkuma cikiqengesqevkenii. Quyalriim-gguq taugaam qakmum qanrutkekunia, tua-i-gguq tauna quyaassiyaallni pitekluku piani, tauna-gguq taugaam inerquucetaituq. Una waniwa wiinga tutgaramnun-llu qanrutkeqtarturalaryaaqaqa, mat'u-mek, cikiqengyaram keneknggucia-llu qanrutekluku. Quyanarpiit-lli.

Qanruyutet maligtaqukuvciki
nepaunaci uputestaunaci-llu yuuciquci

(39) Nicholai Berlin, March 2000:29

Makutgun qanruyutekegtaarteggun nepaunaci uputestaunaci-llu ma-ligtaqukuvciki ayuqucirtuumauci maa-i. . . .

Canek tukuuterugarnek piicaaqukut yugni wangkuta, taugaam cat tua-i makut, una-llu arcaqerluku pilallruat neqaitunritlerkaq-gguq. Ne-qa'armek-llu kiagmi quyuqcaarallerminek pingqellria, qemangqaang-qellria, tukuuguq-gguq tauna. Tua-i ilaminek ayuqnianrilami, cali-llu iliiraluni ilaminek pinrilami. Tukuulriamek aprumaluni yuk tuaten qan-rutkumauq. Makut tua-i arcaqerluteng negtaarumaluteng-llu pilartut, elluarrluci pillerkarci ayagyuani arcaqerluci.

Yuunguicisciigatua

(40) Frank Andrew, June 2001:18–20

Camek waniwa aturangqerciqua cam iliini ikiulrianek uqlarluteng, pii-turlua tua-i kemka-llu alaunani, ilamtun ayuqevkenii tua-i pikailama-wa tua-i aturanek, atamnek-llu wall'u anelgutemnek pikarcurtailama. Elli-raat tuaten ayuqellruut. Tua-llu-gguq elpet wangtun ayuqenrilkuvet, aturaqegciluten aulukestengqerravet nuqlitenrilngurmek atu'urkaitevke-nak neqaiturpek'nak-llu. Tuaten-gguq ayuqelria imutun yuunguilluku-gguq tua-i, umyuan quyigluni amta-llu camek cikirpek'naku, ikayurciiga-naku. Taugaam canek anglanarqellrianek umyuan aturluku anglaniluten nuuqitenrilavet ayuqniarutailavet-llu taum umyuaqenrilkiinek ayuqnial-riim ilami piyuumiurluryaaqengermi. Tua-i-gguq yuunguiciiqan tuaten ayuqluten, umyugaa iluteqevkarluku. Iquggliquq-gguq tamana.

Taugken-gguq tuaten ayuqellria tangerquvgu kenekluku nerevkarluku-llu wall'u pikangqerkuvet atu'urkilluku, wall'u mingeqsugngakuvet aklull-

son. That is what my father told me. He told me not to brag that I gave a person something. He said that the only thing that does not have an admonition is when a grateful person expresses his gratitude. I always tell my grandchildren this about giving, and I talk about how it is a way of loving. Thank you very much.

Following instructions, you will lead a quiet, sensible life with no one complaining about you
(39) Nicholai Berlin, March 2000:29

Through these great instructions you are being taught to live harmonious and unaggravated lives without being a cause for complaint. . . .

We were not wealthy people, but they placed importance on having enough to eat. A person who fished in the summer and stored them for winter use was considered wealthy, because that type of person did not envy others and did not beg for food from his relatives. That kind of person was called a wealthy person. Instructions like these have been impressed on you young people.

I cannot act superior toward others
(40) Frank Andrew, June 2001:18–20

I might be wearing torn and soiled clothing sometime with my skin showing, unlike others around me, because I don't have clothing or a father or siblings to obtain it for me. That is how orphans were. And they said if you are not in my situation, you would have nice clothing, because you have a caretaker who is not poor and you do not lack clothing and food. They say you will have no sympathy for one in that situation, acting superior to him and not giving him anything or helping him. But here you do as you wish, having a good time because you do not lack anything or wish for things that are unimaginable to that poor person. They say that you will be unsympathetic if you treat him that way, making him feel inferior and upset. They say that has a bad consequence.

However, they say you will be fortunate if you are kind to and feed one who is like that and give him clothing if you have extras or sew his cloth-

rai callmagluki ikayualuku. Piluaqerciquten-gguq tuaten pikuvet, yuungui-
tevkenaku. Umyuamek-gguq assilriamek cikirciqaaten taum quyallmikun
nalluyagusngaunak-llu-gguq picurlagmek-llu akingaunani-gguq quyate-
karpenek-gguq taugaam. Tua-i-llu-gguq piinanerpeni anelngutvet wall'u
cam allam yuum angniutekarpenek assilriamek cikirciqaaten. Tua-i-gguq
taum ikayullerpet tauna cikiutekaa, yuum allam taitengraaku. Tuaggun pi-
yugngastiikun-gguq cikiutekumaa, akinaurucimatuuq.

Yuunguilluki tua-i ilaput pisqevkenaki aarluta cali inerqualuta pitullruitkut; elliraat imkut aulukestairutellriit, aatairutellriit, wall'u makut arnassagaat angutessagaat-llu cangallrunritliniut tamakut. Pingnatutullru-
ngermeng pisciigalilriit elli'irtun ayuqliritulliniut. Yuum-llu tua-i camek
cikiqaqani quyaluni tua-i cakneq temni tamalkirrluku quyanarqetullini-
luni tuaten ilakuarunani. Iliini-llu quyam iliini iluteqnarqaqluni. Augna
ava-i tuaten qalarutkumatullruuq, yuunguiluta yuunguiciluta ilamtenek
pinritlerkarput taugaam ikayuutekangqerkumta ikayurluki, wall'u-q' qan-
rramteggun ilaliurluki pisqelluki.

ing if you can sew, helping him. If you are sympathetic toward him, that person will only bestow good thoughts on you in gratitude and will not forget you and will not repay you with something bad, but good. And while you are living, your sibling or some other person will give you something that will make you happy. They say that gift is actually coming from the person you helped, even though it came from a different source. They say the gift is reciprocated through a means that is possible.

They told us not to act superior toward orphans who have no one to provide for them, those who lost their fathers, as well as elderly women and men. Those who become incapable after being self-sufficient become like orphans. And when someone gives them [a gift], they are genuinely grateful, and their whole being is deeply moved. And sometimes they are so happy that it causes them to be choked up with tears. That is how that was explained when we were told not to look down on those who are less fortunate but to help them if we had something to give or be friendly with them by just talking to them.

Qanruyutet-gguq Egelrutaakut

Ulu Mik'lengermi akngirnarquq
(41) Paul John, April 2001:56–58

Cali aug'na uum nuliacungama qanellra piciuqapiaralria ava-i aipam tungiinun ikia naluumasqevkenaku wall'u unani uitavimini qanmiknun 'gguun nep'ngevkarillerkaq. Tauna tua-i piciuqapiarluni maa-i taringumaluku ernerni atullra. Yuum iliin yuucia qinuitqapiararaqluni yuut ilami akuliitni. Camek aviranarqutkamek yuucia imangssagaunani, tangellra tua-i tunulluku unilluku pingermiu, qanemcikutekaunani. Qinuaraunani nunani taukuni uitaluni. Ilii taugken ilaminek apqiitnek uputaarilria, apqiitnek cagcingnaqelria nep'ngutkamek, apqiitnek yuum caullni ulevlaullluku. Qanerkaitulria-am ulevlalriamek cali *meaning*-iirluku pilaamegteggu. Caullni tamalkuan apqiitnek ulevlaulluku, piciunrilnguq piciurrluku, yuum umyugaan akngirutekaa nunaullermegteggun nep'ngutkaat piciurrluku. Tuarpiaq ilumun nalugluku yuut quliitnun, nep'ngutnguvkarluku.

Tamaa-i tamana mulnganarqelria tua-i nunakenrilkemini uitaluni. Qanqatalriani camek qanllerkani yuvriqerrlainarluku. Nep'ngutkaunrilkan qanruteksuumaluku, nep'ngutkauyugngakan taugken tua-i qanrutkeqataryaaqerraarluku taq'icuumaluku. Wiinga ayagyuarlua nulirturpailegma-llu angutngurtellriim qanellra taringellrunricaaqekeka cunaw' ava-i augna qanrutkek'ngaqa. Angutem qanruskiinga, "Yuucuaqaurlullerpeni qanerpeggun ilaten ilakniteksaqunaki. Ulu mik'lengermi akngirnarquq." Taringenritaqa. Maaten tua-i maa-i kinguqvani taringaqa

They Say the *Qanruyutet* Guide Our Lives

A tongue hurts even though small

(41) Paul John, April 2001:56–58

And what my *nuliacungaq* [female cross-cousin, literally, "dear little wife"] said is very true, not to bring up the shortcomings of one's spouse or how one could cause controversy in one's village with one's mouth. That is extremely true, and we understand it because they are living by it these days. However, some people live extremely peaceful and tranquil lives compared to others. Nothing in their lives is troublesome, and one has no stories to tell when one sees them and turns around and walks away. They live in that village in peace and tranquility. But some people gossip about others or instigate controversy. They say that person says anything he wants to others. They called one who was trying to bring up gossip, *ulevlalria* [from *ulevla-*, "to bubble over"]. He says whatever he wants to everyone he sees, making lies into truths, saying things that hurt others, creating trouble in the village. Indeed, it seems they raise it up above people, making it trouble.

That is something that we have to be careful of in another village. We are to always think before we say something. We are to say it if it will not create trouble but refrain from mentioning it if it's going to cause problems. As a young person before I married, I did not understand what an elderly man said, but it turned out to be what I had just spoken about. An elderly man said to me, "Do not say anything you want to a person without considering his feelings during your short life. A tongue hurts even though it's small." I did not understand it then. I understood later that he

qanqata'arqama yuvriqaaqluku pisqellinikiinga, yuullgutemnun akngir-
naqsugngakan nep'ngutnguyugngakan-llu antenrilengraan qemangqaaq-
luku pisqelluku.

Tua-i-llu tangvautelartukut atunem ilaput-llu, ilaput tangvagluki. Ava-
i-am qanqerraallrulrianga qinuarailngurmek yugmek ilani tangvagluki
tuaten tangvalararput, tua-i camek aviranarqutaunani. Ilii taugken tangerrluku tua-i qaneryugtacimitun qanerluni. Ilani umyugait akngirrluki
young-angraata, taqnerungraata, aliayullagavkarluki umyugait akngirqe-
lluki. Tua-i tauna qanmikun yuum ilaknitkiyaraa. Tuaten ayuqekuni qanmikun ilani ilaknitekluki. Tua-i-ll' augna ava-i qinuilnguq yuk qanmikun
ilani ilaknitkevkenaki. Tuaten tua-i man'a yuuguralleq ayuqsugngallini-
luni.

Niitellruaraten qanruyutet
cingiuski cingirpenun angiararucugnairulluki
(42) Paul John, April 2001:55

Augkut-wa ciuliat elitnauripiggluteng ayagyuameggnek ayagyuateng
tamak'acagaita erenrunateng camek ernermek, unugcuutmek-llu camek
cuqaunateng. Ernemeggni piyunarqeqa'arqan tamalkuan elitnauriurlu-
teng ayagyuameggnek qanmegteggun qanruqu'urluki. Taumek tua-i
tamaani nallumciqluteng-wa tua-i yuuvakalriartaitellrulliniuq. Yuung-
naqsaramek cali caliyaranek-llu makunek arnat caliaritnek, angutem-llu
cali caliaranek nallumciqvakalriartaunani piyugngarilriamek. Tua-i elit-
nauriurluteng ayagyuameggnek pillruameng. Tuamtellu *example*-aarluku,
pilugugtutullruut cingilegglainarnek, muruqauvkenateng cingingqerrlai-
narluteng. Qanrutnauraitkut iliini, "Niitellruaraten qanruyutet cingiuski
cingirpenun angiararucugnairulluki." Tua-i piluguuk cingiak taringcetaa-
rutekluku cingitullemteni, cingiutesqelluku qanruyun niitellerput katag-
ngairulluku, nalluyagusngairulluku yuuqallemteni. Tuaten kangilirluku.
Taumek tua-i taringumalallrukait tamaa-i.

Tuamtellu iliini, cam iliini arnaurtellriamek ayagyuamek, waten ayag-
yuaqsilriamek, waten qanruskengelriamek niicugniqaquma; taqungqer-
turatullruameng avani arnat, katagverrluki pisqevkenaki alerquumatull-
ratni, nuyaitnek aqevlalriartangqessuitellruuq. Wagg'uq ilateng camek
aurnermek wall'u apqucimek cikirnayukluki. Tang tamaa-i *healthy*-rluku
temseng cali pillerkaa avaurumavkenaku. Arnat taqungqetullruut ta-

asked me to examine what I had to say and not to bring it up if it was going to hurt others around me.

And now we are always in the company of others and observing one another. We observe those around us. And you know how I just brought up a peaceful person and how there is nothing bothersome about him. But we see others who say anything they want. They hurt others even though they are young or elderly, making them sad, hurting their minds. That is what *qanmikun yuum ilaknitkiyaraa* [saying anything they want and not taking others' feelings into consideration] means. If someone is like that, he says anything he wants, not taking others' feelings into consideration. And one who is quiet always takes others' feelings into consideration before speaking. That is how a person can live.

Tie the few instructions that you heard into your shoelaces, so they will not come loose
(42) Paul John, April 2001:55

Our ancestors taught all of their young people well and did not designate certain days and evenings for instruction. When the time seemed right, they constantly taught their young people oral instructions. That is why there were very few people who didn't know how to live their lives properly or complete women's and men's tasks. It is because they constantly taught their young people. As an example, they always used *piluguut* [skin boots] with laces; they weren't just slip-ons but had laces [to tie around the ankle]. They told us sometimes, "Tie the few instructions that you heard into your bootlaces, so they will not come untied." They used the laces on the *piluguut* as an example back when we had boots with laces. And they told us to tie the instructions we heard to our bootlaces to the point where they will not become lost, so that we would not forget them in our short lives. That is how they explained the meaning. That is why they understood [their teachings] back then.

And once in awhile I would eavesdrop while a young female who had her first menstrual period was given instruction. Because girls always wore braids back then, they told them not to carelessly lose their instructions. Back when they were given instruction no one let their hair hang loose, because they did not want to affect others with their vapor or pass on sickness. The notion of keeping their bodies healthy was al-

marmeng nuyait kepumayuitellruameng. Ilii cali qanrucilria takumni pinaurtuq, "Tauna niitellren qanruyun taquusgu nuyarpenun angiararus-ngairulluku." Tang maa-i makut taringcetaarutellrit elilluaqautekevkall-rit elitnaurameggnun ayagyuanun. Wangkuta-ll' angutni cingimtenek, cingiucesqelluku angiararusngairulluku. Tamaa-i iliin taringelriim yuu-luaqautekaqluku tamana aviranarqevkenaku ilamini yuucurlagpek'nani-llu yuutekaqluku. Tamakunek tamaa-i *example*-iirluteng qanrutlaiceteng taringelriit.

Niiteqainalria
(43) Frank Andrew, September 2000:137

Imna taugken niiteqainalria. Waten pilaraitkut, uuggun-gguq ciutem-teggun niitevkenata ingluakun-llu anevkarluku. Tuaten-gguq pivkenata niicugnilalta, qalartellria-llu-gguq tangvagluku, tangvaurluku niicugni-tukilta, taqkan taugaam ulurluku. Atam-gguq uluqumteggu camek qan-rucia nalluyagutniarput allamek tangvangareskumta. Umyuarput-llu akucetevkenaku-gguq niicugnitukilta qakmani nani umyuarteqluta tau-mek cali. Tamana piciuguq. Piyuumiutailnguq tuaten ayuquq. Tuaten-am ayuqelria makunun alarrnarqellrianun itercivignun, qanercetaarumaaq-luni-llu [pilartuq]. Pivakarluni-llu piunrirluni malluuluni nunat akuliitni, qang'a-llu yuilqumi, qang'a-llu mermi. Imna taugken tamalkirrluni, tama-tumek umyuangqerpek'nani qalartellriim taugaam qanruyutii kiingan nii-cugnilriatun ayuqetullinia, umyuani aakulagcetevkenaku piciatun qak-mani canek.

Mikelnguq assilriatun aklutun ayuquq
(44) Frank Andrew, September 2000:81

Mikelnguq, nasaurluq, tan'gaurluq-llu qanruyutminek angayuqaag-minun maligngaskuni, yuullgutain-llu cailkaungermeng piyunalitek-sugngaluku umyugiurutekluku. Akluuguq yuk irniaq. Atu'urkamtenek wangkuta assirluteng umyugiurutkamtenek, aklukamtenek, cakamtenek, cikiumalartukut mikelngurmek. Tuaten tua-i ayuqsugngaluni tauna yuk. Qaini assiilengraan aturaqliqngermi-ll' assirluni, tua-i akluugarkauluni yuk angayuqaagminun yuullgutminun-llu navguivkenani.

ways on their minds. All women wore braids because their hair was never cut. And a person who was giving instruction in my presence would say, "Braid that instruction that you heard into your hair so that it won't come loose." These were their examples, things they taught their young pupils. And they told us males about our bootlaces, to tie them so that they would not come undone. A person who understood [the teachings] would use them to live a good life, and he would not really lead a bad life compared to his peers. They understood because they spoke to them using these examples.

A person who merely listens

(43) Frank Andrew, September 2000:137

However, the following is a person who merely listens. They tell us not to listen with one ear and let it out the other. They tell us not to listen that way and to watch the speaker, looking away only when he is done. They said we would forget his instructions if we looked away, if we directed our attention elsewhere. They also told us not to listen with our mind preoccupied by different thoughts, thinking about other things. That is true. *Piiyuumiutailnguq* [one with no desire to live according to instructions] is like that. One who is like that becomes involved in bad situations and ends up in jail, goes to court, and eventually dies or is found dead on land or in the wilderness. However, one who is fully attentive and does not think of other things but only about what the speaker is saying is like one who truly listens and is not preoccupied.

A child is like a valued possession

(44) Frank Andrew, September 2000:81

If a child, a girl or boy, is obedient toward his parent, he will be held in high regard by other members of the community. A child is like a valued possession that we can care for and should be treated as such. That is how a person can be. Even though he is not attractive and is wearing tattered clothing, he can be like a valued possession by not harming his parents and others.

Tatailnguq

(45) Frank Andrew, October 2001:163

Tua-llu pinauraitkut, angutem-gguq iliin tan'gaurluq yuk'enrilngermiu ellimeqayunarqellra pitekluku irniaqelriatun ayuqliritua atangqengraan, yagiraurallra assilria pitekluku. Tua-llu makut qatellriit aipaiput tan'gaurluum ilii nasaurluum-llu ilii assirluni calilria calisteksuumilaraat, assikluku calisteksugluku, cucukluku-llu. Cangallruvkenatek. Tamatum-gguq kiingan tuaten pingaitaa. Yuullgutain-gguq taugaam wall'u ciulirneretllu cucukeciqaat nasaurluq, nasaurluuli tan'gaurluuli-llu. Ikayuacunqellrakun anyuqevkenaku, takaqelriatun ayuqevkenaku piqayunaqngalnguq pisciryiin. Tuaten-gguq ayuqelria atengqertuq tatailngurmek.

Taringan tatailnguq? Uunguuq waten pikuma camek egmian nang'erciiquten pinrilengramken. Taunguuq tatailnguq. Imna taugken niiteng'ermi aqumgaluni tua-i uitalria tatervak-gguq tua-i tauna. Makut-llu ungungssiit ilait tatervaugut. Tuntuviit-llu makut ping'ermeng aqumgayugluteng nangertevkenateng. Ilait taugaam pitmeggni nangerrluteng ayagarrluteng. Tamaa-i tuaten ayuquq yuk. Aug'ukun ava-i qalarutketuat caarrluk; apquciarpek'nani-gguq tuaten tamatumek atulria yuugarkauguq. Ilani apquciqetaangraata cakneq piyuunani ellii, apqucim tukniluku piyuunaku. Tuaten qalarutketuat.

Iruk-gguq nanengaituk

(46) Sophie Nicholas, March 2000:83

Maligtaquskumta-llu tamatumun qanruyutmun ilamtenek ayuqniarngairuciiqluta uksuqan cat paivnganriqata pisciigalikata-llu. Tamakut qanruyutet tamaa-i. Cali-llu qanrut'laraitkut wii-gguq pingnatugtemi unuakuarmek tanqigivailgan ayaglua piyuaqapigglua ernerpak tarritqapigglua ping'erma, irugka-gguq kanaken it'gama aluitnek ayaglutek nanengaituk, piyuasciigalilua-llu. Wall'u-gguq canek tegulaupakarlua ernerpak amllernek canek tegulaupakarlua, talligka yuarama nuugatnek ayaglutek talligka nangengaituk.

Ava-i akwaugarpak wanirpak-llu niitarput tegumpangramta alerquallruitkut kevgartualuta tegumpangramta pingnatuktalria tangerqumteggu cirliqualuni, peggluki tegumiaput ullagluki ikayuqilaut. Ca talligka nanilikanirngaituk irugka nanilikanirngaituk. Qaqiskan tauna ukut aqvaluki ataam tekiutevsiarciqaput.

One who quickly responds when asked to do something

(45) Frank Andrew, October 2001:163

They told us that some men begin to consider a boy who is not his real son like his own even though he has a father, because he responds quickly when asked to do something. And these white people who are our counterparts like to keep a young man or woman who is a good worker. [The Yup'ik and Western traditions] are no different. They say [their employer] will not be the only one to regard them highly. They say one's peers or elders will prefer a girl or a boy who displays that behavior as well. They will not be reserved and shy toward one who likes to help and is quick to respond. A name for a person who is like that is *tatailnguq*.

Do you understand what *tatailnguq* means? This is what it means. You will stand up immediately and help me when I'm doing something, even though I did not ask you to help me. That is what *tatailnguq* means. However, one who sits still when asked to do something is a *tatervak*. Some animals do not respond quickly as well. Even moose like to just sit [when shooed] and don't stand. But some stand and run off immediately. A person is like that. They spoke about *caarrluk* [refuse] in that context. They say one who handles repulsive things will live without getting ill. He does not get ill when others do, and his illness is not as serious. They say that.

One's legs will not wear out

(46) Sophie Nicholas, March 2000:83

If we follow that particular instruction, we will not envy others who have enough to survive the winter when things become scarce and impossible to harvest. Those are some of the lessons they taught us. They would say to us who were harvesting food that even if we left early in the morning and walked all day and were unable to walk anymore, our legs, starting from our toes, would not wear away from use. Or my hands working on things all day, my arms, starting from my wrists, would not wear away.

We have heard since yesterday and today to help others even when we are carrying a load in our arms, to drop the things we are holding and help others when we see them struggling. Our arms will not shorten, our legs will not shorten. When we are done assisting them, we may return to what we were doing and pick up the load and continue on.

Qessam angtua

(47) Theresa Moses, June 1995:64

Piyugngaurluta ellimerciuqumta, nangteqenrilkumta egmian niites-qelluta. Qessaluni-gguq uitavakalria qessam angtua, kemga-llu piniaru-lluni, unairulluni. Qessam-gguq tua-i tauna angerluku. Uitang'ermi tua-i canrilngermi qessaluni; qessaurangluni. Makut maa-i wangkutnun aling-cetaarutkellrit. Tuaten tua-i piyugngaurallemteni piuraasqelluta, uitaqa-piarrlainarpek'nata. Caarkangqetuukut yugni tamalkumta enemta iluani elatemteni-llu. Angutngung'ermi arnaungermi-llu ayuqluni piyuilnguq unaqiarulluni kemga piniarulluni. Unairluni-wa tua-i pilallil' qessang-luni.

Qavaq caurailngautnguuq

(48) David Martin, April 2001:76–77

Maa-i makut wangkuta alerquutelput. Piyugngarikan qavaq-llu man'a caurailngautnguniluku, unuakumi qavarturalleq caurailngautnguniluku. Nauwa tua-i caliaqavci kingurautenrilkurrluci tuaten pilartuci. Pissu'urqa-meng-llu tuaten pitulliut, kingurautenrilkurrluteng tua-i angungnaqluku callra ulumallra, entellra-llu. Tuaten ayuquq. Tamaa-i caliaqavci cass'aci cumikluku kingurautenrilkurrluci. *School*-alriim cass'ani tangerrluku kingurautenrilkurrluni. Ayuqlun'-am tauna waten yuukan, qavaq atur-luku, qavalleq aturpakaqaku cakairaciqniluku elliinun pitullruat.

Tuqungigcautnguuq-gguq qavam aturyussiyaallra

(49) Frank Andrew, June 2001:37

Apqucimek-gguq call' calilriaruut tamakut makuat. Misvikluku-gguq tua-i apqucirkaanek calilriaruut. Apquciq-gguq tamakut kangautaat makuat, piciatun apquciq.

Taugken-gguq tua-i im' ukvertalria tua-i piciukluki pilria, ilani quseng-raata cakneq qusyuunani. Anyuqluku-gguq apqiitnek tamakut, takaq-luku. Imna-gguq taugken qavaryunqellria piqainiteklukU tua-i misvikaq-luku makuat. Cali waten pitullruluta, qavaq-gguq cali una aturpakartii

He gets consent from sloth

(47) Theresa Moses, June 1995:64

We were told to always get up and do what we were asked to do right away if we weren't sick. They say if a person sat idle for too long, that person *qessam angtua* [gets approval from sloth]. His body would become weak and flimsy. He would feel listless even though he was fine, and he would begin to feel lethargic all the time. These were some of the things they told us to get our attention. They told us not to sit around but to work while our bodies were able. All of us continually have chores inside our homes and outside. This condition can happen to both men and women. I guess a person's body would get soft, and a person would lose interest in work.

Sleep robs one of work and chores

(48) David Martin, April 2001:76–77

This was taught to us. When they were old enough to do things on their own, they were told that sleep robs them of work and chores, that sleeping in the mornings robs them of work and chores. You know how you try to be on time when you have a job. That is probably the same when hunting, trying not to be late, catching high and low tides. That is how it is. When working, you are constantly aware of time and try not to be late. A person who is going to school is aware of his time as well. They were told that sleeping excessively takes things away from them. They used to tell them that it would cause them not to have anything.

They say sleeping too much is an invitation for early death

(49) Frank Andrew, June 2001:37

They say *makuat* [particles of dust] cause illness. They cause people to get sick when landing on them. Disease spreads through *makuat*. This is the way some contagious diseases are spread.

But one who believes in the truth about excessive sleeping and sloth is not as susceptible to colds and sickness. He repels the *makuat*. They avoid contact with him out of respect. However, *makuat* are attracted to those who like to sleep and are lazy. They also told us that one who sleeps exces-

ingna tekilluku unguvayuituq, tuqungigcautnguami-gguq qavam aturyussiyaallra. Ca tamalkuan qanrutketullruat imkut. Taumek qavaarcecuitell-
ruitkut, qavamteni-llu makluta qasgimi qavalangamta makeqnauraitkut
qavangramta, enuurluta pivkenata, teguluta maktaqluta.

Egmianun-llu tua-i ellamun anesqelluta uksumi-llu. An'aqamta tua-i
ceggaqernaurtukut, qavarniirrluta kumlamun an'aqamta. Tuaten tua-i pi-
ciryaraqluki, arnaungraata-llu arnat, irniat tuatnatuluki eneni, taumek arcaqerluteng qavaarayuitellrulriit.

Man'a maa-i caarrluk enem-llu iluani *dust*-aq maa-i mat'um nalliini
uqlautngulalria. Carriumayuilnguut qalirnerit qat'riaqluteng *dust*-amek.
Wall'u cat neqallret-llu tep'ngaqluteng uitatellriit. Pelqevkenaki-gguq tamakut tegulaqilaput. Eneni-llu uitatullrulriit ilait qimugtet imumi. Pirtugmi waten ellametevkarpek'naki, enem iluantelluki, natermi unani
ungelraqluteng. Uqlallrit cali, anait-llu cumacikevkenaki tegularluki
caliaqesqelluki wangkutnun tan'gaurlurnun arcaqerluta pitullrukaitkut.
Tuatnatulit-gguq apquciarpek'nateng yuutuut. Ilateng apqucilangraata
apqucikegtayuunateng, naulluukegtayuunateng. Tamana tamaa-i cali elli-
mertuutektullruarput, arnaungermeng tua-i tuaten ayuqellruluteng cali.
Maa-i tua-i uqlalriamek tangerrnanriryaaqua mat'um nalliini nallevceni
elpeci, taugaam yuunerkelliluteng.

Ciutek-gguq iigtun ayuquk

(50) Frank Andrew, September 2000:87

Waten-gguq niitelallruuq, ciutek-gguq iigtun ayuquk. Tangvanrileng-
raaku-gguq angayuqaan nallunrit'laraa mikelnguq.

Ciutegken camek niiteksaunatek yugmek taumek tuatnalriamek nii-
cuunatek, tangengerpeggu qaillun taungucingengaitan. Elitaqngaitan.
Qaillun ayuqucia nalluluku tua-i niicuilken, niiteksaunaku pillren. Taugken niitelallren caruyatuniluku qaillun tua-i ayuqsugniluku tauna, wall'u
assilriakun cali niitelallren cali, atranek-llu aterpagtaqluku ciutegpeggun
tuaggun niilluku, taringan elpet apertuqatgu elitaqsugngaluku. Ukuk ciu-
tegpet elitaqevkarluku tangertelluku. Ukugnegun [ciutegkun] taugken
niiteksailkuvgu tangengerpegu tangenrrilngurtun ayuqluku, qaillun ayuqluku niiteksailavgu. Tamana pitekluku ciutek-gguq iinguuk, iitun ayuquk.
Ciumek ukuk ciutek, ukuk elitaqivailgagnek iik nallunrircelluku una temvut. Tamaa-i ciutek iingunilukek qanlauciat.

sively will not live for long, as sleeping too much is an invitation for early death. Those people taught us everything. That is why they did not let us sleep excessively, and they would wake us from our sleep in the *qasgi* one by one, not shaking us but physically sitting us up in our sleep.

They told us to go outside immediately, even during wintertime. We would become wide awake when we went outside into the cold. We would lose our sleepiness when we went out into the cold. That was their *piciryaraq* [custom], even for girls. They did that to children inside the houses. That is why we never saw people sleeping late.

Refuse and dust inside the home gets on everything these days. The surfaces of things that are not cleaned become white with dust. And food that is left out starts to stink. We were told to handle it without being repulsed by it. And some dogs stayed inside the houses back then. They did not let them stay out in the blizzard but had them stay in the houses, and they would curl up down on the floor. They told us to clean the mess they made and not be disgusted by their feces, and they especially gave us boys the responsibility of cleaning them. They say people who handle refuse like that do not get sick very often during their lives. Even though others get sick, they do not get sick as much. That was one of our chores as well as women's. I no longer see messes like that today, during your time, but the life-span of people is shorter these days.

They say ears are like eyes

(50) Frank Andrew, September 2000:87

This is what he used to hear, that ears are like eyes. A parent knows what a child is up to, even though he isn't watching him.

If your ears do not hear about a person's behavior, you will not know who he is if you see him. You will not recognize him. You will not know the nature of one whom you do not hear about. But you hear that a particular person committed adultery or behaved a certain way, or you hear good things about someone. You hear his name mentioned with your ears, and you recognize him if they point him out. Your ears allow you to recognize him. But if you had not heard about him with these [ears], you would treat him like you had never seen him because you had not heard of his conduct. That is why they say ears are like eyes, that ears are eyes. Before these eyes recognize [a person], these ears reveal who he is. That is why they say ears are eyes.

Iigpegun-gguq taugaam tangerquvgu tungaunaku nutaan ukveqina

(51) Frank Andrew, June 2001:13

Matuuguq maa-i yuum-llu apqiitnek kelgurluten qanruciqaaten picilir-luku kina imna, wall'u aipan picilirluku. Tamaa-i-gguq tamana niicugni-ciqan taqkan-llu tua-i kiturtelluku egmianun, ayagtelluku tua-i. Iigpegun-gguq taugaam tangerquvgu tungaunaku nutaan ukveqina. Tamaa-i-gguq cali navguilria yugmek. Piciqenrilkiinek uum picilirluku qannguarulluku piciunrilngurnek. Tua-i-llu maligaruskuni umyugaa navegluni, tamana ciuniuquniu. Tuaten pisqenritaitkut taugaam kiturtelluku, qanenermek taqkan ayagtelluku-llu tua-i tamana qanruyutekellra. Tamaa-i tamana cali yuk elluarrluni tua-i yuulria maligarutaarpek'nani canun. Makut maa-i atuusqumaluki qalaruyutektullruaput.

Yuk-gguq qanruyutminek maligtaqutenrilnguq initami agalriatun ayuquq

(52) Alice Rearden and Theresa Moses, April 2001:137

Alice Rearden: Aptellrulrianga amllepianek *example*-aanek iciw' pugcill-rulriaci augkunek, wiinga-ll' tua-i qanrulluci ataucimek niitellrunilua te-gganermek qanelriamek mumigciurallemni yuk-gguq qanruyutminek maligtaqutenrilnguq initami agalriatun ayuquq.

Theresa Moses: Auguungacaaqelliniuq. Maa-i nunani avullugutengqer-tukut niicuilngurnek. Tauna tua-i qanemcikaqluku. Tua-llu taukumiut, tuarpiaq-gguq maniluki, mayuqanirluki allat tua-i nutaan yuut nii-tengaarrluki. Wagg'uq tua-i taukut mayurrluki, nallunarqellret inilriace-tun. Tuacetun ayuquq, auguuguq. Yuum call' ikia nallunritnitekluku qan-rutekurluku.

Yuk muragtun ayuquq

(53) Frank Andrew, September 2000:78

Tuamtellu-gguq qanruyutminun maligtaqutevkenani yuulria murag-tun napalriatun kangrani pikna catarluni, kangra pikna pitarluni, yaaq-sing'ermi alaunani. Nunani taukuni navguilria yuk qanruyutminek pisqut-minek atunrilnguq, atra-llu niitnaugaqluni tangrruuyuileng'ermi.

They say to only believe it if you see it with your own eyes

(51) Frank Andrew, June 2001:13

A person might also make accusations about someone close to you or accuse your husband of something. [They say you should] listen to that person, let the accusation pass immediately, and forget about it. They say to believe only [what you hear] if you see it with your own eyes. That is also a way of destroying people. Accusing a person of things that he did not commit, gossiping about things that are untrue, is a way of harming others. Those who accept that information will get hurt if they believe it. They tell us not to do that but to let it pass, forgetting about what they said after they spoke. A person who is living properly is not persuaded by others. They told us about things they wanted us to live by.

They say a person not following rules is like one hanging on a fish rack

(52) Alice Rearden and Theresa Moses, April 2001:137

Alice Rearden: You know how you brought up many examples yesterday, and I told you that I heard an elder say while I was translating that a person who is not following rules and instructions is like something hanging on a fish rack.

Theresa Moses: What he said seems to be what I've heard before. You know some members of a village are destructive and get into trouble, and the people there talk about him. They say it is like that [troublesome] person makes the people of that village visible to surrounding villages, hoisting them up, and nearby villages start to hear about them. They display a village that was previously obscure like they were hanging them up. That is what it is like. This is the same as gossiping and accusing others of wrongdoing.

A person is like a log

(53) Frank Andrew, September 2000:78

And they said a person who is not following his *qanruyutet* is like a post with something sitting on top that is visible from afar. The name of one who breaks the rules is heard, even though he has not been seen before.

Tuamtellu yuk-gguq waten ayuquq muragtun. Murak-gguq waten ayu-qeciqsaaquq imna *log*-aq, kevraartuq, qainga-llu waten tua-i assirluni makui-llu pikarnirluteng, cakarnirnganateng. Muriit caliaquratuit avani qupurluki-llu assirluteng. Kepluku-gguq qupsaagyaaqnauraat, ilua qamna qiplinilria, qainga taugaam mamkilnguayaarmek matumek sanqeggluni apqiitnek, ilua-gguq taugken qamna tua-i tegusngaluni tua-i cakneq. Tua-i-gguq tauna, tamana tamaa-i yuk qaimikun taugaam assirualria tangller-mikun, ilua taugken caarrluuluni tua-i, cakarniinani, aug'utun ayuqluni qairem egqaqkiitun piciatun mermi pugtalriatun.

Ilii-gguq taugken muriim, qainga man'a arumaluni-llu, arumarrlugluni tua-i, tangnirqevkenani. Yuum ilii waten ayuquq. Aturaqegtaarnek piyug-ngang'ermi aturaqegtaarnek atuyuunani pikangqeng'ermi, tangnirqevke-nani qainga. Arumaluni-gguq qainga, arumarrlugluni, cakarniilnganani. Yuvrirluku-gguq iqua *wedge*-anek piluku, aitaqutnek kaugturluku, qavci-liriami-llu qup'arrluni egmianun. Ilua assiqapiarluni elatii taugken man'a assiinani.

Tuamtellu ilii elatii man'a mamkilnguayaarmek tua-i waten qipluni. Yuvrirluku-gguq tua-i qup'aqatni, ilua qamna assipiarluni, nalqikapiarluni qup'arrluni. Tuaten-gguq tua-i yuk ayuquq. Yuk tua-i tangnirqeng'ermi nunalgutkumanrilnguq nallunarquq ayuqucia nallunaqluni.

Avani ciuliaput waten alerquutengqellruut. "Nunanun nunakenrilkev-nun ayakataquvet aturanek assilrianek pingqengerpet, calissuutevnek taugaam imkunek uqlalrianek aturluten nunanun ayagakina." Pingaklu-ten pikatgen tun'ernarqeciquten. Nunani-llu tuani nunanun ilauskuvet cali kingunerraatgun taugaam piurqina taukut nutem ilakenrilketen nav-guavkenaki. Tuaten-gguq tua-i ayuquq cali, muragtun caliarkarniilngur-tun yuk, nengaugkarniinani, panigkarniinani, ukurrarkarniinani-llu. Yuk tuaten ayuqluni. Yuarutmek niitelartua tamatum yuarucetaanek. Atu-tullruat-llu qalarucirraarluteng yuarun muragmek aug'umek yuum ayu-qucia.

Tuaten tua-i ayuqluku call' augna pituat. Qanruyutminek atunrilnguq aug'utun tua-i, qainga nalmikun assirlun, tangniqluni, ilua taugken qamna teguviinani, cakarniinani, aklukarniinani.

A person is comparable to a log in this way as well. The surface of a spruce-tree log might look good, like it could be made into something. They always worked on pieces of wood back then, splitting them, and some of them were pliable. When they tried to split some logs open, the grain would be uneven and twisted inside, but a thin layer on the surface would be smooth. They say that is a person who is deceptively attractive on the outside but cruel and unpleasant and not good to work on, like that log floating in the water thrown around by the waves in different directions.

However, they say some logs would be rotten on the surface, a little rotten and not pleasant to look at. Some people are like that. Even though he could wear nice clothing and afford to dress nicely, he never does so and is unattractive. Like the wood, his surface would be a little rotten and unfit to handle. They would study the log's edge and split it with a wedge, and it would split effortlessly after a number of strikes. Its inside would be flawless, but it would be rotten on the outside.

And now the grains on the surface of some [logs] are uneven and twisted, but just a thin layer on the surface. Upon splitting it open, one would see that it had straight grains inside and would split easily. They say a person is like that. Even though a person is attractive, it is hard to know the personality of one who is not from the same village. It is hard to know what a person who is not from the same village is like.

Our ancestors passed on the following *alerquun* [prescription] back then. "When you go to another village, even if you own very nice clothing, use only your soiled work clothes." You will be embarrassing if they feel that you are trying to be superior. And if you become a member of that village, always try to follow their lead, trying not to ruin the lives of the people whom you aren't related to. A person can be like a log that is not good to work on and not fit to be a son-in-law, daughter, or daughter-in-law. I heard a song they sang related to this teaching. They sang that song about how a person is like a log after they spoke.

That is how they explain that teaching. A person who does not follow the *qanruyutet* is like [that log] that looks attractive, but his inside is not fit to handle, not good for anything, and not fit to be carved into something useful.

Nulirran-gguq teq'ermun ekluku arullerkaanun

(54) Frank Andrew, September 2001:139

Waten nasaurluq pituat-am augkut. Nasaurlumek-gguq aipangkuni cayunqeggialngurmek caliyugngangermi qessallni maliggluku, piyuumiitellni aturluku uqlautekluki tua-i pitai uimi, caliarkani caliaqesciiganaki tengruluni, uqlautekluki taugaam piciqai. Tuatnayullermikun-gguq uinga imna man'a nerangnaqurallra pinririinarciquq, unangyuirusngiinarluni, kiituan-gguq camek unangesciigaliuq. Nulirran-gguq taum teq'ermun ekluku arullerkaanun. Imkut tepet nunam iluanun elaulluki pitukait, uitacameng-llu tua-i assiirulluteng neryunairulluteng-llu, aruluteng. Angun-gguq tua-i tuaten tuqunrilngermi, unguvang'ermi natlugnerunani picuirutarkauguq. Nulirran-gguq teq'ermun ekluku.

Teglegarkarniituq-gguq yuk

(55) Frank Andrew, September 2000:83

Tan'gaurluq-gguq mikelngurmek kenirmiarluni kangalriatun ayuquq. Arnaq angutmek aipaunani yugmek alairisciigatuq. Teglegkarniituq-gguq yuk. Tamana tamaa-i. Aassaqngermi-llu yugnun-llu nallusqumangermi, qingaquni aqsiigken aperturarkauluku. Kasngunarqelriaruluni-llu tua-i tauna angutmek piinani, uingeksaunani-llu [qingalria]. Teglelriatun ayuqeng'ermi, mikelnguq ilumini anglikan iirviinani.

Nulirtullerkarput cingiim amatiini uitauq

(56) Frank Andrew, September 2000:83

Maa-i tamana pulengtaq qalarutkelallrat wangkutnun angutngungramta. Kasngunaqluni angutnguluni arnamek tuaten pillerkaq. Inerquutaqpiallruaput. Kassuupailemta ciunemteni uitaniluku una cingik angutni uivarkarput waten, yaani-ll' amatiini kassuulluta. Uuggun-gguq kangiakun *short cut*-aryaqunata, man'a qanruyutvut yaaqsiksagulluku. Cingigmek ayuqestassiigucirluku qalarutetullruitkut tan'gaurluni taugaam wangkuta. Nulirtullerkarput-gguq yaa-i amatiini uum cingiim uitauq.

They say his wife has buried him in a pit to rot

(54) Frank Andrew, September 2001:139

This is what they said about a young woman in the past. If a man marries a young woman who is lazy and does not like to work and doesn't take care of her husband's catch, even though she is capable, she will only make a mess out of them. Because of her irresponsibility, her husband's hunting skills will slowly diminish, and he will catch less and less game and eventually not be able to catch game at all. They say his wife has buried him in a pit to rot. You know how they bury fish heads in underground pits to ferment, and they rot and become inedible if they are not consumed and left [to rot]. They make the same reference, that even though a man has not died and is alive and healthy, he will lose his ability to catch animals. They say that his wife has buried him in a pit.

They say one can't get away with stealing a person

(55) Frank Andrew, September 2000:83

They said that a young man is like someone who walks holding a child in the lap of his garment. A woman cannot get pregnant without a partner. *Teglegkarniituq-gguq yuk* [They say one can't get away with stealing a person]. That is what they mean. Even though a woman is secretive and doesn't want others to know she is pregnant, her stomach will reveal [her pregnancy]. And it is shameful to [be pregnant] without having a husband. Even though it is like [a woman] was stealing something, if a child grows inside her stomach, she has nowhere to hide it.

Our time to get a wife is on the other side of a point of land

(56) Frank Andrew, September 2000:83

They gave us this advice repeatedly, even though we were men. It was very shameful for a man to get a woman [pregnant]. We were warned about it constantly. They told us that we must wait to get a wife until we have reached the other side of a point of land. They told us not to take a shortcut over the top of it, taking a detour and becoming impatient with the long journey around the bend. They spoke to only us boys by using a point of land as an example. They said that our time to get a wife was on the other side of the bend.

Nasaurluq-llu, tua-i arnat caliaqetuamegteki taugaam niicugniluaqayuitaput wangkuta imumi anglillemteni. Anguterrlainaat taugaam makunek assinrilngurnek-llu qalarutetullruit, ayagyuarluta pillerkamtenek, kiituan nulirturtukut angutngurrluta-llu. Angutem ayuqucianek qalarutetullruitkut. Arnauyaram ayuqucia elisnganritaqa tamalkuan wii niicuitellruamku. Arnassaagaat caliaqetullruit tamakut arnat aipangllerkaat-llu tekilluku tua-i irniangellerkaat-llu. Tamana-ll' tamaa-i qingallerkaat uingunateng.

Nerangnaqlerput-gguq atam amuniartuq aglumakikumta akusrarutekikumta-llu arnamek

(57) Frank Andrew, September 2000:85

Angutni inerqunqegcaumalallruukut arnamek aipangkumta allamek arnamek kenkisqevkenata, taugaam mat'ukun assilriakun kenkesqelluki, nuliamcetun irniamcetun-llu kenkekngamcetun pitarrluku, aglumayarakun pivkenaku. Tamaa-i tamana assiilnguq cali, assinrilnguq. Arnaqllu call' tuaten, uutun angutem inerqutiitun pimaluni, uingqeng'ermi allamek kenkisqevkenaku, aglumakengraani-llu maligtaquutesqevkenaku.

Augna tua-i tuaten ayuqluku niicugnilaraqa, uingunani qingaryaraq angutnguluni-llu nulirturpailegmi qingiqengyaraq. Man'a nerangnaquciq pik'ngamteggu yugni, wangkuta inerquutaqerput tan'gaurluni, nulirturpailemta arnamek aglumakisqevkenata, akusrarutekisqevkenata-llu. Nerangnaqlerput-gguq atam amuniartuq. Camek pit'esciigaliluta, picuirulluta, elluatuunrirluni-llu temvut. Cucukenritqapiarqeka wii tua-i cakneq. Anelgutemnun-llu augkunun tan'gaurlunun tua-i kesianek qanrutek'laqka. Atamta apa'urlumta-llu qalaruyutii nalluyagutevkenaku tumyaraqluku pingnaquraasqelluki.

Amllerinivkenaku tua-i pissuusqelluta alaitellratni

(58) Frank Andrew, September 2000:144–46

Imkut ellangellemni yuut tua-i iqayaaqut, aturait nallmegteggun iqaluteng tua-i yuuyaaqut makut iqaitnarqelriit alairpailgata, taugaam tua-i iqairituluteng *meal*-amek piilengermeng. Tuaten ayuqellruut. Tua-i-llu nerangnaqsaramek arcaqerluteng yuucingqellruut augkut. Tan'gaurlurni-llu

Because it is the job of women to discipline girls, we did not hear all of their teachings when we were growing up. Only men spoke to us about right and wrong and our responsibilities and continued until we got married and became elders. They spoke to us about men's responsibilities. I do not know much about women's responsibilities, because I didn't hear everything they were taught. Old women taught girls about marriage and raising children. They also taught them about [the consequences of] getting pregnant without a husband.

They said our hunting skills would diminish
if we desired and had sexual contact with a woman
(57) Frank Andrew, September 2000:85

We men were thoroughly admonished not to love another woman when married, but only to love her in an honest way like we love our wives and children, but not through sexual desire. This behavior is unacceptable. A woman should follow the same principle of not loving another if she has a husband and not complying if another man desires her.

That is what I heard about getting pregnant without a husband and about a man impregnating a woman before getting married. Because subsistence is our way of life as Yup'ik people, young men were admonished against desiring women and engaging in sexual activity before getting married. It is said that our hunting skill and abilities will be weakened. We will not be able to catch animals, and our bodies will no longer be strong and healthy. That is why I do not wish that upon anyone. And I am always telling my male family members about it. I encourage them not to forget our grandfathers' *qalaruyutet* [instructions] and to use them as a path.

They told us to hunt when things were available,
not making the excuse that we had already caught a lot
(58) Frank Andrew, September 2000:144–46

When I became aware of my surroundings, people were actually dirty and wore soiled clothing before cleaning amenities were introduced, but they washed clothes and things without soap. Their lives depended on harvesting. They especially taught us young men about hunting and be-

wangkuta qalarutaaruaqamta nerangnaqlerkarput taugaam, pingnaqler-
karput neqkanek ayagaluta arcaqerluku elitnaurutkellruarput. Qanruyun
murilkelluku cakneq tan'gaurlurni arcaqerluta nangtequastengullruamta,
nengelmi, uksumi pirtugmi ayagaaqluta, ellami nengelmi qavaraqluta.
Tuaten ayuqellruukut wangkuta nerangnaqlerput pitekluku.

Taugaam cangalkevkenaku, piitellerkarput taugaam arcaqalriaruvkar-
luku, piitqapiggluta pillerkarput. Tua-i-llu neqkat makut, kiagmi-llu neqet ayuqenrilnguut tungliqu'urluteng avaken ayagluteng alaitulliniut,
ataucikun waten pivkenateng. Makut taugaam naternat, kayut-llu imar-
pinraat-llu kepsuitut, pelluyuitut nunamteni unani. Neqa-am alaitaqan
waten up'nerkami unguvalriit neqekngamteki amllerinivkenaki pisqu-
tengqetullruukut. Amllerinivkenaku tua-i pissuusqelluta alaitellratni. Waten ayuqut tua-i alaunateng tayima-llu tua-i catairulluteng qagaatmun
ayagluteng. Taumek tuaten qaategtevkenata uitaksaunata alaitellrani pis-
qutkellrukvut.

Imkut tua-i uitayulriit-am carrarnek tua-i unangnaurtut nurusngalu-
teng uksumun. Tuamtellu pelluata taryaqvagnek cali tamakunek tuamtellu iqallugnek neqnek tua-i sayagnek, kangitnernek, qakiiyarnek, imar-
pinrarnek, qusuurnek. Tamakunek tamaa-i pissutuluta, Kusquqvagmi-llu
pituluteng. Avaken tua-i ayagluteng pituluteng. Aug'utun-am cangallruv-
kenateng tua-i amllerinivkenaki alaitellratni pituluki. Fish and Wild-anek-
llu piitellruamta tamaani.

Tamana-am alerquun waten ayuqelliniuq. Augkut ava-i qaateggluteng
pilriit, nurutaqluteng neqnek, tamakut-am pitekluki tuaten pitullrulli-
nikaitkut. Nurutellriit-llu neqnek cikiumalallerkaat pitekluki ilakuyutell-
ruameng augkut. Neqet aulukaqamegteki tua-i ilakuivkenaki aturyugngal-
riit caliaqetuluki egqaqevkenaki, piciatun egqaqevkenaki, sagcecuunaki,
unkumiutaat-llu augit sagcecuunaki. Murilkelluki cakneq, angu-llu tut-
maasqevkenaki inerquraqluta neqallret, neq'liurviit-llu tutmaasqevke-
naki. Tuaten tua-i pituluteng. Murilkelluki cakneq neqallret sagtellerkaat,
murilkeqapiarluki enret-llu sagcecuunaki.

Neqnek sagcinrilnguut iqailngurnek aterpagtaqluki

(59) Frank Andrew, September 2000:149

Tua-i-llu tamana pitekluku, imkut neqnek sagcinrilnguut iqailngurnek
aterpagtaqluki, uqlaucinrilnguut neqnek. Murilkeqapiarallruit neqet ma-

ing providers. We paid close attention to our instructions because we were the ones who suffered, traveling in the cold during winter in blizzards and sleeping outside in the cold. We did that to provide for our families.

However, we did not mind the suffering because we entirely depended on our subsistence way of life, and a pattern of migration has been in existence since ancient times. Fish and animals are not available only at one time, but flounder, devil fish, and small whitefish are available in our village year-round. We hunted without the excuse that we caught too much when sea mammals, our [main] source of food, became available during the spring. [Fish and animals] become available and then are gone, traveling north. That is why they told us not to be lazy and sit idle while they were available.

Those who liked to sit around obtained very little and wouldn't have enough to last the winter. After the [seal-hunting season] was over they harvested king salmon, herring, red salmon, chum salmon, silver salmon, whitefish, and smelt. We harvested the same fish that swim up the Kuskokwim River. That has always been the custom for ages. They harvested fish when they were available, without making the excuse that they had obtained enough. There were no restrictions in harvesting, because the Department of Fish and Wildlife did not exist.

That teaching is like this. They told us to harvest food because some might run out of food, because people helped one another back in those days. When they took care of food, they did not waste anything and discard parts that could be used. They did not make a mess out of them, and even sea-mammal blood was used and not discarded. They took proper care of everything, and they taught us not to step on food scraps whatsoever and places where they worked on fish. That was their way. They watched over food scraps closely, and they did not scatter the bones for people to step on.

They called those who did not mess up food iqailnguut

(59) Frank Andrew, September 2000:149

They called those who did not make a mess out of food iqailnguut [ones who are neat and clean, from iqair-, "to wash, to clean"]. They really took

kut. Atam nerlalput tua-i tamakut kinertaqata, neqkarugaput-wa amllel-riit. Tan'gaurlurni arcaqerluta ceturrnat qamiqurritnek kinertarnek tapir-cetaqluta. Pacignek-llu ner'aqluta, enernek imkunek, enrit ciamlluki tua-i tamualuki enrunrirluki igaqluki.

Cali-am neqallermek tua-i pisqevkenata maavet cailkamun. Estuulu-nek-llu waten piilamta, kinguqerput, wavet qantaq piluku, tuavet taugaam tua-i kaimlluki, piurtelluki nerevkatuluta. Elitnaurluta tua-i tuaten cail-kamun unavet kaimevkaqsaunata kingumtenun taugaam. Tua-i-llu taq-ngamta quyurrluki nerluki call' tamakut kaimelput catairutqapiarluku. Tamaa-i tamakut aterpagtetullruit iqailngurnek.

Qalarucilrianek-llu niitnaurtua uqlaulluki-gguq atam saggluki-llu pil-riit pingnaqestait pisciigaliinatuut. Neqet-llu-gguq nurnariinatuluteng. Uqlautekluku sagcesqevkenaku pitullruat neqalleq enrit-llu. Ner'aqamta-llu can'giiret enyagait imkut tevvaarutesqevkenaki taugaam teguqerluki enernun ilaulluki. Cailkamun waten pisqevkenaki. Tamaa-i wangkutni un'gaani cenarmiuni, Kuigilngurmiut avatiitni ayuqucillemtenek nallun-ritua, avaqliinka nalluanka. Tuaten ayuqellilriit cali tua-i cangallruvkena-teng. Tuaten ayuqluku neqa aulukumallruuq.

Quyuqcaaraqumteni-gguq atam atkugkaurrniartuq

(60) Theresa Moses, November 2000:225

Cali-am una yaqulek-gguq atauciuyaaqerraarluni amilek man'a egcug-naunaku quyuqcaarqumteni-gguq atam atkugkaurrniartuq, atkuurqurai-narniartuq. Maa-i tang makut augkut ca egqaqevkenaku angutem pitaa te-guluku quyakluku assircarluku.

Elitaituq-gguq imarpik

(61) Frank Andrew, June 2001:37

Amlleq tua-i katagarput maa-i yuut cayarait qaneryarait-llu. Taumek ilait aptelaqiitnga cayaraucianek tauna, nalqigutaqluki tua-i. Ca tamal-kuan elitnaurutkelallruarput nunavut-llu unegna, nunamta aug'um nunal-gem avatii man'a, *area*-ra. Qertulriit nanvat kuiggaat-llu atrit-llu nalluvkar-pek'naki, unkut-llu cali imarpigmi kiiguyuut. Up'nerkami pissuayaraput

good care of fish. When the fish we ate dried, we had a great variety of food to eat. We boys especially ate tomcod heads with other dried food. We also ate dried fish gills, smashing and chewing those bones until they were dissolved.

They also told us not to drop food on the floor. Because we did not have tables, we would put our bowls on our laps, and we were trained to let the crumbs drop only onto our laps while we ate. And when we were done, we would gather the crumbs that we had dropped and eat them until they were completely gone. They called those people clean people.

I heard those who were instructing say that the improper care of food will cause their providers' hunting skills to weaken and diminish. And food will become scarce. They told us not to make a mess out of fish and their bones. And they did not let us spit and blow out tiny blackfish bones when eating, but we carefully took and placed them with the other bones. That was the way we coastal people were, those of us from around Kwigillingok. I don't know about the surrounding villages, but they are probably no different. That was how food was cared for.

They said if we collected them,
they would soon be enough to make a parka

(60) Theresa Moses, November 2000:225

They also told us that if we did not throw the skin of one bird away whatsoever, that we would eventually have enough to make a parka. It would eventually become a parka. They never discarded things but were grateful for a man's catch, took it, and made it into something.

They say the ocean cannot be learned

(61) Frank Andrew, June 2001:37

We have lost a lot of our traditions and words with them. That is why some people ask me how to do something, and I explain it to them these days. We were taught about everything having to do with our land on the coast, the area around our village. They let us know about deep lakes and sloughs and taught us the names and the channels down in the ocean.

cali elitelluki, nallunrirtelluki, carvanrit, cikunek imiraluteng pitulriit, aarnarqelriit nallunrirtelluki. Cat-llu avitarvigkaput nallunrirtelluki.

Taugaam tua-i tuaten ayuqengraata elitnaurluta nallunrircetengramegtekut waten pitullruitkut, imarpik-gguq elisngaitaput. Elitaituq-gguq imarpik. Mat'utun-gguq nunatun ayuqenrituq. Nunam-gguq qainga pekcuituq mer'em-llu atercuunaku uruyuunaku-llu. Imarpik-gguq taugken un'a cikutuluku uksumi, evunret-llu piciatun nauqluki, kiagami-ll' urugluku tamana cikullra ayagluni. Tamaa-i tamana tuaten ayuqucia up'nerkami-llu navgurluni ayallra piyaraunani ernermek-llu taumek piyuunani. Taumek pitullrukaitkut, imarpik-gguq tuaten piqatarniluni qanyuituq. Tamana pitekluku tua-i elisngaitniluku, elitaitniluku pitullruitkut imarpik un'a. Unkut tua-i marayat nugtaqtaayuilameng evunertangqetullruut nallunaunateng tua-i. Tamakut tamaa-i tua-i elisngaluki, nugtaringavkenateng pitulit, marayat, qaugyat-wa, qikertat.

Nuna-gguq taugken tua-i man'a enemini tua-i uitaluni, qertulriit-llu enemeggni uitaluteng cangariyuunateng. Kavirlit-llu napat wall'u caranglluut cimiyuunateng. Allamiaqan tua-i uitatuluteng enemeggni. Taugaam maa-i ilii kit'elanguq waten catairulluni acitmun nuna. Nanvat-llu makut cingigluteng wall'u takluteng uivenqeggluteng, kavirlinek-llu napaliraqluteng cenait. Tua-i tamakut enemeggni uitaluteng, tamayuunateng. Elisngallra tua-i uunguciitnaunani, enemeggni uitiimeng nunami. Tuaten-am qanrutketullruit. Taugaam aarnarqutai cali nalluvkarpek'naki, aarnariyaraat.

Pitqerraalriim ciuqlirmek tamalkuan cikiutektua

(62) Frank Andrew, September 2000:93

Tua-llu una cikiqengyaraq. Elaqlini qakemkut umyuaqluki neqmekllu una pingnaqesteseng pill'uni tekitaqan, unani nunamni navgutuat neqa. Taqngamegteggu-llu qakemkut qayagaurluki tamalkuita nunalguteng aqvatesqelluki tuaken. Maa-i-llu call' aturaat nunamni. Tamaq'apiaraan avvluku nunanun tamalkuitnun. Uum-llu pitqerraalriim ciuqlirmek pitaa tamalkuan tua-i tuntuluku piciryaraqluku.

They also taught us spring hunting routes, currents, places where ice formed. They taught us dangerous areas, and they let us know about areas we needed to avoid.

But even though they taught us [about our environment], they told us that we will not learn the ocean. They said the ocean cannot be learned. They said it is not like land. They said that the surface of the land doesn't move and cannot float away or melt. They said on the contrary, the ocean freezes during the winter, and ice piles up in different places, and the ice melts during summer and goes. There is no set time in the spring when it breaks up and no certain date. That is why they said that the ocean does not tell us what it is going to do. They said we cannot predict what the ocean is going to do. Because sandbars do not move around, the places where ice piled up were obvious. We knew where the sandbars that did not move were located.

On the contrary they said the land stays in one place, and steep areas stay in their places and do not change. And the bushes and grass and other plants do not change. They stay in one place year after year. But some areas of the land are starting to sink and disappear. And these lakes have rounded bends or are long, and their banks have a lot of alder tree growth. Those things stay in one place. They do not disappear. The land is not confusing because it stays in one place. That is what they told us. However, they pointed out dangerous areas.

One who has had his first catch gives it all away

(62) Frank Andrew, September 2000:93

And now about giving to others. In my village down here, when their provider arrives with animals, thinking of their neighbors, they divide up the catch. And when they are done, they call their fellow villagers to come and get a share. They are still practicing that tradition in my village today. They divide the whole animal up for all of the village residents. And it is their tradition to give away a person's first catch.

Neqa-gguq man'a ilakuyutnguuq

(63) Frank Andrew, September 2000:95

Arnat arcaqerluteng tamana cikiqengyaraq neqnek caliaqellruat. Angutni wangkuta pillrunritarput, arnat taugaam neq'liurtekngamteki. Waniwa pissutullruukut qanruyutvut aturluku. Unguvalriamek-llu pic'amta, wangkuta pikarput tua-i wangkuta pikluku tuqucamteggu, uterrluta-llu. Enemtenun-llu-gguq tua-i tekicamta aanangqerqumta wall'u nuliarluta, taumun tunkumteggu wangkuta tua-i ataniumanrirluku. Pikenrirluku, arnam taugaam aulukarkaurrluku tua-i elliin ataniumaluku. Irniarin-llu pisciiganaku aanaseng apqa'arpek'naku. Tuaten ayuqluni.

Qaneryaram-am tuamtellu nalqigtaa. Wangkuta-gguq quyatuilngurni qunuyulriani-llu ilakuyutekaq navgumalararput. Arnaq-gguq ilii qunutungatuuq. Uini piyungraan tuaten qunullmikun tungayairutelluku. Angutem-llu-gguq cali nuliani tungayairucecugngaluku tuaten cali unangkengani makut pitani atanirturluki elliin, tungayairutelluku-llu. Neqa-gguq man'a ilakuyutnguuq. Tamakut-llu tamaa-i quyatmegteggun-gguq taugaam tua-i camek assirluni pillerkaanek akinautuat. Tangrrumanrilnguum-gguq akinaurcecetua Ellam Yuan. Ellam Yuanek qanerturatullruut. Maaten tua-i alairtuq, taringnariuq Agayutngullinilria Ellam Yuanek pitullrat.

Amllenminek-gguq cimingetuuq

(64) Frank Andrew and Alice Rearden, June 2001:33

Alice Rearden: Augumek-llu cali iciw' neqmek-wa tuvkaqiuraasqelluta, wall'u tamatuuguq, iciw' neqmek cikirtuurilaasqelluki nangengaitniluku neqkautiit, amlleriinarciqniluki. Niitelartuten?

Frank Andrew: Tamaa-i tua-i cali tamana. Taumek unani nunamteni piciryaraqerput arcaqerluku up'nerkami waten. Unguvalriamek tua-i una unaken atrarluni tagutaqan nulirran ciamtetua tamalkuan tua-i, qaqicamiu-llu nutaan elaqlini qakemkut qayagaurluki tamalkuita, keni'irkaaraminek taugaam tegulluni. Nangqapiarluku-llu tua-i aruqutekluku. Tuaten ayuqut unegkut cenarmiut. Neqngungraata tua-i ca tamalkuan-llu avegvilek umyuaqekngaminun cikiutekluku ilii pituluku. Amllenminek-gguq cimingetuuq.

Quyallagallermegteggun-gguq tamakut tuatnatulit tauna tua-i cingqa-

They say food helps to create family bonds

(63) Frank Andrew, September 2000:95

Women especially were responsible for distributing food. It wasn't our responsibility as men, because women were the caretakers of the food. We hunted following *qanruyutet*. And when we caught a sea mammal, it belonged to us because we killed it. But when we returned and arrived home, when we gave it to our mothers or wives, we were no longer in charge of it. It no longer belonged to us, but a woman was responsible for taking care of it, and she would be in charge of it. And his children could not take it before asking their mother first. That is how it was.

There is an explanation for [hunting and sharing]. They say those who are continually ungrateful and stingy break family bonds. They say that some women are stingy. Even though her husband wants to share, she causes him to lose relatives by being stingy. A man, by being in charge of what he caught, can also cause his wife to lose relatives. They say food helps to create family bonds. They say [elders and orphans] wish good fortune upon those who helped them. They say that an unseen entity, Ellam Yua, repays them. They always spoke of Ellam Yua. It was soon revealed that they were talking about God.

They say that it will be replaced by more than was given

(64) Frank Andrew and Alice Rearden, June 2001:33

Alice Rearden: And what about when they ask us to be generous with food, or is it that? To always give food away because it won't finish, that it will be replaced by more. Have you heard that?

Frank Andrew: That is another saying. That is an important *piciryaraq* down in our village, especially during the spring. When one goes down to the ocean and brings back a sea mammal, his wife divides it all up and, when done, calls all her neighbors out there to come take enough for a meal. She gives it all away. That is how coastal people are. Food and everything that can be divided is given to those one thinks about. They say that it will be replaced by more.

They say because of the overwhelming gratitude they felt, they push the animals toward the hunter. That is why some say, *"Anirtaqulluk, am-*

qutuat pitarkainek, quyallagallermegteggun. Ilait taumek waten pitullrul-riit, "Anirtaqulluk amllenminek cimingeciqvalria." Umyuaqegcilrianek-llu qanernaurtut cunaw' makunek ciulirnernek, arnassagarnek-llu. Tua-i tamaani cali tua-i atullruat augkut tangvallemta. Tuvqatarluteng. Una tuv-qataryaraq cali ilani umyuaqsugluki, qunuyugpek'nani.

Pinqigcuumiirngaituten qanruyuten atungnaqu'urquvgu

(65) Hilary Kairaiuak, November 2000:125

Cali-llu makuni augkuni ciulirnerni ak'allani Yup'igni qanrumauq. Umyuarrluuqerrngaituten, aliayugngaituten, pinqigcuumiirangaituten qanruyuten atungnaqu'urquvgu piyugngallerpeni. Taugken niitellrunger-pegu atungnaqenrilkuvgu, pairrluku pillrukuvgu, arenqiallugmun tekicii-quten — umyuarniullerkarpenun tekiciiquten, aliayullerkarpenun tekicii-quten. Tuaten qanrutkaat.

Qanruyutmek-gguq maligtaqutellria alerquatmun pinialillerkani tekilluku unguvatuuq

(66) David Martin, April 2001:111

Ayagyuakacagaq-gguq qanruyutminun maligtaqutellria yaaqvaarnun ayatuuq. Ellminek navenrilami tua-i qanruyutni tamakut maliggluki piami yaaqvaarnun ayatuuq, unguvamaqerluni. Taugken-gguq-am qan-ruyutminek maligtaquinrilnguq iqukliciisciigatuq-gguq mat'umek pinia-lillmi tungiinun. Pinialillerkaminun iqukliciisciigatuq qanruyutminek maligtaquinrilnguq. *Meaning*-aarit augkut ciuliat apertunqegcaarluki pi-tullruit. Qanruyutmek-gguq maligtaqutellria alerquatmun pinialillerkani tekilluku unguvatuuq. Tuaten qanrutekluku.

Ciunerpeceni caningqauq tauna tekitarkarci

(67) John Phillip Sr., March 2000:14

Yaani wani ciuliamta qaneryaraicetun, ciunerpeceni cangingqauq tauna tekitarkarci. Nasaurlurni uingellerkarci cangingqauq yaani ciuner-peceni. Tan'gaurlurni nulirtullerkarci ciunerpeceni caningqauq. Caning-qaniluku naugguirngaunani tauna.

llenminek cimingeciqvalria [*Anirtaqulluk,* it will be replaced by more than was given]." And they spoke of *umyuaqeggilriit* [those who have become wise]. They were apparently referring to elders and elderly women. Those people whom we observed practiced that custom. They were generous with food. *Tuvqataryaraq* [Being generous] also means that one thinks of others and is not stingy.

You will not feel regret if you always try to live by the rules

(65) Hilary Kairaiuak, November 2000:125

Also, there is a saying among our past elders. You will not feel remorse, you will not be filled with sadness and regret, if you always try to live according to your *qanruyun* while you are able. But if you do not try to follow your teachings even though you hear them, and you go against them, you will come to harm — you will feel remorseful, you will come to sadness. That is how they said it.

They say one who follows
his teachings lives until he becomes frail

(66) David Martin, April 2001:111

They say a young person who adheres to the *qanruyun* lives a longer life, because he is not living a destructive life. However, they say a person who does not adhere to his instructions and teachings does not reach old age. Our ancestors thoroughly explained the difference between right and wrong. One who follows his teachings lives until he becomes frail. That is how they explained it.

Your future is ahead of you

(67) John Phillip Sr., March 2000:14

Like the saying of our ancestors, *Ciunerpeceni caningqauq tauna tekitarkarci* [Your future is placed in front of you, and you can't go around it]. The time for you young girls to marry is already set in your future. The time for you young boys to marry is in your future. They told us that it was our future and couldn't be avoided.

Maani-gguq nunam qaingani aka'arnun nangerngaciqukut

(68) Wassilie Berlin, September 1998:35

Tua-i taugaam alerquutem qaneryaram elluarrluku pillerkaa akqutkell-ruarput wangkuta. Maani-gguq nunam qaingani aka'arnun nangengqa-qerciquq. Maaten tang murilkua ilumuullinilria tua-i ilumuupiarluni.

Mikelngurtun-gguq ellirluteng, uterrluteng-gguq

(69) Frank Andrew, June 2001:40

Unguvanrirluteng angulluat nurnariluteng. Qasgimi-llu maqiqata'ar-qameng tuntunek inguqirluki piyuasciigalilriit, arturyagutellriit, nau-lluuvkenateng taugken, angukara'urluut, maqiqata'arqata tegulaucirluki anutaqluki qasgim elaturraanun, patuluki taugken tua-i kumlamun pingairutelluki. Maqillrat, taqngata-llu egmian itrulluki cali.

Murilkelluki tua-i arcaqerluki tamakut tuaten ellilriit. Ilait-llu inglutun ayarurluteng pekaqtarangnaurtut. Keggutait-llu cimirluteng-gguq alla-yugnek, keggutait cimingluteng allanek, tuaten-llu-gguq elliraqameng.

Qanrit keggutairutqapiararraarluteng keggutengaqluteng tamakunek, allayugnek, ungungsilinrarngalngurnek-gguq. Keggukarangluteng-gguq. Usviirutellrianek mikelngurtun ayuqluteng tanglallruunga. Arnassagar-nek-llu augkunek tutgarameng-llu makut qaill' piaqaceteng qiagaqluteng, capengssagaunateng mikelngurtun. Mikelngurtun tua-i ellirluteng, uterr-luteng-gguq. Tua-i tamakunek tamaa-i pitairulluni maa-i mat'um nalliini, angukara'urlurnek arnassagarnek-llu. Enrit-llu ukut yuupengaqluteng makut arivnerit, qatagtengluteng.

Calisciigaliluteng tuaten elliraqameng naulluuvkenateng taugken. Tamaa-i-gguq tamakut qanruyutem maligtaqustai.

They said we would stand on this land for a longer time
(68) Wassilie Berlin, September 1998:35

We were promised a better life if we adhered to the teachings. A person was told that he would live a longer life. By observing I've realized that this teaching is true.

They'd say they would become like children, going back to childhood
(69) Frank Andrew, June 2001:40

There are fewer older men alive these days. And when they were going to take a sweat bath in the *qasgi*, they transported those who could not walk and had difficulty moving by placing them on caribou skins, yet those old men weren't sick. When they were going to take a sweat bath, they carried them out and put them in the porch of the *qasgi*, but they covered them so they would not be exposed to the cold. And they brought them in immediately when their sweat bath was over.

They especially cared for those who reached that age. And some would walk with canes in both hands. And their teeth were replaced by a strange set when they reached that age.

After losing all of the teeth in their mouths, they grew a strange set of teeth, ones that resembled animal teeth. They called those *keggukarangelriit*. But I saw those who lost their minds and acted like children. And some elderly women cried when their grandchildren picked on them a little, and they didn't have any emotional control, like children. They became like children, *uterrluteng-gguq* [they said they returned to their childhood]. There are no longer elderly men and women who behave that way these days. And their joints would become uneven and crooked.

They were unable to work when they got to that point, yet they weren't ill. They said those people had adhered to the *qanruyutet*.

Qanernaunak yuuluaqautekan yuarluku, nataqeciqan

(70) David Martin, November 2000:103

Qanrupakarlua-am qanqertuq yuuluaqautekaqa-gguq yuarlaku, na-
llunrilkeka yuuluaqautekaqa yuarluku. Ayagyuaruama tuaten qanrut-
linianga. Elluarrlua piurallerkaqa yuaresqelluku. Kingunerrluku-am qanertuq, "Qanernaunak yuuluaqautekan yuarluku, nataqeciqan." Tuaten
tua-i tamana tamariyuilkengaqa tua-i tuaten ayuquq. Ayagyuakacagarlua
taum tua-i anirta wangnun alerquatellra.

Search for ways of living your life
without being a source of trouble, you will find it
(70) David Martin, November 2000:103

After instructing me numerous times [that elderly man] told me to search for advice that would help me to live a proper life. He told me this because I was a young person. He told me to search for ways to lead a good life. After saying that he added, "Search for ways of living your life without being a source of trouble, you will find it." I never forgot that advice. I am grateful for that person who taught me that when I was very young.

Angayuqat Mikelnguut-llu

Ungungssit-gguq alikait uqlautekumalriit
(71) Frank Andrew, October 2001:42, 104

Tan'gaurluum-gguq tua-i eyagnani ciuketua, nasaurluum-gguq taugken kingukluku. Arnaq-gguq tua-i waniwa qagrumariaqami eyagnarituuq.

Qalarutkelallermeggni, tan'gaurlurni wangkuta nalluvkarpek'naku nulirtullerkarput yaaqsingraan, pitsaqevkenata aipangkumta, arnamek irniangekumta, tuaten piyukan, inerquusqelluku. Arnat-llu aanaita nalluvkarpek'naki ayagmek uingvailgata mikelngiullerkaatnek uingekata. Akimek taugaam piinata avani ellangellruukut taugaam yuilqumun ayagaluta pissualuta. Ungungssit-gguq nallutaitut ellangqerrameng allamek. Imarpiim yui mermek nunaluteng, nunam-llu yui nunamek nunaluteng. Wangkucicetun enenek piinateng. Alikait-gguq tamakut, nalluvkenaki tua-i anyuqluki, alikluki, tuaten pimalriit, uqlautekluku pivkaqiit tan'gaurluq nasaurluq-llu miktellrani. Ayagaaqan yuilqumi, yaaqsingraan qimagaqluku tangercecuunateng. Anyuqluku-gguq, alikluku tua-i. Piciuluni tua-i tamana, piciuqapiartuq.

CHAPTER 4

Parents and Children

They say animals fear those who were exposed to [infant saliva and urine]
(71) Frank Andrew, October 2001:42, 104

They say that one must follow strict abstinence rules when the new-born infant is a male, but one needs to follow strict abstinence rules for a female when she reaches puberty. They say one must follow strict abstinence rules for a female when she has had her first menstrual period.

When they spoke about that topic, they talked to us young men about [the care of infants]. Even though we weren't of marriageable age, they told us young men to admonish our wives when we married and had children if she tended to be [careless with an infant's saliva and urine]. Mothers also taught their daughters about raising infants before they got married. We became aware of our surroundings not relying on a cash economy, but we were always out on the land hunting. They told us that animals are aware of everything, because their perception of the world is different than ours. The inhabitants of the sea live in water, and the land is the home of the land animals. They do not have homes like us. They say [animals] can detect and don't want to go near [hunters who are exposed to the saliva and urine of] male or female infants. While a hunter is traveling in the wilderness, the animal would run off although he was a good distance away, and it would not allow itself to be seen. They fear [those who are exposed to saliva and urine]. That is true, that is very true.

Mikelngurmek anglicarilleq

(72) Sophie Agimuk, November 2000:216

Cakviungermi arnaq caliyaramek elitengnaqciquq. Eliciiquq cakviur-turangermi. Mat'umek maa-i arcaqerlua inerqutullruanga [maurluma]. Tuamtellu irniangama, irniangeqarrallemni pianga, "Kitak irniartuuma qavan peggluku qavaryungerpet. Qavaq caunrituq." Tua-llu irniangama-am ciuqlikacaarmek cumikaanga, tua-i cumiklua irniaqa tauna qerruk-suarmek pilirluku. "Kitak irnian tupagaqan tuavet qurrevkaraqluku pikiu, atam elitniartuq." Una-wa irniacuayaaq uunguciinani camek-llu eliteller-kailnganani. Wiinga asgurayugyaaqlua. Alerquucia makugteng'erma atungnaqluku cakviurlua, iluteqaqlua-llu tuaten pingnaqngamni elilluni. Elisngailngalngermi elilluni. Cali unuakumi taklaurautesqevkenaku. Cali-llu atiinun qurqallra agtuusqevkenaku. Tang qanruyutengqellria yuk ama-ken ciutengyugallerminek ayagluni. Maa-i-llu tamarluni. Tua-i-wa una arcaqalria qanrutkeqaqeka makunek ayagyuaqegtaarnek tangrraqama ta-mana umyuaqerrlainatuamku.

Mikelnguut nallunritut

(73) Nastasia Andrew, November 2000:114

Piyuumiuteka waniwa irniangkuvci. Tua-i aug'utun nauwa qanelria mi-kelnguq aanani elpekaqamiu anqallerkaa-llu nacitua, aanani taugaam kii-ngan pisteksugluku, tua-i-wa nallunrilameng. Elluarrluku pingnaqluku anglivkangnaqluku pillra assinruuq. Niitetuut, taringtuut mikyaanger-meng. Pirrlainanrilengraan qanqautaqluku ciunerkaanek wall'u ernerpak atullerkaanek anglillranun. Qanpagatevkenaki anglicangnaqluku irniaci. Iciwa ilamta-llu qanllagalluta piaqatkut assiliyuitukut. Taugaam qanpa-gatevkenaku elluarrluku qanrulluku taringevkarluku pingnaqluku assin-ruuq. Tua-i-wa mikelnguut wangkucicetun temircetun ayuqut. Mikyaa-ngermeng *feeling*-aaput-llu nalluvkenaku aanemeggni, angayuqameggni. Tamana tua-i tamaa-i kenkun.

Ilallugutengqengraata taugaam kenekluku, ciumuratekevkenaku, pin-rituatekevkenaku, pegtetuavkenaku, assikluku, kenekluku taugaam qan-

Raising a child

(72) Sophie Agimuk, November 2000:216

Even though a woman suffers, she will try to learn how to work. She will learn, even though she has a difficult time. [My grandmother] especially cautioned me about this. And when I had my first child, she said to me, "Now, take care of your baby by letting go of your sleep. Even though you want to sleep, sleep is nothing." Then she observed me when I had my first child and placed a small urine bucket under my baby and said, "Let your child pee in here when he wakes up. He will learn." This little baby seemed to have no sense of awareness or ability to learn. I didn't think it was possible [the baby would learn to pee in the bucket]. As advised, I tried to train the baby with a lot of effort and frustration, and eventually he learned. He learned, even though it seemed like he would never learn. She also told me not to lie around with him in the morning. And she also told me not to let his father touch his urine. You see, teaching was administered from the time a child was beginning to comprehend, and now that way of caring is no longer practiced. Since I'm noticing beautiful young people here I'm mentioning this, because it's always on my mind.

Children know

(73) Nastasia Andrew, November 2000:114

These are my hopes for you when you have children. Like someone said earlier, when a child becomes aware of his mother, he even cries when she [leaves home], and he only wants his mother to take care of him, because he knows [that she is trying to raise him well]. It is better if [parents] try to raise [children] well. They hear, they understand, even though they are very young. Instruct him about what he will encounter in his future or how to behave all day as he is growing, even though it is not all the time. Raise your child by trying not to yell at him. You know that we feel awful when others speak to us negatively. It is better to have him try to understand by speaking to him clearly and thoroughly instead of yelling at him. Children are like adults. They know our feelings as mothers and parents, even though they are very young. That is love.

Even though they are troublemakers, love them. Do not give up on them or brush them aside, but be kind to them, love them, and always talk

ruquraraqluku. Ilaitni nallunrituci ciumuqertelartukut, "Tua-i pili pi-yugtacimitun." Umyuangqerrngamta-wa ilumun malrugnek — aipaan elluarrluni egelrutengnaqluta, aipaan-llu iqlutmun.

Yuk irniangqerrluni ellminek arcaqakngaitelliniuq
(74) Nicholai Berlin, March 2000:3–4

Anglicariyaramek arnaulrianun, angutngulrianun-llu uksurpak niiske-ngaqerput, assirluki auluklerkaitnek. Tua-i-llu elliraurtellruukut wang-kuta tuaten ayuqluta. Taugaam waten yuk irniangqerrluni, anglicarar-kangqerrluni, ayuqucirturarkangqerrluni ellminek arcaqakngaitelliniuq. Tangvallemnek ata'urlumnek waniwa umyuaqa calilartuq. Elitellemkun-llu waniwa waten ellirlua nangengqalua elliinek.

Ellminek arcaqakevkenani, allanek-llu aiparluni, aipaminun tua-i-w' ar-caqanrurrluku ellmini ayuqellrunrituq tangvallemni. Wangkuta taugaam eskaurtellerkarput, calligtellerkarput tamana arcaqakluta ayuqucingqell-ruuq, ayuqucingqellrulliniuq. Tamaani ayuquciitellruyaaqaqa.

Arnanek-llu allanek, taugaam tua-i takumcukesteminek tamaaggun ikayuumalallruyaaquq. Taugaam wangkuta pitekluta tayima umyuaqel-lemni tamakut arnat aipani pivkalaryaaqellriit takumcukestekaminek ar-caqakellrunritai. Wangkuta taugaam murilkelluta-wa tua-i pillruakut.

Wangkuk-llu amaqliirutka-llu ayagyaurteksaunanuk. Tamaa-i tua-i-wa qayangeksaunanuk; pissuryaurteksaunanuk. Kiituani pissuryaurtukuk. Pissuryaurcamegnuk pitapuk aulukluki elliin taum angutem, neqtapuk-llu aulukluki. Tamaa-i ellminek arcaqakenrilucia, tamaaggun tangvalqa maa-i mat'um nalliini.

Quyanarqelliniuq waten irniaminek aulukilleq assirluki. Ilavci teki-ciqaat. Ilavci aturciqaat tuaten ayuqellerkaq tamana. Waten ayuqura-rarkauyukellrung'ermi ayuqurnarqenritliniuq, nangtequayarat amllera-meng.

Ayagyaurcamegnuk-llu, ayagayaurcamta tekitnaurtukut, unugmi-llu up'nerkami ayagalaamta, kanaqliit pissulaamteki, tekitnaurtukut neqai-cugnaunata, kenirarkaicugnaunani, taum angutem aulukaarini. Tamaa-i tang yuk aulukilria arnarrlainaq aulukingaitelliniuq assirluki.

Naugg'un elitellruvkenii tuaggun taugaam atamkun. Elitellemnek ma-

to them. You all know that some days we give up and say, "Well, let him do what he wants." It is because we have two minds, indeed — one trying to lead us toward good and the other leading us in the wrong direction.

One with children will not be selfish
(74) Nicholai Berlin, March 2000:3–4

This past winter we've been hearing about how it is to be a parent as a woman and as a man. How to be good caregivers. We became orphans [as children]. When a person has children to raise and teach, a person will not be selfish. I've been thinking a lot about the things I observed my father do. I am standing with the things I learned from him.

As I observed my father, he didn't think of himself first or bring in others to fill in the void [of having no spouse]. His only concern was for our welfare and making sure we got all the preparation and training for adulthood and family life. I wasn't particularly aware of his priorities when I was younger.

[He had no interest] in other women, but he allowed other women who had compassion for his responsibilities to assist him. Now, when I think of those times, it was because of us that he didn't turn his attention to the women who helped him and tried to gain his interest. He only cared for us.

The two of us, my older brother and I, weren't going out on the land alone yet. We didn't own our own kayaks yet; we had not begun to hunt yet, but eventually we were able to hunt. When we started hunting, that man would take care of the animals and fish we caught. Looking back now, I've come to know that he was an unselfish person.

It is gratifying to take good care of children. Some of you will come to that time and also experience that in your lifetime. Even though one feels that things will always stay the same, they don't, because people run into much hardship and suffering.

When we started to hunt we'd go out hunting, and we would return at night when we started traveling in springtime hunting muskrat. Upon our return we'd find food prepared for us to eat. That man always had something cooked for his children to eat. It is not only the women who are able to care for children well.

Everything I learned, I learned from my father. I am telling you these

kunek tua-i ciuqlilirluci qanertua. Waten ayuqerrlainarnarqenritliniuq. Waten wiinga ayuqlua aipanglua irnianglua-llu camek umyuarniurutaunii nangengqallruunga.

Ataucikun tumyarakun ayanritut irniaput
(75) Frank Andrew, September 2000:138

Pulengtaq-llu man'a maa-i qalarutkelaraqa kasngukngamku, wii irnianka kenekngamki. Tua-i pulengtaq tamiini ikayungcaraqluteng tamakunek. Yuk tua-i assirluku tamiin pisqumaluku pituyaaqerput taugaam nallunrituci, atam nallunritaci makut angayuqaulriik ukuk irniangqelartuk qavcinek, ataucikun tumyarakun ayanritut. Ilangqelartut-am iqlutmuryulriamek.

Tuamtellu imkut qimugtet cuqyutngulalriit wangkutnun. Yugtarmek maa-i qalartelartua nunamni niirqelallemnek ciulirnernek. Nunat allat elaqlimta ayuqucirtuutait allarraulartut ilait. Tamakunun ekuravekenii nunamni taugaam yaani tangvakemni ellangellemni niicugnilallemnek qallatelartua yuungama allaurtevkenaki. Ukut-am qimugtet waten, ciulistiit-wa ingna, akiqliqluteng waten ayuqetuut, wall'u malrugnek ciulisterluteng. Tua-i-gguq waniwa cali aanaulriim angayuqrulriim-llu irniaminek maryarcillerkaa — qalarteqainarpek'natek ayuqucimegnegun nepaunatek angayuqrulriik, irniatek-llu tamatumek nepailutevkenaki. Qimugtet maligngatellriit ciulistegnun ingkugnun, kenegnarqut cakneq nunaniqlunillu atuqatarluki ayakatalleq. Nunaniqlun' tua-i ayalleq, ayuqluteng tua-i angayuqaagmeggnek aanameggnek ciulisterluteng-llu pitulriit tua-i assirluteng cakneq, angnirnaqluteng.

Arcaqerluta angayuqrulriani wangkuta qalartenrilengramta irniamtagguq ayuqucimteggun tangvagaitkut. Qanrutkelaqeka iciw' mikelnguum angayuqaagni tangvagak. Tuaten pitukagnek, tuaten-llu pituciquq ellii anglikuni.

Ayagyuaq, irniaq, caliaqekagnegu assirluku, assirluni yuuciquq. Qanrucuunaku taugken irniaqekagnegu, umyugiurtelluku assirpek'nani yuuciquq. Qanruyun arcaqalriaruuq aanaulriami aataulriami-llu. Naugg'un caliaqviituq yuum ayuqucia. Angayuqrulriim aanaulriim-llu aturaitgun irniani caliaqelarai neqkaitgun-llu, temii taugaam pitekluku. Una taugken ayuqucia qanruyutekun taugaam caliaqsugngaa yuum irniani, inerqualuku canek aarnarqelrianek-llu maniilluku nallunrilkengarraminek.

things I've learned to begin my presentation. Things do not always remain the same. I married and had children and lived my life without any worries.

Our children do not follow the same path

(75) Frank Andrew, September 2000:138

And I speak of this constantly these days because I am ashamed of it, because I love my children. And they have asked me to help them many times. We would like everyone to always do well, but you all know that parents have a number of children who do not follow the same path. They might have a child who is disobedient, going in the wrong direction.

They used to compare dogs to us as well. I have been speaking about Yup'ik teachings that I heard from elders in my area. Some of the teachings of the surrounding villages vary. I do not use other teachings, but I speak of things I learned and how I heard them when I became aware down in my village. Dogs were harnessed and lined up in pairs like this with their leader up front, or they might have two leaders. This is also the way a mother, a parent, is supposed to lead her children — not just by speaking, but also by their quiet relationship and guidance and not being silent toward their children. Dogs that follow their leaders are extremely lovable and make you very happy when you are about to travel with them. It is wonderful to travel with them, just like [children] being led by their parents and mothers, and they are just wonderful and cause us to be joyful.

They say as parents, especially, children watch our behavior and actions, even though we are not speaking. You know how I said that a child is always watching his parents. If they behave a certain way, he, too, will behave like that when he gets older.

If a young child is raised carefully [by his parents], he will lead a good life. But if they do not instruct their child and let him do whatever he wants, he will not live a good life. *Qanruyutet* are especially important for mothers and fathers to know. A person's character cannot be worked on by any other means. A mother is responsible for providing clothing and food for her child, for his body's health and well-being. However, one can only work on the disposition of his child through the *qanruyutet*, admonishing him about harmful situations that he knows of. That is

Tamaa-i yuucim uum nerqumalallra. Makuuvkenani atuqengaput, tang-ssunarqelriit aturaqegtaaraat, neqkat-llu assilriit. Tamatutgun assiringai-tuq yuk piniringaunani-llu. Taugaam qanruyutekun tan'gaurluq nasaur-luq-llu nauluaqeryugngaluni, wall'u angayuqaagni tangvallermikun nepaunatek malignallutek-llu pillragnegun, assirluni tangviimikek, nau-yugngaluni.

Tua-ll'-am tuaten ayuqengraan irniarin iliit iqlutmuryulria, umyuani atuqeryugluku, ilallugutnguluni, ilani-llu ukut qinucetaaryugluki. Tama-kutangqertuq-am cali. Yagiraluku, alqunaraluku-llu angayuqrulriani pi-narqenrituq. Tuaten ayuqellra pitekluku nunuraqluku, ilai ukut nunuyuu-naki. Tuaten pinarqenrituq, taugaam qarulluku, assilriamek erinamek cikiraqluku, maqarcelngurmek, engelqerranek, akngirnarqenrilngur-mek. Ukutun assilriacetun qimugtet iliit tua-i imutun qimugyunrilngur-tun ayuqelartuq, tamaa-i tamana. Pitatekluku tua-i assilrianun piyunaq-luku, taugaam qanruqu'urluku, qalaruqu'urluku. Qanruyutekun taugaam yuk assirluni elitnaurutmikun nangerngatulliniuq.

Ciuqliq-gguq elluarrluni tuaten pimakan-gguq atam, kinguqlian ayuqniaraa

(76) Frank Andrew, October 2001:13

Taugaam-am yuut makut tua-i ukugnek ataucimek yuurteng'ermeng ayuqeqapiarciigatliniut-am angliaqameng. Taumek qalarucilrianek imku-nek niigartaqama ciuqlirmek arnaq qingalria qalarutetullrukiit ankan tua-ten qaillun auluklerkaanek qanruqaarluku, pinaurait, tautun pimakegtan-rilngermi, tumii-gguq aturluku, aturyugluku.

Tuamtellu arnaq wall'u tan'gaurluq tuaten-gguq ayuqsukan, qetunraan-gguq, qetunrangkuni, anglikuni atami ayuqucia maligcugngaa. Nasaur-luum-llu-gguq aanami cali ayuqucia aturyugngaluku. Man'a piciuguq.

Irniat kegginaqliniaput

(77) Evan Alexie, March 2000:13

Waten ellangqengnaqluni yuulleq, cali-llu angayuqrulleq caknernar-quq.

Cali-llu apquciilengraata apqucimek cali cikitullinilalliaput wang-kuta. Tamaa-i, tamaaggun wangkuta angayuqaput keneknluki qalarteng-

how the character of a person is fed, not through material goods that we use, through beautiful clothing and good food. A person will not become strong through material wealth. A young man or woman can only grow properly through instructions, or they can develop properly by observing peaceful and cooperative parents.

Even though the parents are like that, one of their children tends to head in the wrong direction, likes to do as he pleases, is a troublemaker, and deliberately teases and annoys his siblings. There are children like that. Parents should not mishandle him and act rashly or violently toward him because of his behavior, scolding him for his bad behavior and not his siblings. [Parents] must not treat him like that, but one must talk to him in a gentle voice, one that is soft, one that fits him and does not hurt. [Children who are disobedient] are like dogs that don't pull vigorously like the others. That is what he is like. He must be treated the same as those who are obedient, continually encouraged and always instructed. A person is only standing by the *qanruyutet* he has learned.

They say if the firstborn is raised properly, his younger siblings will be like him
(76) Frank Andrew, October 2001:13

Even though they are born from one set of parents, children do not have the same nature and disposition when they grow older. That is why I heard those who were instructing a newly pregnant woman about how to raise her newborn child say that if the firstborn is taken care of properly and carefully, his younger sibling will emulate him and aspire to be like him, even though he is not raised as carefully.

And if a young man or woman tends to [behave inappropriately], a son can follow the example of his father when he grows older. And a young woman can also imitate her mother. This is true.

Children are the faces [of their parents]
(77) Evan Alexie, March 2000:13

Trying to be aware and responsible in life and be a parent is hard work.

We can cause our parents to get sick [by misbehaving]. We may say we love our parents, but when we don't follow their instructions, we hurt

ramta tamaaggun maligtaqutenritlemteggun akngirtelalliniaput cakneq qiavkaraqluki-llu. Waten tang qanrut'lallrukaitkut, wiinga-llu taringell-runricaaqaqa, taringelallrunricaaqaqa, angayuqamta-gguq aanamta, atamta-llu kegginaqaitkut. Ilumun irniat wangkuta kegginaqliniaput. Talluryugcet'laraitkut irniamta.

Tan'gaurluq atami piciryaraa aturluku nangerngauq

(78) Frank Andrew, September 2000:5

Arnam nasaurluut elitnauraqai; tan'gaurluum atami piciryaraa atur-yutua, nasaurluum-llu aanami piciryaraa aturyutua. Aanani pitukan, aa-namitun piyugngauq, tan'gaurluum-llu atani tuaten pitukan, tan'gaur-luum-llu atami pitullra aturyugarkauluku. Taumek qalarucitulit imkut waten qantullrulriit augna-gguq-am atami piciryaraa aturluku ava-i na-ngerngalliniuq, wall'u nasaurluq.

Elisngaut augkut ciulirneput qanruyutmek murilkelluteng elitnauru-malriit igausnganrilengraan. Maa-i tua-i wii qanruyun tamalkuan niite-lalqa nallunritaqa taugaam aturrlainayuunaku, navkayuunaku-llu piyuu-nii waten yuk alartaqluni pitulliniami. Taugaam qanruyutni neq'aqaquniu taum inerqurarkaugaa. Waten-llu qanrutpigainarciqluku, "Qanruyutet narureskuvki tuaten pilarciquten." Taumek alerquumaukut mikelngung-luta ellakengnaqluta angayuqrusqelluta. Ilumun mikelnguq una anga-yuqaagni aturyutulliniak.

Tua-i-llu cali mikelnguq ullagtaarusngalria waten agalkaurtetuuq-gguq. Angayuqaagken tuatnatuluku pikunek anglikuni cakviurutkaqaak elkenka. Inerquayuunaku-llu, apertuucuunaku-llu pikagni, anglikuni angayuqaagni akngirtelarciqak, iluteqevkaraqlukek-llu qiavkaraqlukek-llu. Tua-i-wa elkenka angayuqaagken caliaqenrilagnegu.

Man'a maa-i angayuqrulriim arcaqerluku qanruyun qemangqaarka-qenritaa iirumalriatun ayuqluku. Irniaminek wall'u irniaqenrilkeminek cingumainrilkuni, naucurlaasqumalriatun taugaam ayuqluku, iirusnga-luku qanruyutmek.

Irniarita-gguq angayuqateng tuqullrungraata unguvavkatuit.

them very much and make them cry. I did not understand this at first, I did not understand it then, but they said that we children can be seen on the faces of our parents. It is true that children are our faces. Our children shame and embarrass us [and it shows on our faces].

A boy is standing using his father's ways
(78) Frank Andrew, September 2000:5

A woman teaches girls; a boy likes to imitate his father's ways, and a girl likes to follow her mother's ways. If her mother does something, she can, too, and if a boy's father behaves in a certain way, a boy will want to behave the way his father did. That is why our instructors said that a boy is standing using his father's ways.

Our elders who diligently learned oral instructions, even though they weren't written down, are wise. I am knowledgeable about all of the instructions I heard, but I do not always live by them, and I do not live without breaking them sometimes, because a person makes mistakes. But the *qanruyutet* one remembers will guide him. And it will warn him, "This will happen to you if you disobey the rules." That is why we are taught to be attentive and responsible when we become parents. Indeed, a child likes to behave like his parents.

They also say a child who is brought from place to place becomes restless and unsettled. If his parents [take him from place to place], they will suffer over him when he grows older. And he will hurt his parents when he grows older if they do not admonish him. He will cause them pain and will bring them to tears because his parents didn't raise him properly.

A parent is not supposed to keep the *qanruyun* stored away, like they are hiding them. If he does not encourage his children and others, it will be as though he is wishing them to grow up improperly by hiding instructions from them.

They say children allow their parents to continue to live, even though they have died.

Tan'gaurluq-gguq tauna atani catairutengraan, atami caliara alaicetaa, unguvavkaraa-gguq

(79) Frank Andrew, October 2001:18

Qetunraulriim wall'u paniulriim angayuqaagni-am tua-i ayuqlutek pilaagnek qigciklukek, ayuqucirtuatekek-llu ataneqlukek, cakaaqsaunakek caqatallni tamalkuan. Ayagayaurteng'ermi-llu natmun ayakataucini nalluvkayuunaku, ayagyuucini. Atami-llu aklui, pingnaqutminek elliin avpailegmiu aklungutni, elliin ataniumavkenaki, ataminun taugaam uumun pikevkarluki. Elliin ataniumavkenaki, kiputellrung'ermiki naken apepailegmiu atani, apelcirrlainarluku. Unangkenani-llu ukut tamalkuita maaggun akingutmikun-llu pitamikun-llu cat wall'u caliyaureskuni taqellni cat qaqitaqata, ataminun tua-i piinun ilaulluki, umyugiurutkevkenaki. Ataneqluku taugaam atani tauna.

Tua-i-llu nutaan aipangkuni ataminek avvluni, avteng'ermi-am atani una taqevkenaku. Atami pisqutii nutaan aturluku elliin atami piitun pitarrluki unangkengani. Tuacetun atami pillruciatun akluni aklungkuni aulukarkaurrluki, elluarrluki tua-i murilkelluki. Tua-i-llu nutaan una atani piunriqan, nutaan aklui elliin teguciqai. Atani unguvavkarluku tua-i nutaan temii taklartengraan nunami, calillrakun ellminun ayuqucirtuutaikun, aklungqerrsaram-llu mat'um ayuqucirtuutai tangvagtelluni aulukellruciatun, calissuutai-llu tamalkuita murilkelluki. Caliyaraa-llu man'a nerangnaqellra tangvallermini aturluku tamana nutaan nerangnaqerkauluni atani catairuskan. Tuaten-llu pilria navgurpek'naku atami man'a pisqutii, caliara-llu calilallra, aterpagtetuat-am waten: Tan'gaurluq-gguq tauna atani catairutengraan, atami caliara alaicetaa, unguvavkaraa-gguq. Tua-i tuaten alerquumaukut.

Nasaurluq aanani unguvallrani ataneqerkaugaa, maligtaquluku calillra tangvagluku. Anngarmi angutem ataminek murilkellruciatun, maligtaquluku, waten pisqaqani piaqluni arnauyaram ayuqucianek. Anngaa-wa tan'gaurluq angutnguyaramek atiin elitnauraa. Ataminek tua-i murilkiyaraq, qetunraulria, nasaurluq-llu cali aanaminek murilkiyaraq, paniulria, aug'utun cangallruvkenani-am. Ikayualuku, callra tamalkuan piyugngarillerminun, qigcikluki makut elliin ataniumavkenaki, aanaminun taugaam

They say a young man who does not break his father's instructions has kept his father alive, even though his father has died
(79) Frank Andrew, October 2001:18

A son and daughter will honor and respect their parents because they get along and treat each other with respect, and they will obey their teachings and will not disregard them but will always consult them before making decisions. When he begins to travel on his own, [a son] should tell [his parents] where he is planning to travel and ask for their permission. And he shouldn't take charge of the tools and materials belonging to his father before he is able to provide for himself, but his father should own them. He should not be in charge of [the tools] and should always ask his father's permission to use them, even though [his son] bought them himself. And he should include all the things he bought with his own money, the animals he caught, tools and implements he made with his father's things and not use them as he pleases. He should regard his father as his superior and shouldn't do things without his father's permission.

And he should not cut ties with his father completely when he marries and lives on his own. He should continue to live according to his father's teachings with the things that he acquired and caught on his own. He must take good care of his belongings and tools like his father does. He will then inherit his [father's] tools and belongings when his father dies. He will let his father live on, even though his body is laid in the ground, by continuing to follow his teachings and perpetuating the way his father lived, caring for his belongings the same way he observed his father do. And he should work and subsist in the same way he had seen his father do, after his death. They say the following about one who does not break his father's instructions and way of working. They say that young man has kept his father's work alive, even though his father has died. That is what we are taught.

A young woman must obey her mother while she is alive, doing what she does by observing her work. Just as her older brother observed his father, she must do as she is told and follow her mother's commands concerning women's work. The following is a way for a son to learn from his father and a daughter from her mother. [She should] help her, and she should respect the things around her and not be in charge of them when she becomes capable of completing tasks, but she should let her mother

pikevkarluki. Apelcirluku aanani aturaqluki elliin pik'ngermiki. Aug'utun cangallruvkenani angutetun anngarmitun. Tua-i-ll'-am tuaten cali tuaten ayuqellermikun, aani tauna piunriquni nunami, aug'utun cangallruvkenani. Taum piluaqerluku nasaurluum tamalkirrluni caliara pillrukuniu, calituluni yuuyugngaluni nallumciqelriaruvkenani. Waten-llu aug'utun aterpagtetuat, tauna-ggur-am nasaurluq aanani tuqungraan caliarakun unguvavkallinia. Aanamitun ayuqliriluni, ayuqliriluni tua-i taqellra.

Ca tamarmi qanruyutekun taugaam kitugngauq. Tua-llu tan'gaurluq tuaten alerquumangermi malrugnek umyualek, una piyaaqeng'ermiu tamalkirtevkenani, murilkevkenani, qessayugluni, qavaryunqeggluni, aug'utun ayuqenrituq tamalkirrluni murilkellriatun atani tangvallermini atamitun. Tua-llu-gguq tauna tan'gaurluq atani unguvallrani akluinek tua-i akluiturpek'nani, aklui amllerraata cassuutai. Ikayuangnaqevkenaku tua-i murilkevkenani. Tua-i-llu-gguq atii tauna tuquluni. Tuqullran-gguq kinguani aklui tamakut aturciqai piunrirtaqluteng tua-i, nangluteng-llu. Tua-i-llu cumigutellrunrilamiu ayuqucirtuutii atami, tan'gaurluq imna tauna akluirulluni. Caliyaraq cumigutellrunrilamiu qaillun calisciiganani. Waten aterpagtaat, tauna-gguq tan'gaurluq atani tuquan maliggluku tuquuq unguvaqtang'ermi atamitun calinrilami.

Una waniwa qetunraqa calilria camek piaqami tailuni apqaularaanga qaillun ayuqucirkaanek. Tuaten piyunaqluta tua-i. Maligtaqutellria tua-i caliyarakun tua-i caliyugngauq niilluku pillermikun. Tuaten tua-i nasaurluq tan'gaurluq-llu unguvallermini atamitun aanamitun-llu ayuqerkauguq. Piyunaqluni, atami umyugaa ilulliqevkaqsaunaku, iluteqevkaqsaunaku-llu, qiavkaqsaunaku-llu, nasaurluuli, tan'gaurluuli-llu.

Ciuqliim irniam kinguqliq maryarcugngaa

(80) Frank Andrew, June 2001:1, 27

Ukuk nulirqelriik ciumek yuak anngauluni una angutngukuni, wall'u arnaukuni alqauluni. Waten-am qanruyucetangqertuq. Angutngukuni-gguq angucetaryaraq nallunritarkaugaa. Cali-llu ukut kinguqlini maryarcugngaluki-gguq atani ikayurluku angutnguyaram ayuqucianek, kinguqlini ukut assirluki cali malignggalluki-wa tua-i nepaitellerkaitgun pillerkaat.

be in charge of everything. She should use them after asking her mother, even though she owns them. She would be no different than her older brothers. If her mother dies and is buried, if a young woman was trained and learned how to work skillfully, she will be capable and not ignorant. They used the same comparison they did for the male, that she has allowed her mother to live on, even though she has died, through the way that she worked. She becomes like her mother, the things she works on and creates look like her mother's.

Everything is adjusted and fixed through oral instructions. Though taught, a young man who isn't serious and determined and who does not give his fullest effort when working, one who is not careful but is lazy and likes to sleep excessively, will not be like the one who pays close attention and gives his full effort while observing his father. Now that young man, while his father is alive, will not lack many tools that belong to his father. But he wouldn't help his father or watch him. Then one day his father died. After he died, he will use his tools, and they will break and disappear. Because he was not willing to learn his father's ways, that young man will run out of belongings and tools. He will not know how to work because he was not willing to learn. They say that young man has died along with his father, even though he is still alive, because he isn't carrying on his father's work.

My son comes to me and asks how something is done while working. That is what we should do. One can accomplish something by listening to instructions. That is how a young man and woman should be toward their father and mother while alive. That is what they should do, not causing his father anguish and pain and not making him cry. This applies to both young women and men.

The oldest child can lead the younger sibling
(80) Frank Andrew, June 2001:1, 27

The parents' first child is an *anngaq* [older brother] if male and an *alqaq* [older sister] if female. There is the following *qanruyun*. If he is a male, he is to know about men's ways and responsibilities. He can also be a role model for his younger siblings by assisting his father with men's responsibilities, teaching them to be obedient, cooperative, and peaceful.

Tuamtellu una arnaukuni cali-am elitellni aanaminek, arnam tegu-laryarai ukunun-am arnanun cali kinguqliminun nallunricetengnaqar-kauluki aanani ikayurluku, assirluki cali pillerkaat arturnarqevkenaki. Tuaten-gguq ayuqelriit *family*-teng amllengrraata nepaitetuut, maligngallluteng-llu.

Una-gguq arcaqalriaruuq tua-i, cakneq-gguq murilkarkaugaa irniange-qarraarutni, murilkelluku tua-i cakneq qanruyutni aturluku, unugmi-ll' qavairatekluku, murilkelluku atunem uingan-llu. Atam-gguq kinguqling-kuni ciuqlimi tauna tumii aturniaraa, tuaten pitaluku murilkumanril-ngermi. Anngani una yung'eqarraarun ayuqucia-gguq atam aturyugnia-raa tautun pitaluni murilkumanrilngermi. Tuaten qanruyutetangqertuq mikelnguq.

Teggutngungnaqluten kitak tauna mikelnguq aulukekiu

(81) Martina Chugluak, November 2000:221

Tuamtellu irnianglua ciuqlirmek. Allam cali arnam qanrullua, "Kitek tua-i irnianguten. Ciuqlikacaaq irniaq takarnarquq, qigcignarquq. Teggutngungnaqluten kitak tua-i elpet tauna mikelnguq aulukekiu." Imuce-tun-gguq waten angayuqaulriani wangkuta mikelnguyagarmun nanger-ngalriamun teggutngulartukut.

Angayuqaitni wangkuta kenkuterrlainarluta yuuyuilngukut erneq ta-malkuan, kenkutengramta. Tua-i-llu-gguq tauna mikelnguyagaq imna, qaillun pikata, aipaak waten pikan, iggluni. Tauna-gguq tua-i mikelnguya-gaq teggutnguuq kinguqlirkaminun. Takarnaqluni elluarrluni auluknaq-luni. Pitacirramtun wiinga irniamnun qanellratun taum teggutngungnaq-lua yuullruunga. Tauna-gguq ciuqlikacaaq irniaqa piciunrilkan, qaillun irniamek unangesciigaciiqua egmirturluteng irnianka piciqut. Pitacirram-tun tauna wiinga teggutngungaqlua mikelnguq aulukellruaqa.

Ayuqluki angutet arnat-llu qalarutetullruit

(82) Frank Andrew, October 2001:72

Mat'umek-wa taugaam qanernaunata assirluta ilamtenek navguivke-nata piaqameng ayuqluta arnaungraata-llu qalarutetullrukaitkut. Tua-i-llu nutaan angutnguyaramek, angutni arnanek ilaluta qalarucuitellruit-kut qasgimi, angutem caliarkaanek, yuullerkaanek-llu. Angayuqamta

And if [the first child] is a female, she would teach her younger siblings about women's responsibilities and tasks she learned from her mother. She should also teach them about being obedient and not being a burden. They say a family that is like that will be peaceful and cooperative, even though they are a large family.

They say it's most important [for a mother] to take extremely good care of her firstborn child, watching over him closely by following the teachings she learned and losing sleep over him at night. The husband should take care of him as well. They say the younger sibling will follow the same path as his older sibling, even though he isn't given the same amount of attention and care. They say he will want to behave like his older sibling, the firstborn, even though he isn't being cared for as closely [as the older sibling]. That is an oral teaching concerning children.

Raise your child by trying to be a strong foundation
(81) Martina Chugluak, November 2000:221

Then I had my first child. A woman told me, "You now have a child. The firstborn must be cared for with respect and honor. Now, raise that child by trying to be a strong foundation." She said we parents are like a pillar for a child to lean on when standing on his feet.

You know that we parents do not always get along, even though we love each other. They say that small child will fall when the parents do something disruptive. They say the oldest child is like a pillar to his younger siblings. They must be raised with respect and honor. I truly tried to be a pillar to my children. They say if my firstborn fails to live, I will not be able to keep my children, and they will continually die. I made a big effort to be a support when raising my [first] child.

They spoke to boys and girls equally
(82) Frank Andrew, October 2001:72

They spoke to us equally, including females, about not being a source of trouble, treating others kindly, and not hurting anyone. Then in the *qasgi*, they spoke to us about men's work and responsibilities without women around. However, our parents and grandparents would gather all of us

taugaam tamakut apa'urlumta quyumta waten ilakelriani, arnaungraata-
llu qalarutetullruitkut mat'umek yuullerkamtenek, ilamtenek waten
navguivkenata qanernarqu'urpek'nata assirluta taugaam nunani catail-
ngurtun ayuqluta. Tegliuyuunata, picirkartuyarcuunata, ilamtenek eq'u-
kiyuunata, piciliqengyuunata, umyuarrliquciyuunata, taugaam kenek-
luki assirluta, assirluta ilamtenun nunaullgutemtenun, yuullgutemtenun
tamiin pillerkamtenek quyumta arnartuumamta qalarutetullruitkut.
Augna taugken allakarrauluni. Tan'gaurluut allakarmeng angutem cang-
naqsarainek, yuungnaqsarainek, yuuyarainek, pingnatugyarainek. Arnaq-llu cali tuaten, arnam cayaraminek, arnauyaram ayuqucianek. Qasgimi pimatullruamta wii arnanek tangssuitellruunga qasgimi.

Irniangama, nallunrilkengamnek qanruquratullruanka

(83) Theresa Moses, November 2000:3

Tua-i-llu tuani uingama cali tua-i tuaten uituumallerkamnek qanru-
tetullruatnga. Tuamtellu qingallemni cali qavallerkarput man'a nepliu-
tekluku pitullrukiit, inangqaurautesqevkenaki, egmianun tupakumta
ellamun anqertesqelluta. Qessanaqtuyaaqluni tamatum qanruyutem ma-
ligtaqungnaqellra. Tua-i-llu irniangama tuamtellu aug'um cali arnassagaam alerquagaqlua, kitak-gguq waniwa irniangua iliini-llu piluku-gguq
qanrusnguarturluku pitukilaku niicuuraasqelluku ernerpak. Cali-llu
ayuqluta yugni unuakullugtetukiikut. Irniaput-llu cali tamakut unuakumi cam iliini makuggluteng tupagaqluteng. Qanrucetullruitkut ilalqe-
ravkenaki aulukesqelluku. Atam-gguq ernerpak mikelnguq tuaten pillrukuni, ernerpak tuacetun unuakumi tupallermitun ernerpak ayuqniartuq
umyugaa assiinani, assiicugluni, nicuunani. Tua-i tuaten alerqutullrukii-
kut.

Cali kegginaakun yagiprasqevkenaki makut tan'gurraat alerquuma-
luta. Anglirikuni-gguq tan'gurraq yagipramallerkaa amllertuq — ellallug-
mek, pirtugmek, anuqmek-llu. Tua-i-gguq tamaa-i tan'gurraam uluryalla-
gatii. Tuaten kegginaitgun yagipraluki pisqessuitait, nulluakun taugaam
ping'ermi caksaitniluku.

Tuaten qanqegtaaqauqurluku tuani unuakumi qatguurutevkenaku mikelnguq cali tuaten ungilegtengraan pisqumaluku. Atam-gguq tuaten qat-
guuruquurluku anglicaqumteni apqiitnek wagg'uq tatervaurrluni. Qan-

siblings together, even females, and speak to us about how we should live our lives properly, about not harming others and not being a source of trouble, living like we were invisible in the community. They spoke to us in a group along with women about not stealing, not living recklessly, not picking on others, not accusing others, about not having malicious and deceitful thoughts about others, but being kind and friendly toward others, to everyone around us. But they would separate us for that other [form of instruction]. Young men were told about men's roles and responsibilities separately, about hunting and being a provider to the family and community. And women were taught at home about women's work, roles, and responsibilities. I never saw females in the *qasgi*, because we were the only ones taught in the *qasgi*.

When I had children, I taught them what I had learned

(83) Theresa Moses, November 2000:3

And when I married, they advised me about the roles and responsibilities of being a wife. And when I became pregnant, they constantly instructed me about what to do, and [they told me] not to sleep excessively in the morning and to go outside immediately when I woke up. Following this custom is very difficult. When I had a child, that old woman told me that I should sometimes talk to my child in the morning about being good and obedient all day. We all sometimes feel irritated in the morning. Our children will sometimes wake up in a bad mood, too. They advised us not to make it worse for them when they are like that. They said if we did that, our child would behave badly all day and would be disobedient and misbehave. That is what they taught us.

They also advised us not to slap boys on their faces. They said there are many things that will hit a boy's face when he grows older — rain, blizzards, and wind. Those are things that a boy has to turn his head away from. They told us not to hit their faces or abuse them, but they said that it would not do him harm if we spanked him on his buttocks.

They told us to speak to a child softly and kindly in the mornings, not to shout at him even though he is whining. They said if we raised him by yelling at him repeatedly, he would become stubborn and unrelenting. It

qegtaaralluku qanrutengramteni elliini tauna cauvkenani, imna taugaam erinaq angelria kiingan taugaam tauna utaqaluku-gguq. Tamaa-i tuaten ayuqerkauluni. Tamakunek inerqunqegcaarluta.

Tuamtellu tua-i irniaqerraallemteni qurrailitanek yagarucillrunrituallu wiinga. Caitellruamta aturallramnek taugaam pilirturluku. Tua-i-llu tamaa-i tuani-llu aamarciqarrallemni, taum-am tua-i qanrutaqlua unugmi-gguq aamareskumku tauna qurrailitaa mecungenrilkan qurruksuarmek atlilirluku aamareskilaku, atam-gguq elitniartuq. Ilumun ca tamarmi elitengqerrami—pinrilkurcaraq ca tamarmi elitengqerrngami, pingnaqurallra, piciunrilngalengraan atullra, elluarrluni piyarauliniami. Tuaten tua-i inerqutullruitkut.

Cali qanruqu'urluki, ilangekan mikelnguq, irniaput, inglukuquraasqevkenaki qanruqu'urluki enemta iluani piuraasqelluki. Cali imumek imkurrlainarpek'naku manigikan qanrutesqelluku yugnun cangaketuciqniluta, waten usvituriqertaqata, yugnun cangaketuciqniluta tuaten ayuqekata. Ayuqsuitelliniameng makut irniat, ilait tua-i apqiitnek ilallugutngululuteng tuaten aqsamek ataucimek anngermeng, umyugaat ayuqevkenateng yuut irniarutulliniameng.

Taugaam mikelnguq man'a qanrusnguarturluku piyunarqetulliniluni wangkuta qanruyuteklemtenek inerquruarturluku. Cali-llu waten wii pitullruanka neqkenrilkemtenek nerkata nerengraata kainriyuiruciiqniluki. Cali-llu inerqutullruitkut ilamta piitnek tegletungramta tukuurrngaitniluta teglegamtenek tuaten. Wiinga niitellemtun irniangama tuaten ellangarcata qanrutetullruanka wii qanruyutellemnek.

Irniaten-gguq cenirtaaruqu'uryaqunaki

(84) Theresa Moses, November 2000:14–15

Irniarqamta tamaa-i-llu waten qanrut'lallruitkut, irniaten-gguq ilaknitekluki cenirtaaruqu'uryaqunaki. Atam-gguq tauna mikelnguq tuaten anglicaqumteni agamyauluni yuuniartuq, nek'enrilkemeggnun wagg'uq tua-i cenirtaarayuluni. Ilakengramteki-gguq irniaput ullauqurpek'naki enelleramta iluani anglicaqilaput. Ilii-gguq mikelnguum tuaten qanqaucunarquq, inerquyunaqluni-llu. Ilumun tamakut qaneryarat egmirtellriani tua-i, tuaten ayuqetulliniluteng. Una kangauquraumalria, wagg'uq cenirtaarulluku tua-i-gguq agamyauguq, uitaurasciiganani enemta iluani.

would mean nothing to him if we spoke to him softly and kindly, but he would wait for a loud voice before responding. That is how he would behave. They warned us thoroughly about those things.

And when we took care of children for the first time, I wasn't busy with store-bought disposable diapers. Because there was nothing around, we used old clothing as diapers. And when I had my first child and started breast-feeding, someone told me to always put a small urine bucket underneath him at night when I nursed him if his diaper was dry, saying he would learn [to pee in the bucket]. Because everything that is done over and over can become a learned habit — even if you think something is impossible, it can be done. That's the instruction we received.

And they told us to always speak to our children, when they got siblings, about not fighting and arguing at home. And they told us not to constantly scold him but to tell him, when he is in a good mood and old enough to know right from wrong, that other people would be critical of us when they learned of his bad behavior. Since every child has a different temperament, some will be troublemakers, even though they came out of one stomach.

But it is important to constantly speak to a child kindly, to constantly admonish him with lessons we learned. And I told [my children] that when they ate nontraditional food, they would no longer be satisfied. They also warned us that we would not become wealthy with things we stole from others. When I had children, I taught them instructions I learned when they became aware of their surroundings.

They told us not to always bring our children visiting

(84) Theresa Moses, November 2000:14–15

When we had children, they told us not to always take our children visiting just because those particular people were our relatives. They said if we raised our child that way, he will be unsettled and restless, and he will constantly visit other people's homes when older. They told us not to always bring our children visiting, even though they were our relatives, but to raise them inside our own homes. They say some children are easy to instruct and admonish. They end up that way when you pass on instructions to them. They say [a child] who is always taken from house to house becomes an *agamyak* [unsettled and restless person] and cannot stay put inside our houses.

Tamaa-i tuaten cali tua-i-w' akusraruqurpek'naki mikelnguut piuraas-qelluki, usviircalaraput-gguq teggiguqu'urluki-llu piaqamteki, qanruyut-nek pivkenaki, qaill' piqa'arqata-llu engelallagatekluki. Tamaa-i-gguq as-guraircarluki.

Ilulngukeksaunaku irnian

(85) Toksook Elder, November 2000:105

Una-wa waniwa arcaqerluni alerquutellrat ilulngukesqevkenaku, mi-kelnguullgutiin-llu pikaku, wall'u-qaa temirnerem pikaku ilulngukesqev-kenaku aaniinun. Waten-llu alerqualuku pikaku, nani ellami-llu pikaku, ayuqucirkaanek qanruskaku, ilulngukesqevkenaku. Ilulnguk'laquvgu qanrut'larciqaa aanani, iqlungariluni-llu mikelnguuluni, iqlungariyug-ngaluni mik'nani usviturivailegmi. Tuaten aaniin ilulnguk'laqaku ing'u-mun piniluni [pilarciquq].

Tuaten pinarqenrituq. Ilulnguksaqunaciu. *School*-ami-llu qaillun *school*-artiin pikaku tauna ilulnguksaqunaku irnian, taugaam elpet irnian nunu-qiu, niicungnaqluku malingngasqelluku *school*-artii. Tamakut tamaa-i ilul-nguksugngaitaten irnian elluarrluku *school*-aasqumakuvgu, elliin taugaam qanruskaten ilulngukevkenaku alerquayakiu. Tuaten nutaan mikelnguq tua-i-wa ikiussiyaagpek'nani angliciquq. Waten umyuarteqciquq mikel-nguq, 'Aanaka-am qanruskumni nunurciqaanga.' Tuaten tua-i man'a mi-kelnguq ayuquq anglicallra. Waniwa tuaten augna alerquutengqertuq mikelnguum anglicallra. Elluarrluni anagutevkenani angliurararkauguq elpet taugaam aaniini cumikekuvgu, cumikelaquvgu.

Nunurpegnaki qanpiaraulluki inerquraqluki

(86) Louise Tall, September 1998:25

Waten maa-i aanaulriani irniaci qanerturyarluki yuusqumakuvciki: Qatguuruteksaunaki, qanpallagateksaunaki, taugaam qanpiaraulluki, iner-quraqluki. Nunurnarqaqata-llu elitniartut atam qanpiaraulluteng inerqu-tukuvciteng. Qanqaquvci ak'a-llu niilluteng, qanpiarauqurluki qatguuru-teksaunaki piuraquvteng.

Cali aanaulriani waten nallunriraqata alerquagurluki ilaitneng-llu tu-ngelquitneng qanruqu'urluki, una cakniluku piaqluku. Taugai nanikua-

They also told us not to constantly have too much fun and play with our children, that we cause them to become mentally unstable when we constantly have too much fun with them, not teaching them instructions but laughing at them when they do something. We teach them to have no reserve and to lack boundaries.

Do not defend your child

(85) Toksook Elder, November 2000:105

The most important *alerquun* was for a mother not to defend [her child] when another child or adult picked on or offended him. And they told [the parents] not to come to his defense when others instructed and disciplined him [outside the home]. He will become a tattler if you constantly defend him, and he will become a liar while he is a small child before he knows right from wrong if his mother pities him in that way. And he will constantly tell his mother that another picked on him.

One should not do that. Do not defend [your child]. And do not defend your child if his schoolteacher disciplines him in any way, but admonish your child to pay attention and to be obedient. If you want him to go to school successfully, you will not feel sorry for him if he tells you that something happened, but you will discipline him. A child will not be too troublesome if raised that way. This is how the child will think, "If I tell my mother, she will scold me." That is an *alerquun* for raising a child. That is a teaching concerning raising a child. If you as a mother take good care of him, he will grow up well without being too troublesome.

Do not scold them but admonish them gently

(86) Louise Tall, September 1998:25

If you want your children to live [obediently], you mothers should speak to them like this: Do not shout at them or yell at them, but admonish them gently. And when they need discipline, they will learn if you warn and talk to them calmly and gently. If you correct them gently without yelling at them, they will obey right away when you talk.

And you mothers, always tell them who their relatives are when they become aware of their surroundings. If they are in a desperate situation

kata nalluvcini tauna nanikuavikarkaungatgu. Tavaten ilakutengnaqura-lleq assinruuq. Mikelnguq tatamallagaluni qategpagalluni yuukuni waten-guuq qaneryarangqerrluni, qatguq-gguq atanqessagucamiu qa-nengremta nicuitaakut. Qategpagalluta pikumteni qategpagatellerput atanqelluku uitatuuq. Tamaa-i tamana mikelngurnun elluarrluku angli-cangnaqlerkarput.

Cali qanerturaucugluku waten angturikuni-llu wagg'uq kiuluta, angtu-rikuni cakenriciiqaakut. Qanraqamta-llu qanerturautaqluta ellaita wang-kuta-llu aanaitni arulairluta qanenrirluta niicugniluku. Wagg'uq tang taum qanerturauteyagatullemta mik'nani kiuluta. Tavaten man'a qanerya-raq pitangqertuq. Irniamineng aulukiyaraq tavaten ayuquq.

Qalarutaqluki irniavtun pitarrluki
(87) Frank Andrew, September 2000:142

Man'a maa-i cali tekilluku elluarrluta mikelngurmek anglicarillerkam-tenek yug'eurlurni wangkuta imumi qalarucimatullruukut. Caleryagav-kenaki, naucurlallerkaat una assinrilnguq piteluku. Tuaten-gguq tua-i angayuqaagminek ciuliqagterluni qalarucimalria elluarrluni ayagciquq. Ayuqelilukek augkuk angayuqaagni qamulriik ellii-llu qamurluni. Cali-luteng, qamurluni augkugtun angayuqaagmitun. Amna erinalkiartaqan angayuqaak caq'iqertaqlutek egmianun niisngalutek. Maa-i makut ayu-qestassiigutngulallret, yugni wangkuta niicugnilalput qalarucimaaqamta.

Tuamtellu qanrutnauraitkut qalaruciyugngalriit-gguq amlletuyaa-qut, angutem-gguq ilii arnam-llu ilii mikelngurmek inerquringaituq ir-niaqenrilkeminek, irniani taugaam ukut nallaita. Waten-am qanrutkaat. Tua-i-gguq tauna umyuarrliqelria, angutnguli arnauli-llu angayuqrulria. Imna-gguq taugken arnauli angutnguli-llu angayuqrurtellria irniamitun ukutun qanrutaamitun pitarrluku yuum irniara ellami qagaani tanger-quniu egmianun inerquryugngaluku, tua-i-gguq tauna umyuangqellria. Irniani nallaitgun assiisqumavkenaki. Allat irniaqengraitni angayuqa-meng nalluatni tuaten pilriit tapqulluki, irniamitun inerquraqluki qala-ruarrluki-llu. Assilria-gguq tua-i yuk tauna qanruyutem pisqutii aturluku pilria.

"Those pictures are great." — *Frank Andrew, February 2003*

Mother and child at fish camp. Note the large dip net leaning against the fish rack in the background. L2365. Leuman Waugh Collection, courtesy of the National Museum of the American Indian, Smithsonian Institution.

Mother and children in their tent at fish camp on the lower Kuskokwim River, summer 1935 or 1937. L2692. Leuman Waugh Collection, courtesy of the National Museum of the American Indian, Smithsonian Institution.

Women and children pose for Dr. Waugh, summer 1935 or 1937. L2693. Leuman Waugh Collection, courtesy of the National Museum of the American Indian, Smithsonian Institution.

Girl with a quizzical smile, summer 1935 or 1937. L2703. Leuman Waugh Collection, courtesy of the National Museum of the American Indian, Smithsonian Institution.

Woman cooking *assaliaq* (pancake or bread fried in oil) at summer fish camp, 1935 or 1937. L2716. Leuman Waugh Collection, courtesy of the National Museum of the American Indian, Smithsonian Institution.

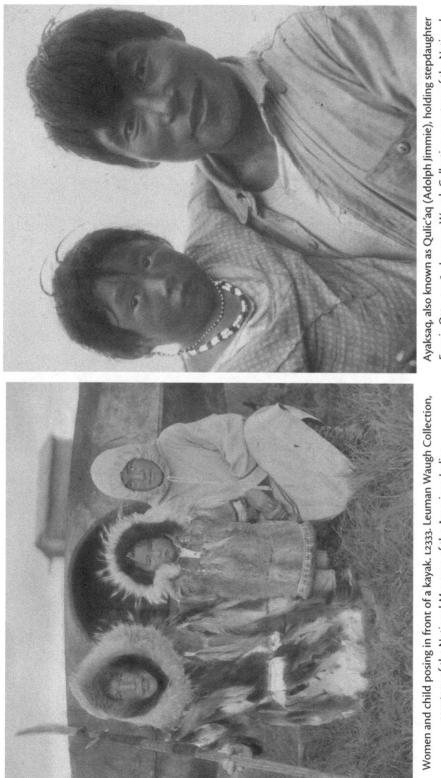

Women and child posing in front of a kayak. L2333. Leuman Waugh Collection, courtesy of the National Museum of the American Indian, Smithsonian Institution.

Ayaksaq, also known as Qulic'aq (Adolph Jimmie), holding stepdaughter Fannie Otto. L2765. Leuman Waugh Collection, courtesy of the National Museum of the American Indian, Smithsonian Institution.

Nagyuk (Katie Albrite) of Kasigluk. L2775. Leuman Waugh Collection, courtesy of the National Museum of the American Indian, Smithsonian Institution.

Child at fish camp. L2737. Leuman Waugh Collection, courtesy of the National Museum of the American Indian, Smithsonian Institution.

Iqcak (Ina Sheppard) of Nunacuaq wearing *agluirutet*, earrings connected with strands of beads hanging under the jaw like a necklace, literally, "device for an *agluquq*, or jaw." L2760. Leuman Waugh Collection, courtesy of the National Museum of the American Indian, Smithsonian Institution.

Young mother and child. L2296. Leuman Waugh Collection, courtesy of the National Museum of the American Indian, Smithsonian Institution.

Unguiralria's mother with *tamlurutet* (chin decorations). L2763. Leuman Waugh Collection, courtesy of the National Museum of the American Indian, Smithsonian Institution.

Man at fish camp. L2777. Leuman Waugh Collection, courtesy of the
National Museum of the American Indian, Smithsonian Institution.

Women and children at the entrance to a semisubterranean sod house. L2359. Leuman
Waugh Collection, courtesy of the National Museum of the American Indian,
Smithsonian Institution.

Ilurall'er (Kenneth Samson) and Kanglek (John Gunlik) from Cal'itmiut wearing warm, hoodless bird-skin parkas. Looking at the photo, Frank Andrew recalled: "Here is a swan parka with other kinds of birds. They don't always have parkas of one species of bird, but they add other ones — swans, common loons, red-throated loons, long-tailed ducks, king eiders, scoters — those all make thick parkas." L2297. Leuman Waugh Collection, courtesy of the National Museum of the American Indian, Smithsonian Institution.

A man carries a child past a sod house with open skylight. L2772. Leuman Waugh Collection, courtesy of the National Museum of the American Indian, Smithsonian Institution.

Girl in a calf-skin parka. L2360. Leuman Waugh Collection, courtesy of the National Museum of the American Indian, Smithsonian Institution.

Women gathered by the shore at fish camp. L2773. Leuman Waugh Collection, courtesy of the National Museum of the American Indian, Smithsonian Institution.

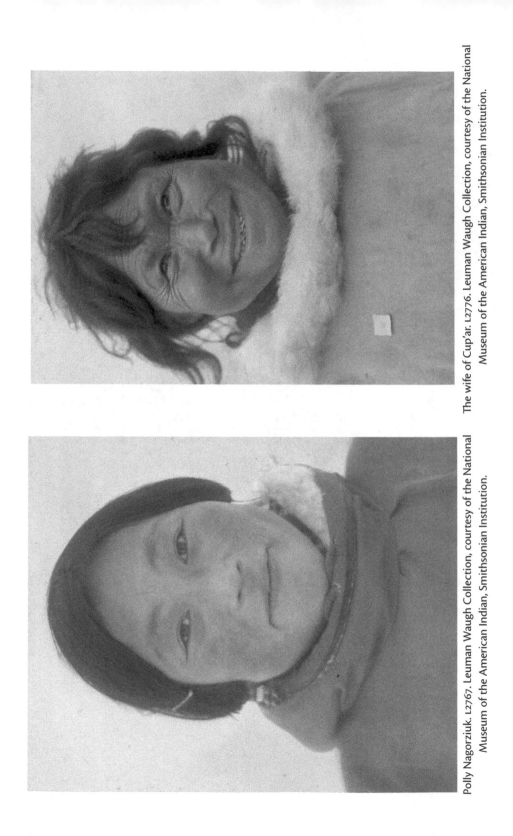

Polly Nagorziuk. L2767. Leuman Waugh Collection, courtesy of the National Museum of the American Indian, Smithsonian Institution.

The wife of Cup'ar. L2776. Leuman Waugh Collection, courtesy of the National Museum of the American Indian, Smithsonian Institution.

Nursing mother in her tent at fish camp. L2340. Leuman Waugh Collection, courtesy of the National Museum of the American Indian, Smithsonian Institution.

Paniquaq (Peter Jacobs, *far right*) enjoying *tepeq* (aged fish heads) with Pac'aq (Joseph Jenkins) and friend. L2319. Leuman Waugh Collection, courtesy of the National Museum of the American Indian, Smithsonian Institution.

Woman wearing a traditional parka with rounded edges and inset strips of caribou-fawn skin, called *uminguak* (two pretend arrow-point designs) recalling the days of bow-and-arrow warfare. L2780. Leuman Waugh Collection, courtesy of the National Museum of the American Indian, Smithsonian Institution.

Tundra grave with *alailutet* (objects placed on burials as memorials to the deceased). L2306. Leuman Waugh Collection, courtesy of the National Museum of the American Indian, Smithsonian Institution.

Men riding an *angyapiaq* (large, open skin boat), towing a kayak. L2787. Leuman Waugh Collection, courtesy of the National Museum of the American Indian, Smithsonian Institution.

Young boy practicing with bow and arrow. L2345. Leuman Waugh Collection, courtesy of the National Museum of the American Indian, Smithsonian Institution.

Girls with buckets and packs preparing to gather greens from the tundra. L2317. Leuman Waugh Collection, courtesy of the National Museum of the American Indian, Smithsonian Institution.

Man and child. L2761. Leuman Waugh Collection, courtesy of the National Museum of the American Indian, Smithsonian Institution.

Angutekayak, originally from Iiqaquq and later from Kongiganak, cradling a child. L2759. Leuman Waugh Collection, courtesy of the National Museum of the American Indian, Smithsonian Institution.

Mary Ann Sundown smiling out from a "sunshine" ruff made from sealskin, wolverine, and the guard hairs of wolf on the outer rim. L2270. Leuman Waugh Collection, courtesy of the National Museum of the American Indian, Smithsonian Institution.

Man wearing a bird-skin parka, with a pair of snow goggles high on his forehead. L2366. Leuman Waugh Collection, courtesy of the National Museum of the American Indian, Smithsonian Institution.

Girl with a welcoming smile. L2268. Leuman Waugh Collection, courtesy of the National Museum of the American Indian, Smithsonian Institution.

Qaurtuculi (James Anaver's father) of Kipnuk. L2239. Leuman Waugh Collection, courtesy of the National Museum of the American Indian, Smithsonian Institution.

Paniluar (Minnie Strauss) of Kwigillingok, with chin tatoos. L2232. Leuman Waugh Collection, courtesy of the National Museum of the American Indian, Smithsonian Institution.

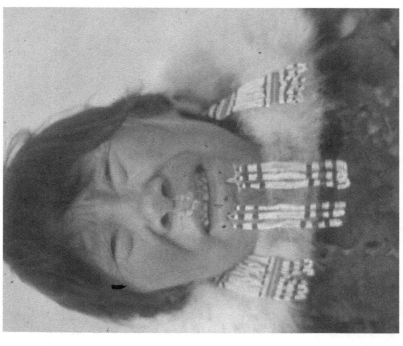

Nussaalarpag of Nunivak Island wearing elaborate bead *aqlitet* (earrings), *cigviit* (nose beads), and *caqiqsiik* (sickle-shaped chin labrets), winter 1937. L2257. Leuman Waugh Collection, courtesy of the National Museum of the American Indian, Smithsonian Institution.

Mary Gunlik's mother (right) and friend. L2233. Leuman Waugh Collection, courtesy of the National Museum of the American Indian, Smithsonian Institution.

Man in murre-skin parka. L2234. Leuman Waugh Collection, courtesy of the National Museum of the American Indian, Smithsonian Institution.

Mother and children in calico *qasperet* (thin, hooded garments). L2302. Leuman Waugh Collection, courtesy of the National Museum of the American Indian, Smithsonian Institution.

Ik'atak (Julia K. Paul) wearing a beaded headdress, accompanied by Asgiilleq and Nagyuk modeling dance headdresses topped with caribou-beard hair, Kipnuk. L2251. Leuman Waugh Collection, courtesy of the National Museum of the American Indian, Smithsonian Institution.

Mary Gunlik's mother wearing a parka decorated with bell and clock parts. L2250. Leuman Waugh Collection, courtesy of the National Museum of the American Indian, Smithsonian Institution.

Man using a kayak to set his fish net, equipped with poles and floats made of inflated stomachs. L2355. Leuman Waugh Collection, courtesy of the National Museum of the American Indian, Smithsonian Institution.

and you aren't around, they will have someone to turn to in time of need. It is better if people know who their relatives are. The following is a saying for one who is yelled at constantly and frightened. Because yelling has become the child's only means of discipline, he won't listen to us when we talk calmly and gently. Because we yelled at him constantly, he has become accustomed to it and can only respond to that kind of command. We should take this advice on raising children seriously.

If we continue to yell and speak to a child inappropriately, he will talk back and not respect us when he grows older. And he will begin to talk back to us when we speak, and we mothers will stop speaking altogether and listen to him. They will talk back to us because we yelled at them when they were small. That is a *qaneryaraq* for raising children.

Speak to them like they are your own children
(87) Frank Andrew, September 2000:142

Even up to this day, we poor Yupiit are instructed about raising a child properly. We were told not to be abrupt toward them or mistreat them, so that they would not be scared. They say one who is guided properly by his parents will lead a good and healthy life. [The child] will imitate his parents, who are pulling him, and he, too, will pull right along with his parents. They would all be working together, and he will pull like his parents. When he calls out, they would turn immediately. They would be obedient. We Yupiit heard those examples when we were instructed.

They also told us that there are many capable of giving instruction and guidance to others, that some men and women will not admonish other children but only their own. That is what they say about them. They say that male or female parent is *umyuarrliqelria* [one who doesn't have good wishes toward others and is mean and selfish]. However, they say a male or female parent who immediately admonishes another's child when he sees that child misbehaving outside, like he would his own child, is referred to as *umyuangqellria* [one with good wishes toward others, who is thoughtful and unselfish]. He doesn't want only his own children to be obedient and well behaved. They disciplined other children who were misbehaving without their parents around. They say that person [who admonishes others] is a good person, one who is following and perpetuating the instructions and teachings he learned.

Makut maa-i niicugnilallrenka wii tan'gaurluullemnek ayaglua, tua-i qasgi taugaam enekellruamku wii kiima pivkenii pitatenka-llu. Enemi qavayuunata. Qavayuirucet'laraitkut qaillun allrakungeqerluta, qasgi taugaam eneksagutelluku. Tuaten ayuqellruukut wangkuta ciuqlirpeceni.

Man'a cali qavaryaraq inerquutnguuq umyugiurutkesqevkenaku. Waniwa tamalkumta qavatuukut qavarningaqamta unugmi. Angayuqrulriik cali caliarkaqaak irniamegnun. Naklekumanrilngurtun ayuqellruukut tamaani. Qavamtenek qasgimi makcetaqluta ciulirneret, egmianun-llu ellamun anevkarluta, uksuuli kiaguli-llu ayuqluku. Ca tamalkuan tua-i caliaqellruat qavamek-llu umyugiurcetevkenata. Tamaani-llu elitnaurvigtailengraan makunek elkarcetetullruluta, inarcelluta. Piciryaraqluku tua-i tamana. Unugmi-ll' tan'germi maktelluta, pillgucirrlainartelluteng tua-i. Cunawa kenekngamegtekut tua-i tuaten piluaqallerkamtenun cingumaluta piamta angayuqallemta pillrullinikaitkut wall'u apa'urlumta. Wall'u allaungermeng yuut atakenrilengramteng-llu qalarutetullruatnga elluarrlua yuullerkamnek. Maa-i angayuqrulriim atu'urkaa ellimertuutnguuq angayuqrurtellrianun. Irniaqenrilngerpeciki qalarutaqluki ukucetun irniavcetun pitarrluki, assilria assitellria-llu maniurturluku.

Nutaan tamatumi-gguq tepsarqelriami uqlautngunruluni akngirnaqluni-llu piyugngaluni mikelnguq kencikumanrilnguq

(88) Frank Andrew, June 2001:21

Elpet waniwa tepsarqelria wall'u uqlarnarqelria agturngaitan nallunrilkuvgu narniilkan-llu tua-i agturngaunaku, kencikluten elpenek uqlallerkan tepsariciqngavet agturaluku pikuvgu tauna. Tua-llu ayuqestassiigutnguuq waten tauna, yuk-gguq, irniaten wall'u mikelnguut kencikulluki assinrilngurmek elitellerkaat. Nutaan tamatumi-gguq tepsarqelriami uqlautngunruluni akngirnaqluni-llu piyugngaluni mikelnguq kencikumanrilnguq. Murilkenrilkuvgu akngirtaqluten anglikuni piyugngaluni, iluteqevkaraqluten-llu. Umyuan navgurluku tua-i qanrucuilavni elpet ayuqucirtuayuilavni-llu, kencikevkenaku piavgu. Tuaten kangingqertuq tamana.

I heard these instructions from the time I was a young man, because the *qasgi* was my home. And I wasn't the only one, but others my age [heard them] as well. We did not sleep in houses. They had us quit sleeping at home at a certain age, but the *qasgi* became our home. Those of us who were born before your time lived like that.

It is also an admonishment not to be careless and indulgent with sleep. We all sleep when we become sleepy at night. Parents are responsible for teaching their children about [sleep]. They didn't feel sorry for us back then. The elders woke us from our sleep in the *qasgi* and had us go outside immediately, both in winter and summer. They took responsibility for all aspects of our lives and did not let us overindulge in sleep. And they had set bedtimes for us, even though there was no formal schooling back then. That was our routine. And they woke us during the night in the dark and had us stay awake with them. It appears that our parents and grandfathers did this because they loved us and wanted us to lead good lives. Other parents spoke to me about proper conduct as well. Parents are asked to follow the proper roles of parenting. Speak to them like your own children even if they aren't your own, always revealing good and bad to them.

They say a child who is not raised carefully can potentially be more unpleasant than stinky things
(88) Frank Andrew, June 2001:21

You will not touch something stinky or dirty that smells bad, being careful not to dirty your body, because you will stink if you touch it. In the same way people should be careful not to let their child learn about improper behavior. They say a child who is not raised carefully can potentially be more unpleasant and hurtful than stinky things. A child who is not raised carefully can hurt you when he gets older and will cause you grief. He will hurt you because you do not talk to him and give him advice, because you are not taking good care of him. That is the explanation for that.

Mikelnguq-gguq piyuayaurpailegmi qaneryaurpailegmi-llu elitetuuq
(89) Frank Andrew and Alice Rearden, October 2001:117–22

Frank Andrew: Alerquutengqetullrulria mik'nani-gguq mikelnguq piyua-yaurpailegmi qaneryaurpailegmi-llu tungaunani elitetuuq, elicugnga-rituuq, taringyugngariluni-llu, inerqulriani-llu niicugngariluni. Tua-i-llu-gguq angayuqaagken murilkelluku cakneq tua-i piarkauluku tuaten ayuqellrani. Aurrsungareskan-llu picurlautekani nallua mikelnguum, uq-lautekani-llu. Tepsarqellria-llu uqlautek'ngermi, uqlauteklerkani nallu-luku. Tamakut tamaa-i qaneqsailengraan assiitniaqluki qanrutaqluku. Murilkelluku tua-i piiyuangareskan-llu tua-i, imumek piiyuangareskuni tua-i ca ullagluku pingareskuni, nutaan murilkenaqluni. Akngirrnayuk-luni aarnaqluni, wall'u kenermun pinayukluni. Murilkelluku nutaan cak-neq murilkelluku, inerquagurluku assiitniurluki aarnarqelriit niitelluku.

Tua-i-llu una taringuullra atauciureskan, taringyuriqerreskan, nutaan ayuqucirtuutnek ayagnirluku, niisngaluni irniarullerkaanek, malignga-lukek angayuqaak irniarullerkaanek. Assirluni tuaten pikan elkenka niisngaciqniluku. Assiinani taugken inerquutet makut navgurluki pila-qan kenekngaitniluku elkenka. Elliinek-llu camek neqkassaagluku piller-kaa capeqniluku, atu'urkaanek pisciigatniluku, atiinun taugaam uumun atu'urkainek neqkainek-llu pingnaq'larniluku, aaniin-llu mingeqluk' atu'urkiularniluku, elliinek pisciigatniluku. Taringyuriqerreskan tamaku-nek tamaa-i-gguq elicungcarluku. Umyugiurcetevkenaku-llu makunek neqkanek mermek-llu elliinek-llu tegulluku pivkaqsaunaku.

Tamana-gguq tamaa-i mikelnguum ilangcimayuilkuni angayuqaagmi-nek tuaten tegulautengraan ancurtuirutlerkaminek elicaraqaa. Pikenril-ngermegteggu angayuqaagmi inerquyuilagni aglumakuniu teguluku pi-yugngaluku.

Tua-i-llu cali umyugiurturtelluku, waten inerquyuunaku enemi neq-kanek-llu pikuni-gguq angayuqaagni ataneqngairuciiqak. Elliini cauv-kenatek tua-i angayuqaak inerquyuilkagni. Taumek mikelnguut avani angayuqateng tua-i apterrlainarluki, qanqerraarrlainarluteng camek ner-yugaqameng. Angayuqrita, aanaita taugken tua-i cikiqerluki. Taumek elisngalalriit tuatnamalriit, nepaunateng-llu angayuqateng malignga-luki, inerquqayunaqluteng.

Qaingakun-llu maaggun, kegginaakun arcaqerluku yagiraksaunaku,

They say a child learns before being able to walk and talk
(89) Frank Andrew and Alice Rearden, October 2001:117–22

Frank Andrew: It is said that a child is capable of learning and understanding when he is little and unable to walk and talk yet and capable of obeying when admonished. And they say parents are supposed to watch over them carefully during that time. A child does not know about dangerous or dirty things when starting to crawl. [Parents] are to continually tell him about dangerous and harmful places before he is able to speak. They are responsible for watching him closely, and they should really watch him when he begins walking, when he starts to walk toward things. The possibility of getting hurt or going toward fire is especially frightening at that time. They [should] watch him very closely, continually admonishing and warning him about harmful things.

When [a child] is able to comprehend, they should start teaching him about good behavior and being obedient toward his parents. He should be told that his parents will listen to him if he is well behaved. He should also be told that they will not love him if he misbehaves and breaks their rules. They should also tell him that it is difficult for him to hunt for food on his own, that he cannot provide his own clothing, that only his father acquires clothing and food for him, and that his mother sews clothing for him, that he cannot provide for himself. They should begin to teach him those things when he is big enough to understand and comprehend instructions. And they should not let him eat and drink whenever he wants and take things on his own.

They say if a child's parents do not pay attention to him and allow him to take whatever he wants, they are teaching him to lack self-control. He can take things that do not belong to him because his parents do not admonish him, and he can take whatever he wants.

And if they let him do as he pleases and do not admonish him at home when he takes food, he will no longer regard his parents as his superiors. He will not have respect for his parents if they do not admonish him. That is why children constantly asked their parents first in the past, and they always asked when they wanted to eat. Only their parents, their mothers, would give it to them. That is why those who are raised that way are quiet and obey their parents and are easily admonished.

And they told us not to hit or spank [children] on their bodies and es-

qacartaaqsaunaku-llu. Ellangcaquniu-gguq taugaam atiin-llu nulluug-ken'gun qacartaararkauluku, qaingakun maaggun pivkenaku akngirteller-kaa murilkelluku, kemegturragnegun taugaam nulluugken'gun. Kegginaa-kun angu pivkenaku inerquutengqellruukut mikelngurmun.

Alice Rearden: Niitellruunga arcaqerluku tan'gurraq pilaasqevkenaku amllertut-gguq ellami-llu pillerkaa kegginaa.

Frank Andrew: Tuaten ayuquq tan'gaurlull'er. Tan'gaurluq-gguq una ir-niaq wangkutni-wa ciuliamteni arcaqerluku umyugiurrlainartelluku piar-kaqenritarput. Piyungraan iliini pivkaqsaunaku, iliini tua-i qanrutiini egmian cikiraqluku. Mikelnguut makut nallunritaput usviilameng catai-lengraan, tamakutailengraan aanameggnun-llu kaigalartut qailuteng tua-ten. Tua-i-llu pitailan qiarraarluteng egmianun assiriluteng, umyuarrlug-carautekevkenaku-llu.

Tan'gaurluq tuaten tua-i allauluku piat augkut ayagastekaungan-gguq anglikuni pingnaqestekauluni, ernerpak neraunani yuilqumi neqtail-ngurmi kangaryugngaluni, arenqiallugguni-llu qavartarluni, neqkailami-llu nerevkenani. Tamana pitekluku tuaten umyugiurrlainarcetevkenaku tan'gaurluq pitullrulliniat. Nasaurluq tua-i ping'ermegteggu tuaten pitav-kenaku enem-gguq iluanek ayagayuilan arnaq arcaqerluni, angucetun ayuqevekenani.

Ayuqniarturalleq ellminek piiyaureskuni assinrakun ayagyugngauq
(90) Theresa Moses, April 2001:121

Cali-llu irniaq anagulluku ataniussiyaagluku cayullra qunulluku ta-malkuan iliini maligtetungermiu. Malruulartuk-am inerquutak. Tauna-gguq piyugngarikuni cucullni niilluku teglengariciquq, tegletuciquq, anagulluku tamaa-i qunuqurassiyaagluku pikumteggu irniaput tauna. Pi-yugngarikuni-gguq teglengariciquq. Taugaam tua-i anagulluku qunuce-tungramteggu maligtaquaqluku iliini pinaqluni. Tuacetun ayuquq ava-i anagulluku cali ataniussiyaagluku pisqevkenaku, teglengariciquq-gguq ellminek piyaureskuni. Pikenrilngermiki nalluatni canek tegucaurrluni, tegutetuluni tua-i-w' cucussiyaagluni piluni, tuatnaluni.

Mikelnguq-am man'a nepailutevkenaku anglicaasqelaqiit tamaa-i iner-quutarnek qanruqu'urluku. Niicunarqelria waniwa una: "Assircaartur-luten-at' ernerpak piurqina, ilavet pikatgen nayurpek'naki unitniaten." Tuacetun ayuqluni. Murilkesqelluku-llu niicugniurluku aatiit. Ayuqnia-

pecially their faces. But if they want to get their attention, [the parents] should only spank them on their buttocks, not on their bodies, being careful not to hurt them, but only spanking on the thickest skin, the buttocks. We were told not to hit a child on his face whatsoever.

Alice Rearden: I heard they should especially not do that to a boy, that there are many things outside that hit his face.

Frank Andrew: That is what it is like for a boy. Our elders said that we should especially not let a boy do as he pleased all the time. That we should not allow him when he wanted to do something sometimes, but we should give him something right away when he asks at other times. We know that children ask and cry for something from their mothers even though it is not there, because they are too little to reason and understand. And because there isn't any, they stop crying, and they don't stay angry.

They treated a boy differently in the past because he traveled as the hunter and provider, walking all day in the wilderness with an empty stomach and sleeping in bad conditions and not eating because he had no food. They did not let a boy do as he pleased all the time for that reason. And even though a girl was treated the same, they weren't as strict because a girl does not travel from home as much as a male.

One who always envied others can live a better life when on his own
(90) Theresa Moses, April 2001:121

Also, one should not be too domineering over a child, never allowing him to have things, but one should submit to his requests once in a great while. There are two teachings concerning this. They say our child will become a thief and will take things that he desires if we never allow him to have things that he wants. They say he will become a thief when capable. But even though we don't follow his requests all the time, we should give him what he wants once in a while. They told us not to be too domineering toward him, that he will become a thief when he's older. He will take things that do not belong to him because he desired them too much.

They tell us to raise a child by not being silent toward him, always admonishing him, giving him positive advice and discipline like the following: "You should behave all day, and do not stay around, but leave, if others pick on you." That is what it is like. Tell him to observe and obey

qan-llu piluku, cucutukan, anglirikan, tuacetun piurqan, cat ikiulriit ma-
ligtaqurrlainanrilkaki, tamakut cat akusrarutet anglanarqellriit maligta-
quyuilkaki, anglirikan, elliinek piyaureskan tuacetun piyaurciiqniluku,
cucullratun. Nauwa tua-i maa-i mikelnguut irniaput-llu cangyugluteng
ingna pikegciniluku cuculuteng qantulriit. Ing'utun *friend*-amitun piyugyaaqluni, canek nurnarqelriamek piluni. Tua-i tamakut cali tamaa-i taum
qanellratun, elliraulleq umyuarpayagaunarquq, umyuartunarquq ayuq-
nialleq taugaam ilaminek makunek mikelnguullgutminek.

Iciw' maa-i cumikelriani aquiciquq igvarluni-llu uumek piluni tuarpiaq
cucucetaarluku maniirqelluku taum mikelnguum. Taunaurluq-llu tua-i
kia pingailani ayuqniaurlurluni elliitun piyugyaaqluni. Tuaten ayuqnaq-
luni. Irniat tamaa-i anagulluki-llu qunuqurassiyaagpek'naki pisqelaqait.
Tua-i-am ciunrat aipaa tauna atam-gguq teglengariniartuq, iqlungariluni-
llu anagulluku ataniussiyaakumteggu. Tua-i taugaam maligtaquaqluku
iliini pinaqluni. Malruulukek taum qanrutkelaqii, malruulutek, assilria
ikiulria-wa. Tuaten ayuqluni. Tuaggun taum tungiikun anglicaquni mikelnguq, ikiulriim tungiinun tamaa-i cat qaneryagciluni-llu anglirikuni teg-
lengariluni, iqlungariluni tuaggun tua-i ikiulriakun pikuni.

Una-wa ayuqniarturalleq ellminek-llu piyaureskuni umyuami qanru-
tetullruani, makut-llu alerquagilriit niitetullruamiki assinrakun ayagluni.
Nauwa tua-i avani alerquitulriit qanrutestailngurnek. Ellimerciqaat-gguq
pilu'ugluku anevkarluku, "Kitek-at' qasgiluten qaneryaramek teglessaa-
gaa. Qanrutestekaituten aatavnek." Tauna tua-i qasgiluku qanerturalria-
nek niicugniuryartuusqelluku. Teglekan-gguq qaneryaramek tamaa-i
qanrutestailan, nalluyagutevkenaku atullerkaa tekiskan, elliinun aturciq-
niluku. Tuarpiaq cayailkutnek, akngircailkutnek cikisqelluku, teglesqe-
lluku tuaken qasgimek.

Mikelnguq alingurnarqelriatun ayuquq angayuqaulriignun

(91) Frank Andrew, October 2001:145, September 2000:90

Taugaam waten niigartelallruunga mikelnguq alingurnaqniluku, ali-
ngurnaqelriatun ayuqniluku angayuqaulriignun. Nauwa mikelnguq
assirluku anglisqumakii taugaam. Tamana pitekluku tuaten pitulliniut,
alingurnaqluku pikenrilngurtun tua-i ayuqluku navraqelriatun murilkelluku carrlugmun pivkallerkaa. Tamatumek taugaam niigartelallruunga.

Angayuqrulriik-wa tua-i qanruyutengqellriik mikelngiuryaramek,

his father as well. And when he wants what others have, tell him that he can get the things that he desires or be like one he envies if he does not always get into mischief or trouble or become involved in things that are frivolous when older. You know how our children sometimes come to us wanting something that another person has. They want to have the rare thing their friend has. And like that person said, being an orphan and envying other children causes one to be more wise.

You know how [children] come to us wanting something after playing when another child deliberately displays what he has, trying to make others envious. And because no one can get that thing for him, that poor person is envious. That is what happens. You know how they ask us not to be too stingy toward children. They say [our child] will become a thief and liar if we deprive him too much, but they say we must follow his requests sometimes. They explain both the good and bad. That is what that is like. If a child is raised improperly, he will become a thief and liar when he gets older.

One who always envies others will go on the right path when he starts to provide for himself, because of his own will and because he had heard advice from others. Back then they told one who had no one to give him instruction while putting on his boots, "Now go to the *qasgi* and try to steal instructions. You don't have a father to teach you." They told him to go and listen to those who were giving instruction in the *qasgi*. They said he will not forget the rules he stole and will use them as needed. It was like they were telling him to steal information from the *qasgi* that will protect him from harm.

A child is like something parents should be fearful of harming

(91) Frank Andrew, October 2001:145, September 2000:90

I've heard that, to the parents, a child is like something that they should fear to injure or harm. You know we all want a child to grow healthy. For that reason they raised a child carefully, fearing doing harm, like something that doesn't belong to them, caring for him like something that is borrowed. I only heard that.

Parents are instructed about raising children, how to raise a child

assirluku anglivkallerkaanek mikelnguum. Waten qanemyuugauteksau-
natek-llu, umyuarak assiirarulluku inglukullukek waten piksaunakek mi-
kelngiurlukek pisqellukek. Atam-gguq mikluni qaneryaurpailegmi ak'a
elituq taukugnek angayuqaagminek. Mikelnguut-gguq makut wangkucicetun ayuqenritut. Egmianun-gguq patmeggnun ektuit, tua-i nalluyagus-
ngairulluki. Taumek tuaten qanrutkumalria, alinguqluki-wa tua-i anglica-
llerkaatnek. . . .

Tua-i mikelnguum mat'um kingum yuan inerquutaa amllertuq makunun temyigilrianun tamiinun, tua-i mikelnguq wangkuta kinguqlirput,
nasaurluuli tan'gaurluuli-llu yuk'enritniluku picurlaasqevkenaku. "Yuk'en-
ritaqa una yumtun pivkenaku cikinrillaku-llu kaingraan neqmek." Wall'u
nunurluku, ik'ikluku, tangcurlagluku, tangnikevkenaku. Tuaten pisqenritaitkut wangkuta. Kingumta-gguq yua alingnarquq. Angliniartuq-gguq
atam wangkuta-llu cirlaurrngiinarluta. Yuum-gguq iliin picurlaumallni
nalluyagucuita mik'nani uum temirtem qaillun picurlallrukani nangel-
rakluku-llu pillrukani. Ilii-gguq akinautuuq angliaqami tauna pisteni
cirlaurtaqan. Kingumta-gguq yua alingnarquq umyugaa navlerkaa. Na-
lluyaguciyuituq-gguq mikelnguq ayagyuaq. Assilriamek-gguq taugken
pillrukani tua-i cali assilriakun ingluliurluni akinauryugngaluni taumun
assirluni pistek'lallminun. Tamana taugaam atuusqaat wangkutnun: Yuk
mikelnguq tangellren ayuqluku tua-i kenekluku taugaam pinqegcaarluku.
Nakmiin-gguq irniarunrilngermi alla arnaq aanakenrilkeni wall'u-q' aa-
takenrilkeni assilriamek pisteklallni nalluyagucuitaa. Ilumuullininiluni-llu,
ilumuuqapiarluni.

Inerquumanrilnguq teglengariyugngauq

(92) Frank Andrew, June 2001:28, 31

Inerquatullruit teglegyaramek mat'umek. Tua-i inerquatekluku tegleg-
yaraq. "Aanavet nalluani camek teguteksaunak, aatavet-llu tua-i nalluani
camek teguteksaunak." Alingcira'arturluki-llu pitullruamegteki, apelciyuu-
naki pisqevkenaki. Tuaten pirraarluta pinauraitkut, angayuqrulriik-gguq
irniartek murilkenrilkagni tuaten ayuqeciquq. Mikelnguq-gguq ellminek
elicuituq assilriamek, assiilngurmek taugaam elicugngaluni ellminek mu-
rilkumanrilkuni. Teglengarluni tua-i ca tamarmi tangellni aglumakeku-
niu teguyugngaluku.

Angayuqaagni-llu-gguq cakenrirarkaulukek inerquumayuilami, tegle-

properly. They told [parents] to raise children by not arguing and fighting when angry. They say [a child] learns from his parents before learning how to speak. They say children are not like us. Things stick in their minds immediately, and they never forget them. That is why it is said to raise them with fear and worry. . . .

There are many admonitions for adults concerning [the treatment] of the younger generation, for all children younger than us, male or female. They tell us not to make the excuse that they aren't our children, saying, "He isn't my child, so I will not treat him like my own and I will not give him food, even though he is hungry." Or they told us not to scold him, dislike him, give him a dirty look, or think he is ugly. They tell us [adults] not to do that. They say the younger generation is something to fear. It is inevitable that the child will grow older and become an adult and we will become old and weak. It is said that some children never forget being mistreated when they were little. They say some will seek revenge when they get older and the person who mistreated them becomes weak. They say harming a child is dangerous. They say a child never forgets. But if [the child] had been treated with kindness by an adult, he can return the kindness later. They ask us to live by this principle: Treat every child you see with sincere kindness and compassion. They say they never forget those who treated them well, even other parents. This is true, this is extremely true.

One who is not admonished can become a thief
(92) Frank Andrew, June 2001:28, 31

They admonished them about stealing. They were constantly warned about stealing. "Do not take things without informing your mother and your father, too." And they always tried to caution them not to take things without asking. After they told us that, they'd say that if parents didn't watch over their children, they would become like that. They say a child does not learn good things on his own but can learn bad things on his own if not properly cared for. He can become a thief and take everything he desires.

And one who is not admonished can lose respect for his parents and

ngariluni tua-i, umyugiulria inerquqaumayuunani camek piyullminek pingraan inerquyuunaku anglivkaqagni ilangciyuunaku. Tuamtellu-gguq kaigaaqan amllernek neqnek, camek-llu tamalkuan cikilaasqevkenaku, naivarrarmek taugaam carrarmek cikilaasqelluku. Atam-gguq amlleriluku cikitukuvceni elaratuniartuq. Taugken-gguq elpeci tua-i cuqlirluku cikitukuvciu amllenrilengraan elisngarikuni elarasciiganani. Elitelluku tua-i. Qunguturatun-gguq ayuqut mikelnguut cumikluki-gguq taumek elitnauyunarqekai. Maa-i ungungssit-llu makut kanarluki pitullrukait, cumikluki-gguq qimugtengungraata-llu elitnaurumalria elitelartuq, takartariluni-llu, inerquqayunariluni-llu. Yuunrilngermi, qimugtengungermi, niisngariluku yun'i. Tua-i ilumuuluni.

Tua-i yaqulgung'ermi cat ungungssit tamarmeng; maa-i aipaimta makut elitnauraqatni elisngarilalria. Tangniqluni-llu tua-i tangvayunaqluni piaqluni. Tua-i mikelnguut makut tangnirqellerkaatgun malingngatelluki tua-i pingnaqurayunarquq. Qanruyun taugaam assilria atungnaqu'urluku anglicayunarqai. Tuaten-gguq ayuqekuni teglengarngaituq. Qanrucimayuilnguq-gguq inerquumayuilnguq-llu tuaten ayuqeciqluni. Calillu mayiteqevkaumalria; kaigangraan tua-i niicuunaku. Taumek waten pitullrukaitkut, "Tua-i kaigaaqan cikilaqiu tuaten amllertaluku, elarangraan niitevkenaku. Uumikuan-ll' kaigangraan niitevkenaku. Uumikuanillu kaigakan cikirluku nutaan." Tua-i-gguq tuaten umyugiurcetevkenaku, pirrlainarpek'naku. Tua-i-gguq elluarrluni taugaam tuaten tuatnakuni angliyugngaciquq. Anuraqtarluni tua-i. Ca-wa cucungermiu tegusciiganaku apelcirraarpek'nani. Tuaten qalarucetullruitkut. Aanaput aataputllu qanruqaarpek'naki tegucetukumta neqkamtenek cucunarqellrianek wall'u canek allanek, teglengariciqniluta. Tua-i-llu-gguq pivakarluta unateput cetuita aciit qanngeciqut. Aglumakengarput-llu neqkaq teguyaaqaqamteggu unatemta ner'aqluku. Tua-i alingnaqnaurtuq tuaten tamana tua-i piciukluku, alingcetaarturluta tua-i pitullruamegtekut. Tamaa-i-gguq tua-i ciuqvani, tamakut avani ciuqvani tuatnatullruut, yuaraita nuugit qanngaqluteng. Taumek camek iirusngavkenata pitullrukaitkut. Tuaten ellirciqniluta apelciyuunata pikumta.

Tuamtellu-gguq teglengarikumta elluariciquq-gguq callerput teglegyarani arenqialliqngaunata-llu, asvairqumangraan-llu tua-i qacikluku ikircugngariluku nak'rikan tegliullerput. Tamakunek tamaa-i cali qalarutetullruitkut.

become a thief. [That will happen] if they allow him to take whatever he wants and ignore him, not reprimanding him. And they told us not to give him things in large quantities when he asks for something but just a little bit. They say he will learn to complain and cry for more if we give him things in large amounts. But if you give him things in limited quantities, he will not complain, even though it is not a lot when he starts to learn. Let him learn in that way. They say that children are like *qunguturat* [wild animals kept as pets]. That is why they should give their full attention when teaching and caring for them. They also said that any animal that is taught carefully, including dogs, learns and gains respect for others easily and is easy to admonish. Even though it isn't human, a dog becomes obedient toward its owner. That is very true.

That applies to all animals, even birds; they learn when our Western counterparts train them. And they become pleasant to watch. One must try to always let children become pleasant to watch, letting them become cooperative. One must raise them by using the good *qanruyutet*. They say they will not become thieves if raised that way. But one who is not given instruction and not admonished will be like that. And also one who has been deprived [will be that way]; not listening to them even though they ask for something. They told us, "Give your children small quantities of things when they ask for something, ignoring their complaints. And when they ask the next time, deny them. Give it to them when they ask the next time." They didn't let them have whatever they wanted. Do not always give him things. He will only grow properly if you do that. *Anuraqtarluni* [He will want to do something but will feel restrained by authority]. He will not take things he wants without asking first. They told us that. They said if we took food or other things that we wanted without informing our mothers or fathers first, we would become thieves. And if we kept doing this, we would develop mouths underneath our nails. And when we took food we wanted, our hand would eat it. That sounded frightening to us, and we would believe it because they continually warned us. They said that happened to people long ago. The edges of their fingers developed mouths. That is why they told us everything and didn't hide things from us. They said we would end up like that if we took things without asking.

And stealing would become easier for us if we became thieves, and things would be easy for us to open, even though they seemed difficult, when we become expert thieves. That is what they told us as well.

Picurlautekanka nalluluki

(93) Frank Andrew, June 1995:45

Ellangyuallemni wii yugtarkun ayagniucimallruunga niisngallerkamnek mikcuaraulua murilkenglua. Alerquamallruunga maligngatlerkamnek angayuqaagma qanruyuutiignun, inerquatiignun, cat aarnarqellriit
nalluamki mikelnguullemni. Picurlautekanka nalluluki, enem iluanek
anlua ellami kangaryaurpailegma. Niisngallerkamnek ciumek elitnauru-
mallruunga, maligngatlerkamnek angayuqaagemnek, enem-llu iluani um-
yugiunritlerkamnek. Miklemni murilkellua, murilkumalua tuaten ayuqellruunga.

Kangangarcama-llu tuarpiaq murilkevsiangarrlua. Cayulqa tamalkuan
maligtaqurrlainarpek'naku, piyulqa aturrlainarcetevkenaku. Taumek tamana qigcikillerkamnek eliteluaqautekellruaqa. Angayuqaagemnek taka-
qillerkamnek eliteluaqautekellruaqa. Murilkellruagnga angayuqaagma.
Cunawa kenkelliniamegennga umyugiurcetevkenii.

Tua-i cali tamatumek pirraarlua, ellami akusrartelangama, nutaan cali
assirlua, ilaliurutevkenii, nangelrakivkenii-llu kenkilua ilamnek tamalkuita pillerkamnek cali qalarucimatullrulua; assirlua irniarullerkamnek
angayuqaagma umyugaak navguavkenaku.

Cailkakun nerevkayuunata

(94) Wassilie Evan, July 2000:4

Tamaani yuut tua-i arenqiliqapiaqsaunateng pilalrulliniut, waten ayuqevkenateng. Elpeci maa-i umyuarteq'lallilriaci, wangkuta-llu tuaten um-
yugiurtullruyukluta elpecicetun maa-i mat'um nalliini. Kipusviit-llu amlleriluteng nunamteni. Cailkakun-llu neryuitellruluta. Enemun-llu iterluta,
enemtenun iterluta aquirraarluta nereksaitellruukut. Taugaam nerlallruu-
kut waten kiingan cailkakun-llu *cracker*-aanek-llu tangaayuunata neqkanek. Estuuluq neqkartangqerturpek'nani. Ner'aqluta unuakumi makta-
qamta imna assaliaq, cetamauluku pirraarluku wangkuta tua-i taumek
assaliamek, *only one,* cikirluta, nerluta. Ernerpak-llu nereksaunata cailkakun, nerevkayuunata cailkakun. Ner'aqluta unuakumi, *twelve*-kella'a-
gan-llu cali nerngata aipiriluta, pingayiriluta-llu atakutami. Nauwa ataam
ava-i atakutallrulriakut aqsiluta piyugtacimcetun maani. Tua-i tuaten ayuqellruukut wangkuta.

I was unaware of dangers around me

(93) Frank Andrew, June 1995:45

When I was little and starting to become aware of my surroundings, I was taught about proper behavior. Since I was little and ignorant of life's dangers, I was taught the importance of following the instructions of my parents. Before I was able to leave the house and move about out there, I was unaware of dangers that lay ahead of me. I was taught to respect my parents and listen to their advice. I was taught not to run around in the house, do as I wish, or grab what I wanted. When I was little they took care of me and paid close attention to me.

And it seemed like they paid closer attention when I began to walk. I was not allowed to do as I wished all the time. That kind of child rearing taught me greatly about respect and self-control. It taught me a great deal about respecting my parents. My parents took great care of me and paid very close attention to me. Apparently they didn't allow me to act as I wished because they loved me.

Then after that period of instruction, when I was big enough to play outside, they began to teach me about having respect and compassion for everyone around me, teaching about proper behavior around others and how to avoid doing things that might cause humiliation to my parents.

We only ate at set times

(94) Wassilie Evan, July 2000:4

Life was sometimes hard back in those days, not like it is for you today. You probably think life was easy like it is today. And there are many stores today in our villages. We didn't eat anytime we wanted to eat. After playing outside we didn't go into our homes and eat whenever we wanted. We only ate at set times, not anytime we wanted to. We never saw pilot-bread crackers. The table never had food set on it. For breakfast we would eat fried bread that was cut in four parts. We would eat only one portion of it. We wouldn't eat again until twelve o'clock, and that would be our second meal, and we would have a third meal at suppertime. Remember, we just had supper, and filled ourselves up as much as we wanted to. That's how we were.

School-ayuilengramta inangqauraasqumavkenata unuakumi

(95) Theresa Moses, November 2000:226

School-ayuilengramta-llu tamaa-i inangqauraasqumavkenata unuakumi. Makeskuneng cegg'asciigalkumta pinauraitkut, "Atam ella paqteqerru." Ukverluta egmian anqerreskumta ellam menglii kiarrluku alerquallracetun nauw' im' qavarnilleq, qavarniyugnaunata tua-i. Kuuvviaryugnaunata, mukaartuquyugnaunanta, tua-llu aqumluta uitaurluta. Nernarikan neqliuqakut nerluta. Waten-llu pivkenka, "Cayugtua." Taugaam ellait kiimeng yuurqerluteng, cakaiteurlullruamta.

Talluryuarluta yuullruukut

(96) Theresa Moses, November 2000:222

Wangkuk waniwa, tang waniw' una uyu'urqa—tua-i uyuuqlunuk yuulunuk. Tamaa-i wiinga ellangellruunga camek nallulua, yaassiirugarnek-llu enemta iluani cataunani, cuukiirtulriamek-llu tangyuunii. Tua-i ava-i qagkut qagaa-i can'get arulalriit. Tamakut can'get elliluki tua-llu waten piluki nemerluki piluguput-llu all'uki. Kesianek tamakunek aturluta qerrulliput-wa qecigkitkacagaat. Cali-wa makut qamiqum wagg'uq nerestai allauluteng maavet-llu atrayuunateng. Qaim-wa cali nerestai allat qamiqumun mayuyuunateng. Qamiqum nerestai tungunruluteng qaim-llu nerestai qatenruluteng. Tang tukuullrunrilngukut wangkuta, enemta-llu ilua catangssagaunani.

Tuamtellu alqairutvut augna George-am aanallra tuquqatallrani enecualleramta tamaa-i iluani, *measle*-am assirivkallrunrilani, putuskaa qertuqutarluni canegnek. Tang tukuungssaagallrunrilngukut wangkuta. Tuaten talluryulriani-llu talluryuarluta yuullruukut tan'gaurluq-llu tangerciiganaku iliini. Waten-llu iterpaalulriani, *friend*-ama enemeggnun aguskanga, tua-i pekviini nerestem keggengraanga tua-i kumegyungramku talluryuglua pekviini uitalua. Tua-llu keggsiyaakanga alqunaq waten pileryallalriatun pileryaglua. Iliini taugken aliingqakuma, una-llu aliingqakan aliirciigani call' uitalua. Naugg'un kegkanga tua-i pinrilnguarturlua cav-

They told us not to lie around in the morning, even though we did not attend school

(95) Theresa Moses, November 2000:226

They did not want us to lie around in the morning, even though we did not attend school. When they got up, if we could not become fully awake, they would tell us, "Go and check the weather." We would believe them and run outside. And once outside, when we scanned the horizon like they told us, we would suddenly be fully awake. We wouldn't even have coffee or bread, and we would just sit still. When it was time to eat, when they served us food, we would eat. And we would not say, "I want this." But [our parents] would be the only ones to have a hot beverage, because we didn't have anything.

We were timid and shy

(96) Theresa Moses, November 2000:222

This is my younger sibling — we lived as siblings. I became aware of my surroundings without having seen or owned [modern goods], and there weren't piles of boxes inside our homes, and I never saw anyone wear socks. You see the grass that is moving out there. We would take that grass and wrap our [feet] with it and put on our boots. We always used those, and our pants were made of thin hide. And [lice] on our heads were different, and they never went down to our bodies. And the lice on our bodies were different, and they never crawled up to our heads. The lice on our heads were darker, and the lice on our bodies were lighter. You see that we were not wealthy, and we did not have many things inside our homes.

And when our older sister, George's mother, was dying inside our little house, because the measles did not allow her to recover, her pillow was just stacked grass. You see that we were not wealthy whatsoever. And we were very timid and could not look at young men sometimes. And when a friend would bring me inside her home, I could not move, even when lice bit me. Even though I wanted to scratch, I was so shy that I did not move and stayed still. And if it suddenly bit too hard, I jerked. But sometimes, if my arms weren't in my sleeves, I couldn't put my arms back in my sleeves and stay still. When it bit me on my body, I would pretend noth-

teqataarciqaqa waniwa. Ayuqluta nerestengqellruukut wangkuta. Elpeci Kassauluci yuurcavci nerestengssagaituci.

Wangkutnek angkengssaagallrunritukut avani. Talluryutullruukut nunanun-llu ayagayuitellruamta. Talluryuarluta yuullruukut. Waniwa tang una uyu'urqa, tua-i tungekluku uyu'uqluku. Enem iluani anglaniyarpiarqamegnuk, aanavuk tauna tuquvailegmi, pinauraakuk, "Neplirpiiqnatek yuut atam cangakniaraatek qakmani. Waten qanerciqut, 'Tua-ll'-am qamkut nep'ngeqatartut.'" Maa-i tang qanruyutektulput wangkuta. Inglukuurutetukumta-gguq enemta iluani anngaput-llu alqaput-llu waten qakmani yuut qantuniartut. "Atam qamkut neptuut, atam qama-i kiutaagutut." Tua-i tamana qanruyutektullrat. Wangkuta anglillruukut nepliulluta taugaam, tuarpiaq pinerrluirturluta.

Aanaka petugvikellruaqa

(97) David Martin, April 2001:183

Qimugtet iciw' kangirtangqellriit petugvigmek. Tuaten wii tangrruallruaqa aanaka piunrillrani. Tuar petugvika tauna tayima iquluni. Imutun tua-i ayuqekutelartua wiinga wangnek piyaurpailegma tuaten angayuqairutellruama, qimugkauyara'urlurtun natmun ayagviilngurtun. Ca ullagluku uitavigkailngurtun ayuqellruunga wiinga, tua-i-wa aanamnek taumek petuumavimnek pistairtellemni. Ataka augna piunrillrani uunguciiterrluglua cali pillruama maligcaurpailemni cali tauna atalqa piunrirluni. Tauna taugaam tua-i aanalqa tua-i akaarnun petuumavikluku.

Aanam tuqullra alianarquq cakneq

(98) Theresa Moses, April 2001:133–34

Wiinga-wa aanaka tuqullrulria-llu aipangvailegma. Aanam tuqullra call' alianaqluni cakneq. Ena tua-i aatamek yungqeng'ermi, yungssagaunani. Itellra kumlanani catangssagaunani, aataq-llu uitang'ermi cassuutnguvkenani. Wiinga nanikuallruunga cakneq aanaka tuqullrani.

Maa-i upagatullrulriit up'nerkillermun, maa-i-llu upayuirulluteng. Up'nerkiyarameggnun ayagatulriit enet tua-i yungssagairulluteng. Aanaka

ing was wrong and would rub it. We all had lice. You have no lice whatsoever, because you were born in modern times.

We did not think much of ourselves back then. We were humble and
shy partly because we never traveled to other villages. We were shy. This
here is my younger sister. She was born right after me. When we were getting a little rambunctious in the house before our mother died, she would
say, "Quit making noise, people will be critical of you, and they will say
out there, 'Oh no, those people next door are going to be noisy and rambunctious!'" Those were our *qanruyutet*. She said that if we did not get
along inside our homes with our older brothers and older sisters, this is
what those people out there would say. "Those people next door are loud
and unruly, and they are bickering even now." That was one of their sayings. They continually gave us advice as we were growing up, like they
were preventing us from making mistakes.

My mother was a post
(97) David Martin, April 2001:183

You know how dogs are tied to a post. That is how I imagined my mother
when she died. It seemed that post that I was tied to fell over. That is what
I compare my experience to, because I lost my parents before I was able
to provide for myself. I was like a puppy who had nowhere to go. Losing
my mother made me feel like I had nowhere to go, like I went somewhere
and had no place to stay. This was when I no longer had a mother to care
for me. It was also because I didn't really remember my father's death. My
father also died before I started to go out on the land with him. But my
mother was a post that I was tied to for a longer time.

Having a mother die is extremely lonesome
(98) Theresa Moses, April 2001:133–34

My mother died before I married. Having a mother die is extremely
lonesome. Even though a home has a father in it, it is like no one is inside whatsoever. Going inside feels cold and empty, and even though a father is inside, he doesn't fill that void. I was full of desperation when my
mother died.

They used to travel to spring camp every year, and they no longer move
these days. They traveled to spring camps, and houses would become

assiinani. Tuaten-llu tua-i yungssagairutenratgun aanaka tuquluni. Nani-kuallruunga angelriamek aipaqa-llu tuqullrungraan tuani nanikualqa tauna tekitellrunrilnguq. Aanaka tuqullrani nanikuallruunga, anngalqa, ukuk-wa ellirrak malruk, kinguqliqa-wa, wiinga-wa, aataka-wa, anerne-rillrani wani tangssugluku. Umyuarteqa'artua, tuartang wangni nanevpall-raam qukaani qikercisngalriakut natmun ayagvigkailnganata, nanikua-naqluni angelriaruluni-llu.

Avani tuqullret-am kinguatni ernernek *five*-aanek naacirturituut. Naa-kata-llu tua-i erenret ukut *five*-aat kinguatni cayaurrluteng. Tauna tekis-ngapailgan tumairutsiyaakataakut, aqvasteput tekican ayageurlurluta ka-navet up'nerkiyarvigmun.

Tekicarturtukut tauna up'nerkiyarvik Aqumgallermimek pitukiit, maani-w' kialirneratni cali kuik Pairrlirmek pitukiit. Tua-i tamaaggun anelrarluta, kiugna-wa meq waten. Una tua-i mer'uluni. Tua-llu ayaglu-teng, ikamrak-llu kinguak qaill' pellukarluku, tuarpiaq qagrulluni tauna carvullagluni tua-i tumairrluni, tua-i alqunaq tumairulluku. Tauna um-yuaqetuaqa. Tua-llu kiagluni tua-i egmian urugluni. Taum tua-i utaqanga-naku, nayumiqaurnganaku qagercungraan.

Aanangqellriani elpeci aanaci quyavkangnaqu'urluki piyunaqluteng. Wangkuta tuaten wiinga pitullruunga. Cali-am inerqutullruatnga aanaka-gguq yuum allam uputaaqaku, aanaka qanruskumku, iluteqaarrluni aa-naka tuquciquq. Tuacetun-am qanrutaqluta pitullrukaitkut. Qaill' qanru-tekqangraatgu, aanavut, wiinga-wa aanaka qanrutenrilkurrluk' taugaam nunaniryugcetengnaqu'urluku. Tuaten pitullruukut. Aanam tuqullra aa-taq anerteq'ngermi nanikuanarquq. Aanaq-wa tua-i enem tamatum yuk-ngaku. Ayagaqluni aataq cakneq uitavigkailnganani. Aataput-llu wang-kuta takaqellrukput.

Piyugngarikuvet angayuqaagken akinauqikek

(99) Elena Martin, April 2001:131

Pilallruanga maurluma, "Piyugngarikuvet angayuqaagken akinauqi-kek." Qaillun akinaurciqseta? Kanakecuayaaq ayagluki maa-i aulukingel-riakut mikelngurnek. Taqsuqnaqpialliniuq. Ellaita-llu wangkuta anga-yuqamta tuaten pillruakut, qavairatekluta tuaten. Tua-llu pinauraitkut, angayuqaput akinauqilaput piyugngarikumta.

empty. My mother was not in good heath. My mother died when there was hardly anyone around. I was filled with extreme desperation, and even though my husband died, I did not feel the same sense of desperation as when my mother died. I was desperate when my mother died, and my deceased older brother, the two orphans, my sister, myself, and my father watched as she died. I felt like we were stranded on an island in the middle of a huge lake not having anywhere to go. The situation made us feel gravely desperate.

Back then, they abstained from activity for five days after the deaths of [relatives]. They carried on with their usual activities after five days. Before those days passed, when it seemed like we would not have a way to travel anymore, we traveled to our spring camp when the person who came for us arrived.

When we got close to the spring camp they called Aqumgallermiq, there was a river up above it that they called Pairrliq. As we went down that river, there was water at the place we left behind. As we left the place where there was a lot of water, something seemed to break loose, and water rushed and flowed in a strong current all of a sudden, and the trail was lost. The trail was lost all of a sudden. I always remember that. And summer came and [the snow] melted quickly. There seemed to be one place that kept it from breaking apart, like it was waiting for us to pass.

For those of you who have mothers, always try to make your mothers happy. That is what I did. And they warned me that my mother would die out of grief if I told her that another gossiped about her. That is what they told us. Even though they said some unfavorable things about her, I never told my mother and always tried to make her happy. That is what we did. Even though a father is alive, when a mother dies we feel desperate because a mother is always at home. The father leaves and seems out of place in a home. We were respectful of our father.

Repay your parents when you are able

(99) Elena Martin, April 2001:131

My grandmother said to me, "Repay your parents when you are able." How will we repay them? You know how we take care of children from the time they are little. It is extremely tiresome. And our parents did the same for us. They lost sleep over us. And they told us to return the care our parents gave us when we became capable.

Qunutungaunata-gguq yuulta

(100) Frank Andrew, October 2001:24–26

Avaken-wa tua-i ayagluteng piulliniuq tamana, arcaqalriaruluni tua-i. Waniwa-wa una ayuqestassiigutiit neqa. Qunutungaunata-gguq yuulta. Yuullgutput avegvingqerraqamta neqrarnek neqerrlainaunrilengraata-llu cikiqaqluki, ikayuagurluki. Atam-gguq tuaten ilakutaqengramceteng piyuilkumceteng ellaita-llu ilakenrirniaraitkut iliirangramta-llu niitnan-rirluta. Ilakuyun ilangarrluni-gguq tamaa-i. Anelgutkeng'ermi ilakenrir-telluni qunuyullermikun. Tamaa-i kangia.

Taugken-gguq ilakutaqenrilngermiu, tapqulluku ilaminun tuaten-gguq piqaquurteni, taum-gguq tungayaksaguciiqaa. Ilakutaqelriatun tua-i ayuqlirilluku.

Qanrutetuluta, yuullgutvut-gguq malrugnek umyugiutevkenaku piar-kaqerput. Neqa-gguq, neqngunrilngermi-llu tungayagturinarquq. Yuum-gguq arenqiallugtellermini ikayuqaquurteni nalluyagucuitai. Irniaminun-llu-gguq qalarutketuluki.

Avani ciuqvani man'a qalarutkaqamegteggu neq'erituut nulirqellriik taukuk irniarlutek malrunlegnek, *seven*-aanek, ukuk-wa-gguq cali nu-lirqelriik irniarunatek. Uksut iliitni neqa nurnalliniuq avani Caninermi Akulmi-llu. Tua-i tauna *seven*-aanek irnialek cirlaurpailegmeng avavet Caninermun neq'liata, kainiqenrilata tumairupailgan ayautellinii irniani taukut. Taukuk-llu imkuk nulirqelriik cali ayaglutek. Taukuk tua-i *seven*-aanek irnialgek taukunek uciaramek tua-i cakviurleurlutek, taukuk taug-ken malruungamek cakviurpek'natek, neqengqenrulutek-llu nerestaila-mek. Angulliniakek taukuk. Ikayuayugnaunakek tua-i mengliignegun tumyarakun kituamegnek angutiin taum pilliniak, "Irnialilriit-am maa-i mat'um nalliini ayuqnianaiteqertut," ngel'arluni-llu-gguq, ikayurpek'na-kek unillukek.

Taum kinguani irniari taukut *seven*-aat, arnarluteng malrugnek anglilli-niut, angliriluteng tua-i. Allrakut amlleriluteng taukuk-llu tuquksaunatek irniarilnguuk. Cirlaurteurlulliniuk tua-i taukuk, cirlaurtenglliniuk. Cirli-qenritlermegni temsek ukvekluku yuulriik quyiutekluku-llu irniarilnger-mek tua-i canrilngacia. Up'nerkiyaqcaaralliniuk tua-i cirlaurtenglutek tamaani. Atam piqerluteng angyamek kasmurrarluteng anguyartullini-

They said we should live by being generous

(100) Frank Andrew, October 2001:24–26

That tradition has existed since long ago, and it was very important. Food was the example they used. They told us not to be stingy. They said we should give others a little food and other things we could spare. We should always help them. They said even our real relatives [will no longer consider us relatives] if we do not share with them, and they will ignore our requests for help. They said that hindered family bonds. They break their ties even with their siblings because of stinginess. That is the meaning of that.

But if one gives to others just as they do to their relatives, those people will become like relatives, even though they are not a real relative. They will start to treat them like a real relative.

They tell us not to be deceitful and insincere toward others. They said that giving a little food and other things results in closer ties. They say a person does not forget those who helped him when he was going through hardship. And they will tell their children about it.

When they spoke about this long ago, they brought up what happened to a married couple with seven children and a childless couple. One winter food was scarce out in Canineq and in the tundra area. That one with seven children brought his family out to Canineq before they became weak, because food was available there and people weren't starving, before their trail was gone. That childless couple left at the same time. The couple with seven children suffered because they had a load to carry, but the other couple did not have a difficult time because there were just the two of them, and they had more food because no one ate their food. Those two came upon [the family]. They did not attempt to help them, and when they passed them on the trail, the husband said to [the father], "Those with children are not a cause for envy during this time." He laughed and left and did not help them.

After that their seven children, with two girls among them, grew older. After many years the childless couple had not died. They were starting to become feeble. The couple who had so much faith in their strength when younger had boasted about not having children. They were on their way to spring camp and had become weaker and older. One day [the family with children] came upon those two while pushing their boat and saw

kegket. Canimellilliniut imkuk taukuk qanellrek, "Irnialilriit-am ayuq-nianaiteqertut maa-i," engelarauteklukek-llu. Angayuqaagket-wa-gguq ekumauralriik angyami, irniagkenka-llu kasemlukek taukuk ikamrak. Cukanrarluteng-llu tua-i kituryartuamegtegket akinaullinia tauna, aki-nauresqevkenaki inerquutnguyaaqelria. Taum nulirran uinga qanlliniuq, "Irniarilnguut-am qakma ayuqnianaiteqertut."

Engellicameng tua-i irniani taukut pillinii imkuk aqvasqellukek. Cu-kanraullukek taitesqellukek irniagkenka am taukuk maligngiimegenkek aqvalukek taukuk irniariteurlulriik elkegtun piyugnaunakek, cakaarpek-nakek. Tamaa-i-gguq tamana pitekluku inerquusngauq. Ikayurtalria-gguq yuk camek-llu cikirrlainarluki pilria wall'u qalaruartaqluki, yugnik-sagutetuat, tungayaksagulluku tua-i, nalluyuqenrirluku.

that it was that couple who had said that to them, "Those with children are not a cause for envy these days," and they had laughed and made fun of them. Their parents were inside [the boat], while the children pushed their sled. As they quickly passed, he repaid the couple, although it is an admonition not to repay someone. The husband of the wife said, "Those without children are not a cause for envy at this time."

When they got to their destination, he told his children to get that couple. He told them to bring them back quickly, and because their children were obedient, they went to get that poor childless couple. They did not treat them the same way [the childless couple had treated them], not ignoring them. That is the reason for that admonishment. They say one who is generous, one who not only gives but gives instruction freely, becomes a friend and relative. One no longer feels uncomfortable around them.

Angutet Arnat-llu

Angun-gguq nerangnaqestenguan mulngakutetuat

(101) Frank Andrew, September 2000:59

Tamaa-i tamakut tamaani ciuqvani [atutullrit], maa-i cali pilaqait. Una-gguq angun nerangnaqestenguan mulngakutetuat. Mikelnguq-gguq eyag-narquq an'aqami. Tan'gaurluum-gguq eyagnani ciukluku antuuq. Nuaga tequrra-llu mulngananruluni angutmun uumun, qainganun pillerkaa wall'u aturainun. Nasaurluq-gguq taugken eyagnani kinguqliqtuamiu mulnganaillruluni angutmi. Tuaten-am nalqigcetuagket. Tan'gaurluq-gguq tua-i qasqiartaqami, aanami emuanek pinriqertaqami eyagnani pe-llularaa. Nasaurluum-gguq taugken utumallni eyagnamek, agleraqami nutaan eyagnarituuq; mulnganariluni tua-i.

Aglenraraullemteni

(102) Theresa Moses, November 2000:224

Aunraama piatnga, tua-i-gguq waniwa arnaurtua. "Tang arnaurtell-riaten usviturivailegpet tua-i." Angurrlugmek-gguq tan'gaurluq tepsak-luku qanqeryaqunii. Arnat-gguq angutni teptunruut. Tangerrluku kina ungacirliu tan'gaurluq arnam. Maaggun-gguq tepeput eltetuut [akuni enirluku]. Angun-gguq tepaillruuq angutnguami, arnaq taugken aun-ratuami teptunruluni. Maaggun-gguq eltetuuq. Wangkuta tang maa-i qungvagyutullemta ilii tan'gurrarnun. Assikituyaaqukut elpecicetun, assi-

Men and Women

They say they take special care [raising] a boy because he is a hunter

(101) Frank Andrew, September 2000:59

These are things they followed long ago, and they still follow them to-day. They say that they take special care when raising a boy because they are hunters. It is said that abstinence rules must be followed when a child is born. When a newborn child is a boy, there are strict rules one must follow when caring for him. One should be careful not to let his saliva and urine touch a man's body. But it is safe to be exposed to [the urine and saliva] of an infant girl, because the time for one to follow strict abstinence rules regarding girls comes later. They say that about [a boy and girl]. The abstinence rules that one has to follow end when a boy reaches the end of infancy and stops breast-feeding. When a girl reaches puberty, she develops a power to affect a man's hunting ability; she requires special care then.

When we had our first menstrual periods

(102) Theresa Moses, November 2000:224

When I had my first menstruation, they said I became a woman. "You have become a woman before becoming wise." They told me never to say a young man stank. They said women emit a stronger scent than men. We were told that our odor leaks out through [the opening of our garments]. They said that a man has less [body] odor because he is male, but a woman emits a stronger scent because she bleeds. They said her odor leaks out here. That is why we were careful toward a young man. We ad-

kitullruyaaqukut, tangerrluku, umyuarput taugken atullruvkenaku. Tua-ten talluryuarturluta, alingurluta yuullruamta ayuqluta. Wiinga-llu assi-kinguaqtatullruyaaqlua taugaam caumasciiganaku alikluku caumalerkaa. Yuk ayuquq, ayuqukut tamalkumta.

Inerqullruitkut tan'gaurlurni nasaurlurni-llu
nulirturpailemta uingvailemta-llu

(103) Paul John, David Martin, Theresa Moses, Lucy Sparck, Alice Rearden, and Marie Meade, April 2001:79–91

Paul John: Nulirturpailemta arnaq agturallerkaa qularyugnaunateng apertualuku. Tua-i nall'arqelluku apaaluku inerquanauraitkut. Taumek alikellrukvut wangkuta arnam mallguullerkaa nulirturpailemta. Una-llu aperluku pilaatgu, "Nulirturpailegpet tuaten pikuvet tuaten ayuqeciqu-ten. Ciunerpeni arnaq caningqauq pinarikuvgu nulirtuquvet tekiciiqan." Tua-i tamana wangkuta taringumaluku nulirtuqumta tekitarkaullerput. Taringumangramteggu arnam agturayaraa ancurtukluku cakneq, arnam aquiteklerkaa. Cali-llu apqiitnek aqliinek arnam, aqlii tua-i cali aarcir-tuutekluku. Arnaq-gguq aglerumariaqami, qagrumariaqami aqlii angut-mek navguyaqliurtelartuq waten aquitekluku atuquniu nulirqevkenaku. Tamaa-i tamakut wangkutnun taringumavkarluki tan'gurraungramta qa-larutaqluta taringevkarluta.

David Martin: Tan'gaurlurnun alerquutii qanemcikaa. Arnam nasaur-luq cali arnauyaram ayuqucia qanemciksugngaluku. Ava-i tan'gaurluum ayuqucia qanruyutii ciulianek ava-i qanemcikaa. Caurailngauteksugngaa-gguq arnaq waten umyuamikun pissiyaakuniu tan'gaurlullraam waten angtarilriim. Caurailngauteksugngaa callerkaminun kenkessiyaakuniu tauna ayagyuarluni. Cali-llu-gguq-am tamana waten nalqigtaat tan'gaur-lurnun taugaam. Pingnatungekan, catuluku, pissutuluku pikan, arnaq tauna nasaurluq pitatii akusrarutekekaku, tua-i-gguq elliinun tut'uq navgutkaa. Tamana tamaa-i iirpek'naku cali qanrutkaat. Pingnaturtug-yaramun-gguq-am cali tamana tamaa-i cali canrilngalnguq nasaurluq. Akusrarutekekuniu pingnatugturyarani pingnatullerkani man'a, cat paiv-ngalutellerkaat tamaaggun navgaa, nasaurlurkun tuaggun. Ca tamalkuan iirpek'naku qanrutkaat augkut ciuliat, yuum picurlautii waten ayagyuar-luni.

mired [boys] just as you do now after looking at them, but we did not do as we wished. We were always shy because we were fearful. I even liked boys, but I could not face them, and I was afraid of being face-to-face with them. All people are alike, we are all the same.

They admonished young men and women before marriage
(103) Paul John, David Martin, Theresa Moses, Lucy Sparck, Alice Rearden, and Marie Meade, April 2001:79–91

Paul John: Before we got wives they spoke to us without shame about touching a woman. They admonished us clearly by explaining the consequences of our actions. That is why we were afraid of getting close to a woman before marrying. And they told us, "This will happen to you if you behave this way before getting a wife. A woman is in your future. You will marry her when the time comes." Even though we understood that we would eventually marry, we were extremely afraid of touching and having sexual contact with a woman. We were also warned about the scent that a female emanates. They say that when a woman begins menstruating, her scent is capable of ruining a man if they have intercourse while unmarried. They explained these things clearly and thoroughly, even though we were young men.

David Martin: He just spoke about what young men were taught. A woman can also speak of the ways of women. He just spoke about the ways of young men and their instructions from elders. They say a young man who reaches a certain age will be unable to accomplish tasks if his mind is too preoccupied by a woman. They will not accomplish tasks if they are too infatuated with women while young. They only explained this to young men. They told [a young man] that he would only harm himself when he began to hunt if he messed around with a woman his age. They revealed that without remorse and shame. They also said a young woman was a detriment to the hunting ability of a man. They said he would ruin chances of animals being available to him if he had sex with a young woman. Those elders brought up harmful situations that young men could get into without keeping them secret.

Lucy Sparck: Tamana cal' kaynqukluku, kangia apraluku piksaicugnar-qaat amllermi qanrutkaqamegteggu agturayaraq.

Paul John: Wiinga-wa ellangeqataarallemni aperluku tua-i taringevkar-luku pilallrukiit. Waten maa-i akusrarutekiyaramek ap'laraat qacuniarya-raq, aperluku tua-i. Pissungengnaq'ngekumta pingnatullemtenun nakii-lutekciqniluku. Pitarkaput-llu tuaten pissu'urqamteki pitarkamtenun tangvalallerkarput, pitarkamtenun tangvagciqniluta.

Theresa Moses: Wangkuta-llu cali wiinga-wa inerqutullrukiitnga ava-litngusqevkenii tan'gaurlurmun. Tua-llu waten arnassagaam qanrucii-qaangaa, "Cuyayunqellriaten-llu tua-i iqugkualleruarmek, kuingim iqugkuallranek qelluniqerluten, tua-i aipaa-wa nunuliqerluten, inarucug-ciqkiiten piyugluten. Tua-i navegciqan tuaten manimakuvet maligtaqu-kuvgu tauna." Arnam-gguq avalitai amllertut. Aunraryaureskuni-llu cali aunrallruluni, qalugnera-gguq tua-i tukniriluni. Arnam-gguq ilii picui-rutnarquq. Maa-i tang wiinga-llu niicugniaqama alingkacagarlua. Cu-yam-llu im'um iruluarii-gguq cakuinraungraan cuyayulqa niilluku manii-llua taumek inarucukanga, maligtaquskuma tua-i-gguq avalitnguciqua tan'gaurlurmun, angayuqaagken-gguq wiinga eq'uklua. Yuum-gguq ne-kayullra quyallra-llu tukniuq. Waten akunliqaaqluku. Tua-i-gguq tuatna-kuma anerteqngaitelliunga ingna tekilluku taukuk angayuqaagken tuk-nian wii tungemnun qetunrarmegnek ilulngulutek. Tuaten pivkarluku wii manimalua taum qetunraagnek inarucuglua maligtaquskuma.

Lucy Sparck: Cauga tauna qalugnera?

Theresa Moses: Iciw' tukniriluni aqlii arnam. Tua-llu wangkuta elilluta amlliq'ngengaunata-llu waten angutem irua pikan angutet qukaat pikan, yuut-llu qukaat waten piqerluta [akuni teguluki quyu'urrluki] kituryartur-luku.

Paul John: Tua-i-gguq aurneni makunun tumemini uitalrianun cagcuu-miinaku, aqlani.

Theresa Moses: [Aqlii] naresquuravkenaku. Arnam-gguq tepii tukniuq, angutem-llu tepii tukniallruluni. Inerqutullrulua-am cali angutmek tep-sakisqevkenii. Arnaq-gguq teptunruuq, tua-i-w' aunraryaurcami. Angu-tem-gguq tepii cakaniyuituq. Ayayuilnguq-gguq taugaam angun arnar-pagnimek tep'ngetuuq. Tamaa-i tan'gaurluq-gguq tuaten atullrukuniu tauna nasaurluq kiingan-gguq tua-i tangvagyugturluku, callerkani-llu, neqsullerkani-llu peggluku, ingna taugaam tauna nasaurluq atullni tang-vagyugturluku. Tua-i-gguq ungalluku. Wiinga-llu tua-i taum angayuqaag-

Lucy Sparck: I don't think they spoke about touching [women] inappropriately a lot of times, because they were ashamed.

Paul John: When I was starting to gain awareness of my surroundings, they explained it to us so that we would understand it. They use the term *akusrarutekiyaraq* [engaging in illicit sexual relations] for *qacuniaryaraq* [engaging in sexual intercourse] these days. They said it would hinder our ability to hunt when we are old enough. They said our catches would be able to detect our behavior when we hunted.

Theresa Moses: They also told me not to be the source of a man's demise. An elderly woman told me, "You like tobacco, he will try to pay you with a cigarette butt to sleep with you. If you follow his request, you will ruin him." She said a woman is at fault for many things. And they told her that *qalugnera* [her scent] would become strong after she had her first menstrual period. They say some women cause men to become unskilled hunters. I would become terrified when I heard them speak. They also told me that if a man shows me a small end of a tobacco leaf, wanting to sleep with me, if I submit I would be at fault for the young man's demise, and his parents would despise me. They said a person's hurtful feelings and gratitude were strong. That is what they ended with. They said I would probably not be alive for a long time if I [ruined a man] because of the hatred his parents felt toward me over their son, if I submitted when he wanted to sleep with me.

Lucy Sparck: What does *qalugnera* mean?

Theresa Moses: You know, it's the strong scent of a woman. We learned not to step over a man's leg if it was extended if one was walking among men, and we learned to pass by [holding and closing the skirts of our *qasperet* (hooded garments)] when we walked among people.

Paul John: It is because she did not want to expose those around her to her *aurneq* [vapor], *aqlii* [her scent].

Theresa Moses: They didn't want [the men] to smell the scent. They say a woman's scent is stronger, and a man's body odor is weaker. And they told me never to say that a man is smelly. A woman's scent is stronger because she menstruates. They say a man's scent never changes. But they said a man who does not travel starts to smell like a woman. If a man had intercourse with a woman, he would only want to stare at that young woman and would no longer have any desire to work and fish. He would only want to be in the company of that young woman whom he had in-

ken taum tan'gaurluum umyugaa-w' navegluku tuatnallrukuma, manill-
rukuma ataam qetunrarmek aturyuglua taumek nunulirlua. Alikaqluku
tuatnallerkaput. Angun-llu tan'gaurluq tangerrluku waten quuskegcircii-
ganaku ugaan ungacinayukluku.

Marie Meade: Yuut-llu-q' waten takuatni waten angun nasaurluq-llu
tua-i qaill' mallgullutek pingaunatek, mallgutaarlutek?

Theresa Moses: Mallgutaayuitellruukut wangkuta. Tamatumek nangya-
qitelallruama-llu wiinga angutem-llu tangllerkaa uluryakluku. Cali-llu
angun waken anuqliqan asguakun maaggun pekngaunii taugaam uqrakun. Tuaten-am arnaq-gguq tepturituuq. Maa-i-ll' egmiulluku tua-i
tepengqerrsuklua tuaten piuraraqlua. Tunrikaqluku tamana tepka egmiulluku call maa-i tuaten umyuarteqaqlua. Angutmek asguakun pekte-
llerkaqa alikluku tepka narnayukluku.

Paul John: Tayima *example*-iirlua augkut qanlallrat qanrutkekumku ta-
ringciqngatan. Arnaunricaaqua taugaam augkut tegganret angullugaat arnam qageryaraa aurnengqerrsaraa wangkutnun tan'gurrarnun qanrutkaqamegteggu, tayima ca imna keniraq qaill' pitariaqami tepii cagtelaruq
enem iluanun, narnariluni enem iluani. Tua-i-gguq arnam aurnera tuaten agelrumarilriim, qagrumariami-gguq ilua qamna wangkutnun tan'gurrarnun navguutngurcugngarilartuq pitengnaqlerkamtenun, kememta
piniatellerkaanun. Tua-i mat'umun yuucimtenun navguut'nguluni.

Tamaa-i qularyugnaunateng augkut ciuliat taringepiartelluki ayagyuateng qanrutetullrukait tamaa-i. Tua-llu elitnaurvilegnun maligarucaur-
cama nunanun ayalrianun elitnaurvilegnun tekitnaurtua, ak'a-llu ukuk
tan'gurraankuk nasaurluq-llu caumallutek qalarullutek, tua-i qigcikutev-
kenatek. Tamakut taugken elitnaurvingnaciallruameng, agayulirtem-llu
igvarnaciarluki anglivillrenka caumatellriamek watqapik tua-i tangerr-
naitqapigtetullruluni. Tan'gurraankuk nasaurluq-llu caumallukek watqapik tangerrnaunani. Qigcikullutek. Anelgutkellriit cali qigcikulluteng.
Anngaqelriit nayagaqellriit qigcikulluteng. Elitnaurvilegnun maligutnaq-
naurtuq nasaurluum uum an'ngani caugarrluku qigciksugnaunaku cau-
maluku. Allayuugaqluteng elitnaurvilget. Avukulertengvailegmi tamaani
Kass'at igvarpailgata, Yupiit ellmeggnek auluklermeggni ayuqucirtuumar-
meng elluarrluteng yuullrullinivagtat.

David Martin: Ik'um cali qanrutkellra qaqivsiaqerlaku nasaurluq, nasaurluum ayuqucia. Tua-i-gguq apqiitnek agelrumariaqami tan'gaurluum ken-

tercourse with. He would be preoccupied with her. I would hurt a young man's parents if I submitted to a young man. We were afraid of doing that. And we could not smile at [young men] because we were afraid they would develop affection for us.

Marie Meade: And would a male and a young woman not be near one another?

Theresa Moses: We were never near each other. Believing and being fearful of that rule, I was afraid to look at a man. And if the wind blew from this direction, I would not walk on his windward side but on his leeward side. They said a woman's scent becomes strong. I continue to follow that custom today, thinking that I smell. I am embarrassed by my odor, and I have continued to think that way today. I still pass a man on his leeward side, because I'm afraid he will smell my odor.

Paul John: You will probably understand this teaching more clearly if I tell you what they said in the past using an example. I am not a female, but when those elderly men spoke to us about a woman's scent, it can be compared to the scent that fills a house when food is cooking in a pot. They say a female's scent is capable of ruining a man after her first menstrual period, when her inside has exploded, [harming] our hunting ability and our health. They say that their vapor affects our health.

Those elders did not keep things from their young people but taught them everything they needed to know and understand. And when I began to travel with others to villages with schools, I saw young men and women facing and speaking to one another without respect for each other. But in the place where I grew up, we did not see [young people] facing one another whatsoever, because schools were built much later and priests arrived later. There were no young men and women seen facing each other whatsoever. They respected one another. And siblings respected one another. Older brothers and younger sisters honored one another. When we traveled with others to villages with schools, we saw a young woman facing her older brother with no shame. The places with schools were different. They apparently lived decent lives before our culture began to change, before white people arrived, back when Yupiit were self-sufficient.

David Martin: Let me add to what that person said concerning a young woman's ways. They say a young woman is capable of becoming pregnant

kekani, taum pikani, nasaurlull'er ayagyuakacagalria yugmek qumingyug-
ngariarkauguq agelrumariaqami.

Theresa Moses: Waten taringcetaarucirluta qanrutetullruakut. Waten-
gguq angun kangangelartuq kenirmiarrarluni, tua-llu taumun maligta-
qusteminun, maligtaqukani, tua-i aturcelluni, katagluku tuavet unilluku.
Tua-i qingirluku, ilua qingangluni.

Paul John: Arnaq, imna kalngaggaq, tua-i tauna arnam taringcetaarutii
kalngaggaq tua-i. Tua-i-llu angun cali taringcetaaruterluni aug'utun kenirmiarrarluni kangarluni tarralluni. Tua-llu kalngaggarmun tekicami,
ciuniuqani, kenirmiarrani tauna kalngarrarmun tuavet egmian igcetell-
riatun, arnaq tauna maligtaquskan, atuquniu tua-i kenirmiani tauna ar-
namun tunluku. Makut tang maa-i *example*-at, taringcetaarutkegtaa-
raat niicimayuirulluteng agayumaciq igvallrani waten qanturillruameng,
"Assiilnguuguq tauna aperyaqunaku."

Alice Rearden: Kalngaq cauga?

Theresa Moses: Assigtaa arnam. Tauna tua-i. Taum-llu tua-i angutem
kenirmiarrani tuavet, arnaq maligtaquskan, tuavet tua-i katagluku ekluku unilluku-ll' tua-i taqkuniu ayagluni taum tua-i piksagulluku. Tua-ll'
tauna nauluni qamani taum kenirmillra.

Paul John: Nutaan maniisngatarci *example*-aaq avanillaq. Kusquqvag-
miut-wa makut kalngagnek pitukait wangkuta-llu issratnek.

David Martin: Nasaurluq tua-i angutem cikiryugngaluku yugkamek arnaq tauna maligtaqullrukan.

Theresa Moses: Manimakan.

Marie Meade: Tua-llu manimaluni ayuqellria qaillun ayuqerkauga?

Theresa Moses: Tua-i-w' niilluni qessavkenani taum unayaqkani angutem waten piyugluku, tua-llu arnaq maligtaquluni akilirluni piani, akilirluni taugaam. Avani-wa ilait akiinateng pitullilriit, wagg'uq ung'aqercingnaqellriit. Maligtaqulluni tua-ll' tuaken piyugngaluni. Qingatuli,
qingayuilnguq taugaam piyuitetullilria tuaten.

David Martin: Avani cali cumigyagucugallemni augkut wii murilkelluki
tanglallrenka arnat ilait uingnaciarumatullruut, tua-i akaurrluni aanaur-
tellriatun ilait ayuqliriluteng. Tamakut tamaa-i uilgarnek aperluki. Uilgarnek, uingilata, angutmek pistailata.

with a child when she has had her menstrual period, if a young man has intercourse with her.

Theresa Moses: They gave us the following example. They said a man walks around holding [a prospective child in] the skirt of his *qaspeq* [hooded garment], and if a woman consents, if she allows him to have sex with her, he will drop it and leave it there. He will impregnate her, and she will become pregnant.

Paul John: They used to say that a woman was like a *kalngaggaq* [little storage bag], and a man, like she said, walked around holding [a prospective child] in the lap of his garment. And when he got to that small bag, if she consented, he would drop what he was holding in his lap into the bag. If that woman consents, and he has intercourse with her, he will be giving what he was holding inside the lap of his garment to the woman. These examples, these wonderful metaphors, are no longer heard because when Christianity arrived, they started saying, "Do not speak of it, it is a sin."

Alice Rearden: What is a *kalngaq* [storage bag]?

Theresa Moses: It is a woman's bag. If a woman consents, a man will drop the object in the bag and leave it there, and the woman will then own it. And what that man held in the skirt of his garment will grow inside her.

Paul John: You just revealed an example that was used long ago. These people of the Kuskokwim River area call them *kalngat* [storage bags], and we call them *issratet* [grass storage bags].

David Martin: A man can give that woman [a prospective child] if that woman consents.

Theresa Moses: If she displays herself without inhibitions.

Marie Meade: And how would one who was displaying herself behave?

Theresa Moses: She would consent and would not be unwilling if a man [wanted to have intercourse] with her because he paid her, only through payment. Some people who were trying to make a person develop affection for them probably consented without payment in the past, those they called *ung'aqercingnaqellriit* [those who are trying to get affection from others]. That can happen to them if they consent. That did not happen to a person who could not get pregnant.

David Martin: When I observed people in the past, I saw husbandless women, and some started to look like mothers after a while. They called those *uilgaat* [husbandless women]. They called them *uilgaat* because they did not have husbands, because they did not have men to support them.

Theresa Moses: Maa-i cali aatailngurnek tanglalriit. Ak'a-llu avani acunia-qenganek. Tuaten pikan aatailngurmek acirarkauluku tauna manimallru-kan arnaq angutmun unayaqesteminun. Irniangekuni tua-i tauna acunia-qengamek piaqluku. Maa-i-llu "Augna aataituq." Waten piyugnagaluku.

Ilait-llu qanritnun uilgirniaqluki arnat. Qanran-gguq uilgiraa. Waten niitnarqaqluteng. Qanran-gguq uilgiraa.

David Martin: Qanqataitellran.
Paul John: Uingnacialria uilgarmek piaqluku. Tua-i ayuqengraan waten wangkucicetun uingnaciallra taugaam pitekluku uilgarmek piaqluku.

Marie Meade: Angutet-mi? Nuliangnacialriit-llu-qaa aprutengqelartut?

Paul John: Nuliangnacialriarpakartaitellruuq *food stamp*-ataitellrani. Wagg'uq, "Cikum ukicugngaurtii, ayakuaryaqunaku iinga-llu ingluileng-raan, kegginaa-llu qaillun ayuqengraan." Cikum-gguq ukicugngaurtii ca-maken uksumi anguyugngauq. Angutmek aipailngurpakartangqellrunri-cugnarquq. Angussaagyugngauralria qessakesciiganaku.

Tamaa-i arnaq ellminek uksumi nengelmi nerangnaqesciigalami ne-rangnaqestekaminek qaill' ayuqengraan angutelqurrarmek qessakisciiga-nani.

Qimugkauyartun-gguq tan'gaurluq ayuquq
(104) Theresa Moses, April 2001:201

Una waniwa arcaqalriarungatellrulliniluni tan'gurraq nasaurlurmek akusrarutekiluni, nasaurluq-llu unangluni tan'gurrarmek. Tamaa-i iner-qutullrukaitkut, qimugkauyartun-gguq tan'gaurluq ayuquq, ung'aqer-cukaartuq-gguq. Tua-i ingluliuqumteggu tamaa-i tan'gaurleurluq imna pi-tullni peggluki, catullni, umyugaani taugaam tauna nasaurluq uitaurluni, tangvagyugturluku kesianek. Tuaten qanrutektullruit. Wangkuta wiinga-llu alingetullruunga tuaten pivkarnayuklua. Wiinga-wa alingcetaarlua pi-

Theresa Moses: And there are fatherless children these days. They used to call those *acuniaqengat* [illegitimate children] back then. If one is a product of that situation, they call him an *aatailnguq* [one without a father] if a woman has sex with a man who asked her. That would be her illegitimate child if she has a child. And today they say, "That person does not have a father." That is how they refer to them.

And they said that the mouths of some women caused them to be husbandless. *Qanran-gguq uilgiraa* [They say her mouth has caused her to be husbandless]. That is what people say about them. They say her mouth has caused her to be husbandless.

David Martin: The fact that she could not keep her mouth shut.

Paul John: They called one who could not get a husband right away a *uilgaq*. Even though she was like us, they would call her a *uilgaq* because she did not get a husband right away.

Marie Meade: What about men? Were those who did not get wives right away referred to by a certain term?

Paul John: There weren't many [men] without wives back when there weren't food stamps. And they said, "Do not refuse one who can make a hole through the ice, even though he is missing one eye and his face is disfigured." They say that one who can make a hole through the ice can get food from underneath during the winter. There probably weren't many women who did not have male partners. They could not refuse a hunter and provider.

Because a woman could not go out and hunt during the winter in the cold, she could not refuse a man who could provide no matter how he looked.

They say a boy is like a puppy
(104) Theresa Moses, April 2001:201

The worst situation seemed to be a young man having sexual relations with a woman and a young woman ruining a young man. They warned us that a young man is like a puppy, that he develops affection easily. If we consent and have sex with him, he will stop living like he did, stop working like he used to, and constantly think about and be with us. That is what they said about him. I was afraid that I would cause someone to go through that, and they warned me that his parents would be angry at me

tullruanga tuaten pivkarikuma angayuqaagkenun qenruciiqnilua. Tuaten ayuqluni. Alikumaluki tan'gurraat tangerciigatnaqluteng-llu kegginaitgun, tallurnaqluteng. Tamaa-i cali maa-i umyuamnek aug'ayuilnguq, arnaq-gguq teptunruuq angutmi.

Arnaq-gguq tuquuguq

(105) Paul John, November 2000:235

Wangkuta tan'gurrarni ellangarteqarraallemteni qularluteng pillrunritut tungemtenun, arcaqerluku mat'um arnam tungiinun. Nulirturnarillerkamta ciungani tan'gurrarni arnamek aquicikumta qaillun wangkutnek navgullerkarput aperturluku taringevkarluku. Cali-llu aquicinrilkumta piluaqerluta anglillerput piyugngarillerput tekitellerkaanek. Wangkuta tan'gaurrarni arnaq una qanrutkaqamegteggu wangkutnun una nancecuitaat, arnaq-gguq tuquuguq. Tua-llu tua-i tuquucia una maaten taringluku pinaurput, ava-i augna nulirturpailemta arnamek agturakengkumta tua-i tuqutellriatun ayuqluta man'a unguvaqallemteni tememta qaillun kayutacirkaa. Arnamek agturakengkumta imutun piniarcalriatun apqucingellerkaanun-llu tua-i piciqelliniaput. Cali man'a pingnatugturallerkarput atrartellriatun, pitengnaqlerkarput pitarkamta nuyurrsagutellerkaat tamaa-i. Qulautekevkenaku navguuteklerkaa uum arnam ap'lallinikiit wangkutnun. Tua-i qularpek'nateng.

Tua-i-llu cali maurlungqertua, uingeksailnguugnek malrugnek panigluni, aanama uyuragkenek. Cali tua-i taum maurlurma ukuk niicugniaqamku paniigni aarnaurak tan'gurrarmek uingnarivailngagnek ung'aqercingnaqesqevkenakek. Tuamtallu avani mat'um nalliini apyuirutarput. Waten pinaurak, "Agelrumariutek angutmek navguryarturtutek ung'aqercecingnaqkuvtek. Tan'gurraq navguryuumariartek, qagrumariutek." Tang maa-i makut ciuliamta wangkutnun miktellemtenek ayagluta kangingepiartelluta qanruyuteklallrit. Mat'um nalliini ayagyuaput utumaluki pisqumangramteki aassaqulluki makunek, nutaan aturluki ellmeggnek mulngakluteng anglingnaqlerkaatnek.

Tuamtellu wangkuta tan'gurrarni inerqurnauraitkut. "Waniwa elpeci 'gguun anertevkallerpeciuggun arnam tepii, camek naruralriatun imutun pilaquvciu, yuucirpeci cali akngirutekciqaa." Tua-i alerqurnauraitkut, "Kitaki tuaten arnam tepii narenrilkurrluku pillerkarci waniwa. Anciquci pitsaqevkenaci-llu pairkengqataqerciquci arnamek. Pairkengqataquvci

if I caused him to become like that. That is how it was. We were fearful of young men and could not look into their faces because they were embarrassing. That is why I have not forgotten even up to this day that a female emits more scent than a male.

They say a woman is death
(105) Paul John, November 2000:235

When we young men first became aware of our surroundings, those people did not withhold things from us, especially about women. They let us understand that we would only harm ourselves if we young men copulated with a woman before marriage. They also told us that we would be fortunate in adulthood and able to provide for ourselves if we did not have sex. When we young men were instructed about women, they never failed to include *"Arnaq-gguq tuquuguq"* [They say a woman is death]. When I came to understand what they meant when they said that a woman is death, it was like a woman caught and killed us if we touched her before getting married, affecting our health and well-being while we were alive. If we touched a woman, it would cause us to become weak and have health problems. And it would diminish our ability to provide for ourselves and affect our hunting abilities, and animals would become afraid of us. They told us ways a woman can harm and ruin us without remorse. They did not withhold things from us.

I also had a grandmother who had two daughters who weren't married yet, my mother's younger sisters. And while I listened, my grandmother warned her daughters not to cause a young man to feel affection for them before getting married. Today we do not mention that anymore. She would say to them, "You are now menstruating. You will ruin a man if you cause him to develop affection for you. You are capable of harming a man now that you have started to menstruate." Our elders explained and had us understand these teachings thoroughly from the time we were small. These days, even though we want our young people's lives to improve, we are not talking to them about being careful while growing older.

They would caution us young men about the following. "Your health will be harmed if you breathe in the scent of a woman like you are smelling something." This is how you must avoid smelling a woman's scent. "You

anernerci nucup'akiciu tauna arnaq kiturnatkarpecenun." Tua-i-gguq carrluanek yuurrminritlerkarput pitekluku.

Nutaan-llu tua-i wangkuta taringumiimteggu tan'gurrarni tua-i aturluku. Arnaq pairteqatarqamteggu amigmi anernerput nucugaqluku. Iliini-llu ellavarnatkamtenun aneryaaqsaunata tua-i nutaan ellamun ellireskumta aneryaarluta. Tepii-gguq narkumteggu, yuucimtenun agtuuskan, tua-i agturaluku pinrilengramteggu, tamana-gguq ayuqucimta navgutkeciqaa. Tuamtallu arnamek tangvagnaqnaurtuq angun un' malkataquniu akuni kankut qecugmigluki ankuni. Aqlagtenrilkurrluku-gguq tauna angun menglairluku.

Aullu-llu angun irua nengingangraan amllirciqevkenaku arnam. Kencikulluteng ellmeggnek arnat. Tuamtellu angutem aklua ataarciiganaku. Ataallmikun arnam angun tauna pingnatugturallra atrarrnayukluku. Waten man'a nerangnaquciq yuungnaquciq nunam taugaam qairrlainainek atullermeggni, makut maa-i pinerrlugtenritengnaqluku yuusqumaluki ayagyuameggnun apertualallrit.

Cali-llu ellami wangkuta tan'gurrarni arnamek pairkengqata'arqamta anuqii imumek anurvanrilkan qakemna, maaten piciqukut waken aqlalluni, tua-i-ll man'a pairteqataq'ngarput ukalirnerkun taugaam aqlaqurallran taum anuqem tungiikun pairtengnaqluku. Uqriiskevkenaku cali arnaq ellami aarutekluku.

Nasaurluum aarnarqutii amllertuq

(106) Toksook Elder, November 2000:214–15

Yaa tua-i-llu waten ayagyuarulriani elpeci murilkenqegcaarluci avaunritengnaqluku-llu niicugniurqici qanaacimayuituci. Arcaqerluni nasaurluq waten angliqataarallermini qanruyutengqertuq, tua-i-wa aarnaqngami cam ikiulriim piqeryuka'arani. Wiinga atam aanairutellruunga qaillun angtaurlua kemyunarivailegma-llu. Tua-i-llu maurlurma iciw' tua-i taugaam makunek kevgartuayaranek pilua. Tua-i-llu maurlurma nunaqlilirlua pianga waten, "Elpet angliuralriami yuuciquten elpenek cumikurluten." Waten inerqurturlua, "Aquissiyaagpek'nak, caliyaraq elissangnaqiu, elpenek pistekuten." Amtallu ilanka amllerrluteng anaananka, alqankallu. Nasaurluum tang aarnarqutii amllellria, tua-i elpet arnaureskuvet angliurallerpeni. Cali makut tan'gurraat arcaqerluki aarcirtuutekluki. Arnaq-gguq tepailngalngermi tepsarquq. Inerquraqlua cali waten. "Tumya-

will go outside and might meet a woman. When you are about to pass her, hold your breath completely until you pass that woman." They didn't want us to inhale her scent, which could cause our health to decline.

We young men did that because we understood [the teaching and its consequence]. We held our breath when we were about to pass a woman at an entryway. And sometimes we held our breath until we got outside. They said inhaling their scent would harm our health and well-being even if we didn't touch them. We also saw a woman taking the hem of her garment and closing the skirt before passing a man when she was going outside. She would go out of her way not to affect him with her presence or let him smell her scent.

And a woman would never step over a man's extended legs. Women were careful with their bodies. And they could not put on a man's clothing. She was afraid of diminishing a man's ability to hunt if she put on his clothing. They told their young people about these things because they did not want them to experience hardship, as their livelihood depended entirely on harvesting food from the land.

And when we young men were about to pass by a woman outside when it wasn't extremely windy, when a breeze was blowing from this direction, we only tried to pass a woman on the windward side. They warned us not to pass by a woman on the leeward side.

There are numerous warnings against young women
(106) Toksook Elder, November 2000:214–15

And now pay attention and listen very closely, you young people, and try not to forget because you haven't been given oral instructions. A young woman has to follow rules and instructions because she can harm others and can get into bad situations easily. I lost my mother when I was this age and before I became confident in my ability to complete tasks independently. My grandmother taught me about working and completing tasks. When my grandmother took me in she said, "You who are growing older — you must watch yourself closely." She always admonished me, "Do not play around too much and try to learn how to work. You are your own caretaker." And here I had many relatives, aunts and older sisters. There are many warnings against young women. They especially warned us about young men. They said a woman has a strong scent even though

ratgun ayakuvet ciuneren tan'gaurlurtangqerqan angu asguakun kiturya-qunaku — tepsarquten. Uqrakun taugaam kitungnaqkiu."

"Cali-llu tan'gaurluq kegginaa qukarturluku tangssugyaqunaku. Tan'gaur-luq kangatuuq mikelnguyagarmek kenirmiarluni. Tan'gaurluq agtuquvgu qingarciquten. Iringqacaqunaku tan'gurraq tumyarami." Tangrru aarnar-qutii maa-i inerquutnguluni-llu angelriaruluni.

Nauwa maa-i kenka atuusqessaaqaat, wangkutnun taugaam kangia apertuyuitaat, kemegkun taugaam kiingan kenka aptuat. Kangingyuitar-put kenka. Maa-i tang man'a ilii kenkem. Tan'gaurluq assikeng'erpegu kegginaa qukarturluku caumayaqunaku. Inerquutngullruluni man'a el-pecenun nasaurlurnun. Maa-i tamana tass'uqelriignek-llu tangrraqama neq'aqerrlainatuaqa, ikiungerma, wiinga maurlurma inerquuqurallra aar-naqluni cakneq. Tua-i-llu waten cali pianga, "Tuaten yuugurqina tan'gu-rraq keggina qukarturluku tangeqsaileng'erpegu eq'ukenrilngerpegu, assikeng'erpegu." Umyuaqaqa wiinga kesianek tamaani nasekcugglugau-llemni tuaten qanellra.

Tua-i-llu pianga, "Caliyaraq elitengnaqiu. Atam canritlikuvet allakar-pet yuurtellinikuvet iluteq'laryaaqniartuten una piyugluku." Maa-i-tang man'a qanruyutekellra, "Elitengnaqluku cayaraq, arnam yuungnaqsaraa. "Elitengnaqluku ca iluteqngairulluten allakarpet yuureskuvet." Wiingal-kuk qemangqaaqa tamana irniamnun-llu. Tua-i-wa irniama umyugaat navegnayukluku iqlutun.

Inerquumatullruanga caknerpak maurlurma taum, kiituan wii aquiller-kaqa, nunat-llu akuliitni pillerkaqa talluryagutaqa qanrucesciurturlua. Aquiyaqliquma alaiterpagnganii yuut nasaurluullgutma akuliitni. Arca-qerluku man'a tan'gurraq inerquutekluku cakneq. Tua-i tuaten qanrullua, tan'gaurluq-gguq mikelnguyagarmek kenirmiarluni kangatuuq tumyarat akuliitni. Agtuquvgu qingarciquten. Tangrriu, kasngunaqluni, tallurnaq-luni. Elpeci ayagyuaqegtaarni qanruyuteci avaunritengnaqluku anglikeg-taarci. Assirtuci. Ayagyuaqegtaarauguci, assiisqumaluci-llu wangkuta.

she seems odorless. She also cautioned me about this, "If there is a young man heading in your direction while you are walking along a path, do not pass him on his windward side — you have a strong scent. Only try to pass him on his leeward side."

"And do not look directly into a young man's face. A young man walks around holding a child in the skirt of his garment. You will become pregnant if you touch a young man. Do not display yourself on his path." See how potentially dangerous a woman is today and how the warning against her is great.

You know that they ask us to love others, but they do not reveal the meaning to us but only mention physical love. We do not fully understand love. The following is a part of what love means. Even though you like a young man, do not look directly into his face. This was an admonition for young women. My grandmother's warning always comes to mind when I see a couple holding hands these days, even though I myself am not perfect. It was extremely dangerous, and she said to me, "Continue to live by not looking directly at a young man's face even though you aren't angry at him, even though you like him." I always remember everything she told me as a young girl.

Then she said to me, "Try to learn how to work. If nothing happens to you and you start living independently, you will become frustrated over wanting to complete a particular task." The following was what she taught me. "Try to learn the ways of a woman, their livelihood. Try to learn how to do something until you will no longer be frustrated when working on a task independently." I am so horrible, I have kept this [instruction] from others and also from my children. I thought that my children would feel hurt and take it the wrong way if I told them.

My grandmother strictly admonished me, and it got to where I was shy to play and walk around in the village, because I was spoken to all the time about proper conduct. When I finally played outside, it seemed that I was completely visible among girls my age. They especially warned us against young men. She told me that a young man walks around in the middle of the path holding a prospective child in the skirt of his garment. You will become pregnant if you touch him. You see that it's shameful and embarrassing. You wonderful young people should lead healthy lives and not forget your rules and instructions. You are good. You are wonderful young people, and we would like you to be well and healthy.

Nulirrualria, uingualria-llu

(107) Theresa Moses, Paul John, David Martin, and Lucy Sparck, April 2001:98

Theresa Moses: Arnamek tangerkengaileng'ermi arnamek tua-i aturuallagluni, arnamek tangerquni. Tauna-am angenruluni pillrularngatuq tuatnaluni tuqulleq kanani Qaluyaani. Tua-i unguvangairucan arnat-llu itercecuirulluki allat. Arnamek allamek itellriartangaqan, tua-i tuaten arnatulriatun tua-i uaciungartaqluni tua-i. Tua-i-llu una uinguaryaraq wall'u nulirruaryaraq, tangvanrilkiitgun ilami tangerkengami tungiinun [tangrruarluni], aipaak nulirruarluni.

David Martin: Ilami tangvanrilkiitgun tangrruarluni.

Paul John: Ii-i tuaten cali tua-i qanemciulartuq, arnaq wall'u angun. Arnaq-llu uinguaquni tuaten cali. Cali tua-i ilami tangvanrilkiitni uinguaminek taumek tangerkengarluni.

Ellaita tua-i aassaqevkenateng taugaam qanaaluteng ellmeggnek kitugcuumaut. Ellmeggnek aasaqevkenateng qanrutarkameggnun qanaatekaqluteng. Augna angakellrukeka-wa nallunrilken-llu. Tua-i tamaa-i ayagyuanrirluku-llu wii aanama qanrutketullrungraaku qagaantellruan tangyuitellruaqa. Utertellmi kinguani tamatumek qanemciuq. Ava-i-gguq tang avani aarutiit elliin pitsaqutmek atullrunricaaqekii arnam aurnera. Tua-i-gguq ilumun piciullinilria. Elliin tua-i assiiruyutekellruniluku. Tauna-gguq ilu'urnikaa arnaq. Nalluani ullagluku agtuqiini tatamluni tungiinun tuigquallrani, tua-i tepii-gguq tua-i tuarpiaq-gguq ayuqucianun nuvutellria. Ell'allagvikluku-gguq uyaqumikun atkuminek. Cunawa-gguq tua-i assiiruyutekaanek. Tan'gurrauluni-gguq tamaa-i.

Tua-i taum atiin aaniin-llu kangiitularyaaqelliniluku tangerrluku assiirucan. Aassaqkacaagarluni tua-i qanruteksuumiinaku, kiituani-gguq enemeggnek anyuirutuq tua-i assiirucami. Apqaungraagni tua-i nalqigcuunani kasnguyuum pitacianek. Ell'allagvikqainallruluku-gguq uyaqumikun, tepiinek-gguq kesianek tua-i narumaluni pelluyuunaku. Tua-i-am piyunarqucilegmun angalkumun atiin taum kaigatliniluku ellamun anenanrillran kinguani. Piinanrani atiin taum tayim' pistekagkenun malrugnun yun'erraagnun inguqicirluk' tua-i qasgicetlliniluku, qasgimun-llu

One having a pretend wife or a pretend husband

(107) Theresa Moses, Paul John, David Martin, and Lucy Sparck, April 2001:98

Theresa Moses: [One with that condition] fantasizes and acts like he's sexually involved as soon as he sees a woman. A man dying from that condition was probably the worst case down on Nelson Island. Because he was so ill and about to die, they would not let other women come [into the house] at all. When a woman came in, he would [begin to touch himself] as if he was with a woman. One with the condition *uinguaryaraq* [from *uinguaq*, "pretend husband"] or *nulirruaryaraq* [from *nulirruaq*, "pretend wife"] begins to imagine and act like he or she has a sexual partner.

David Martin: He imagines things that others do not see.

Paul John: That is what they say about men or women [who become ill with that condition]. A woman can also suffer and imagine that she has a male partner. She imagines and acts like she has a husband while others can't see her partner.

They can only get better if they speak about it and do not keep it a secret, if they do not hide it and speak to those whom they can confide in. That man was my *angak* [mother's brother], and you know him. My mother spoke about him even though he was not young anymore. I never saw him, because he lived up north. She told that story after returning home. He said that he did not purposely smell the scent of a woman. He said that teaching was indeed true. It was the cause of his demise. The woman was his *iluraq* [cross-cousin]. When she got startled and turned abruptly toward him after he snuck up to her and tapped her shoulder, when she did that, it seemed like her scent came out through the neck area of her parka and permeated his body. After that he got weak and sick. He was a young man at the time.

His father and mother would ask what was wrong, because they saw that he was not well. He kept it secret and did not want to talk about it. He eventually stopped leaving their home, because his health was deteriorating. He did not explain what happened to him even though they asked, because he was so ashamed. The scent had gushed out of the neck opening of her garment and struck him, and the smell stayed with him and would not go away. His father consulted an *angalkuq* [shaman] after he quit going outside. After a time his father had two young people carry

iturcamegteggu kanavet, canegnek-gguq curillrulliniluku tupiganek, tak-lartelluku tuavet.

Tua-i piinanrani angalkut tauna iliit taukut tuunrilluku yuarutmek atur-luteng. Atuutestai piqanratgun tua-i ellani qaill' piqernganaku nalluya-guqaarluku, ellangumaaralliniuq ellami kiiqapigmi tua-i aqumgaurluni natlugcugnaunani ayuqucia tua-i camek natlugutengqerrsugnaunani. Pii-nanrani yugnikekngaqapiarii imna ak'anek-llu tangerpaalugluku, agiir-quralliniuq yaatiinek quuyurrarmi ullagturluku. Tekicamiu canianun aqumluni pillinia, "Aling aren tangerrsaqlirpaa-ll'. Cam waniwa tangyui-rucetaten tua-i, ellami-llu kiarqurangramken tangyuirulluten?" Atam aa-ssaqucumiirutlinikii tua-i yugnikucamek aassaquyucuunatek. Nutaan tua-i ayuquciminek taumek tua-i ilu'urminek tatamlluku pillermini ell'a-llagvikellranek qanemcitliniluku, tua-i ayuquciminek qanemcilluku. Tuani-gguq tua-i qanemcitqerluku iquklitqerluku ellangartelliniuq qas-gim qukaani imumi enemini-w' tua-i uitayaaqellinilria. Taum tua-i angal-kuum yugnikekngaanek amilirluni ellalinqigaartelluku qanrucell'uni, makut-llu-gguq qasgimiut niicugniluku tamarmeng, niicugnilliniluku. Tua-i-gguq nutaan assiriluni. Taugaam-gguq assiringermi qaillun tua-i pi-qatalliniaqami tuani narqengaqeqatuniluku pellukapigtevkenaku.

Tua-i-w' ell'allagvikluku-wa uyaquni qaillun qipcillakallermini narler-luku tua-i qainganun nuvulluni. Taumek tamaa-i tan'gurraq una alerqua-gaqamegteggu: "Arnamek pairkengkuvet amigmi paircartuquvgu," waten piluta anerneriteqaasqelluta, kituqumteggu taugaam natmun aneryaa-qerraaresqelluta.

Tuamtellu arnamek pairkengqataqumta angu uqrakun kituqaasqevke-naku, asgurrlainaakun taugaam, tepii narenritlerkamteggun. Tamaa-i.

Lucy Sparck: Aug'um cal' Cevvarmium qanemcitqalqaanga. Piunrill-ruuq ak'a. *Lapp game*-arluteng, *lapp game*-atulriit. Qerrerrarluni, nuu qe-rraqsaunan' ellii an'urluni ilikluku-ll' tauna arnaq. Naqungqaluni taun' ar-naq. An'urngami aqvaqurturluni piluni takuyaqerlun' pillermini, ellii call' takuyarlun' arnaq tauna, pukaullutek. Pukauteqanrakun waten takuyar-qami narqalliniluku. Aquiluteng. Pitsaqaartevkenateng puukaullutek el-kek, narluku taugaam. Tavaken-llu-gguq ayagnirluni tavaten ayuqlirilun', qaill' taugaam kinkut imkut kitugtelliniluku.

him to the *qasgi* and set him down on a twined grass mat they had prepared for him to lie on. They had him lie down on it.

The *angalkuq* began to use his powers on him, and the singers started to sing. Just as they started singing, he lost consciousness and soon became aware outside, sitting all alone, and there was nothing wrong with him at all. After a time his best friend, whom he hadn't seen for a long time, came toward him from a distance, smiling. He sat down next to him when he got to him and said, "I haven't seen you for a long time. What has kept me from seeing you, and I no longer see you, even though I search for you outside?" He did not want to keep it secret anymore, and, because they were such good friends, they did not keep secrets from each other. He finally told him why he was like that, how his cousin's scent permeated him accidentally, and he told him why he was like that. After telling him, as he finished, he became aware of his surroundings and saw that he was actually sitting in the *qasgi*. That *angalkuq* had disguised himself as his friend and had him appear in a different setting and confess while many people in the *qasgi* listened. He finally got better. But even though he was better, he still smelled [her scent] once in a while. He did not get over it completely.

When she expelled the scent on him as she turned her neck somehow, he smelled it suddenly and it permeated his body. That is why they told a young man the following: "If you pass by a woman, when you are about to pass by her at a door," to hold our breath for a moment and to breathe out after we passed.

And they told us not to pass a woman on her leeward side but to always pass on her windward side, so that we would not smell her scent. That is what that is.

Lucy Sparck: A person from Chevak also told me a story. He died some time ago. They were playing lapp game [a ball game similar to baseball]. You know how they played lapp game then. After running across — or no, he hadn't crossed, but he was out and that young woman was on his team. That young woman was wearing a belt. When he finally [got out], he ran, and when he looked away for just a moment, that girl and he ran into each other. As they ran into each other, he moved his head like this and unintentionally smelled her scent. They were playing. They ran into each other accidentally, and that young man just smelled her scent. And from that moment he became like that, but some people healed him somehow.

Theresa Moses: Iciw' ava-i akuteng-llu waten piqerluki naqungqang'er-meng. Mikelnguq assiirucugngaluni tamaa-i aurneraniqluni-gguq arnam aurneranek.

Arnaurrluteng angutngurrluteng-llu taqmiggluteng
(108) Frank Andrew, October 2001:46–47

Neq'akestain qanruyun tamana tuaten piaqameng tua-i pegtetuat. Pi-qalang'ermeng tua-i naanguaq man'a pegtellriatun ayuqluku piqalang'er-megteggu, caliamun taugaam mat'umun, tua-i aglenraraurtaqameng. Tua-i-gguq arnaurrluni tua-i taqmiggluni, mikelnguunrirluni, nasaur-luunrirluni, neviarcaraunrirluni, arnaurrluni taugaam taqmiggluni. Te-mirtem caliaranek caliangyugngariluni tua-i aglellrurrluni taqmiggluni.

Tan'gaurluq tuamtell' qiugucingengami angutngurtuq-gguq tua-i. Angutngurrluni tan'gaurluunrirluni. Temirtem caliarinek caliyugngari-luni tua-i ak'a calilangeng'ermi. Piyugngarillmeggnek tua-i ayagluteng yuut makut ataita caliameggnek elicetetuit pinercirpek'naku, qaillun pita-rikan tuatnalangevkararkauluku, pivkenaki tuaten, ayagmek taugaam.

Pillguteklutek nulirqellriik calilallrak
(109) Frank Andrew, October 2001:1–4

Maa-i mat'um nalliini angayuqerpeci ayagmek arnaulriani uingvaileg-peci uingyaramek-llu qalarucimananrirtuci. Tan'gaurluq tuamtellu nu-lirturpailegmi nulirtuumayaramek qalarucimananrirluni. Tekitnercir-pek'nata nuliangellerkamtenun uingellerkamtenun-llu pimallrunritukut wangkuta. Arnamek-llu umyuangvailemta tamana uituumayaraq, uing-yaraq nulirtuumayaraq-llu ayuqucirtuutek'ngellruarput. Taumek arnaq tan'gurluq wall'u nulirturaqami, arnaq-llu uingaqami, ayuqucirkaitevke-nani uiminek caliyugngallrulria. Nepaunani tua-i umyugaanun-llu uimi nall'arusngaluni arnaq. Irniaminun ukunun irniangekuni irniaminun tap-qulluku uini aulukarkauluku. Enem-llu ilua man'a uimi caliaran enem ilua elluarrluku aulukluku, cali irniaminun ukunun tapqulluku ataminun-llu. Cali-llu neqkat aturait-llu. Qanrucimalartukut tua-i arnaq caliara am-llertuq enem iluani, yugni wangkuta. Aturanek caliluni, akluit kituggluki,

Theresa Moses: You know how he stated earlier that they also held the lower part of their garments like this [against their legs], even though they were wearing belts. It is possible for a child to get sick from contact with a woman's vapor.

They became fully grown men and women

(108) Frank Andrew, October 2001:46–47

Those who remember their instructions stop [playing like children] when that happens to them. Even though they do that once in a while, it is like they quit playing like children and only work on tasks when they begin menstruating. They said that one who becomes a woman and is fully grown is no longer a child, no longer a girl, no longer a young woman, but has become a fully grown woman. She can take on adult responsibilities because she has had her menstrual period and is fully grown.

And they said a boy became a man when he grew whiskers. He has become a man and is no longer a boy. He can take on adult tasks, even though he has other responsibilities. Their fathers taught them about their responsibilities when they became capable, not waiting for them to reach a certain age, and they didn't use age as an excuse for not having them work but taught them from the beginning.

How a married couple works together

(109) Frank Andrew, October 2001:1–4

These days your parents no longer tell you women about the ways of having husbands from the beginning of your lives. And a young man is no longer told about how to treat his spouse before getting married. They did not wait for us to get wives and husbands before giving us guidance. And we were told about having husbands and wives before the thought of a woman entered our minds. That is why [a newly married woman] knew how to treat her husband. She was quiet and didn't go against her husband. She was supposed to care for her husband and her children, when she had children. And she was to work hard on chores inside the home and what was caught by her husband, along with taking care of her children. And she was to take care of their food and their clothing as well. We were told that women have a lot of responsibilities inside the home. She sews and mends clothing, cooks food, and cleans the house. That is what

neqkiurluku, enem-llu ilua kituggluku. Tamaa-i tamakut tapeqluki tuaten qanrucimaut arnat. Uimi umyugaa camek assinrilngurmek umyuang-
qertessngaunaku-gguq tuaten ayuqekuni. Taugaam elluarrluku piarkauluku nuliani.

Uingan waten ayuqucugngaa nuliani ilukegcivkarluni calikan, elliin-llu
calillgutkeciqaa ayuqeliluku. Angutngunivkenani neqkiuraqan ikayuraq-
luku eruritaqluku-llu. Ca tua-i arnam caliaqsarai wii-llu waniwa nallunritanka yuuyaram. Mingeqsarat nalluvkenaki tuaten ayagmek elitnauru-
mallruama.

Tuaten tua-i ayuquq pillguteklutek nulirqelriik. Una arnaq wall'u
angun, arnam pingraani ellmikutuucimikun cirlakarkauluku nuliani
wall'u uini, carrlugmek naucingnaqengraan akinauyuitellermikun, ilang-
ciyuunaku-llu, ingluliuqsaunaku. Tua-i-gguq tuaten ayuqelria, cali uimi
uum wall'u nuliami akinaurngairutaqani umyualinqiggluni assilriamun
maligutetuuq, ayuqucilinqiggluni tua-i, elluarrlutek-llu nepaunatek ping-
lutek.

Imkuk-gguq taugken arnam uingekuni uini mernuqrutaqluku, elluarrluni-gguq angutem uitavikngaitaa. Nasperturluku-llu unicugngaluku
ayuqucini cimirngairutaqaku. Tamaa-i tamana pitekluku augkut angayuqamta wangkuta umyuarput aturluku arnamek aiparkamtenek piyuitell-
ruitkut. Ellaita taugaam ciulirneret ayuquciit yurvirluki, elluarrluki piste-
kamtenek arnanek aipangevkatullruitkut. Makut-ggem-tam' kinguqliput
angayuqateng cakenrirait. Taumek neplilriit, avvulluteng, irnialing'ermeng-llu unilluki avtaqluteng aulukumanriameng, ayagmek caliaqumanri-
ameng. Assirpek'nani tamana tangvallra.

Waten. Callaganritestekaanek, elluarrluni aulukiyugngalriamek tegu-
lallmikun. Atam waten ellilriani tan'gaurluq wall'u nasaurluq tangllermi-
kun tuaten ayuqucia nallunrirnaritulliniuq. Qaneryaramta wii niicugni-
lallma tuaten ayuqevkaraanga. Tuaten yuarutetullrulliniit qetunrateng.
Arnaq-llu cali angayuqaagken ukuk nallunrilkengamek tan'gaurluum
angayuqaagken carrliulriim angayuqaagken pingraagnek niiyuteksuu-
naku-gguq. Tauna qetunraak nallunrilamegnegu tua-i ayuquciakun assinrilan. Tamaa-i tamana atullruat ciuqlimta taumek nepaitellrulriit, arcaqerluteng neplirpek'nateng. Avvutaalriartaunani-llu tua-i caqapkacagalriit
taugaam.

Inerquutaqluku-ll' tua-i nallukengamtenek cucukliisqevkenata. Nepai-
telleq taugaam pitekluku, nepaunaki pisqumacim kenkem qaneryaraq

women were told, also. They told her that she would not allow her husband to have bad thoughts toward her if she was like that. But a husband was also supposed to treat his wife well.

A husband can cause his wife to feel a sense of joy and satisfaction while working, and he will work alongside her and do as she is doing. He will not use the excuse that he is a man but help her while she is cooking and wash dishes as well. I also know how to do women's work. I know how to sew, because I was taught that from the beginning.

That is how a married couple work together. Even though the male or female is trying to provoke the other, one can overpower his spouse by being composed and calm, by not retaliating, ignoring him and not countering him. The one who [starts arguments] changes when a husband or wife does not counter that person, and he begins to behave better, changing his disposition, and their relationship becomes healthy and peaceful.

But a man will not be happy in a relationship where a woman gets tired of her husband easily. And he could leave her if he wants to get back at her, if she isn't going to change her ways. Our parents did not allow us to choose our own partners for that reason in the past. However, the elders would observe the disposition [of young people] and choose partners for us who would treat us well. But those who were born after us do not respect their parents anymore. That is why they are experiencing turmoil, divorcing, and leaving their spouses even though they have many children. They get divorces because they are no longer raised properly, because they have not been disciplined in the right manner from the beginning of their lives. That is not good to see.

The following was [how they chose their partners]. [They would find their son a wife] who would not be abusive and rash, one who could take proper care of things with her hands. When one [becomes elderly], one knows what a young man or woman is like through observation. The instructions that I heard have taught me to be like that. That is how they searched for partners for their sons. And the parents of a girl would not accept the requests of the parents of a young man whom they knew was not a good person, and they could tell by his behavior. That is the custom our ancestors followed, and that is why they led peaceful lives. There wasn't much disorder in their lives. And divorces occurred only once in a great while.

And we were admonished not to choose a person we did not know. These instructions for living exist only because they wanted people to live

man'a alaicetaa nunam yui nepaunaki pisqumaluki. Assiitesqevkenaki. Qaneryaraq tua-i man'a alaitelluk' nunam qaingani. Yugni taugaam wangkuta, makunun aklunun pinrituq. Yugnun taugaam calilriaruuq qanruyun.

Nasaurluq-gguq tangerqumku kegginaqegtaariinun alarcaqunii
(110) David Martin, April 2001:229

Tan'gaurlunun cali ayuqucirtuun, arnanun pivkenani. Wangnun qanruyutelleq cali. Nasaurluq-gguq tangerqumku kegginaqegtaariinun alarcaqunii. Nutaan tangerrluku tauna nasaurluq camiungulria kegginaqegtaariinun alarcaqunii, nunalgutkenritaqa tauna. Nunalgutma-gguq taugaam ukut tua-i ayuquciat man'a piurallrat nallunrilkengamnun tauna tua-i taugaam pikilaku, umyuama cumiguskiliu.

Kegginaqegtaariinun-gguq alartevkenii nasaurluum. Iignegun tangellra assirluni qamna taugken iluani, umyugaan alerquutii qipumalriatun ayuqluni. Qanlartut-am yuk-gguq, yuut ayuqenrilameng, kegginamegteggun tangkegcinarqut, tangellra tua-i assirluni, natlugnerunani, taugaam-gguq umyuara. Ava-i qanrutkelaragka malruk. Aipaan taum picurlautmek imalgem picurlagcetaa tauna kegginaqegcingraan, umyugaan.

Maa-i mat'um nallini *high school*-anun ayagaluteng kass'aciryaramun ekngameng makut kinguliaput camiumek taumek ukurrangaarrnaurtut tua-i nunalgutkumayugnailngurmek. Kegginaqegtaaraitnun alarrluteng, ayuquciat man'a yuvrinrilamegteggu. Qipumatem-am ava-i *meaning*-aara. Yuum ilii-gguq kegginarrluni tangkegcinarquq, ilua-gguq taugken qipumaluni. Qipumalriim nalqigutii-am *meaning*-aaq tamana ayuquq. Tan'gaurlurnun-am ava-i augna ayagyuanun tua-i aarutngulleq ava-i cali qanrutkarci. Nutaranun taugaam makunun alerquatnek ayagyualrianun taugaam akwaugaq-gguq maa-i inerquutautulinek niicugniurtuci, nasaurlurmun tan'gaurlurmun-llu.

Puqlakellguteksagutukuk-gguq aipaqa-llu
(111) Theresa Moses and David Martin, April 2001:209

Theresa Moses: Pingayuatni-wa pilallilriit.
David Martin: Maa-i aipaqsagutaqamta puqlakellguteksagutukuk-gguq aipaqa-llu. Tamatum-am tamaa-i una kinguvrak canimelutessiyaalriik, waten ilakutsiyaalriik kinguvrak tauna pisciigatetulliniuq. Kinguqvaarni-

in harmony and love, for people here on this earth to live peacefully. They didn't want people to be bad members of society. This has caused these instructions to exist here on earth. This only applies to people and not material things. Our instructions only apply to people.

They said I should not mistakenly choose a girl based on her beautiful face
(110) David Martin, April 2001:229

Here is another teaching that applies to boys and not girls. I was also instructed about this. They said that when I see a girl for the first time, I should not be deceived by her beautiful face. They said I should not be deceived by the beautiful face of a girl whom I see from another village. They said that I should only prefer a woman from my village whom I know.

They said that I should not be misled by a girl's beautiful face. She might look attractive when looking at her with these eyes, but inside, her mind is like something that is twisted. They say that because people are different, some have beautiful faces, are attractive and flawless, but their minds [are twisted]. I spoke of two minds earlier. Her other mind, which is filled with dishonesty, causes her grief even though she has a beautiful face.

Because our young people are traveling to high schools these days and are living by Western ways, their parents gain in-laws from other towns, ones who are not even close to their village. They are deceived by their beautiful faces, because they did not study their characters. That is the concept behind being twisted. They say some people have attractive faces, but they are twisted inside. That is the concept of *qipumalria* [one who is twisted]. You just spoke about what young men, young people were warned about. You have been hearing only about admonitions for young men and women.

They say that the body heat of my spouse and me becomes one
(111) Theresa Moses and David Martin, April 2001:209

Theresa Moses: I think they [marry] when they are third cousins.

David Martin: They say when my spouse and I have become a couple, *puqlakellguteksagutukuk* [our body heat becomes one]. The descendants of [a couple] who are too closely related cannot function normally. But if

gguq taugaam yaaqsigingaqan tua-i nutaan piurcugngariaqluni ilakuteng-raagnek taukuk. Ilakutsiyaaglutek-wa tua-i pilriik nauvimegnegun, yuurr-vimegnegun.

Puqlaput-gguq quyurcetuuq atauciurrluni. Tua-i-llu-gguq tua-i ilakut-siyaagamegnuk kinguverpuk tauna qaillun ayuqsugluni, allayuuluni yuu-luni. *Meaning*-aaq tamana tuaten ayuqelliniuq. Kinguqvaarni-gguq tua-i piyuirulluni pituyaaquq. Tamana-am pitekluku ilaita tamana mallgutsii-yaallerteng pitekluku avvuqurainatullrulliniut irniateng waten qaillukua-ssiiyaangaqata-llu. Avvuqurainautekluku tamana tamaa-i pitullrulliniut.

Cakik ukuk ukurratek
nengaugtek-llu irniamegtun pitaluku piarkaugaak
(112) Frank Andrew and Alice Rearden, October 2001:73

Frank Andrew: Angutngukuni, arnaungermi-llu uimi ilai ukut, wall'u nuliami ilai, cakiraqai. Taukut-llu cakirain tamarmeng nengaumeggnek tuqluraqluku tauna, arnaukan-llu ukurrameggnek. Arnam-llu tua-i aug'u-tun angutetun cakiraminek taukut cakiqluki. Arnaukan-llu taukut caki-rain ukurraqluku, angutngukan-llu nengaugaqluku. Tuaten aterpagtaa-tuit.

Cakik cali ukuk ukurrartek nengaugtek-llu irniamegtun pitaluku uita-curlagcetevkenaku, ayuqucirtuatuluku irniamegtun ukugtun pitaluku, na-lluyurniurceteksaunaku, takaqitevkarpek'naku, yum'egtun ukutun ayuqu-lluku. Yuut ilait qanlartut ukurrarrlugtuq-gguq, ukurrarrlugtellriamek, wall'u nengauggluggluni. Cakik taukuk nalluyurnaqlutek-gguq, allakauk-luku. Angutem wall'u nasaurluum-llu uitacurlallni pitekluku uini unitar-kauluku angutem-llu cali nuliani unitarkauluku. Panigtek tua-i uillugte-lluku wall'u qetunrartek nuliarrlugtelluku.

Tuaten-gguq ayuqut *family*-t angayuqrit ilaita, ukut qetunrateng aipa-ngaqata. Ukucetun ayuqulluki pisciiganaki, nalluyurniuravkarluki. Ta-ringnaqluni kenkinrilnguut tamaa-i tuaten ayuqut. Maa-i cali yuum iliin aturaqluku, nengauggluglluteng ukurrarrluglluteng-llu.

a couple marries even though they are related, their children [can't marry] and their descendants will be able to marry and be okay. Ones who are too closely related through their parents, from their birth parents.

They say when we marry our body heat becomes one. And because we are too closely related, our descendants will not be normal. That is how that is. The birth defect usually diminishes as the descendants of that couple become more distant. That is why some couples who realize that they are close in blood separate when they produce children who are not normal.

In-laws are to treat their
son-in-law and daughter-in-law like their own children
(112) Frank Andrew and Alice Rearden, October 2001:73

Frank Andrew: A male or a female, her husband's relatives or his wife's relatives, are *cakiraat* [in-laws]. And all the *cakiraat* would call the male son-in-law *nengauk* and the female daughter-in-law *ukurraq*. Like the man, the woman would call her in-laws *cakiraat*. And a female would be the *ukurraq* of her *cakiraat,* and a male would be their *nengauk.* That is what they called them.

In-laws are to treat their son-in-law and daughter-in-law like their own children, not causing them hardship, instructing them like their own children, not causing them to feel uncomfortable, not causing them embarrassment, but treating them like their own children. Some people refer to those who are having a difficult time as a daughter- or son-in-law as *ukurrarrlugtellria* [one having a hard time as a daughter-in-law] and *nengaugglugtellria* [one having a hard time as a son-in-law]. Their in-laws are unfriendly and uncomfortable to be around, and they treat them differently. Some young women leave their husbands because they are having a difficult time, and a man will also leave his wife. They cause their daughter to have a bad relationship with her husband, or they cause their son to have a bad relationship with his wife.

They say some parents are that way when their sons marry. They don't treat [their spouses] like their [own children], causing them to feel uncomfortable. One can easily see and know that they have no affection [for her]. It still happens today. Some have a difficult time as sons-in-law and as daughters-in-law.

Iliin taugaam angayuqaagminek tuaken uini wall'u-q arnaq nuliani angayuqaagminun elluarrluku pinrilucia pitekluku anutetua angayuqaagminek, nuliqsullni pitekluku, angayuqaagmitun ayuqutevkenaku nuliani tauna pinritaqan'gu. Angutngungraan ilii tuaten pituuq cali. Angayuqaagni maligtevkenakek, aipaqsullni tauna pitekluku. Angayuqaagminek tauna unilluku. Taum aiparmi angayuqaagkenun nugtarrluni. Pitangqelartuq tua-i makunek assinrilngurnek inerquusngang'ermeng.

Angayuqaagmi uitacurlagtelluku taringekuniu nuliani angutem, aataminun aanaminun-llu angayuqaagminun ellmegcecicetun aulukenrilucia elpekekuniu, nuliqsukuniu angayuqaagni taukuk unitarkaulukek tauna maliggluku. Tuaten tamana aturaat cali.

Nunanun allanun nugtarrluni nengaugicaraq wall'u ukurricaraq qaneryarartangqertuq cali ineruutnek. Nengaugiskuni nunanun allanun anglivikenrilkengaminun, taukumiumek nuliangekuni, tuancukan, taukunun ilausngallerkaa nunanun anglivikenrilkeminun, yuurvikluki uitavikurluki anglivikenrilkeminun, murilkengnaqluni tuani uitallerkaa qanernarqellerkani murilkelluku cakneq ayuqucini. Taukut assikenrilkiitnek nunalget, nunat taukut piqallerkaanek murilkengnaqluku. Tuaten alerquucetangqertuq. Ellmikutuungnaqluku cakneq tuantesqelluku umyugaa angevkenaku. Camek-llu picirkiqsaunaki taukut nunat. Quyurrluteng camek piaqata atanrussaalriatun ayuqeksaunaku. Tuaten tua-i ayuqucirtutullruitkut arnat-llu tua-i pilallikait ukurritellriit nunanun allanun.

Alice Rearden: Niitelallruunga-llu ukurritellrukuni tuavet nunamun iciw' qanmikun uini allanun qanrutkesqeksaunaku, uingan calallra, wall'u-q camek assikinrilkuni uiminek allanun tuavet nunanun qanmikun qanaalaasqevkenaku piciatun.

Frank Andrew: Tamaa-i tamana inerquatnguuq. Kenertun-gguq ayuquq ekuagilriatun. Nunat umyuaqegtaariit ekualuku pilriatun ayuqsugngaluku assilriamek umyuaqegtariit navgurluku, navguryugngaluku. Kelguqengyaraq tamana inerquutnguuq. Uivet ayuqucia nunanun taukunun qanrutkaqluku, tua-i-gguq kelguqengluten. Nalluani qalarutkaqluku ayuqucia. Navguilriaruuq-gguq tamana yugnek kelguqengyaraq.

Alice Rearden: Camek-llu-qaa nengaugiskuvet wall'u-q ukurriskuvet camek piyukuvet tuani nunami angayuqavkun taugaam piyugngaluten,

But some spouses take their husbands or wives out of their parents' home when their in-laws mistreat them, because they want to stay married to them and do not treat their wives or husbands like their parents. That even happens to some men. They do not treat their spouses like their parents, because they want to stay married to their wives. A man can move away from his parents to his wife's parents if he wants to stay married to her. These unfortunate situations occur, even though people are admonished.

If a man realizes that his parents are mistreating his wife, he will leave his parents and go with her if he wants to stay married to her. That still occurs today.

There are instructions and rules to follow when moving to other villages and becoming a son-in-law or daughter-in-law. When one becomes a son-in-law in a place where he did not grow up and marries someone from that village, he must really watch his behavior while living there and try not to be the source of trouble in that village if he wants to live in that place where he was not raised. He should be careful not to do something that is unfavorable to the villagers. There is a teaching like that. They tell him to live there by minding his own business and being reserved, not acting like he is better than others. He should not tell others from that village what to do. He should not try to be the boss when they gather and plan something. That is what they told us, and they probably told women who became daughters-in-law in other villages the same thing.

Alice Rearden: I also heard that when one becomes a daughter-in-law in another village, she is not supposed to speak about her husband to others, revealing what her husband does, or to tell people of that village if she does not like something about her husband.

Frank Andrew: That is an admonition. They say it is like fire that is burning, like burning the wonderful [minds] of the village. They are capable of ruining the wonderful peace and tranquility of that village. *Kelguqengyaraq* [passing on unfavorable information, telling another what someone else said about him or her] is an admonition. Speaking about what your husband does to members of that village, what they call *kelguqengyaraq,* talking to others about his behavior and conduct. They say *kelguqengyaraq* hurts others.

Alice Rearden: And if you want to do something in that village or if you want to tell the villagers what to do or advise them about something when

wall'u-q iciw' taukuni nunani picirkiuryukuvet wall'u-q camek qanrucu-kuvki.

Frank Andrew: Uimi aanii wall'u irniari arnaullgutni, tamakut aturluki-gguq piarkauguq. Cakirani aturluki wall'u-q cakini arnaq.

Avani neqet nulirrita tua-i auluktullruit

(113) Frank Andrew, October 2001:73

Avani neqet nulirrita tua-i auluktullruit nalluvkenaki-llu tua-i angutet pitait caqumalriit tuaten amllertaciit. Uingan taugken aulukesciiganaki nulirran taugaam nalluvkenaki, elliin ataniumaluki tua-i. Neqkaitnek-llu tegulaucugngaluni tamaaken neqnek, irniarin-llu agturasciiganaki, ata-tuumarmeng. Tuaten ayuqellruut-gguq avani.

Tua-i-llu caqerluteng neqa nurnalliniluni — nani pia, qagaani-llu elaq-limteni pillilria — nurulluteng neqait up'nerkami. Akulmi avani nangute-lliniluteng tua-i. Nulirqelriik tua-i taukuk. Nulirra tua-i tauna neqkaara-tek tua-i nangniluki qanlliniluni caqerluni. Cunawa-gguq uini iqluluku. Keviraun akakiignek imalek iirluku, nalluani taugaam ner'aqluni. Ayaga-qan-llu canek tua-i neqkangengnaqluni ayagaqan ner'aqluni.

Tekilluni-am caqerluni itrami tua-i ugayarluni nuliani unangkengami-nek tua-i camek piluku neqkaarmek, tangllinia manuani akakiigem qel-tii nepingalria atkuani. Uingan taum egmian taringartelliniluku piciunril-ngurmek ellminun pillinicia. Taringamiu pillinia, "Manun tauna alkartuq, alkartuq." Manuni tanglellinia, akakiigem qeltii nepingalria.

Assinrituq-gguq tamana. Tayarnerikun teguluku, nuliani nangerrluku anutelliniluku apluku nanlucianek. Apertuaku tua-i nengelmi uksumi kevirautaq tauna painga angiqaarluku tallia iterrluk qamavet, uqumek imarluni, akakiignek imarluni kumlamek, qillertelliniluku tuaggun kau-mavkarluku. Kumlam-llu tua-i mayuani tuqullinilun tua-i. Taugaam iner-quun cali ilangluni-gguq tuaggun nangusnguarillerminek uiminek.

Waten-llu qanrut'laraitkut waniwa-gguq waten aipaqelriani kenkulluta aipaq'lartukut, arnaq-llu uini kenkullutek tua-i, umyugaak natlugneru-

you become a son or daughter-in-law, you can only do so through your spouse's parents.

Frank Andrew: They are supposed to do so only through the mother of her husband or their female children. They are supposed to ask for permission through their in-laws or her female in-laws.

Their wives took care of their catches

(113) Frank Andrew, October 2001:73

Their wives took care of their catches back then, and they kept track of the amount of stored food. Her husband wasn't responsible for animals that were caught and brought home, but his wife knew how to take care of them and was in charge of them. She could take food from storage, and neither her children nor their father could handle it. They say they were like that in the past.

Once when food was scarce — I don't know where this happened, perhaps it was at a place to the north of us — they ran out of food during spring. They ran out of food at a place in the tundra area. There was a couple. The wife said that they were out of food one day. She apparently lied to her husband. She had hidden a seal poke filled with whitefish and ate from it without her husband's knowledge. And she would eat when he would leave and hunt for food.

One day when he got home and took off his garments and mentioned his little catch, he noticed a whitefish scale stuck on the front of her garment. Her husband immediately understood that she was deceiving him. When he understood, he said, "Your front garment has ripped, it has a small rip." She looked at the front of her garment and saw the whitefish scale stuck there.

They say what happened here was not pleasant. He took her by the wrist and pulled her outside and asked where the food was. When she showed him where it was out in the cold winter, after loosening the opening of the seal poke filled with cold whitefish and oil, he shoved her arm in through the hole and tied it closed. She died from exposure when the cold rose up. An admonition came to exist from that one who lied to her husband about running out of food.

They also tell us that we who are married care for and love each other. A woman would love her husband. They say a time of food shortage is a

nani. Tamana-gguq tauna piitnaq, neqaituryaraq nutaan kenekmek yuv-ririttuuq. Nulirqelriik-gguq kenkutellrak nutaan nallunaituak tamatum kainiqsaram. Yuk-llu umyuangqellria, qunutungailnguq nallunrirtelluku cali. Tauna-am tua-i uini tauna tamalkirrluni kenkenritliniluku, ellmi-nun tuc'elluku tamana umyuarrliqun. Tamatum-gguq tamaa-i maniluku ayuqucia taum, kenkinrilucia nakmiin uiminek.

Yuk-gguq ayuqucilinqigcuqngauq
(114) Frank Andrew, October 2001:73

Qanemcimek-wa tua-i piciatun niitelaryaaqelrianga, Qanagaarniarut-mek taugaam taumek nengaugarmek niitetullruunga cali. Waten tua-i ayu-qucirturraarluta pilaraitkut yuk-gguq temyigingermi angutngurteng'ermi ayuqucilinqigcugngauq. Tauna nutaan qanemciktuat Qanagaarniarun.

Nulirtulliniuq nengaugilluni nunani taukuni. Akiqliqut-gguq waten kuigem paingani nunat, akiqliqluteng nunauluteng. Nani pia? Nani aper-tuqsaitaat. Cassuyuunani-gguq tauna maaten piat pissullerkani-llu teng-rukevkenaku. Cakigken tua-i kenkenrillinikiit catngunrilan cassuyuu-nani uitiin, tua-i ikayuuvkenani.

Qasgimi maqitullruut avani tua-i maqiuratuluteng qasgimi.

Taukut uksumi caqerluteng maqikaiturangellinilriit qanikcangellrani. Qanikcalingellrani tua-i maqikaiturangluteng, muragat patuluki, kiituan tua-i maqingnatulanglliniut ikayuqluteng canek muralqurrarluteng. Tuat-navakarluteng-am, tuatnavakartelluki tauna im' cakia taum cassuyuil-nguum qanlliniuq, nengauni tauna piluku, nirluku tauna, qanalleruar-mek una piyugtiinun navertesqelluku ilatarkaminek. Catngunrilan tua-i tauna nengauni maqikamek navercesqelluku imumek qanagmekenem qaniinek. Tamakucimek ataucimek kiputesqelluku. Nukalpiat-am tau-kut iliita pistekangengairucan tua-i elliin piyulliniluku, takumcukluku tua-i arenqialamiu takumcukestailan. Tuaten ayuqengraan tua-i takum-cukngamiu taum cakian pisquciatun qanagmek augaulluni yuksagutelli-niluku tua-i.

Taunaurluq tua-i im' pissuyuilnguq umyugaa tua-i akngirtellinilria cak-neq. Cunawa-gguq tua-i qavanermek taqluni. Unugaqan-gguq kangara-

real test of love. They say starvation reveals a couple who truly love each other. And it reveals a person who thinks of others, one who is generous. That woman apparently did not love her husband unconditionally, and her cruelty came back to her. That experience revealed her true nature, that she did not truly love her husband.

They told us that a person can change
(114) Frank Andrew, October 2001:73

I heard many different stories, and I used to hear the story of Qanagaar-niarun, the son-in-law. After giving us instruction they told us that a person can change even though he became an adult. They then told the story of Qanagaarniarun.

He had married and became a son-in-law in a village. The two villages were situated across from each other along the river. The villages were across from each other. Where were they? They did not mention the village. They saw that he did not obtain anything and was not eager to hunt. His in-laws no longer loved him because he didn't help out, because he stayed and did not obtain anything and did not help.

They took fire baths constantly in the *qasgi* back then. They always took sweat baths in the *qasgi*.

Sometime during the winter when it started to snow, they started to lack firewood for fire baths. They started to lack firewood for a fire bath when there was a lot of snow and firewood was covered, and they began to help one another prepare for fire baths using whatever they could for wood. After some time the father-in-law of that one who did not get anything spoke up. Pointing to his son-in-law, he said that someone should buy him with one *qanak* [plank from the frame of a *qasgi*]. Because his son-in-law was good-for-nothing, he wanted to trade him for a *qanak* to use for firewood. He said one of the men in the *qasgi* should buy him for one of those. When no one took his offer, one of the *nukalpiat* [good hunters] announced that he would [buy him], because he felt pity for him when no one else pitied him. Out of pity, even though he had a bad reputation, [the *nukalpiaq*] took off a log like his father-in-law requested and took him.

That poor [son-in-law] who did not hunt was extremely hurt and quit sleeping after that. He would walk around outside during the nighttime

qelria ellami enet amiigit qanikcarcecuunaki, elakat-llu cikuvkayuunaki. Qasgimun-gguq qaqitaqamiki unugmi itraqami, caniqamun aqumqer-luni, Evvcuutangqetuut muraggarnek, tamakuni, iqua cingigluni, rest-aqa'arqami unugmi qes'arrluku-gguq waten una-gguq tugrulluku iqua, waten-llu-gguq tua-i piqerluku. Qavaryartuami-gguq taugken qamiqurra atrariinarluni, taum-llu-gguq tua-i evcuutam iqua cingiumalria qauraa-nun wavet tugrulluni, cugican tua-i mak'arrluni. Tua-i-gguq tauna qavar-yaraqsagulluku. Cugican-gguq taugken tua-i makcami egmian ellamun anluni, tua-i qavanqiggngaunani unugpak errvianun.

Allrakuni-gguq tallimani waten arulaiyuunani. Wani-gguq cakaninri-tuq. Wani-gguq taugken pitqalangluni caqa'arqami. Wani-llu-gguq picuri-kanirluni. Wani-llu-gguq cali quyigikanirluni cali. Tallimiitni-llu-gguq tua-i caviirulluni tua-i, picuriluni tua-i. Ayallra tamalkuan neqtangluni-gguq, cayunairulluni, nukalpiarurrluni. Taum imumi takumcukluku pis-tellran paniminek nuliangevkalliniluku. Tauna-llu imna nuliara nakmiin carumilegmek uingelliniluni, akiqliitni ikani uitiin tauna. Iqsulegmek ui-ngevkarluku taum cakian, uingluni tauna, nakmiin nuliara unicetellrat.

Pissulangami tua-i tamaani pissungengami uurcaraqami unaken imar-pigmek maklaggluni tag'aqami up'nerkami iqsuminek ayarurturluni alai-tullinilria piyualuni, nunat waten akiqliqngata. Elitaqnariqatarluni-gguq taugken tua-i ayaruni-am tallirpiminun nugtara'arrluku akiqliitnun ika-vet caqiqanirluni. Cakigni taukuk iqluquurlukek. Akinaurlukek-gguq tua-i kiituan-gguq taum arnam cakian qayagaulangyaqaa, "Cangallrunri-tuten atak' tang nulian ullaggu."

Tamana-am cali inerquutngurrluni, yuk tuaten ayuqengraan cimiryug-nganiluk' ayuqucianek—tautun pisqevkenaku, qanagmun tun'illertun pisqevkenaku inerquutngurrlun' nasaurluq wall'u tan'gaurluq-llu. Tua-ten taktaluku qanemciktullruat qalaruqaarluta, cimirilleq tauna taqmig-tenermikun ayuqucilinqigtelleq. Qanruyutiit tamaani ciuniurpek'naku ayagyuallermini nulirturpailegmi tamaani. Ciuniuryunritlermikun tua-ten tua-i pimaluni, cakian cakegtakevkenaku qanagmun taugaam nav-

cleaning entryways of homes, not letting snow cover them, and making sure ice holes on the river were free of ice. When he was done clearing them, he'd go into the *qasgi* at night and sit down on the side. They had *evcuutat* [tools to remove snow from garments] made of wood with a sharp point at one end. He would hold onto it like this [putting both hands around the stick] and would poke the tip like this [underneath his chin]. They say when he rested briefly and began to doze off, his head would fall when he started to fall asleep, and he would wake suddenly when the sharp end of the *evcuun* [snow removal tool] gauged his head and hurt him. They say that is how he started to sleep. When he started to feel pain and woke up, he would immediately go outside, and he would not sleep for the rest of the night.

He did this nonstop for five years. Nothing happened the first year, but he started to catch game once in a while during the [second year], his hunting ability was better the [third year], he became even better the [fourth year], and he couldn't improve his skills any further on the fifth year and became a good hunter. They say he caught animals every time he went out. He became a *nukalpiaq*. The one who felt pity for him had him marry his daughter. And his original wife married a left-handed man who lived in the village across from them. His in-law had her marry a man who was left-handed. His original wife, who had left him, remarried.

When he started to hunt in the spring and caught a bearded seal, when he would announce his success from down in the ocean and head toward the village, he would appear holding a walking stick in his left hand. Because those villages were across from each other, right before they could recognize him, he would move his walking stick to his right hand and walk in the direction of the other village. He would deceive his [previous] in-laws. He was repaying them, and eventually his mother-in-law started to shout at him, "You are no different [from the other man]. Why don't you go back to your wife."

That also became an admonition after that incident, that a person can change his ways — not to treat a girl or boy like that man who was sold for a log. They used to tell that story after giving us instruction about the one who changed his ways just as he became an adult. He did not live by their instructions as a young person before getting married. He was like that because he would not follow them, and his in-laws did not value him and sold him for a log. He changed his ways then, through the log that he

rulluku. Tua-i cimiriluni nutaan tuani tamaaggun qanagkun akimikun, cirlakluku tamatum. Ayuqucini mumiggluku nutaan, elluarrluni pingllerkaminun pingnatungluni.

Qalaruqaarluta tua-i iliini tamana iqukluku pitullruitkut.

Cakigka taugaam ataneqlukek nulirtuquma

(115) David Martin and Theresa Moses, April 2001:49

David Martin: Cali wangnun alerquatekellra maurluma yinqigeskumagguq yugnun allanun ilakumanrilngurnun, atanrussaagpek'nii pikilii. Taumun cakimnun, irniangqerqan irniarinun ilaliuskilii, wii umyuaqa qaillun pingraan wangnek piyuglua piksaunii piyugngangerma. Taugaamgguq ukuk wani cakiigma camek pisqumakagnga, tua-i piyugngakumku tauna, egmianun tua-i irniarinun ilaliullua tua-i pisqellua. Irniarinun ilaliullua tua-i ukunun ellimeqiignun ilaliullua.

Tan'gaurluq allakarmi, nasaurluukuni-llu allakarmi alerquastengqertuq. Alerquastengqellruut tuaten. Tua-i umyuani elliin taugaam aturpek'naku taukunun tua-i ilausngaarkauluni piyugngang'ermi, tuaten piyugngang'ermi. Ukuk cakigni apqegni aanakelriatun atakelriatun-llu ellimerrutekaak tamana ciullguurangnaqluku cali pisqumalukek, pisqumaluku — enem iluani ellimerkaq amllerniluku. Tamana aqumgaurluku waten elisngaitniluku qanruteklluku. Tuaten wii qanemciksugngaaqa. Arnam taugaam tayima nalqigucugngayugnarqaaten arnartaryaram ayuqucianek. Wiinga angucetaryaraq tuaten qanemciksugngaaqa. Cakigka taugaam ukuk aipaqa tauna aipaqsaguskumku angayuqaqngakek taukuk taugaam atanqellukek tua-i wii umyuaqa assilria aturpek'naku.

Theresa Moses: Avani inerqutullruitkut nunalinqigeskumta taukurmiumek uingekumta tuani-gguq uitakilta wangkutnek murilkelluta. Ciuqliuluku maa-i man'a inerquutaqtullruat. Qanllerkaqa murilkelluku, taukurmiunek qanemkun navguillerkaqa avalitngullerkaqa murilkelluku taukurmiungureskuma. Angayuqaak-llu aug'utun, angayuqaqelriatun pisqellukek. Qanellra ikiungalengraan qanellrak maligtaquurangnaqesqellukek.

Cali uima taum picilirtungraanga piksailkuma ilangciksaunaku uitat'laasqelluku, kiuksaunaku, allanun angutnun ellilangraanga qanqaqsaunii-gguq uitauratukilii. Tua-i-gguq nunakenrilamki taukurmiut. Wangkuta man'a, atam-gguq qannguatukumta taukut nepngurrniaput tau-

was sold for, which caused him to change his ways. He finally changed his ways, and he started to try to live a good life.

After giving us instruction they sometimes ended with that story.

My in-laws are supposed to be my superiors when I marry
(115) David Martin and Theresa Moses, April 2001:49

David Martin: My grandmother told me that if I became part of another family that I am not related to, I should not try to be in charge. She said that I should join my in-laws and their children, if they have children, and not follow my own mind even though I was tempted and capable. But they said that I should do as my in-laws requested if I could, working with their children. They said I should join their children when they asked them to complete tasks.

A young man and woman were instructed separately. That is how they were instructed. [A young man] was told to join the other family and not do as he pleased even though he was capable. He [was told to] treat his in-laws like a mother and father and try to complete his tasks before they asked him to — that there are many tasks to complete inside a home. They told him that he would not learn anything by sitting around. That is what I can say about that. A woman can tell you about women's ways. That is what I can say about a man's ways. But my in-laws are supposed to be my superiors when I marry, if [my partner] has parents, and I cannot do whatever I wish.

Theresa Moses: They warned us to watch our behavior when we married someone from another village and moved. That was the first instruction given. They told me to be careful not to damage the reputation of others from that village with my mouth, to be careful about being blamed for something when I became a member of that village. And they told me to treat his parents like my own. They told me to always obey them, even though I didn't agree with what they said.

And they told me to ignore my husband and not respond, even though he accused me of having relationships with other men, to sit [without responding], since I was not from that village. They said if I gossiped, I would cause the villagers to become noisy and to blame me. They gave us that advice if we lived [in another village]. And they told us not to

kurmiut, wiinga-gguq avalitkaqlua. Tua-i tuaten inerqutullruitkut tuani uitakumta. Yuk-llu qannguangraan tauna qanemcicesqevkenaku waten ing'umun qanrutkellruniluku, piniluku. Wiinga-gguq atam ayagneqlua nepengniartut, nunat-llu allat niitengluteng qanengluteng-gguq, wiinga-gguq taukurmiut inianka, inilriacetun ayuqanka. Mayurrluki, niitevkar-luki, wiinga avaliteklua taumek qanllemnek. Maa-i tamakut pinerrluir-turluki tuarpiaq pitullrukait. Taugken-gguq wangkutnek murilkurluta piuratukumta, imucetun tua-i nallunaqluteng taukurmiut nallunarqeller-megteggun uitaluteng. Taugken-gguq tuaten yuukuma tuarpiaq-gguq iniluki mayurrluki taukut nunat, nunat piciatun niilluki waten piniluki taukut, wiinga tua-i qanllemkun, qanemkun taugaam, qanemciklemkun. Pinerrluirturluta pitullruitkut wangkuta.

Wiinga qessangerma uingevkallruanga aatama, aanaka taugken tuqull-ruluni. Taukuk-llu cakiigka qanenrullinilutek tamarmek alerquagiller-mek, iliini yugmek-llu qanmegnegun iliini nekayugcecitullinilutek. Wii taugaam tuaten alerqumiimta qanqaqsaunata qemaggluki cat ikiulriit nii-tellrenka yuukilii. Alingcetaarturluta pitullruitkut.

Taum-gguq uima-llu ilai tungelqurri neqmek-llu avegvilegmek tauna uika tekiuskan ciukurluki-gguq maa-i tuvkaqtukilaki. Avani ilumun kass'artarnek pivailemta neqa taugaam man'a tungelqiurutkurluku. Ilang-qeng'erma-gguq angayuqangqeng'erma-llu ilait taugaam taum uima ciu-kerrlainarluki. Atam-gguq tuaten ayuqeng'erma uima-llu taum taukut ilanka pillininiarai, wangcetun caullininiarai. Nakmiin ilaksagulluki tua-i tuarpiaq ilaksagulluki, anngaqluki nayagaqluki. Wiinga-llu alqanka anngaanka, uima tamaa-i ilai. Anrutaq una avani alerquutngullruuq an-rutakun taugaam kass'allanek canek akinek piyuitellratni tamaa-i. Kal-maaniurluni tamaani cikiqengyaraunritellrani, una tua-i neqalleruar aler-quutekluku.

Tua-llu waten pinariqataqan upluki cali anguteput imarpigmi pissuu-tekaitnek. Imarniciluki, ivrucililuki, issratnek taquarvigkaitnek, arilluli-luki, pinerrluirturluki tamaa-i. Tuaten ayuqellruukut wangkuta. Tuarpiaq upeskata tamaa-i pinerrluirturluki. Ivruciit imangengaunateng, imar-nitait all'uki pikuneng mecungengaunateng. Aliumatait iluita maa-i ima-ngengaunateng mermun akurtengraitki.

tell someone if another gossiped about them, that someone spoke about them. They said the village would become noisy because of me, and other villages would start to hear and say that I have "hung" those villagers in the air. I have hoisted them up, and I would be at fault for what I had said. It seemed they gave people advice so that they would not make mistakes in the past. But they said if we were careful, it would be like people of that village would be unheard of and would live anonymously. But they said if I lived my life in the previous way, it would be like I was hanging them up in the air, raising that village up, and other villages would hear what was happening in that village through the stories I told. They always gave us advice to help us make wise decisions.

My father made me marry, even though I was unwilling. My mother had died already. Both of my in-laws turned out to be unrelenting when it came to giving instructions, and they sometimes caused a person to become angry when they spoke. However, we were told never to say anything but to keep negative things we heard inside. They always tried to frighten us.

And they said when my husband arrived with food that could be divided and shared, my priority should always be to give it out to my husband's relatives. Indeed, back when we did not have store-bought goods, food was a way of developing close family bonds. They said that I should always try to give to my husband's family first, even though I had relatives and parents. They said that if I was like that, my husband would start to treat my relatives like I treated his. They would become like my real family, like my older brothers and younger sisters. And my own older sisters and older brothers would be like that to my husband. We were taught about the [importance of one's] stomach back when they did not have money. This was back when people did not give to others by digging into their pockets, but food was important in keeping families together.

And before it was time [to hunt], we got our husbands' ocean hunting gear ready for them. We made them *imarnitet* [seal-gut raincoats], *ivrucit* [waterproof boots], and *issratet* [grass storage bags] for their provisions, *arilluut* [waterproof mittens], always making it easier for them [to hunt]. That is how we lived. It seemed we would make life easier for them when we prepared things. Their waterproof boots would not fill up with water, and they would not get wet if they put on their seal-gut raincoats. The insides of their mittens would not fill with water, even though they immersed them in water.

Tekitaq

(116) Paul John, April 2001:58

Tuamtellu ava-i ilu'urqa nengaugicaram iliinek qanelria cakigni tua-i takaqlukek pillerkam tungiinun. Nuliacungaqa-llu cali una arnam tungiinun cali ukurricaramek [qanertuq]. Nunakenrilkeminun waten yuk ayagaqan nengaugilluni wall'u ukurrilluni tekitauyaaqelalliniuq. Taugaam taukut ciunrin tangerrluku, ukuni nunalepiamini wagg'uq umyuartunruan nakmikengtulliniat casteknaluku nunameng tuani iluani. Makut-wa ilaita upucaaqekiit, "Makumiungunrituq. Tekitauguq." Tuaten piyaaqekiit taugaam ciulirnerita tangerrluku ayuqucia nakmikengyuumalliniluku, imutun castekelriatun, tua-i-w' ikayurtekelriatun pillerkaan tungiinun, ayuqucia tangerrluku. Ayuquciqegcikan, ayuquciqegcivakaan ilaminek elluarrluni ikayuringnaqvakaan, mulngakluni ilaminun pivakaan, tangerrluku casteksuumingarkaulliniluku. Tua-i taugken tekitaungraan castekarniilkekunegteggu cali casteksugngaitniluku.

Avani-llu ciuqvaaraungraan navguilria pitsaqaartevkenani ciunerminek ilaita caqalriit nunat wagg'uq anlluku, kingunranun utercetetulliniluku, tua-i-wa anagulluni ilakarniipakaan. Wagg'uq anlluku tuaken nunanek. Tauna taugken tauna aipaa tekitauyaaqluni taugaam tua-i teguyaraqluku, teguyugturluku apqiitnek, imutun kevganuugaqelriatun tua-i nakmiknaqvakaan tangerrluku tuaten ayqucugngaluku.

Irniamini nakmiin iluqsinrurtellria

(117) David Martin and Theresa Moses, April 2001:204

David Martin: Angucetaryarakun cali nalqignaurqa augna allamun yinqiggluni nengauguyaram alerquatii. Wani-gguq aipaqa tauna angayuqangqerqan tua-i taukunun eyiuskuma aiparma ilainun, tua-i taukut enem-gguq iluani ellimerrutekat amllertut. Tang ca tamalkuan nalqigeskiit augkut ciuliamta. Enem-gguq iluani ellimerrutekat cali amllertut ayuqenritut: Mer'et, qerrutet, cat erullerkait. Taukuk-gguq tegganrek angayuqaak qanerpailgagnek-am taum ullautellriim qanllerkaak ciullengnaqluku. Ellimerrutekakek tamakut ciulleguurniaqluki pisqutem tamaa-i *meaning*-aara cali tuaten ayuqelliniluni. Ukuk wani enem tamatum atanrek ellimerrutekakek-gguq ciulleglukek tua-i aperpailgatki pingnaqluki.

One who moved from another village

(116) Paul John, April 2001:58

My cousin just spoke a little about being a son-in-law and about respecting the in-laws. And my *nuliacungaq* [female cross-cousin] spoke a little about the responsibilities of a daughter-in-law. Indeed, when a person gets married and moves to another village and becomes a son-in-law or daughter-in-law, he or she is regarded as a newcomer. But by observing him and seeing his wisdom, the residents of that village would begin looking up to him and choose him to become a leader. Others in the village might say, "He is not from here, he moved from another village." Others might say that, but their elders would observe his character and look up to him as a leader. They would want him as a worker after observing him because he was good-natured, because he tried his best to help others and was careful around his peers. On the other hand they wouldn't want one they felt would not be a good worker to work for them, even though he moved from another village.

Long ago the villagers would banish a person who was harming others or the community, and they would let him return to his old village because he was too difficult to live with. They would kick him out of that village. However, even though someone moved from another village, he would become their helper. They would begin depending on him and gain trust in him.

One who is more valued than one's own children

(117) David Martin and Theresa Moses, April 2001:204

David Martin: Let me explain the instructions for a son-in-law moving in with another family. They said if my wife had parents and I moved in with her family, there are many chores to be completed inside the home. Our ancestors explained everything. They said there are many chores to complete inside the home: packing water, dumping honey buckets, washing things. They said a person who moved in with [their in-laws] should try to complete chores before the older people of the household, the parents, asked him to work on those tasks. That is the advice about completing chores before being asked. They said one should try to complete chores before being asked by the head of the household. They say that

Qanernaunani-gguq tauna tua-i nengaugaq cucukenruluku-llu ukuni ir-niamegni, ciullguuralutek piatek ellimerrutekanek tamakunek. *Meaning-aaq tamana tuaten ayuquq.*

Theresa Moses: Ayuqluni. Atam-aarluta. Atam panimini-llu umyugaani iluqsinrurtellininiartuq. Irniamini nakmiin umyuarteqellrani iluqsin-rurtellininiartuq tamaa-i qanruyutekait ciullguuraluki, ellimerrutekait ciullguuraluki. Tamaa-i tuaten ayuqluni; angucetun ayuqluni arnaq tauna. Ellimerrutekait qanrutekvailgatki ciullguuraluki. Ciullguuraluki tua-i kituggluki, apqiitnek pegtangitakevkenaki uimi pitai, ciuniurtur-luki taugaam, assirluki auluku'urluki. Ilumun keneknarqetuuq man'a ukurraungermi tuaten assirluku-llu nuliqluku. Tun'ernaqluteng cali ma-kut ukurrat nengaugat-llu.

Angussaayuilkumteggu-gguq aiparput
nulirturuarluta kainiqevkararkamtenek nulirturciqukut

(118) Paul John, November 2000:80

Wangkuta tan'gurrarni elitnaurqamegtekut aipangllerkamtenek uum aiparkamta ayuqucirkaanek qanrutaqluta. Aiparput una aturall'erkainek pisciigalkumteggu, man'a pingnaqsaraq aturluku pinrilkumta, aturall'er-kainek aiparput pisciigalkumteggu nulirturuarluta-gguq kepqevkararkam-tenek nulirturciqukut. Tuamtellu angussayuilkumteggu-gguq aiparput nulirturuarluta kainiqevkararkamtenek nulirturciqukut. Cali-llu irnia-ngekumta irniarput unatminek meluulangareskuni, tua-i-gguq taum ir-niamta ellimerraakut, "Angungnaqia aataaq neqkamnek." Unataikun cali tua-i umyuarteqlerkamtenek irniamta cikiumaluta. Irniaput unatmegg-nek meluuyungareskata ellimerciutekarput irniamtenek, "Aataa neqka-ngengnaqia." Tamakutgun tamaa-i wangkuta elissallruitkut aipangllerkar-put tekilluku tua-i aipangkumta.

Cali-llu aiparput-gguq una piipaaraluni enem iluani qanquni, tua-i-gguq taum aipamta taumek atu'urkaminek unangengnaqutesqelluni pii-parakuni qanrutaakut. Tua-i tamakunek tamaa-i nallunritevkallruitkut. Nengaugisnguaurluqumta-gguq taum aipaqliuskengamta ilainun ullau-lluta, cassurpek'nata-gguq neqkaaraitnek nanguluugutnguyarturciqukut wangkuta ikayuulluta taukunun ciunemtenun nengaugisvimtenun neq-

son-in-law who does things before he is told would not be criticized by his in-laws; he would be valued by his in-laws more than their children, because he is completing chores before he is asked. That is the explanation for that.

Theresa Moses: It is the same [for women]. They would say to us, "Look!" They would say she would become more cherished than even one's own daughter. He would be more valued than their own children if he completed tasks before he was asked. That instruction for men is the same for women. Always try to complete chores before one is asked. Fixing things before one is asked, trying not to be careless with her husband's catch but always working on things immediately and taking proper care of them. Indeed [a person], even a daughter-in-law, who displays that behavior is desirable. Some daughters-in-law and sons-in-law can cause one to be embarrassed and ashamed.

They said that if we did not hunt for our spouse, we deceptively married one who we would let starve

(118) Paul John, November 2000:80

When they taught us young men about marriage, they told us what to expect from our partners. [They said] if we could not obtain clothing for our partners, if we did not subsist, if we could not provide clothing for our spouses, that we deceptively married someone who we would deprive. They also told us that if we did not hunt for our partner, we would deceptively marry someone who we would let starve. Also, when we had children, a child who started to suck on his hand was actually saying, "Father, try to catch food for me." Our children were also giving us something to think about with their hands. If our children started to suck on their hands, our children were asking us, "Father, try to catch some food for me." They taught us up to the point where we would marry if we did get a partner.

Also, if our partner said that she was lacking something inside the house, she was actually asking us to get that thing she needed. Those are the things that they taught us. If we became sons-in-law, we would have no purpose in being there but to contribute to finishing their food if we do not help them obtain food and wood. They said that if we were lazy, we would not be a contributor to our in-laws, but we would finish their food

kaarkun maaggun muragkun-llu pinrilkumta. Tua-i-gguq cauvkenata tau-kunun nengaugisvimtenun nangulugutnguciqukut neqkaitnek wall'u ika-yuanrilkumteki muraggarkun qessaluta-gguq uitastenguciqukut. Tua-i tamakunek tamaa-i elitnaurucirluta waten aipangyaram tungiinun pill-ruitkut. Ayagmek-llu wangkuta tua-i-w' aipangnaluta umyuarteqaqamta una enemek uqisviggaitellerkaq ciuqliuluku umyuaqetullruarput. Aipa-put-llu quyumta uitangkumta enemun uqisvigkaitellerkaq una umyuam ciuqliqluku.

Cali-llu aipangkumta nernariaqan qantacunguar teguluku tungelqurra-nek imiqassaagallerkaa neqkanek, tauna cali kasgunaqluni, waten aipa-ngellrem kinguani. Tua-i tamaa-i elissaumiitkut ciulirnemta waten nulir-turluni aipaqliutnerrarluni ayuqucirkamek.

Nulirqelriik caliarkauguq ikayuqlutek

(119) Frank Andrew, September 2000:9

Waniwa-llu waten aipaqsagutellriik, angun ciuqliugarkauluni. Nuli-rran naigtaarluku pingaunaku. Ayuqlutek-llu tuaten aipaqutarkaulutek. Kenkullutek, narurtaarutevkenatek, maligtaquuraullutek.

Tua-i-llu cali una wani arnaq angutiin ilangqerrameng-am qanruyun man'a navkaquluku pitulimek, arnam iliin uini qalaruqualaraa, qatpaga-lluku tuaten, wall'u angutem nuliani qancurlagalluku wall'u yagiraluku. Tamakut tamaa-i assinrilnguut aipaqucecurlagluni pillerkaat. Angutem-gguq arcaqerluni nuliani kenkarkaqaa. Irniani, enem-llu ilua, uini tapqu-lluki aklukait tegumiaqluki, neqkiurluki, caliaqluki. Caliara amllerrluni arnam, nangteqluni. Angutem-gguq ilalqerluku yagiraluku pingaitaa, ika-yualuku taugaam ikayuangnaqluku, pillgucirluku. Arnaq wall'u angun. Angun angutnguniteklluni-gguq uitaurngaituq arnam uum yagirallra ar-nartaryaraq piyugngang'ermiu. Kenkekuniu-gguq nuliani, aipani, arnar-taryaraungraan caliarkaqaa ikayurluku.

Iqluvkenii waniwa wii elitnaurutemnek mingeqsaraq nallunritaqa. Ca tua-i mingeqsaraq, neqkiuryaraq-llu nalluvkenaku. Tuamtellu aiparma angucetaryaraq qaqilluku pinrilngermiu cali ikayuagaqlua, tua-i qanruci-malallrulliniami cali tamatumek. Tamaa-i tamana assilria.

if we did not help obtain food and gather wood. They taught us those things when they talked about marriage. And from the time we were very young, having fuel to warm our homes was foremost in our thoughts. Not having fuel in our homes when we lived with our partners was foremost in our minds.

Also, after getting married, the idea of taking a small bowl and asking one's relatives to fill it with food when it was time to eat was shameful. Our elders taught us about what was expected of newlyweds.

A husband and wife must work together
(119) Frank Andrew, September 2000:9

When a couple marries, the man is supposed to be the superior. The wife should not disobey him. They should treat each other the same when married. They should love one other. They should not fight and always cooperate with one another.

Because there were people who broke rules and instructions among them, some women spoke inappropriately toward their husbands and yelled at them, or a man would speak abusively toward his wife or hit her. That is not good in a relationship. They say a man, especially, must love his wife. She suffers more, taking care of kids and doing chores inside the house, along with her husband and their belongings, serving them food, working for them, because a woman's work is plentiful. They say a man [should not] mistreat her but should try to help her and work alongside her. This goes for both a woman and a man. A man will not sit around because he is a man, even though he can complete women's tasks. If he loves his wife, his spouse, it is his duty to help her work, even though it's considered women's work.

I am not lying now when I say that I know how to sew because I was taught. I know how to sew and cook. And even though my wife is not capable of completing all of men's tasks, she also helps me because she was also taught. That is good.

Waten-llu tuaten ayuqullutek pilriik, waten elliqunek irnialing'ermek nanikuaklutek tua-i. Aanakelriatun aipani ayuqsagulluku, nuliaran-llu aataksagutellriatun ayuqsagulluku. Tuaten ayuqliriukuk aipaqa-llu. Atuyunaqsaaqluni tamana, assilriaruluni.

Angutet-gguq kiimeng mer'em acianek tegutetuut

(120) Theresa Moses, June 5, 1995:68

Wangkuta ca tamalkuan alerquutekluku yuullruukut. Uingekumta, tuai-wa angussaagtekaqngamteggu, takaqluku uikesqelluku, pirpakluku, pirpakluku uikesqelluku tangnerrlugnarqengraan, tangellra ikiungraan. Wangkuta-gguq arnani yag'arrluta mer'em-llu akuliinek tegusngaitukut. Uksumi-llu cali yag'arrluta neqkamek tegusngaitukut. Angutet-gguq kiimeng mer'em acianek tegutetuut. Nengelvagmi-llu yuilqumek cali tekiulluteng. Upeskumteki pinerrluirturluki uptesqelluki, ellaitnun pivkarpek'naki.

Umyuallguteksagutellriik

(121) Theresa Moses and David Martin, April 2001:202

Theresa Moses: Arnaq-am uingan [tungiinun] tamaa-i qanruyuterluni. Agamyavkenaku uinga ayakan neqkanun tekitevkangnaqesqelluku. Tekiskan-llu, aklurugaitellruameng avani, mernurluni tekiskan, qimugtai matarqelluki petugluki tamakut-llu cingyaari quyurrluki tua-i iterrluki. Tuaten ayuqluni. Akluarakek cumikurluki, kitumun picisngairutnilukek. Tuaten nuliqsagutnilukek, atunem paukullutek, pauksagutnilukek. Angutiin cak'ngaarai murilkesqelluku atauciungraan, ca yaqulek neqa-llu itruskaku, keninrilkaku ikiurtenritlerkaanun ellisqelluku.

Atam-gguq atauciungermi uingan tekiuqurallra neqkaq tamaa-i kiagmi ikiurtevkarpeknaku kinertevkarluku auluku'urkumteni amlleriluni-gguq atam ernerni qavcini neqkaurrniartuq. Wall'u-q yaqulegnek atkungqetullemteni yaqulek-gguq atauciungraan amilek, qessavkenii ciuniuturluki

When a couple treat each other like that and become elderly together, they feel helpless without one another although they have many children. His wife becomes like a mother, and he becomes like a father to his wife. That is how my wife and I feel today. That is how it should be. It is a good thing.

They say men are the only ones capable of taking food from the water
(120) Theresa Moses, June 5, 1995:68

In everything we did in our lives there were rules to follow. Since they were to be our providers, when we married we were to respect and love our husband, even though he wasn't handsome or attractive. They said we women couldn't reach out and take food from the water. And we couldn't just extend our arms to find food in the winter. They'd say men were the only ones capable of taking food from the water. And they were able to bring home food from the wilderness in severe cold weather. We were told to prepare things for them to make it easier for them, not for them to prepare things themselves.

Two working together with one mind
(121) Theresa Moses and David Martin, April 2001:202

Theresa Moses: The following instruction was given to a woman concerning her husband. They told her not to be restless and go visiting when her husband left but to try to make it so that her husband would come home to food. And when he returned home exhausted, because they did not have a lot of tools and equipment back then, she should unharness his dogs and tie them, bring his tarps inside. That's what she would do. She would watch out for his belongings, that no one would do it for them anymore now that they were married, that they had become dependent on one another. She was told to care for her man's catches, even though it was just one bird or fish, to store it if she did not cook it so that it would not spoil.

They said that even though our husband returned home with only one animal during the summer, and we took care of it and dried it and didn't let it spoil, it would become larger in volume and could be edible after a number of days. Or back when we owned bird parkas, they told me to al-

egmian piuraasqellua—atam-gguq atauciuyaaqerraarluni atkugkanrurr-
luni. Wall'u-qaa irniam tauna atauciuyaaqerraarluni engelqaqkaku irnia-
mun piliyugngariniartuq.

   Aklui cali tamaa-i pegtangitagpek'naki elluarrluki cumikluki aulukesqelluki. Kitumun picisngairutnilunuk—wangkugnek aulukengqatarni-
lunuk. Arnartaq-llu nallunrilkaku nulirra tangerrluku mernurtevkar-
pek'naku ikayuusqelluku.

   David Martin: Unakellrungramki aipallma nuqlitaqami ellimelaraanga,
"Ukut tang natmun enekegtellerkaitnun-llu piqerki. Ukut taqimariut."
Tua-i tamaa-i cali tamatum aipaqutengermi yagarcenani callerkamek pillerkam *meaning*-aara. Tuaten-am taukuk ikayuqlutek pilriik nalqigcameg-
teki, qanertut, ukuk-gguq umyugaak atauciurtellrulliniuq, ca-gguq tamalkuan umyuarcirluku piamek. *Meaning*-aaq cali tamana tuaten ayuqluni.
Umyuallguteksagullutek-gguq tua-i taukuk nulirqelriik, ikayuqullutek
waten pilriik, paqnakutaanrilnguuk. Taukuk tua-i umyuamegen'gun um-
yuallguteksagutellriignek aterpagglukek. Tuaten nalqigcimauq tamana.

Angutem iliin pitani cumiketua yaavet nangvianun
(122) Theresa Moses, April 2001:227–28

   Alerqutuitkut uingekumta tuaten ayuqesqelluta, angun-llu cali nulia-
ngekan tuaten ayuqesqelluku. Tua-i-gguq teguaqamiu qemangqaani atu-
ngetua, yuucirluni tamana ikiulria. Tua-i kamakurluku nuliani piksailengraan. Tamatuuluni. Neqsuqngaminek cumikluku nangturnilrianek.
Tamakut tamaa-i piksailengraan apqiitnek tanemkurluku qanrutaqluku.
Neqsuyuitnitekluku nuliani canek kipukengyuitnitekluku. Tua-i tamaa-i
tuaten angutem ili ayuqetulliniuq, qungutungakluki, cukakluki cak'ngani
tamaa-i.

   Taugken-gguq angutem cak'ngani tua-i itruskuniki peggluki tua-i nu-
lirran-llu taum aulukluki. Ilai ciumek tuvqakluki, elliin-llu ilani arcaqa-
kevkenaki, kingumek taugaam tua-i ilani tuvqakluki. Tuaten-am tua-i
qanruyutnguuq tamana. Angutem-gguq pitani pegcugnaunaku ellinger-
miu tanemketua nuliani. Iliin taugken tua-i pitani itruskuniu tua-i pegg-

ways prepare it immediately and not be lazy, even though it was just one bird with the skin on — that it would become enough for a parka after it was only one piece of skin. Or it could be made into a child's garment if it fit, even though it was just one piece of skin to begin with.

They also asked us not to be careless with [a man's] clothing but to take good care of it. They told us that no one would do things for us — that we were going to start taking care of ourselves. And they told him to help his wife if he knew how to complete women's chores, not allowing a woman to get exhausted.

David Martin: Even though I had caught the animal, my late wife would tell me if she was falling behind, "Store these in a good place. These are done." That is what one is supposed to do when busy with chores. When they spoke of a couple who worked well together, they said that their minds had become one because they made decisions together. That is another piece of advice. They say two who are helping each other are starting to have one mind — [they are] ones who are not suspicious of one another. They referred to them as *umyuallguteksagutellriik* [two with the same mind, in consensus]. That is how that is explained.

Some men watch over their catches up until they are all gone
(122) Theresa Moses, April 2001:227–28

They instruct us to behave a certain way when we get a husband, and a man is told to behave a certain way when he marries as well. They say they start to display the behavior they had inside them when they marry. They start to display the bad side of their personality. [A man is] suspicious of his wife, even though she hasn't done anything. That is what that is. They really watch over their catches. Even though she hasn't done anything, he will always harass her. He always brings up the fact that his wife does not hunt for food or buy anything. That is how some men are stingy with their catches and worried about them finishing too soon.

But a man is to completely turn over the responsibility of his catch to his wife to care for when he brings it into the home. She would share the catch with his family members first, then she would think of her own family. That is a *qanruyun*. They say a man who does not give up his catch to his wife completely harasses his wife about it. But some give all of the

luku, pegteqapiggluku, aprarkaunrirluku pituniluku. Arniin taugaam aulukluku. Avani ilaliurutngullruan neqa, anrutaq.

Tamaa-i tuaten nulirran taum ilainun piarkauluku, angayuqaagkenun
ciumek. Ilaling'ermeng-llu nulirra tauna, ilai taugaam uimi arcaqakluki.
Atam-gguq uingan-llu ilai pingniarai, pitaminek taumek cingumatengnia-
rai. Ilii-gguq angutem pit'aqami pegtevkenaku pitua, nuliaminun tamana
tanemkuutekluku. Aulukeksailkaku auluksuitniluku qanevlugutekluku
nuliami umyuarteqellra unirvagluku, navgurluku qanaatekluku.

Tua-i tamaa-i qemangqaani tamana nuliangqerrsukuni yuk'egtaarmek
all'uni piarkauluni. Wall'u-q nuliqsaguskuniu-llu qemangqaani tamana
atungluku, nulirra kesianek aliayugturluni. Tuaten ayuqluni. Ava-i qung-
yarluni, piksailengraan tanemkurluku. Cumikelria pitaminek tuaten
tamaa-i ilaluku qanngutengluku, nulirra kesianek aliayugturluni. Taugken-gguq tua-i imumi angutem ilii pitani tua-i itruskuniu ellikuniu
tua-i peggluku, umyuaqngairulluku, nulirran taugaam aulukluku tuacetun. Iliin nuliami cali tuaten tua-i, ilai cali tuacetun nuliamitun piarkauluki, pitaminek neresqumaluku. Tuaten ayuqetuniaqait. Angutem iliin
pitani cumiketua yaavet nangvianun. Iliin-gguq taugken tua-i pitani
tekiuskuniu, ut'ruskuniu enemun umyuaqngairulluku.

Nulirran-gguq taum qessayulriim teq'ermun ekluku arullerkaanun
(123) Frank Andrew, October 2001:142

Taugaam augna waten nasaurluq pituat-am augkut: Nasaurlumek-
gguq aipangkuni cayunqeggialngurmek, caliyugngang'ermi qessallni maliggluku, piyuumiitellni aturluku uingeng'ermi, uqlautekluki tua-i pitai
uimi. Caliarkani caliaqesciiganaki tengruluni, uqlautekluki taugaam, tuat-
nayuullermikun-gguq uinga imna man'a nerangnaqurallra pinririinarciquq, unangyuirusngiinarluni, kiituan-gguq camek unangesciigaliuq amlleq ilii. Nulirran-gguq taum teq'ermun ekluku arullerkaanun. Imkut
tepet nunam iluanun elaulluk pitukait, uitacameng-llu tua-i assiirulluteng neryunairulluteng-llu, aruluteng. Angun-gguq tua-i tuaten tuqun-

responsibility of one's catch over to his wife when he brings it into the home. He should not have anything to do with it and would not bring it up again. But his wife should take care of it. It is because food, a stomach, was a way of strengthening family relationships.

His wife is to give his catch to his family, to his parents first. His wife is supposed to consider her husband's family first, though she has many relatives. They say her husband will eventually want to give his catch to her family. They say some men do not give all the responsibility of their catch to their wives, and they harass their wives about it. If she did not take care of it, he would argue with her about not taking care of it, hurting his wife's feelings by speaking about it.

If he wants to have a wife, he should become a wonderful person, expressing his good character traits. Or if he starts to express his bad traits when married, his wife ends up being sad all the time. That is how it is. Even though she is innocent, he accuses her and always harasses her. One who watches over the animals he caught pesters his wife about them, causing his wife to be depressed. But when some men bring their catch inside and put it down, they no longer want anything to do with it and do not think of it anymore, but his wife takes care of it. That man would treat her family like he does his own wife, wanting them to eat his catch. That is what they say they are like. Some men watch over their catch up until it is all gone. But some do not think about their catch anymore once they arrive with it and bring it in the home.

A lazy wife buries her husband in a pit to rot

(123) Frank Andrew, October 2001:142

Those people of the past said the following about a young woman: If one marries a girl who does not like to work and is lazy, even though she is capable of working, and does not do anything when she doesn't want to and makes a mess out of her husband's catches after getting married and cannot work eagerly on her chores because she is not eager but only makes a mess out of them, her husband's hunting skills will slowly diminish because of her behavior. And he will catch less and less game and eventually not be able to catch animals most of the time. They say his wife has buried him in a pit to rot. You know how they bury fish heads in un-

rilngermi, unguvang'ermi natlugnerunani picuirutarkauguq. Nulirran-gguq teq'ermun ekluku.

Nasaurluut neryugniluki camek qanesqumayuitait
(124) Edward Shavings Sr., November 2000:91

Cali *young adults married*-aumalriit qakma waten qanruyutengqelli-niukut kwangkuta yugni. Elpecenun aipaqsagutnerrarnun wall'u aapaqsa-guteksaalengerpeci illiini *married*-aarciquci, waten qanruyutengqelliniut makut nasaurluut *married*-aaraqameng-gguq uiteng kwaten cellimertur-luki kiiki qanrulluki yuilqumegg-llu apqiiluteng wall'u imarpigmek pi-yugniluteng, neryugniluteng tamakut qanesqumayuitelliniit tavaten.

Waten-gguq ilii yuum pissurluni neqsurluni-llu yuilqumi uksumi-llu aapaagni imarpigmi-llu ayagaqami imum aiparmi qanellra neq'akluku pissurnaringraan imarpik wall'u yuilqur callungraan uterrnaciatuuq nutaan-llu ilii picurlagluni tayima tekitevkenani unangengnaqluni kiiki ella assirutengraan pingnaqviirluni. Tamana qanruyutet ilakliniat. Maku-nun ayagyuanun tava wangkutnun qanruyutnguller nayagamtenun-llu ai-pamtenun-llu neq'akngamku qanrutkaqa.

Cali-llu *married*-aarpaalegmeng *girls*-at makut mingqeneq nalluarka-qenritliniat. Murilkelluki aanaci piarkaqliniaci mingqenermek wall'u *cook*-anermek keninermek nalluvkenaci piarkaulliniuci. Wii angutnguq-tangerma kenituunga, keniutetuanka irnianka augkut kiiran aipaqa ke-nirturcetevkenaku. Nutaan-llu ner'erraarluteng quyaviklua *good cook*-au-nilua irniama augkut.

Arnaq kiingan calivkarpek'naku
(125) Bennedict Tucker, November 2000:77

Wiinga aiparma imum ayagatullemni camek piqangerma inerqulallrua-nga cegganqellermini, watua maani aiparma uum. "Tauna caliaqenritan wiinga piciqaqa." Tua-llu allragnirpak casciigaliami, casciigalivkenani iru-minek pektaarciiganani, cakneq wiinga nallumciqlua, eruriyaraq man'a nallumciqluku. Cunawa tua-i cakneq iluteqem tusngalallinikii ellii alar-

derground pits, and they become inedible and rot if left alone. They make the same reference, that a man will lose his ability to catch game even though he has not died, even though he is alive and healthy. They say that his wife has buried him in a pit.

They tell women not to request specific foods to eat
(124) Edward Shavings Sr., November 2000:91

There is a *qanruyun* for young married couples. For those new couples or even unmarried couples, when you get married someday there is a rule for girls not to request [their husbands] to acquire [animals] in the wilderness or ocean, not to ask for specific food to eat.

When some people are hunting and fishing in the wilderness during the winter or even in the ocean, they will remember what their partner said while traveling. And even though the conditions are not good out in the ocean and the weather is bad in the wilderness, they return home late, and some get into fatal accidents and don't return home, trying to catch game in bad weather. That is one of the *qanruyutet* for these young people. It was a rule to us, our younger sisters, and to our partners. I am telling you about it because I have remembered it.

And these girls are supposed to know how to sew before getting married. You are supposed to observe your mothers and know how to sew and cook. Even though I am a male, I cook. I cook for my children, not letting my wife be the only one to cook. And after eating, my children thank me and tell me that I am a good cook.

Do not let a woman work on tasks alone
(125) Bennedict Tucker, November 2000:77

When I was young and able to travel and did housework, whenever I did some housework my wife would tell me when she was healthy, "That is not your task, I will do it." And this past year, now that she is not able to work, she is not fully incapable but cannot move around with her legs, I try to do housework and do dishes not really knowing how. And now

tellrulliniluni-gguq tuaten inerqulallruanga, erurisqevkenii ellii piciqniluni.

Waten aiparluni caarkaicugnaqlartuq iliini angun. Arnaq tuaten kiingan calivkarpek'naku enem iluani carrirnarqellria carrirluku, tua-i cat aiparminun caliaqerrlainarcetevkenaki. Pitsaqevkenani una waten piyunairtellerkaq alqunaq una pistaunani, panini-llu tayima nani uinglutengllu *school*-arluteng-llu *high school*-arluteng. Tua-i alqunaq una pilleq atawaunritliniuq, nallumciqnaqluni. Tua-i iliikun temciklartua wangnek aipaqa-llu qanrulluku alarvikaqama canek. Cakneq tua-i yuut itraqata tua-i qanrut'larai arnaullgutni, "Alartelallrullinilrianga tang tua-i ilumun. Enem iluani piyukan angun tua-i ikayuqlutek tua-i piarkauguk."

Qanaatepigainalriatun wangni ayuqelarapuk

(126) Paul John, November 2000:82–84

Ava-i qanqertua irniamnek wii elissarinritqapiarallemnek wii aipaqucaram tungiinek. Taugaam tuaten elicarinrilngerma waniwa aanasengllu pinerrluatevkarlunuk tangerpailgatkuk man'a tekitarpuk. Tamaaggun tamaa-i qaneqsailengramegnuk irniapuk tangalilingnaqluki aipaqutellerkaatnek elluarrluteng tua-i qanaatepigainalriatun wangni ayuqelarapuk. Tangalilinrilkurtellmegnegun, qanllemegnegun tallimegnegun, tua-i man'a maa-i erneq tekilluku.

Cali-llu ava-i kan'a qanelria aipaagni pinqigcuumilallragnek keniryaramek mat'umek nalluniqellranek. Wiinga kenillerkaqa-wa tua-i uivaksiyaanrilamku makunek keniryaranek cumikluki pilaamki. Waten cali yuilqumun ayagangyaurteqarrallemteni alerquumatullruamta, una-gguq ciulirnerput maligeskengarput keniuskilaut yuilqumi. Tamaa-i wangkuta waten tan'gurrameggni ciulirnemta malikaqamegtekut imutun tua-i tegussuukelriatun ayuqetullruitkut. Arulaiquneng kenirnarqellriamek neqkangqerquneng ellimerrluta, "Kitak muragkiurluten kenia." Tua-i tamaa-i maligtaquluki tamaaggun ayagniutekluku kenineq imutun nallunrilriatun ayuqluku.

she regrets and feels sad that she made a mistake not allowing me to wash dishes, telling me that she would do chores herself.

Men sometimes don't have much to do at home when they have partners. [A man shouldn't] let a woman do all the work at home, cleaning things that need to be cleaned inside the house. He shouldn't leave everything up to the spouse, [keeping in mind] that she could suddenly become handicapped, leaving no one around to complete tasks while their daughters are now on their own with husbands or attending high school. It is not good when one suddenly has to do things and no one else is around to complete tasks. It causes one to feel helpless. Sometimes I laugh at myself, and I tell my wife when I make mistakes. When people come inside our home, she tells her female friends, "I indeed made a mistake. If a man wants to complete tasks inside the home, a couple is supposed to help each other."

We taught them through our actions
(126) Paul John, November 2000:82–84

Earlier I said that I did not teach my children about responsibilities of marriage whatsoever. Even though I did not teach them, they have not seen their mother and me fight and argue up to this day. Even though we have not spoken to them about these ways, I believe we have taught them through our actions. By not being abusive to each other through our words and arms, we have taught them something.

That person said earlier that his wife regretted not letting him cook — that he did not know how to cook. Because I am not so helpless when it comes to cooking, I used to watch others cooking. When we first started traveling to the wilderness, we were told to cook for our elders traveling with us in the wilderness. When our elders brought us young men along, we were their helpers. If they had food to be cooked when they stopped, they would say to us, "Gather some wood and cook." By following their requests, we learned how to cook for the first time.

Ingluilkuni-gguq angun cimirciquq

(127) Frank Andrew, September 2000:141

Tuamtellu yuk temirtengurtellni tekilluku-llu aug'ariyugngaluni, ayuqu-ciminek katagiyugngaluni. Cali-llu waten qalarucimalallruukut tan'gaur-luq-gguq nasaurluq-llu aipaqsaguskunek, waten ilii aipaan umyugaa piniallrukuni, arnam wall'u angutem, angutem nuliani qanleralluku pilar-ciqaa umyugaa navgumaluni, kenekluku imumun aipaqsagutellerminun qancurlagalluku. Arnam-gguq taum inglulirpek'naku nepaunani niicug-niciqaa wall'u unilluku anluni. Tua-i-llu-gguq tauna angun nuliani tuat-nalaryaaqerraarluku ingluilkuni, ingluliunrilani ayuqeliluku pivakarluni umyuangluni, "Wii tang picurlagkun pilalrianga. Aug'utun atak aipam-tun ayuqlirilii." Tua-i-gguq tauna kiturcecinrilnguq. Umyuarput uuggun erinamek tapirluku anpailemteni taq'lartuq wani, ircaqumtenun pilartuq, assilria assinrilnguq-llu. Tauna-gguq tua-i arnaq qanruyutem atullrakun taugaam pilria, ingluliurpek'naku cangalliuqsaunani-llu tuaten pingraani kiturcetaqluku ciuniurpek'naku arnauli wall'u angutnguli. Imkuk-gguq taugken waten ingluklutek pilriik nuliqsaaqeng'ermek aiparmi piaqani ayuqeliluku piaqluni, kiituan yagirat'nguk. Mikelngungqerngaituk-gguq assilrianek; irniangqerngaunatek assilrianek tuaten pitukunek. Carrlug-nek-gguq calilriaruciquk irniamegnek, arcaqanruarkanek-llu tayima ell-megni.

Nalluskariinnek taugaam nuliangeciqniluku

(128) Theresa Moses, April 2001:137

Tuamtell-am qanrutkumayuilan tan'gurraq, qaillun tua-i ikiuluni yuu-luni, qanrutkumaksailkan makut piciqut nalluskariinek taugaam nulia-ngeciqniluku. Wall'u tua-i arnaukan nalluskariinun taugaam uingeciq-niluku. Qanrutkuurumayuilkan tauna waten tan'gurraq ayuqniluku, tua-i-llu tauna ikiullra qanrutkumayuilkan piciqut ilait, nalluskariinun taugaam nuliangeciqniluku. Wall'u arnaq cali tuaten ayuqluni. Nallus-kariinek taugaam uingeciqniluku. Nauwa tua-i akwaugaq wiinga niitetull-ruunga uilgarnek. Qanranun uilgirniluku. Tuacetun ayuqluni.

If a man does not have an opponent, he will change

(127) Frank Andrew, September 2000:141

Also, when people become adults they can change their ways and abandon some of their behavior. And we were also told that when a young man and woman became a couple, if either the woman's or man's mind is weaker, a man will speak abusively to his wife when angry, speaking abusively to the one he had loved and married. That woman will listen to him silently and not fight back, or she will go out of the home. They say that if that man does not have an opponent, if she does not counter him, after treating her [badly] he will start to think, "I do things in a troublesome way. Let me be like my wife." That is a person who does not let things pass. Before we express what we are thinking using our voice, whether good or bad, it stops here in our heart. They say that woman who follows the rules, does not counter her husband, and isn't bothered by it and lets it pass is following the rules. But they say a couple who argue and fight, one who reacts the same way when her husband picks on her, eventually will start to hit each other. They will not have good children; they will not have good offspring if they behave that way. They will be teaching their children bad behavior; [their children] will behave worse than them.

A troublesome man can only marry a woman who doesn't know his character

(128) Theresa Moses, April 2001:137

And again, since no one spoke of the young man's behavior, one who was living a disgraceful life, since his behavior was obscure, they'd say he would only marry a girl who doesn't know about him. And if a woman is like that, they would say that she will only marry someone who doesn't know her. If no one talks about what that young man is like, if no one speaks of his bad behavior, some will say that he can only marry a woman who doesn't know what he is like. And a woman is the same way. She can marry a man who doesn't know her. You know how we heard about those husbandless women yesterday. They say their mouths have caused them to be husbandless. That is what that is like.

Tuamtellu ilii piciquq nulirtutuyaaqellruniluku augna nulirtuyuirutni-luku. Tua-i-wa nuliani anagulluku qutgulluku nuliqngani, yagipraluku, caluku tua-i nanglluku. Nallunriqunegteggu niicuirutarkauluku. Tua-i tamaa-i nalluskariinek taugaam piciqniluku. Qaneryarat augkut amllell-riit. Tua-i yuum ikianek qanerturquvet nallunrilkengarpenek tuarpiaq-gguq iniluku, initamun iniissuucirluku agarrluku. Tamaa-i taringcetaa-rutait ayuqenrilnguut.

And someone would say that a particular man had been married before but could not be married anymore. When he married a woman, he would be verbally and physically abusive and act superior to her. If they learned how he was, they would no longer want to marry him. That is what that is, that he can only marry a woman who doesn't know him. There are many instructions. If you continually speak about the bad behavior of a person you know, it would seem that you are hanging him on a clothesline, hanging him on a clothesline with clothespins. Those are some of their many examples.

CHAPTER 6

Ilameggnek Tukuulriit

Nunanun tekiskuvci qanernarqeqallerkarci murilkekiciu

(129) Frank Andrew, June 2001:14

Nunanun ayagalangarcamta tua-i inerqutullruitkut waten: "Kitaki-ata nunanun tekiskuvci murilkelluci pikici, qanernarqeqallerkarci murilkelluku. Takarnarquq nunalgutkumanrilnguut nuniit." Tuamtellu tua-i tamana inerquutaqellruarput. Cat-llu tua-i akluit tegulaasqevkenaki qigcikluki tua-i nunanun tekiskumta pisqelluki. Taugaam arenqiallugeskumta ikayurtekamtenek tua-i nutaan kaigaluta pisqelluta. Tuamtellu waten nunalinqigtellria, nunakenrilkeminun ayagluni tuavet inerquutaqaa cali tamana. Tuantarkauluni nunani alaitenritengnaqluni mulngakluni ellminek, atanirtungnaqevkenaki-llu, yuullrat taugaam ellaita maligqurluki. Atam-gguq umyuani aturluku pilriarukuni nep'ngevkarniarai taukut nunat. Tamaa-i kangia tamatum.

Waten pitullruitkut, waniwa-gguq nunanun tekicarauguq, nunakenrilkengaminun, takaryugluni, natmun-llu ciunillerkaunani. Ilii-gguq taugken nallunrilkengangqerquni tungayuminun ciuniryugngaluni. Taugaamgguq tuatnanrilnguq tua-i aug'utun, natmun tua-i pillerkani nalluluku, takaryugluni tua-i tekilluni nunanun. Waten alerqutullruitkut, kitakigguq allaneq tekiskan egmianun ciuniuqilaut nutaan tangengrramteggu kituucilengramteggu-llu ilaliurluku cakneq. Tamaa-i tamatumek alerquutetangqertuq.

Tua-i kituunivkenaku tua-i ciuniuresqelluku, eneminun-llu ciuniurtelluku nerevkarluku, qanenrilnguarutevkenaku. Atam-gguq tuatnakuni tungayai amllereniartut. Ilumuuluni piciuluni-llu tamana. Nunani tua-i nani uitang'ermi umyuaqnarqetullliniluni. Carrarmek tua-i tuyurluni-llu pinarqetulliniluni, tuaten ayuqutellni umyuaqnaqliniluni.

CHAPTER 6

Those Who Are Rich in Relatives

When you arrive in another village, be careful not to be a source of trouble
(129) Frank Andrew, June 2001:14

When we started traveling to other villages, they admonished us about the following: "Be careful when you arrive in other villages. Be careful about being the source of trouble. If you are not from that village, you have to respect the members and the community." That was how we were admonished. And they told us not to take things that belong to people in other villages but to respect them. They told us to ask for help only when we were in a difficult situation. That is also an admonition for one who has moved to another village that is not his own. He is supposed to live in that village by trying not to be noticeable, being careful and trying not to boss others around and following their ways. They said one who does as he pleases will cause turmoil in the village. That is the meaning of that.

They told us that this is how one should arrive in a village that one doesn't live in, being shy and not knowing where to go. But one who has acquaintances can go to his known relatives first. But one who is not in that situation, one who doesn't know where to go, is shy when he arrives at a village. They told us that we should receive a newly arrived visitor immediately, even if we have never seen him before and don't know who he is, being friendly toward him. That is an *alerquun*.

They told us to greet him and bring him to our home, feed him, and not ignore him just because we don't know him. They say a person who does that gains many relatives. This is a good way to be, and it's true. They are in our thoughts, even if they live in another village. One wants to send [the one who welcomed him] gifts, remembering how one was treated.

Ciuliamta tangelteng tamalkuan ciuniutullruat

(130) David Martin, Theresa Moses, and Lucy Sparck, April 2001:126

David Martin: Camiungungraan tekitellria ilakluku tua-i nutaan tangengermegteggu, ilakelriatun tua-i aulukluku tua-i, ciuniurluku. Man'a makut-wa tua-i qanertet qanrutketukiit nall'arrluku ciuliat augkut ayuqucingqellrulliniut, tangelteng tamalkuan ilakluku tua-i, nutaan tangengermegteggu ilakluki.

Lucy Sparck: Tamana-llu-qaa allaniuryaraq cali qaneryarangqertuq?

David Martin: Allaniuryaraq-am cali waten meaning-aaq tamana qanrutkumauq. Nutaan tangerkeka-am tauna pitateka wall'u ak'allauli, wall'u ayagyuarli, takaryuarnarquq. Wiinga-wa tua-i tangellra tauna tamalkuan takaryuarautekluku pillruamku. Nutaan-gguq tangerkumku piyugngarikuma, canek-llu waten neqalleruarnek qemangqaangqerrsaureskuma nutaan tangengramku tauna tua-i piyugngaaqa, "Kainiqkuvet nerevkaryugngaamken," nutaan-gguq tangengrramku tua-i tauna. Allaniuryaraq apyutii. Tua-i-gguq tauna apeskengaqa kitumek pistailkuni quuyuaqalriatun piciquq. Tuaten tamana cali qanrutekluku.

Tua-i-gguq tamaa-i ilakaqa tauna tua-i nutaan tangengrramku. Ukutun ilamtun tua-i pitarrluku ilakaqa tua-i. Tamana-am *meaning*-aaq tuaten tua-i qanrutkaat cali. Nutaan tangengrraaku tua-i ciuniuresqelluku. Waten taugaam-gguq qanenrilkurtellria takarnarquq. Ilumun tua-i wiinga maa-i elitaqumaaqa cali tamana. Ayagyuangermi qanenrilkurtellria takarnarquq. Taugken cali temyigingermi qanenrilkurtellira cali takarnaqluni, ayagyuarluni. Piqalriani taugken tua-i nutaan nallunairluni tua-i umyugaa takaryunriqerrnganani. Tamana pitekluku wii waniwa tangellrenka tamalkuita tua-i piuratuanka, takaryugyaraa yuum nallunrilamku tua-i. Ayagyuarli, ak'allauli, tangellrenka tamalkuita tua-i piurluki alerquun tamana maliggluku.

Theresa Moses: Mikelnguum-gguq quyallni nalluyagucuitaa. Piyugngariaqami-gguq tauna naklekestellni nalluyagusngaitaa. Akinauryugngaa-gguq ellii call' kingumek quyavkarluku. Maa-i makut wangkutnun qanruyutellret. Tangnerrluknguarpek'naku yuk ayuqluku tangvaasqelluku.

Tua-i-w' allamek alerquacetailngalnguq allaneq una alerquutekellrukvut kaillranek, anrutaanek qaillun ayuqengraan, tangnerrlugnarqengraan nerevkaasqelluku nereksailkan. Tuacetun piluku. Wall'u tangerrluku

Our ancestors welcomed everyone they saw

(130) David Martin, Theresa Moses, and Lucy Sparck, April 2001:126

David Martin: No matter where a stranger who had just arrived was from, we welcomed and took care of him like a relative. These instructors were right when they said our ancestors welcomed everyone they saw, even if they saw them for the first time. They considered them relatives.

Lucy Sparck: And are there instructions for *allaniuryaraq* [the way of treating *allanret* (guests or strangers)]?

David Martin: Allaniuryaraq is also explained in this way. I am shy around a person my age, an elder, or a young adult I see for the first time. I was always shy toward everyone I came across. They said that if I saw them for the first time and I was able to provide for myself and had started storing a little food, I could tell him, even though I saw him for the first time, "I can feed you if you are starving," even if I saw this person for the first time. That is what is said about *allaniuryaraq.* They said that the person whom I asked would be grateful if he did not have anyone to receive him. That is how they explained it also.

They say we are related to someone even though we see him for the first time. They say he is a relative just like my real relatives. That is what they said. They told me to welcome someone even if I saw him for the first time. However, they say that a person who refuses to speak is intimidating. I encounter these situations all the time. A person who refuses to speak causes us to feel shy even if he is a young person. And even an adult is hard to approach and causes us to feel inhibited, and a young person can be the same way. But it seems they lose their inhibitions when we speak to them a little. I always welcome everyone I meet for that reason. I always acknowledge everyone I encounter, be they young or elderly, following that *alerquun* because I know that people can be shy.

Theresa Moses: They say children never forget the gratitude they felt. They never forget the person who felt compassion for them when they get older. They can repay them, causing one who caused them to be grateful to feel the same way. These were our instructions. They told us to treat everyone the same and not treat them badly.

There is not another teaching concerning visitors, but we were told to ask him if he is hungry, always being concerned about his stomach no matter what he looked like, and asking him to eat if he hasn't eaten. That

yuuviksugngakumteggu yuuvikluku aturamta iliinek. Angutngung'ermi-
llu tuaten pilallilria. Tangerrluku yuuvikluku tua-i, wagg'uq iknilluku
tamaa-i qainga tangerrluku iknilluku. Aturaput atauciunrilkan tangerrluku tua-i qailiqengraan qaikegcilriatun pitarrluku allaneqesqelluku
tua-i qainga tangerrluku ataucimek pingqenrilkumta yuuvikluku-gguq
wagg'uq iknilluku.

Neqa tungayagtunarquq

(131) Frank Andrew, October 2001:151

   Nutaan allanret alerquutnguut. Waten tungayailnguq wall'u nallun-
rilkengailnguq nunani tekicartuquni, nunanun natmun ciuniurvigkani
tua-i nalluluku. Tuaten piyugngaluni. Kia tua-i imum pingaunaku tua-i
nunat ilait assiitut avani. Allaneryunqeggianateng. Allaniuyuunateng. Tamatumek qanrucimatuyaaqellilriit. Wangkuta tua-i avani Kuigilngurmi
ellangellemteni qalarucimatullruukut allaneq tekitellrani tangrraarluki
uluusqevkenaku arnaungraan. Egmianun ciuniuresqelluku qanenrilnguarutevkenaku camiungungraan tua-i ciuniurluku pisqelluku, tangrraar-
luku ulurpek'naku. Tuaten-gguq ayuqelria auguuguq, auguuciquq, waten
tungayai amlleriluteng, *friend*-ai amlleriarkauluteng, yugkun ataucikun
apervikuatekaqluku, apervikuatekellrakun kingunranek. Uumikuan-llu
tengruluni nallunrilamiu wall'u carrarnek neqa'arnek cikiutekainek ang'aqluni tuavirtarkauluni nuniinun. Malingqerquni-llu anglirikanirluni. Tu-
ngayagtunarquq tua-i neqa, yuum aqsaqruanun atuulria. Neqallerruar
man'a-llu-gguq qanruyun qaneryaraq ilaliurluku tuaten pillra, qanenrilnguarutevkenaku, takaqevkenaku. Ciulirneret tua-i makut takarnaqsaa-
qut, taugaam allaneq tuaten pisqenritaat, takarnarqengraan ciuniuresqelluku. Arnat-llu cali tuaten alerquutekluku angutet augkut pimaciicetun
cakanirpek'naku. Arnaullgutait camiungungraata qanenrilnguarutevke-
naki ilaliurluki taugaam. Assirluni tua-i ciuniurluki, nalluyurnaunani.

is how they asked us to treat [a stranger]. Or we should give him some of our clothing if we see that he needs it, if we can spare clothing. That is probably the case for men, also. Removing our clothing and giving it to one who needs it, what they called *iknilluku,* giving him our clothing after seeing he needs it. They told us to receive him as a guest and treat him like one who is clean and attractive even though he is unattractive, and give him clothing if we have more than one set.

Food is a source of having a large family
(131) Frank Andrew, October 2001:151

[We were especially] taught about welcoming *allanret* [guests or strangers]. Someone with no relatives or acquaintances will not know where to go when arriving in a village. That is what can happen. No one will welcome him, because some villages were not friendly back then. They were not friendly toward strangers and visitors. They were not open and welcoming. When I became aware of my surroundings in Kwigillingok, we were told not to look at a visitor who had just arrived and then to look away, even if they were women. [They told us to] welcome them immediately and not ignore them no matter where they were from, to welcome them and not look away. They say a person who is like that will gain more relatives and friends, and others will speak of them. And the person they welcomed will be excited to see them again or will take a small amount of food as a gift when they come again. And if they have a traveling companion, they will gain even more [friends]. They say that food that replenishes a person's stomach is a source of gaining a lot of family. *Neqallerruar* [A little food] and also giving instruction, being friendly toward others and not being silent and reserved toward them. Elders are generally very respectable, but they tell us not to treat strangers like that. They tell us to welcome others, even though we are afraid to approach them. That was a teaching for women also, and it is no different than what men were taught. Not to be silent toward other women from other villages but to be friendly. It is better to welcome them, not causing them to feel unwelcome.

Tuqluucaraq

Tuqluutet

(132) Paul and Martina John, Simeon Agnus, and Alice Rearden, June 11, 2000

Alice Rearden: Pisqumaat tuqluucaraq.

Paul John: Tuqluun-llu una arcaqanra ciukluku pinaqsaaqellria. Waniwa ayuqenrilamta Yup'ik, Kass'aq wall'u cakucit, wangkuta ciuliamta Yup'igni ilakuyutellratnek, tua-i imumek ilakuyutellratnek piqatartukut, wagg'uq tuqluutetgun. Tua-i ilakuyutqapiartuq una tuqluun wangkutni Yup'igni, tua-i ilakuyutqapiarauluni.

Taringnanrullrakun piciqaqa tuqluun. Aipaqliuskunek ukuk nulirqelriik irniangekunek, irniaragnek ukuk angayuqakek, aaniin wall'u-qaa cali atiin aanii atii-wa, tua-i taukuk tamalkukenka angayuqakek angayuqaagmi apaurluklukek angutek, arnak-llu maurluqlukek. Tua-i tuaten taringnanruciqngatellrakun. Tua-i-llu taukuk nulirqelriik anelgutengqerramek cali tayima, angutii tauna angutngullgutminek anelgutengqerqan, anelgutii cali angutiin taum irniangluni. Irniangekan, tua-i wangkuta Yup'igni piciryaraqluku, angutngullgutekngamek irniakek anngaqluteng uyu'uqluteng-llu. Cali-llu nulirra arnaullgutminek anelgutengqerquni, cangallruvkenani irniakek cali anelgutni-llu uyu'uqlutek. Tuaten tuqluuteput ayuqluteng.

Tua-i-llu taukuk irniakenka, taum atami *brother*-aa tuqlutuluku ataataminek, *uncle*-aaminek pivkenaku, ataataminek taugaam. Taum-llu cali aaniin *sister*-aara tuqlutuluku anaanaminek. Tua-i arnaullgutekngaku aanami atami-llu cali angutngullgutekngaku, tauna ataatameggnek tua-i tuqlutuluku. Taukuk-llu arnarrlainaak cali alqaqelriik, irniakenka aanamek *sister*-aara anaanakluku.

CHAPTER 7

The Way of Addressing One's Relatives

Kinship terms

(132) Paul and Martina John, Simeon Agnus, and Alice Rearden, June 11, 2000

Alice Rearden: They want you to speak about *tuqluryaraq* [the way of knowing one's relatives].

Paul John: The knowledge of kinship and the terms used by relatives are most important and should be taught first. Because Yup'ik people, white people, and other races have different traditions, we are going to describe how our Yup'ik system of relationships worked through *tuqluutet* [kinship and relational terms]. Our use of *tuqluutet* was a way of knowing our relatives. It is a system that kept families together.

I will describe *tuqluutet* in a way that seems most understandable. If a couple marries and has children, the child's parents' mother and father will be his *maurluq* [grandmother] if female and *apa'urluq* [grandfather] if male. I am describing this in a way that is most understandable. And if the couple have siblings, if the husband has a brother who got married and has children, because they are brothers, their children would consider each other brothers and sisters. And if his wife has a sister, her children and her sister's children would be considered siblings as well. That is how our kinship system works.

And their children would call their father's brother, their paternal uncle *ataata* [father's brother], not uncle, but *ataata*. And the mother's sister, their maternal aunt would be called *anaana*. And the kinship term for his father's brother is *ataata*, and the children of sisters would call their mother's sister *anaana*.

Tua-i-llu cali aatakek *sister*-aangqerquneng arnanek, arnaq tauna *sister*-aara irniangluni, tauna cali *brother*-aara irniangluni, nutaan tauna arnam irniaran tauna angun angakluku, tua-i-wa aanani arnaungan, *brother*-aara-llu tauna angutnguami. Irniaran arnam, tauna angun, tauna *brother*-aara angaminek tuqlutuluku. Arnam irniaran angun tauna tuqlurluku angaminek. Arnaungami-wa tua-i tauna aani, angun tauna *brother*-aara angakluku.

Augna-wa ava-i qanrutekqataryaaqelqa apqen. Angutem irniaran arnaq *sister*-aara atami, acakluku, acacungaqluku tua-i acakluku. Tua-i-llu cali arnam, anngarmi irniara an'gaqluku, wall'u uyu'urmi angutngukan irniara an'gaqluku, arnam. Anelgutmi irniara tua-i, angutem irniara an'gaqluku. Cali taugken arnaullgutmi irniaqekaku nurr'aqluku irniara.

Tua-i taugken taukuk tua-i Kass'at tuqluutiitgun tamarmek taukuk *nephew*-rulutek. Wangkutni taugken Yup'igni ayuqevkenatek, Kass'at ayuqlukek *nephew*-qetungraitkek.

Tua-i-llu taukuk-am angayuqertuumiimek nulirqellriik irniarak irniangluni. Irniangekunek taukuk angayuqertuumiimek ava-i apellruyaaqengramku apa'urluqlukek tua-i irniakenka. Tua-llu taukuk imkuk apa'urluulriik tutgarakek irniangekuneng, irniakenka taukuk amauqlukek. Tamarkenka nulirqellriik, arnak angun-llu atauciuluni tuqluutiik, amaurulutek tamarmek.

Tua-i-llu taukuk tutgarakek cali unguvainanragni taukuk apa'urluunkuk maurluq-llu irniangekata, tutgaramek irniarit tuqlutuluki cali tamarmek taukuk maurluum apa'urluum-llu iluperamegnek. Tua-i tutgarmek irniarit iluperaqluki.

Tua-i-ll'-am cali taukuk unguvainanermegni iluperakek irniangluteng. Cali-am taukuk amauk iluperamek irniakek unguvainanermegni irniangekata wagg'uq maqamyuarutekluki, tua-llu neruvailitaq.

Tua-i-llu tamakut tamaa-i tuqluutet cumikelriani tua-i tungelquni-llu nallunritarkauluki. Atami tuqluqaku tauna caminek, elliin-llu taringluku cakliniaqa wii una. Aanami-llu cali tuqluqaku caminek, cali taringnaqluni. Tua-i tamakut tuqluutet murilkelluki, niicugniluki taringumalriani, tungelqut tamakutgun tuqluutetgun tua-i nallunarqevkenateng, taringumanaqluteng.

Wiinga waniwa taringumiimki tuqluutet, maa-i elpeci nalluvceni ayuqeltassiigutengqelartua uumek *reservation*-aamek. Cakun ayagyugaqavci *reservation*-aalivailegpeci augtaryutuuci, "Ayausngaitellikiinga-wa." Tua-i

And if their father has a sister and she has children, her children would call their maternal uncle *angak*. The man would be the *angak* of his sister's child. That man would be the *angak* because [the child's] mother is a woman and her brother is a man. The children of the sister would call her brother by the kinship term *angak*. A woman's child would call her brother *angak*. Because the mother is a woman, her brother would be [her child's] *angak*.

You just mentioned what I was going to say. The child called his father's sister, his paternal aunt, *acak* or *acacungaq* [little father's sister]. And a female sibling would call her older or younger brother's children [both male and female] *an'garat*. And the female sibling would call her younger or older sister's children [both male and female] *nurr'at*.

But in the Western kinship system, they are both referred to as nephews [whether it is a brother's child or a sister's child]. But in the Yup'ik way, we use different terms for the sister's side and the brother's side.

Then the couple's child has a child of his own, and the couple's parents are still alive. Even though I mentioned it earlier, the couple's parents would be grandparents to their children. And then if those grandparents' grandchild has a child, he would call both the women and the men his *amauq* [great-grandparent].

And if the grandchildren of grandparents have children while they are still alive, they would call their great-grandchildren *iluperat*.

Now, the great-grandparents, while they are still alive, when their *iluperat* have children, they call them *maqamyuarutet* [great-great-grandchildren], then *neruvailitaq* [great-great-great-grandchild].

If one pays close attention to the *tuqluutet*, he would know who his relatives are. If his father uses a certain term when referring to a particular person, he will immediately understand how he is related to that person. And if their mother also uses a kinship term and reveals how she is related to a particular person, they will understand how they are related to that person. If a person pays close attention to the *tuqluutet*, listens to them and understands them, it is easy to know how a person is related. They are easy to understand.

Because I understand *tuqluutet*, I compare it to the way people make reservations. If you want to travel with no reservation, you worry about whether you are going to go or not. And before you call the hotel and make arrangements to stay there, you are also unsure of where you are

augtaryugluci. Tuamtellu ciunerkarci *call*-arpailegpeciu *hotel*-aaq, cali na-nelvigkaunaci umyuarci. Tua-i-llu tengssuun *call*-aquvceni *reservation*-aaliyugniluci, apqevcenek *confirm*-aqaci, caceturiqerrluci, "Tua-i ayau-cestekangua." Tuamtellu *hotel*-aat *call*-aquvciki, *room*-arkangqernikaceci caceturiqerrluci, "Tua-i qavarvigkangua." Tuacetun tang augkut ciuliamta tungelquarateng tuqluutait apertuaguratullermeggni waten irniameggnun ayagyuameggnun-llu, tuacetun ayuqellrullinikait *reservation*-aliural-riatun. Pektaukata nanikuanritlerkaat pitekluku. Naklekestekait nalluv-karpeknaki, tungelquarait apertuagurluki. Tua-i *reservation*-aaliyarami cangallruvkenani tamana. Ayagyuateng *reservation*-aaliuralriatun aper-tuaqurallermegteggun tungelqurritnek ayuqetullrulliniluki.

Tua-i tamaani tuaten ayuqumiiceteng ayagyuateng angayuqrita, aper-tullritnun nunanun ayagluteng, tekitaqameng augtaqevkenaki nereksaita-qameng neryartutuluteng, inarcartutuluteng qavarnariaqameng tamaku-nun ciulirnemi apertualallritnun. Nalluvkenaki piameng augtaqevkenaki tua-i, ullagluki neryugngaluteng, inarcugngaluteng, nanikuavkenateng. Tuarpiaq ak'a *reservation*-alilaiceteng angayuqameng.

Cali-llu angayuqameng atrit nallunrilamegteki, taum ciuneni tanger-qaqsaunaku apertuumalriim atrakun tungelquni, cauciilkani qanruciiq-luku, "Pim yukaanga." Tua-i-llu taum ciunran taringareskuniu, ava-i cak-neq ciuniurluku naklekarkaqlinillni taringarcamiu ciuniurluku cakneq tua-i ikayualuku, kaigcecugnaunaku, qavarviiturcecugnaunaku.

Cali-llu taum ayagyuam tauna apertuamalria tungelquni nani eneng-qerruciilkaku ciuneni, yuut aptesqelluki aterpaggluku tauna nani eneng-qerrucianek. Tua-i-llu apyutkekaku, taum aptestek'ngaan eniinek aper-tuucugngaluku. Apertuuskani tua-i tuavet augtaqevkenaku ag'arkauluni taum ilani tua-i apertuallruatgu ilakniluku.

Tuqluun-qaa cali qanaateklerkani ilangqertuq?
Martina John: Iluraat piksaitaten. Ilu'urqelriit piksaitaten.

going to stay. And if you call the airlines wanting to make a reservation and they confirm your reservations, you feel more secure knowing that you have a way to travel. "I have a way to travel." And then if you call the hotels, when they tell you that you have a room, you feel more secure knowing "I have a place to sleep." That is comparable to how our ancestors used to reveal their relatives' *tuqluutet* to their children and young people, just like they were always making reservations when they were traveling. They let them know who was going to feel compassion and pity for them and always revealed the names of their relatives so that they would not worry. That system [of knowing relatives] is no different than making reservations. When they constantly revealed who their relatives were to their young people, it was like they were always making reservations for them.

Because young people's parents [revealed who their relatives were] back then, when they traveled to villages and arrived, they would go to the relatives they were told about without feeling unsure, and they would go and eat if they hadn't eaten. And when it was time to go to bed, they would sleep at the houses of those people whom their elders told them about. They did not feel uncomfortable, because they knew who they were, and they could go to them to eat and sleep without worry. It was like their parents had already made reservations for them.

And because they knew their parents' names, a person who had never been in a particular village but had been told who his relatives were by name, if he did not know them, he would tell them, "I am a child of this person." And if the person whom he told understood how they were related, he would receive him gladly, because they understood that they were supposed to feel compassion and pity for him, and they would receive him openly, help him, not let him go hungry or be without a place to sleep.

And if a young person who was told who his relatives were didn't know where their home was located, he was told to ask others. And if he asked about [his relatives by name], the person he asked could show him where their home was located, and, when shown, he could go there without feeling uncomfortable, because he was told by his relatives that those particular people were related to him.

Is there any more to say about *tuqluutet?*

Martina John: You haven't described *ilurat* [father's sister's sons, mother's brother's sons]. You have not described the relationship between *ilurat.*

Simeon Agnus: Makut ilu'urqelriit qanrutekluki tua-i piyaaqekai. An'nga-qellriik una wani angun arnaq-llu irniakek nakmiin ilu'urqerkaulutek. Ukuk wani an'ngaa una uyuraa arnaq irniakek tua-i nakmiin ilu'uqlutek. Nakmiin tua-i ilu'urqeqapiarlutek.

Paul John: Ava-i-wa tua-i qanqauteksaaqellrukeka, taugaam waten uumek ilangqerrsugngauq. Aatami ilu'uqnillrukaku, elliin cali taringluku atami iluraan irniari ilu'urquciit. Aatameng iluraita irniarit elliitun ilu'uqluki. Tamaa-i tangeqsaileng'ermiki, taringluku tauna atami ilu'uqnikaku, elliin cali irniari taum ilu'uqnillran taringluku ilu'urquciit. Tuaten tua-i ayuqluni.

Tua-llu cali aanami angun una uicungaminek, nutaan-llu irniaran tangerrluku, aaniin-llu tua-i uicungaminek tuqluqaku, taringnaqluni waten, "Wii angakliniaqa una." Tuamtellu atami tangeqsailkeni tuqluqaku ilu'urminek angutngullgutni, elliin cali taringluku, "Wii una ataatakliniaqa." Tamaa-i tuaten tua-i arnaung'ermeng ayuqluteng angutet-llu. Arnam arnaullgutni tuqluqaqaku ilungaminek, tua-i tuaten augkutun cangallruvkenani, ayuqlutek.

Ava-i apellrungramku, aanami ilungaminek tuqluqaku arnaq angutngulriani, nuliacungaminek cali tuqlullerkaa taringnaqluni. Aanami ilungaminek tuqlullran pania nuliacungaminek tuqlullerkaa tayim taringnaqluni.

Tuqluutet, atret-llu

(133) Frank and Noah Andrew and Alice Rearden, September 2000:64

Frank Andrew: Tuqluutet waten ayuqut ciuliamtenek ayagluta. Nuliqsaguskunek, una allagnek nulirra angayuqerluni, uinga-llu cali allakagnek angayuqerluni. Tua-i aipaqsagullutek. Tua-i-llu irniangekunek, irniaragnek aanaminek arnaq tuqlurluku, angun-llu una ataminek. Tua-i ciuqliq *family*-urrluteng ayakatallrat.

Ciuqliq waniwa. Irniangeqarraarutiignek aanani aanaminek tuqluraqluku, atani-llu ataminek. Atiin-llu qetunraminek, aaniin-llu cali qetunraminek, wall'u paniminek. Uum-llu tua-i tuqluutekek atakenka irniamegnun ayuqlutek.

Waniwa aipan allakarmi angayuqangqertuq. Tua-llu waniwa irniangutek. Atauciungulutek ukuk, waniwa irniarlutek. Irniangavtek, uum ilai aiparpet tapqullukek kat'um irniarpetek.

Simeon Agnus: He has talked about *ilu'urqellriit* [those who are cross-cousins] in the family system. The children of male and female siblings are first cousins. They are real *ilurak*.

Paul John: I talked about it a little earlier, but it can also be this way. If one's father said that a particular person was [the father's] *iluraq*, he would understand that his children are his *ilurat* also. Like his father, the children of his father's *ilurat* are his *ilurat*. Even though he had never seen them before, if his father said that a particular person was his *iluraq*, he would understand that the children of the person who his father said was his *iluraq* would also be his *ilurat*. That is how it is.

And then if a mother of a child calls a man whom her child sees for the first time her *uicungaq* [female's male cross-cousin], the child would know immediately that the man was his *angak* [maternal uncle]. And if his father calls a man his *iluraq*, he would know that the man was his *ataata*, even though he had never seen him before. It is the same for both female and male cross-cousins. The woman calls her female cross-cousin *ilungaq* [father's sister's daughter, mother's brother's daughter].

Even though I mentioned it earlier, if his mother called a woman her *ilungaq*, he knew to call her daughter *nuliacungaq* [father's sister's daughter, mother's brother's daughter]. The daughter of his mother's *ilungaq* would be his *nuliacungaq*.

Kinship terms and names
(133) Frank and Noah Andrew and Alice Rearden, September 2000:64

Frank Andrew: This is how *tuqluutet* have been from the time of our ancestors. When a man and woman get married, they both have mothers and fathers. They would get married and have children. The children would call their father *aata* and their mother *aana*. That's how a family is formed.

This is the way a family begins. Their first child would call his mother *aana* and his father *aata*. And the father would call his son *qetunraq*. The mother would also call him *qetunraq* or her daughter *panik*. The father's [parents] would use the same term for their children.

Your husband has his own set of parents. And now you two have children. They are one nuclear family with children. And since you now have a child, your child is a part of your husband's family.

Uum waniwa irniarpetek elpet aanakaaten. Anelgutengqerquvet-llu nasaurlumek anaanakluku. Tan'gaurlumek-llu anelgutengqerquvet angakluku. Tua-i-llu aatan irniarpet ap'akluku. Aanan-llu maurluqluku irniarpet.

Uum-llu tua-i cali taum aatavet anelgutai arnaukata angutngukata-llu ayuqluki arnat maurluqluki, angutet-llu apa'urluqluki. Aanavet anelgutai, wall'u atavet anelgutai ayuqluki irniarpet uum tuqluryugngaluki augkunek ava-i, maurluminek apa'urluminek wall'u ataataminek, anaanaminek-llu. Tuaten ayuqut.

Tua-i-llu una irniartek irniangekan elpet tutgarpenek piyugngaluku, uivet-llu cali tutgaraminek. Taum-llu tutgarpetek anelguteten tamalkuita apa'urluqluki wall'u maurluqluki. Angutem-llu cali uum atami anelgutai, arnaulit, angutngulit apa'urluqluki maurluqluki-llu.

Tua-i-llu tauna tutgartek-am irniangluni. Irniangekuni-am tuqlurarkauluten amauminek. Amauqsagulluten waten tutgarpet irniaran. Pingayuurtut waten — elpet, qetunraan, tutgaraan, iluperan. Pingayuat, iluperarpet tua-i taum amauminek tuqluryugngaluten.

Tua-i-llu iluperan tauna tuamtellu irniangluni. Irniangekuni-am urumaviminek tuqlurciqaaten, ayuqlutek uin-llu urumaviminek. Elpetek-llu tauna iluperarpetek yua maqanqautmek, maqanqautevnek tuqlurluku. Uivet-llu cali ayuqluku maqanqautminek tuqlurluku. Taum-llu tuqlulallerpetek urumavikluten.

Tuaken tua-i taq'uq yugni wangkuta tuqluutvut. Ping'ermi tauna, kiturluku yaaqvanun unguvayuitut yuut. Tuaken tua-i cauluku allaurrluku apertuyuitait, tuqluutet augkut irniaminek waken.

Tuamtellu qetunrarpet irniari. Augkut-am irniat maa-i makut ciuqlirmek angayuqaagnek tuqluutet ava-i augkut pianka. Tua-llu irniarulriit kinguveqelriit waten ilameggnun makunun tuqluutait, ilakutameggnun, tuaken malrugnek nek'velriatun arnat angutet-llu irniaritnun. Augna ava-i ciuqliq elpetegnek naulria, una qetunrartek, qetunraa-wa cali, cali-wa qetunraa, wall'u pania-llu — kinguvalriit augkut ava-i tuqluutait elpetegnun angayuqaagnun. Ukunek ciuqliignek.

Tua-llu nutaan ilakutellriit waten ukuk irniat makut urelriit tuqluutait ilakutameggnek tuaggun. Waniwa taum aanavet wall'u aatavet anelgutain irniarit, aanan angutmek anelgutengqerqan, irniarit ilu'urqeciqaten. Tamalkuita irniari ilu'uqluki, angutngungraata arngaungraata-llu, ilu'uqluki tamalkuita, ilungaqluki.

You are the *aana* [mother] of your child. If you have a sister, she is your child's *anaana* [mother's sister]. And if you have a brother, he is your child's *angak* [mother's brother]. And your father is your child's *apa'urluq* [grandfather]. And your mother is your child's *maurluq* [grandmother].

Now your child can call your father's siblings, whether they are male or female, his *maurluq* [grandmother] and *apa'urluq* [grandfather]. Your mother's siblings and your father's siblings, your child can call them *maurluq, apa'urluq, ataata* [father's brother], or *anaana,* and so on. That's the way our family system works.

And if your child gets married and has a child, you can call his child your *tutgar* [grandchild], and your husband could also call him *tutgar.* And your grandchild can call all of your siblings *maurluq* or *apa'urluq.* The father's siblings can be his *maurluq* or *apa'urluq,* too.

And now your *tutgar* has a child. His child would then call you *amauq.* You would become *amauq* of your grandchild's child. There are now three descended from you—you, your son, your grandchild, and your *iluperaq* [great-grandchild]. The third one, your *iluperaq,* would call you *amauq.*

And then your *iluperaq* has a child. His child will call you and your husband both *uruvak* [great-great-grandparent]. And you two would call your great-great-grandchild *maqanqaun.*

There are no more kinship terms after that. People usually don't live that long. They do not use other terms besides the ones we talked about, starting from the child.

And now your son's children. I just talked about the *tuqluutet* for the direct lineal descendants starting from the parents. Now the *tuqluutet* used by the descendants to their extended families. The first one I mentioned, the one who grew from you two, your son, then he'll have his own [child], then he in turn will have a son or daughter—they are your descendants, and the terms mentioned are the ones you two would use for them.

And now within a family, the offspring of a couple and the children who are born from their offspring, the terms that are used by that one family member. The children of your mother or father, if your mother has a brother, his children will be your *ilurat.* All of his children, both female and male, will be your *ilurat.* Your female cross-cousin will be called *ilungaq.*

Taugken anguterrlainaukunek waten aatan anelgutii-wa cali angun, irniari ilakluki tua-i anngaqluki piarkauluki tuaten.

Tua-i-llu irniarita taukuk aturlukek-am cali tua-i piyugngayaaqluteng. Waniwa atami nayagaa, ilu'uqluteng tua-i ping'ermeng, angutem taum irniaran ilu'urmi aaniit, atami nayagaa acameggnek tuqluraqluku, acakluku. Taum taugken arnam irniarin, una aanameng anngaa angameggnek, angameggnek tuqlurluku. Taum-llu angiita nayagami irniari usruminek tuqluraqluki, usruin-llu angameggnek. Ukut taugken angutem irniarin acakluku, tauna atameng nayagaa arnaunra. Tuaten ayuqut.

Noah Andrew: Tuqluutet-mi kinguvalriit?

Frank Andrew: Tuqluutet kingutmun ayalriit. Tuqluun una ciuqliq cakaniyuunani waten ciulianek kingutmurtuq. Irniaminek qamurluni cali, cimingluteng tuaten, tuqululeng tuaten. Cimiyuunani tua-i.

Akwaugaq-llu iciw' mallgiinaqemken, avaggun piunrillerteggun ullagluten kiituan taringamken. Yuum pellaatekaqevkenaki tamakut. Nallunrilkuniki pellaangaunani. Atritgun tamakutgun caksugngaluki, nalaqutaqluki. Nuliacungangartaqluni, ilu'urangaʼartaqluni, tutgarangartaqluni-llu. Tua-i makut tuqluutet calilriaruut yugni wangkutni. Ilakutellriit ciuliameggnek nallunailkutaqluki. Waniw' wii piarkaqkumken elpet, angayuqaagken-llu, aipaa piarkaqluku uinga-llu piarkaqevkenaku. Uingakun tuaggun piarkaqenrilkengamkun elpet piarkaqluten wii.

Alice Rearden: Ciin-gguq qanlartat piarkaqniluki?
Frank Andrew: Nuliacungaqluten, ilu'uqluten, una waniwa piarkaqniluku qaneryaraq. Malruuguk-am aug'um piarkaqniluku piyaram. Tua-i aipaagni nuliacungaqaa wall'u ilu'uqluku-llu. Wall'u pingayua augna piaqa. Augna ava-i aatan piarkaqenrilkumku wii nuliacungaqeciqamken, ataataktngamku piarkaqevkenaku. Ataka taugaam taum ilu'uqluku.

Tua-i-llu aanan piarkaqluku wii, nuliacungaqluku, piarkaqenritamken elpet, irniama taugaam piarkaqsugngaluten. Tua-i-gguq tauna amllerutaq. Amllerutamek aterluni. Aipaak una atiikun piarkaqluku, aaniikun-llu piarkaqevkenaku. Amllerutaq-gguq tua-i. Nunamni un'gaani tuaten pimauq. Tuaten ayuqut tua-i.

But if your father has a brother and he has children, his children will be like your siblings. His sons will be your brothers.

And their children, following their fathers, could use the same pattern and use the same terms. Now his father's younger sister, though their children were cousins, the mother's son will call his cousin's mother *acak* [father's sister]. But the women, her children will call her brother their *angak* [mother's brother]. And the *angak* would call his younger sister's child his *usruq* [man's sister's child], and they'd call him *angak*. But the children of a man, they'd call his younger sister *acak*. That's how it is.

Noah Andrew: How about the *tuqluutet* that are passed on from one generation to the next?

Frank Andrew: Tuqluutet are passed on from generation to generation. The same kinship term is used and doesn't change as it goes down the family line. Generations change and they die, but the terms never change.

Remember yesterday, when I inquired about your family, we realized that we were related when you mentioned your deceased family members. If one knows about family lineage and understands the kinship system, one will not get lost. One will find new relations by the use of the kinship terms. One would find new *nuliacungaat, ilurat,* and *tutgaraat.* These *tuqluutet* are important in keeping families connected and stable. Kinship terms help to clarify how people are related. If you are my *piarkaq* [cross-cousin], your parents, she would be my *piarkaq* but not her husband. Since he is not my *piarkaq,* then you become my *piarkaq.*

Alice Rearden: Why do they say one is not his *piarkaq?*

Frank Andrew: When I say that you are my *piarkaq,* you are both my *iluraq* or *nuliacungaq.* When you say someone is your *piarkaq,* he is either your *nuliacungaq* or *uicungaq,* and they are also your *ilurat.* I had just talked about the third option of how one can be a *piarkaq* for another. So if your father is not my *piarkaq,* you will by my *nuliacungaq,* because your father is my *ataata* and not a *piarkaq.* And your father would call my father his *iluraq.*

And if your mother is my *piarkaq,* my *nuliacungaq,* you are not my *piarkaq,* but you can be my children's *piarkaq.* That is what they call an *amllerutaq* [relationship through one's parents, where one is related to someone in multiple ways]. He would be considered a *piarkaq* to another through the father but not through the mother. He would be called an *amllerutaq* by that person. That is how it is out in my village. That is how they are.

Tua-i-llu makut tuqluutet iluriuryarat. Waniwa ilu'urqellriik tuqluutekaak iluq'amegnek, iluracungamegnek, ilurallramegnek, ilurapamegnek, arenqimegnek, qatngutmegnek. Maa-i tuqluutet ilu'urqelriit.

Alice Rearden: Ciin-gguq allaugat?

Frank Andrew: Tua-i-am tuaten ciuliameggnek ayagluteng-am pimalriit. Allaungalngermeng iluqaaryarauluteng tamarmeng. Piarkameggnun tua-i tuaten allaungalngermeng augkut kinguvalriit.

Una waniwa qatngun waten ayuquq. Arnauli angutnguli anelgutkelriit, qatngutekciqamken arnaungerpet wall'u angutmek anngangqerkuvet qatngutekluku cali. Ayuqluki arnaungraata aperyarauguq — ilu'uqluki tamalkuita. Aipaakun tua-i allakun ilu'uqluku, nuliacungaqluku-llu. Aug'ukun taugken qatngutkun, atauciuluku tua-i qatngutekluki, arnauli angutngulillu, cali qatngutekluku. Tuaten tua-i ayuqluteng.

Cali ilii kis'arciaqa-am tayima cali tuqluutem ilu'urminun. Una tua-llu qangiaraminek tuqluqengyaraq. Piarkaqenrilkumken elpet aatan taugken piarkaqluku, aanan-llu piarkaqluku, qaqilluku tua-i, qaqillukek, ukugnegun piarkaqevkenak, qangiaramnek tuqluryugngaluten, elpet-llu ataatavnek wii. Taugken augkuk angayuqaagken aipaa piarkaqkumku, aipaa-llu piarkaqevkenaku aug'ukun pisciiganaku. Aipaakun piarkaqevkenii, aipaggun taugken piarkaqlua. Waten tua-i ayuqut nunamni tuqluutet apertuamalallret.

Ilait arnat un'gaani elisngait cali tuqluutet elisngayaaqait. Ayuqenritut tuqluutet tua-i pilianek-gguq ilangqelartut tuqluutet. Apa'urluita wall'u iluraita pililuteng tua-i ellmeggnun tuqluutngurtaqluni tua-i tamana piurtaqluni. Allarrauluni, augkut tuqluutet ilaluki. Piciryarauluni-gguq-am tua-i, piciryararrauluni. Ava-i ilaita-llu maa-i Kass'angenrakun-am, ilaita nuliacungateng-llu tuqlurnaurait Kass'arngalnguqa, Kass'arngalngumeggnek. Tamaa-i tamakut piliat ilu'urmeggnun tuqluutait.

Family-t tua-i tamakut yaaken ayagluteng *generation*-aat kinguveqelriit tuqluutait. Waniwa wiinga waten pimaunga. Tuyuryarmi yaani Ilgayam nuniini ilakutanka amllertut. Qaluyaani-ll' cali qagaani keggani Nelson Island-aam nuniini cali ilakutanka cali amllerrluteng. Pakmani-

Now, to mention the different terms for *iluriuryarat* [the relationship between cross-cousins]. One can call his cross-cousin *iluq, iluracungaq* [little cross-cousin], *ilurall'er* [bad cross-cousin], *ilurapak* [big cross-cousin], *arenqik* [from *arenqig,* "to be agreeable"], or *qat'ngun* [one related through spouse exchange]. Here are different terms used between cousins.

Alice Rearden: Why are they all different?

Frank Andrew: That's the system used by them, starting from their ancestors. Even though they are different terms, all of them are a way of addressing *ilurat.* Even though they are different, they are terms used to address their *piarkat* from generation to generation.

This is how *qat'ngun* is used. Either a woman or a man are siblings. You will be my *qat'ngun,* even though you are a woman, or if you have an older brother, he will also be my *qat'ngun.* That term applies to women as well —they will all be considered *ilurat.* On the one hand *nuliacungaq* is only used for a female *iluraq,* but on the other hand *qat'ngun* can be used for both female and male cross-cousins. That's how it is.

I can't remember one term used for one's *ilurat.* Now, to mention the use of *qangiar* [man's brother's child]. If you are not my *piarkaq* but both your parents are my *piarkaq,* if you are not my *piarkaq* through them, you'd be my *qangiar* and you'd call me *ataata.* But if one of your parents is my *piarkaq* and one is not, we can't address each other in those terms. I would not be your *piarkaq* through one way, or I would be your *piarkaq* through the other way. The terms that were described worked like that in my village.

Some women down there on the coast are also knowledgeable about *tuqluutet.* There are many different *tuqluutet,* and some are made up as well. Their grandfathers or their *ilurat* create them on their own, and they would exist from then on. They are different, but they are a part of those *tuqluutet.* But they say that it is a custom. And after Kass'at arrived, some people used names like Kass'arngalnguqa [my one who looks like a Kass'aq] for their *nuliacungat.* Those are the *tuqluutet* that were made up for their *ilurat.*

Those are the *tuqluutet* that continue to be passed on from generation to generation. So when they taught us who our relatives were, this is how I was instructed. I know I have many relatives in Togiak, near Bristol Bay, and I have many relatives out near Qaluyaat, near Nelson Island. And

llu Kusquqviim kangrani Selitmiuni-llu iluraanka amllerrluteng. Uaken Qinarmek, Qinarmiunek, Tuntutuliarmiungurtellriit ua-i nugtarcameng. *Move*-aameng allamun Tuntutuliaq cimirluteng nunallerteng, Qinarmiut tuaken sagtellrit.

Maa-i aipaimta-llu aturaat. Tua-i elpet Naparyarrarmiunguyaaquten taugaam nunalinqiggluten maavet Anchorage-aamun. Ilait-llu natmun ayagluteng, akmavet-llu *Lower 48*-aamun ayagluteng natmun akmavet saggluteng. Tuaten ayuqelliiniut yuut. Taumek alerqularaitkut waten yuk tangengramteggu nutaan, ilaliurluku taugaam pisqelluku taringyugnga-kan. Makut maa-i ilaput, wiinga-llu qanerciiganii, Kass'atun pisciiganii ilaliuryungramki. Tua-i taringusngailamegnuk qalartengramegnuk.

Waten pilaraitkut. Ellam-gguq yui ilakut, ilakukut-gguq tamalkumta. Tua-i taringaqa man'a waten qanlallrat. Agayun-gguq piurcillruuq Adam-aankugnek Eva-llu allamek-llu naucivkenani. Tuaken-llu piciuguq man'a, tuaken ayagluni ellarpak man'a yungluni, ciulirneret igaryaramek nallu-ngermeng qanertut "Ella-gguq allamek yuituq. Ilakukut-gguq." Man'a maa-i nallunricet'laraat cali kesianek ciulirneret catairutellret imkut ayu-qucirturiaqameng wangkutnun. Makunek-llu tuqluutnek apertuulluta piaqamta ilakutamtenek.

Maa-i tua-i tamana man'a tuqluun ilakucaraq, ilakutaminek piyaraq, elitnaurutngunrirtuq. Wangkuta tamarcetarput nallunricaaqengramte-ggu maniyuilamteggu kinguvemta yuitnun. Tuqluun assilriaruuq, assir-tuq. Waten tua-i pitaluku augna nallunrilucirramtun qanrutkaqa.

Alice Rearden: Aptuq wani tuqluuten-gguq-qaa allauciquq atevkun. Iciw' acilaqaitkut. Tuqluuten-qaa allauciquq aterpegun? Wall'u tuqluutengyug-ngauten-gguq-qaa aterkun?

Frank Andrew: Tamana aturaat yuut ilaita tamarmirrluteng pingalnger-meng. Waniwa wiinga-llu aturluku iluramnun. Ilu'urqa wall'u nuliacu-ngaqa tayima piunrillruuq, ilu'urqa-llu nakmiin. Atra-llu una, taum at-qestii, tuaggun ilu'urqaqa wii piarkaqsugnganricaaqengramku, atrakun ilu'uqluku, piarkaqeveknaku taugken ukugnegun angayuqaagnegun. Taugken atrakun piarkaqngamku tuqluraqluku taum tuqluutellemnun taumun ateqngaku. Manilaraat-llu tamana, tamaa-i atrakun-gguq una

I have many *ilurat* on the upper part of the Kuskokwim River and in Sleetmiut. When people moved from Qinaq, their village was renamed Tuntutuliak. After people moved from Qinaq, they scattered all over the land.

Aipaiput [Our counterparts, the white people] are also living by this. You [Alice] are originally from Napakiak, but you have moved here to Anchorage. And some people move to different places and even travel and disperse to the Lower Forty-eight states. That is how people are. That is why they advise us to be friendly even if we see a person for the first time, if they can understand [our language]. And I can't speak English to others, even though I want to be friendly toward them. It is because we won't understand each other if we speak to one another.

This is what they tell us. *Ellam-gguq yui ilakut* [They say the world's inhabitants are related]. They say that we are all related. I [now] understand what they used to say. They say God created Adam and Eve and did not create anyone else. These [*tuqluutet*] are true from then on. From then on our huge world became populated, and even though our elders did not know how to write, they said, "*Ella-gguq allamek yuituq. Ilakukut-gguq* [The world is not inhabited by anyone else. We are all related]." This is what our ancestors, those elders who passed away, constantly said when they were teaching us. And they also revealed this when they were telling us about *tuqluutet,* about our relatives.

Tuqluucaraq, the way of knowing whom you are related to, how one should address one's relatives, is no longer taught today. We have caused it to vanish, because we don't teach it to our descendants, even though we have the knowledge. *Tuqluucaraq* is a good thing. I just explained that topic to the best of my knowledge.

Alice Rearden: [Ann Fienup-Riordan] is asking if your *tuqluun* [relational term] would be different because of your name. You know how we are given names. Will your *tuqluun* be different because of your name? Or could you receive a kin term through your name?

Frank Andrew: Some people are still practicing that, even though they aren't following the practice entirely. And I am still practicing it today toward my *ilurat.* My *iluraq* or *nuliacungaq* has passed away, and my real *iluraq* as well. And the namesake of my *iluraq,* the person who was named after him, is my *iluraq* through [his namesake], even though he cannot be my *piarkaq* whatsoever. He is my *iluraq* through his name, but he is not my *piarkaq* through his parents. But because he is my *piarkaq* through

iluurqaa, atrakun-llu nuliacungaqluku. Tuaten piciryarauguq-am cali. At-ritgun piunrillrungraata atqestait atritgun piarkaqluki, ilu'uqluki. Wii-llu wani aturluku cali. Tuaten-am tua-i atulriaruuq augna, atritgun piyaraq.

Alice Rearden: Yuum-llu-qaa atranek qanqeryugtuten? Nalqiga'arcugan-qaa?

Frank Andrew: Makut tang atret ilait, tamarmeng watua piyaaqellilriit, nani yaaqvani avani ciuliamteni wall'u ukatiini, ilu'urqelriit waten angu-tet wall'u arnaulit-llu, camek pitullrat pitekluku lucky-rluteng watua nu-nam qaingani pitekluku atermek tuaten ayuqelriamek at'ngevkatulliniat. Tuaken-llu tua-i piurrluni kingutmun ateq.

Tamaani-llu anguyiim nalliini tamaani wangkuta ciuliarput tauna Pa-ngalgalria ilurain taukut, anguyiit inglumeng takuatni, *caribou*-m irnia-ranek, *young*-alriamek. Uqilaut-gguq tamakut, *caribou*-t irniarit, aana-meggni-llu-gguq uqilanruut. Taum iluriin tuqluutengqertuk-gguq cali piliamegnek Tuqulumegnek. Maa-i makut piliameggnek waten tuqluuci-lallruut. Ellimellinia, augkut inglumeng takuatni, tuntuk taukuk igvaar-cagnek, nuraa tauna pisqelluku tangvagtelluku augkunun. Aurrluni tua-i ullagluku nang'errluni nutaan malirqalliniak, nutaan ayakalliniuk panga-leglutek alingamek. Taum-llu nuraam taum aanani uqilanruami unilluku. Carrilqakun qerallran maligtellinikii, napanun-llu pulavailgan anguamiu tegulliniluku taum tua-i. Akemkut-am tua-i inguit uurangaarcan "Uu-u-u! Cauvkenani augna pangalgalria." Cunawa-gguq tua-i acirluku. Pa-ngalgalriamek piurangluku. Kiturrarmek-am aterpagtetuyaqaat atpiara-nek, taugaam cali cimirluni taumek Pangalgalriamek. Anguyiim tamaani nalliini, anguyak arulairpailgan Yugtaq. Tua-i qimagaqami-gguq nuna-kun, nunamun tut'aqan taqtuat nallunriamegteggu anguyiit. Kuiget-llu nequturrangraata qeckarluki akiatnun tut'aqluni, angumasciiganani tua-i aqvaquraqami nunam qaingakun. Kangia-gguq tua-i tauna Pangalgalria-rurtellra. Pangalgalriamek-wa tua-i atengluni.

Tamaa-i tamakut atret waten ilangutkelallrit. Callritgun tua-i ilait ateq alairaqluni, arturnarqelriatgun pillritgun yuullgutkeng'ermegteki pillrat artuqmegteggun acirluku taumek atrurcetaqluku. Makut maa-i atret ayu-qenrilnguut amllertut tua-i atret Yugtaat atret. Kuimaralria-llu tauna cali

his name, I address him by that special name that I used for his namesake, because he is named after him. They also told me that one can be
my *iluraq* through his namesake or that she is my *nuliacungaq* through
her name. That is also a custom. They are our *piarkat, ilurat* through their
namesake, even though that person whom they were named after passed
away. And I am still practicing that custom. That is also what addressing
someone after his namesake is like.

Alice Rearden: Would you also like to talk about people's names? Would
you like to explain it a little?

Frank Andrew: Some of these names or maybe even all of them, some
of our ancestors of long ago or even recent times, *ilu'urqellriit* [those who
are cross-cousins], both men or women, were given particular names, depending on what they did or when they got lucky here on this earth. And
a name started to exist from then on.

Back when they had bow-and-arrow warfare, our ancestor Pangalgalria
[from *pangaleg-*, "to run at a gallop"] [was pursuing] a young caribou
while his enemies were watching. They say caribou calves are very fast
runners, even faster than their mothers. They said [he and his *iluraq*]
called each other Tuquluk. He told him to pursue its calf when those caribou came into view in front of their enemies, while they watched. He
crawled toward it, finally stood up, and chased them when they ran off
galloping because they were frightened. And that calf left its mother because it was a faster runner. He followed it when it crossed a clearing, and
he grabbed it when he caught up to it, before it disappeared into the trees.
Then their enemies across there started yelling, "Uuuuuu! He is just running like an animal, proving nothing." They apparently named him. They
started calling him Pangalgalria. I forgot what they called him before that,
but they started calling him Pangalgalria. It was back during wartimes,
before Yup'ik wars ended. When those warriors figured out who he was
as he ran away on land [during battles], they would give up when he got
to the land. And even though the rivers were wide, he would jump and
land across from them and could not be chased down when he ran on
land. That is the story of how he became Pangalgalria. That is how he got
the name Pangalgalria.

Those names became a part of the other names. Some names origi-
nated in what people did. They would give their peers names because
of the things they did that seemed impossible, and it would become a
name from then on. There are many different names of Yup'ik origin.

kuimturnirluni, kuimturnillrakun Kuimaralriamek cali at'ngevkarluku. Anglluralria-wa-gguq cali tauna Paallagalria-wa. Maa-i makut anguyiim tamaani nalliini atrurtelallrit. Tauna-gguq am Anglluralria kiagmi waten piaqami anguygami teguqata'arqatni, kuigem-llu cali ceniini uitaaqameng matarrluni mermun qeckatuuq tayima-llu tua-i pugevkenani. Yaaqva-ggun-llu nutaan pugluni. Tamakut yuullgutain artukluku tua-i. Ungung-ssitun ayuqluni imarpigmiutartun.

Una tuamtellu Paallagalria waten qanrutkelaraat. Anguyagmi-gguq nunam qaingani malirqeraqatni, anguqata'arqatni ayainanermini manig-celengraan paallatuuq nunam qainganun. Paallaggaarluni-llu yaaqva-qanirluni nang'errluni allamek qavcinek amllirluni paallagaqluni. Uni-lluki tua-i tuatnaluni. Tua-i-gguq tamana pitekluku cali Paallagalriamek at'ngevkallruat. Maa-i makut atret ilangutait. Tamarmeng tua-i atret tua-ten ayuqelliniluteng. Anguyiim nalliini piurtellret atret amllerrluteng. Ilait-wa nallukenka wii tamakut. Amllerniluki pilaryaaqekait taugaam nalqigcimanrilnguut takumni nalluanka qaillun qanrutkellerkait.

Augna-llu Tangvagmek pilallrat. Ukinqucugpalek-llu. Qayat makut ukinqucungqelartut — tamaa-i ingna ciungani teguyaraq ukinqucugmek atengqertuq. Tauna-gguq ukinqucungqelallruuq angpiamek tua-i. Tauna-am pitekluku ukinqucua atra cimilliniluku Ukinqucugpalegmun. Maa-i makut nalqigtelallrit nalqigcugngaanka wii tuaten pilallrit, at'ngevkalall-rit, atrem allakam ayagneri. Kinguvri-llu tua-i tuaten atengqerrsugngari-luteng. Tua-i taumek pituluki, atret atengluteng.

Tuamtellu Urluvlek tauna. Urluvret nallunritaaten-qaa? *Bows.* Angtua-mek-gguq urluvengqetullruuq anguyiim nalliini tauna. Pinirluni cakneq, kiimenani-llu-gguq urluvni tauna qelusciigataqluku yugnek taugaam na-nercirluni qeluaqluku. Tua-i-am tamana urluvra [pitekluku] Urluverpa-legmek acinqigtelliniluku. Maa-i makut atret piliat nalqigtelallrit wang-nun. Ilait atret tua-i amlleq nalluaqa wii.

Alice Rearden: Piliarunrilnguut-mi atret, yuunrillret. Iciw' yuunriraqata atenglalriit? Qaillun tamana ayuqucianek qanqaasqumayaaqamken.

Frank Andrew: Tamakut tang tua-i atret makut piliarunrilnguut piksai-lamki uunguciilkenka. Taugaam waten kinguveqelriit tamakunek acirtura-

Kuimaralria [from *kuimar-*, "to swim"] was a very good swimmer. They gave him the name Kuimaralria because he was a very good swimmer. Anglluralria [one who dives under water, from *angllur-*, "to dive under water"] and that Paallagalria [one who falls forward, from *paallag-*, "to fall forward"] as well. These names came into existence during wartimes. When warriors were going to overtake Anglluralria near riverbanks during the summer, he would undress and jump into the water and dive. He would finally surface a great distance away. That is how he was in the water. His peers would be in disbelief, because they could not do it themselves. He was like a sea mammal.

This is what they say about Paallagalria. When they would chase after him on land during wartime and almost catch up to him as he was running, he would fall forward onto the ground even though his path was smooth. He would move farther away after falling forward, stand up, take a few more steps, and fall again. He would leave [his pursuers] behind that way. He was given the name Paallagalria because of that. These are names that became a part of our naming system later. That is how all names are. There are a lot of names that came into existence during wartimes. I don't know some of them. They say that there are lots of them, but I don't know how to describe the ones that were not explained in my presence.

And the one they used to call Tangvak and also Ukinqucugpalek. These kayaks have an *ukinqucuk*—the handle that is up in front is called *ukinqucuk*. They say that man's kayak had a huge *ukinqucuk*. They changed his name to Ukinqucugpalek because of the *ukinqucuk* on his kayak. I can tell you about those that they described, those that they made names for, the origin of those other names. And their descendants can acquire those names from then on.

And then that Urluvlek. Do you know what *urluvret* are? Bows. That man owned a large bow during wartimes. He was extremely strong, but he could not pull his bow by himself. He could only pull it by having others hold it down. They renamed him Urluverpalek because of his bow. These are names that were created that they told me about. I don't know some names.

Alice Rearden: How about names that were not created, names of the deceased? You know how when people die, people receive names. I want you to speak a little about that.

Frank Andrew: Because I haven't described them before, I don't know about names that were not created, but they say they named their de-

tullruit-gguq ciuliaritnek. Waniwa-llu wii Miisaugua Yugtun, Avegyaulua-llu, Ayaruaraulua-llu. Taukunek tua-i aterpagtaatullruatnga pingayunek.

Alice Rearden: Qaillun tamakunek at'ngellrusit?

Frank Andrew: Ciuliameggnek-wa tua-i acitullrulliniit tamakut. Una *meaning*-aara Miisaam uunguciitaqa, Avegyam-llu. Una taugaam Aya-ruar, ayaruicuitellruuq-gguq tauna, anguyiim-llu nalliini ayaruni tamana atutullruluku. Tauna-gguq tua-i tuaten piluku pitekluku Ayaruarmek pi-tullruat. Tuamtellu tauna anguyiim nalliini ayaruni-gguq nunamun ka-pulluku kangrani pikani aturatun anuqem elliuqiitun pitullruuq. Pitga-qungraatni avitaarluni pitegcautmun agturcecuunani. Tauna-gguq tua-i Quagguucuarmek at'ngellruuq, imumek *needle fish.* Maa-i makut nalqig-telallrit.

Kangilirluki, aciisqumaaqamegteki mikelnguut taumek kangiliisqe-lluki-am pitullruit aciisqelluku, kangilirluku-gguq.

Alice Rearden: Kangililriamek-qaa tangerqallruuten?

Frank Andrew: Pulengtaq-wa tua-i tuaten pitukait. Mik'lengraata an'a-qata tua-i ciutaitnun pus'arrluteng ilakutameggnek aterpaggluku. "Taiguq tamarmi waniwa." Aterpagqaarluku tainiaqluku waniwa. Tuaten tua-i aci-qengelrianek niicugnilallruunga, ciutaitnun pus'arrluteng. Mik'naki tua-i. Kangilirluki-gguq. Ataucimek tua-i atermek aciyuitait, taugaam ilakuta-meggnek. Tua-i ilaita-llu ilakutameng ateqluku pingraata, atellgutkevkar-luki tua-i kangilirluki. Maa-i nallunritaten atellgutkelartut. Miisaat-llu amllerrluteng, Avegyat-llu amllerrluteng atellgutkelriit. Tua-i ilakutaqel-riit-gguq tamaa-i. Ciuliameggnek waten sagingang'ermeng atellgutkelriit.

Alqairutmeng atqestait al'ameggnek tuqluraqluki. Wall'u aanameng at-ranek atelget aanameggnek tuqluraqluki. Tamaa-i aterteggun tuqluute-teng aturluki cali.

scendants after their ancestors. And [through that custom] my names are Miisaq, Avegyaq, and Ayaruaraq in Yup'ik. They call me by those three names.

Alice Rearden: How did you receive those names?

Frank Andrew: They named those people after their ancestors. I don't know what the meaning of Miisaq and Avegyaq are, but they say Ayaruar never went without an *ayaruq* [walking stick]. And he used his *ayaruq* during wars. They called him Ayaruar for that reason. And he stuck his *ayaruq* in the ground during battles, and the very top of it would be like clothes that are blown by the wind. And even when they shot at him with an arrow, he would move away, and he would never let an arrow hit him. His name was Quagguucuaq, you know, [little] needlefish. These are things they told me.

When they wanted a child to receive the name of the deceased, they were told to do a naming ceremony, *kangiliriyaraq.*

Alice Rearden: Did you ever see anyone give a person a name?

Frank Andrew: That occurs frequently. Even though they are small, when they are newborns, they used to bend down to their ears and name them after their deceased relatives and say, "That person has come and is here now." After saying their name they would say that the person has come and is here now. That is how I saw people naming others, bending down to their ears and giving them names while they are small. They call it *kangilirluku* [giving a person a name]. They never gave them just one name, but they gave them names of their deceased relatives. And even though their relative was already named after him, they would let them become *atellgutet* [those with namesake and name in common], naming them. Now you know that some have the same name. And there are many people who have the name Miisaq, and there are also many Avegyat who have the same names. Those people are said to be *ilakutat* [relatives]. Even though *atellgutkellriit* [those with the same namesake and name] are living in many different places, they have the same names that came from their ancestors. Yes, through their names.

They would use the term *al'aq* [older sister] for those who were named after their late older sister, or they would call those who were named after their mother *aana* [mother]. They called them by their *tuqluutet* through their namesakes.

Alice Rearden: Angutngungraan-llu arnaungraan-llu. Angutmek atengqerrsugngaluni arnaq, angun-llu arnamek atengqerrsugngaluni. Tuaten-llu ayuqut?

Frank Andrew: Tuaten ayuqut. Angutem atqellrungraaku unguvaller-mini aciryugngaluku arnaungraan una taum angutem atranek. Tua-i-llu angutem tauna ilu'urqellrukuniu arnaungraan iluraminek tuqluraqluku, ilurapaminek. Atritgun maa-i makut tuqluutet amllerrluteng.

Tuqluutet

(134) Paul John, Theresa Moses, Wassillie Evan, Agnes Alexie, and Phillip Moses, November 2000

Paul John: Maa-i watua ayagyuaput cakuciiruyutut tua-i ilakeng'ermeng-llu ilateng nalluyagulluki. Ilakeng'ermegteggu-llu taum nalluyagutellmeng tungiinun tua-i ayuqngameng, ilakeng'ermeng maa-i mallgutqapigtengermeng, apeqmeggnek *boyfriend*-aqsaurrluteng, *girlfriend*-aqsaurrluteng-llu. Tua-i cakuciiruyucameng. Tua-i-wa wangkuta angayuqritni tuqluukarait makut ellaitnun elitnaurutkenriamteki.

Tua-llu augkut ciuliaput ilakuyutepiarluki ilakutellruniluki kenkulluki-llu qanrutkelaqvut maa-i. Ellaita angayuqrita ayagyuateng tungelqurritnek apertuaquraiceteng nanlengraata, nunani allani uitangraata tungelqurrit apertuagurluki. Yaaqsingraata aterpagqurluki. Qanrutaqamegteki-llu tuaten qanrutaqluki, "Tuavet nunanun tekiskuvet aterpaggluku yuaqiu. Taum aterpageskuvgu iliita nallunritestiin tuavet ayauciiqaaten. Atam-llu taumun itquvet qanruskiu pimek angayuqangqerrniluten, atan wall'u aanan aterpagglukek."

Tua-llu wiinga ata'urluma aug'um camek qanrucuitellruanga, yuucirkamek qanrucuitellruanga. Qanrucuileng'ermia tungelqurramnek taugaam qanruquratullruanga nunani allanelengraata. Tua-i maa-i kangingaqamku, atama qanrutkelallranun cakniluku yuk una apraqatgu, cakellra-llu tua-i kangingluku.

Tua-i tamaa-i tuqluun una nalluyagucunaicaaqucia wangkutnun cali maa-i kinguvernun Yupiulrianun. Tuqluukar una amllerugauguq ilangqerrucimek kangingutnguami, ilakuyucim kangingutekngani. Tuaten-llu ilakuyutem kangingutekngani, tua-i una naken tekitengraan kina qan-

Alice Rearden: Even though they are men or women. A woman can have a man's name, and a man can have a woman's name. Is it like that?

Frank Andrew: That's right. They can give her that man's name, even though she is a female. And if that deceased person was the man's *iluraq*, he can call her *iluraq* or *ilurapak*, even though she is a woman. There are many *tuqluuтet* that exist through people's names.

Kinship terms

(134) Paul John, Theresa Moses, Wassilie Evan, Agnes Alexie, and Phillip Moses, November 2000

Paul John: These days our young people do not know how they are related to one another, and they don't know who their relatives are. And they have become boyfriends and girlfriends with their relatives, even though they are closely related, because they no longer know how they are related to one another. It is because we, their parents, have not taught them about their *tuqluuтet*.

And today we say that our ancestors lived in great unity and loved one another, when we speak of them. [It is] because parents told their young people who their relatives were no matter where they lived and revealed who their relatives were even if they lived in other villages. And they told them their names even though they lived far away. And they used to tell us, "When you arrive at that village, name that person and look for him. If you reveal that person's name, a resident who knows him will take you there. And when you go inside his home, tell him who your parents are, naming your father or your mother."

Now, my poor father never gave me instructions to live by. Even though he never gave me advice, he always told me about his few relatives, even though they resided in other villages. And today when I come to understand how a person is related to me, that they are related to a person that my father had spoken about, when they name that person, I understand how they are related to him.

That is why our younger Yup'ik generation and we should not forget the kinship system. *Tuqluukar* is extremely valuable because it helps people to understand who their relatives are, because it helps people to understand relationships between people. And because it is a way of un-

qan, "Pimek ciuliangqertua, piuguq ataka wall'u apaurluqa." Tamaaggun kangingartaqamku tauna cakellra-llu taringluku. Maa-i-llu tua-i makut allanerugaat apertuumalallret tua-i-am waniwa cakuciitevkenaki caknilua qanenrilengraata tangrraqamki cakuciit nalluvkenaki, ilakluki umyuamkun. Tua-i man'a maa-i kinguvemta nalluyagutqapigeskaita ilakaat tuqluun apertuatenriamceteng.

Tamaani-llu wii niitaqama waten umyuama taringyuitellrua una, tegganeq qanerciquq, "Ella allamek yuituq. Yuut ilakut tamarmeng. Ella allamek yuituq." Umyuarteqtullruyaaqua, "Qaillun-kiq yaaqsiulluteng ilakat ella allamek yuilkan?" Maaten tang ayagangua una tegganeq qanerciquq, tauna-gguq tuani pimiu tuavet nugtartellruuq maa-i-gguq kinguvri maantut. Tuamtellu piciquq iliit, tauna-gguq naken tekitellruuq camiunek maa-i-gguq kinguvri maantut. Tamaa-i apqiitnek yaaqsingraan-llu ilii ukurritaqluni, yaaqsingraan-llu ilii nengaugitaqluni. Tamaa-i tuatnallermegteggun tua-i ilakuciat ilumun piciulliniluni, asguranaunani-llu. Natetmurtellriani caminek nalkutarnaqluni maa-i nunat yaaqsigngalengraata. Tuaten pinaqngan makunun cali kinguvemtenun tamana utelmun tua-i piyugngacirramcetun apertuaqurayunaqsaaqelliniluki tungelqurritnek nanlengraata.

Kass'at-llu una cali waniwa maaten murilkanka tuqluutiit amllertacirraqlinikii *uncle*-aq, *auntie*-q, *grandpa*-q, *grandma*-q. Tua-i-llu kinguvra tuqluutetaunani. Wangkuta taugken Yup'igeurlurni tuqluutet ayuqenrilnguut amllerrluteng yaaken tua-i yuurtellermeggni angayuqaagminek ayagluni apa'urlua, amaura, amauran-wa cali amani ciungani. Tuamtellu waken tutgarmek ayagluni kingutmun tutgarii iluperaa, neruvailitaa. Tamaa-i cali tamakut wangkuta tuqluuteput tungelququyutelput amllenruluteng Kass'amteni ukuni.

Theresa Moses: Uum waniwa Kangrilnguum atallra ellanguteklluku, ellangutkellruaput. *Uncle*-anek nalluluta, Kass'atun *uncle*-aq nalluluku. Atii tuqlutullruaput angalleramtenek. Tua-ll'-am caqerlua cali piunga, "Ciin

derstanding the relationships between people, even though a person has arrived from another village, if that person says, "My forefather is so-and-so, my father or grandfather is so-and-so." When I come to understand who that person is through that system, I also understand how they are related to me. And today [at this convention] I know how many of these strangers who have revealed their names are related to me, even though they have not told me specifically that they are related to me. When I see them, I know how I am related to them. They are my relatives in my mind. *Tuqluucaraq* is one of the traditions our younger generation has forgotten because we stopped teaching them.

And back then I did not understand when an elder would say, "*Ella allamek yuituq* [The world has no other persons]. All people are related, there are no other inhabitants on this earth." I used to wonder, "How are they all related, being great distances apart, if there are no other inhabitants on this earth?" When I began traveling, it became apparent when an elder would say that they have moved to that place and that today his descendants live in this place. And then another person would say that person came from a certain place, from that particular village, and his descendents now reside here. And, as they say, some people become daughters-in-law and sons-in-law in faraway places. By witnessing how they [move around], it is indeed true that they are related, and it is not surprising to find a relative when traveling to different places, even though they seem so distant. Because [knowing *tuqluutet*] results in [finding relatives in faraway places], it is imperative that we go back to those ways with these descendants of ours, and they should be taught about their relatives no matter where they reside.

When I came to observe these white people, the extent of their *tuqluutet* system is uncles, aunties, grandpas, and grandmas. And their descendants do not have *tuqluutet*. On the contrary, we poor Yupiit have many different *tuqluutet* from the time that they are born, starting from their parents, their grandmother, their great-grandmother, and before their great-grandmother, and then starting from the grandchild down to their great-grandchild, great-great-grandchild. And we have more *tuqluutet*, or terms for relationships between relatives, than these Kass'at.

Theresa Moses: We became aware of our surroundings during the time when Paul John's father was alive. We did not know about uncles, the English term *uncle*. We used the term *angalleraq* [literally, "bad mother's

ikiussiyaalriamek pilirluku pivkalarceciu." Kiugaatnga, tua-i-gguq ava-ken ayagluni tuqluutnguuq tauna. Angalleramtenek aatallra piuraraq-luku. Tuamtell'-am tauna egmircetsaagyaaqluku tauna irniamnun ma-kunun, una taugaam ataataq cucukenruluku ellaitaa. Tauna cali angaller ik'ikluku wangtun.

Nalluvkenani Yugcetun tuqlurturatullruamteki tutgaraanka, makut tuqluutet, angayuqama, aatama, uum-llu aatairutma atallran tuqluutait-nek egmigcetsaagyaaqaqkenka Yugcetun. Ukut wani irniama atallrat ma-kut kinguqliin qulicungameggnek pitullruatgu, qetunraqa augna elliin tua-i tuqluutiinek pivkassaatuaqa. Cali-llu angakestait angacungaramegg-nek pitullruatgu, tuaten-am cali tauna tua-i angacungariitnek pivkassaa-tuyaaqluku, una *uncle*-aq nalluluku. Maurluit-llu, aanalqa imna maacu-ngameggnek pitullruat acakestain-llu acacungameggnek.

Wiinga-llu cali tauna tua-i kiimnuk ellirtukuk uyu'urqa-llu. Ilapuk im-kut, angutek malruk arnak-wa cali malruk tamallruluteng tayima. Wang-kuk tauna-llu uyu'urqa-llu kiimegnuk piurrlunuk. Atalqa imna angagpa-meggnek pillrukiit angakestain, ataatarpameggnek-llu. Tua-i uyuramnun tamana egmircetsaalaryaaqaqa anngarput imna wangkuta tuqlutullruam-teggu anngacungamtenek. Cavut nalluvkenaki Yugcetun taugaam, tuq-luuet piuratullruamteki, nurr'acungat, nurr'at. Imna-llu arnaq tangellra ikiuluni wii kenkellrukeka nurr'acungamnek tuqluvkaraqluku Piunrim-llu Atii imna tauna taringyuitetullruaqa uurapamtenek tuqluvkaraqluki. Tamaa-i makut tuqlurturatulput wangkuta atritnek-llu apertuyuunaki. Apertuutelput tuaggun taugaam niitellemteggun, nallunrillemteggun aperturturluki tuqlutullruaput.

Cali-wa imna Nuyarralgem Atiinek pitullrat an'garpamtenek tuqlutu-luku. Tang tamakut tuqluuteput wangkuta ayuqellrunrilnguut, nurr'a-cungat, anaanat, anaanarpiit. Maa-i tang makut naken nunani allani uitangraata apertullrit, "Tauna tang nurr'acungavnek tuqlurarkauken," ap-

brother"] for his father. And one time I asked, "Why do you let us call him this offensive name?" They told me that it has been a *tuqluun* since long ago. We always called his late father our *angalleraq*. And I tried to pass this tradition down to my children, but they preferred *ataata* [father's brother]. They thought that *angalleq* was offensive like I did.

Because we knew them and constantly called them by their *tuqluutet*, I tried to have my grandchildren continue to use my parents' late father's and my late father's father's *tuqluutet*. Because his younger siblings used to call my children's late father their *qulicungaq*, I have tried to let his siblings address my eldest son with the same *tuqluun*. And his maternal nieces and nephews, his sister's children used to call [my husband] by the term *angacungaq* [little mother's brother]. And in turn I've tried to let my son's maternal nieces and nephews call him *angacungaq* as well, because I don't know how the term *uncle* is used. And the grandmothers, they used to call my late mother their *maacungaq* [little grandmother], and her paternal nieces and nephews, her brothers' children, used to call her their *acacungaq* [little father's sister].

And also, my younger sister and I are the only ones left in our family. Our other siblings, two males and two females, have passed away. My younger sister and I are the only ones who are alive. My late father, his nieces and nephews used to call him their *angagpak* [big mother's brother] and *ataatarpak* [big father's brother]. I am trying to encourage my younger sister to teach her children to use proper kinship terms, because we used to call our older brother our *anngacungaq* [little older brother]. We only used the Yup'ik system, and using the proper terms when we addressed our families, we knew them as *nurr'acungaq* [little woman's sister's child], *nurr'aq*, and so forth. And that homely and unattractive-looking woman whom I adored very much, they used to let me call her my *nurr'acungaq*. And the Father of Piunri, they had us call him our *uurapak*, though I didn't understand why. Those were the *tuqluutet* that we always used, and we never called them by their actual names. We always used the *tuqluutet* that were taught to us when we addressed our immediate and extended family members.

And the man they called the Father of Nuyarralek, we used to call him our *an'garpak*. The *tuqluutet* that we used were terms such as *nurr'acungaq*, *anaanat* [mother's sisters], *anaanarpiit* [big mother's sisters]. They used these terms to address them even though they lived in other villages, and

qaarluku caullranek. Tua-i-am tuaten tangerqumteggu tauna-llu atra aper-tuqatgu, taukut nunat apertuqatgu, tua-i waniwa tauna imna tuaggun tuq-lullrat. Kesianek tuqluutekiullrit wangkuta angayuqamta, augkut ava-i apertullrenka anaanat, acacungaat, nurr'acungaat, an'garaat. Tamakut na-lluvkenaki wangkuta tuqlurturatullrukput atritnek-llu arivqaqsuunaki. Arivarcaaqellemni ilurairutma Joseph-am atallran nunullruanga, ik'atak-gguq aulukliniunga-gguq. Arivcaaqellemni atranek tuqlunripaalugluku nunurlua tuaten nunurnganii qanleqtuutetullrukiinga.

Ava-i augkut cat tuqluutet aperturturaranka. Tua-i angayuqamta, "Una-wa pikeken, ataatan, acacungaan, an'garaan, nurr'acungaan." Una taugaam cali uurapak wiinga tua-i taringellrunrilamku, tua-i-am ellii Piunrim Atii tuqlutullruluku uurapamtenek. Tua-i nalluluki Kass'atun nal-lullemteni tamaa-i apertullritgun taugaam tuqlurturatullruaput. Uum-llu waniwa Kangrilnguum aatallra angalleramtenek, ilaita-llu arnat ui-cunga'urlumeggnek, ataatayagameggnek, ataatameggnek. Maa-i makut tuqluutellret kinguvarcetengnaqsaaqluki-llu wii makunun tutgaramnun aanaurtellrianun, aataurtellrianun. Tua-llu qanerluteng uncle-an, ataa-tarcecilriamek-llu niicuunii. Angutek ukuk anngaqlutek tua-llu irniang-lutek, ataataqarkauluku tauna tua-i, ayuqluni, taugken maa-i, "Uncle-an, uncle-an, uncle-an." Arnam taugken, arnauluni tauna irniangluni, tauna-llu anelgutii angutnguluni, taum arnam uyuraa angutnguluni. Arnam ir-niani piciqai "Tua-i tang angacungaan wall'u angagpiin-llu." Tang maa-i makut tuaten ayuqelriit tuqluutet. Maa-i-llu tungelquq'ngermeng nalluya-gucimalriacetun ayuqluku. Tamana tamaa-i kataumariluni.

Paul John: Tua-llu wiinga aipaqa cimiritellruyaaqaqa tuqluutmek atau-cimek. Amkut Kangirnarmiut aiparma arrsaulluaqellinikai, tua-i-am tuq-luutnguluni. Tua-i-am wiinga quyurniqallerkaa aiparma umyuaqluku piaqa, "Tua-i tang arrsaulluaq una cimiquni Atmaulluarmun assinruyal-ria."

Wassilie Evan: Wiinga apa'urluqa Napaskiarni ellangellemni aug'um apa'urluma imkut, ilurani-llu imna Taawam-wa atii, Assiyam-wa aaniin uncle-aaqlikii tauna, apa'urluma tuqlutullrua yagulluaminek. Iluriurutek-luku yagullua. Elliin-llu cali cali answer-aaraqluku yagulluamek.

Tuamtellu cali Napaskiarni cali cunawa apa'urluqa waten pinauraa, apa'urluminek pivkenaku waten pilallrua, "Apacikaa." Tua-i wiinga-llu taum apa'urlurma apertuutellrani tamatumek aturaqluku. Pia-i-llu kiug-kut taum Assiyam aaniin, Taawam kinguvri kia-i kiugkut, Taawaq augna

when one went to another village and they asked who he was, they'd say to him, "You are supposed to call that person your *nurr'acungaq*." Those were the *tuqluutet* that our parents taught us, those names that I mentioned earlier, including *anaanat, acacungaat, nurr'acungaat, an'garaat*. We always called them by those names and never their real names. When I accidentally called my late *iluraq* Joseph by his actual name, his father scolded me and said how shameful it was that I was trying to do things on my own. When I called him once by his name without thinking of using his *tuqluun*, he scolded me. He instantly corrected me sternly as if he was scolding me.

I have been mentioning those *tuqluutet*. Our parents said to us, "This person is your so-and-so, your *ataata, acacungaq, an'garaq, nurr'acungaq*." But I did not understand why we called the Father of Piunriq our *uurapak*. We did not know how to speak English back then, but we used terms they taught us to address our families. And we used to call Paul John's father our *angalleq*, and some women would call him their *uicunga'urluq* [little cross-cousin] or *ataatayagaq* [cute little father's brother], *ataataq*. These were the *tuqluutet*, and I have been trying to pass them down to my grandchildren, those who are becoming mothers and fathers. But they say "your uncle," and I don't hear them using the term *ataataq*. Children [in the past] called their father's brother their *ataata*, but today they just say, "Your uncle, your uncle, your uncle." But in the case of a female, if she has a child and if her sibling is a male, she says to her child, "He is your *angacungaq* [small mother's brother] or your *angagpak* [big mother's brother]." These are some of the terms they used for relatives. And today it is like they have forgotten their relatives and how they are related. The knowledge of [*tuqluutet*] is lost.

Paul John: And now I tried to change one of the *tuqluutet* my wife used. Those particular people that live in Kongiganak could be referred to by my wife as her *arrsaulluat* [ones who are a little poor]. Keeping in mind that she might smile, I said to her, "It would be better if the term *arrsaulluaq* was changed to *Atmaulluaq* [One from Atmauthluak].

Wassilie Evan: Back when I became aware in Napaskiak, my grandfather used to call the Father of Tawaaq *yagullua*. He was probably Assiyaq's mother's uncle. In return he would call my grandfather *yagullua*.

And he used to call my grandfather in Napaskiak *apacikaa* and not *apa'urluq*. And I also called him this when my grandfather told me to.

yuunrillrulria, tamana-am pitekluku pilallruaku, irniari kia-i qaugkut tan'gaurlurnun tuqluutiitnek taum apa'urluma, pilaranka, yagulluamnek iluranka.

Agnes Alexie: Waniwa Cevv'arnermiungurtelqa akaurtuq. 1953-aami yaavet Cevv'arnermun ellillruunga. Maani ellangellruyaaqua kiani Negtemi. Taugaam waniwa tua-i irniangyuicaaqua, taugaam yuliamnek waniwa anglicarilua pilartua.

Cali ukunun irniamnun anglicaramnun makut nallunrilutacirramtun tuqluvkalaranka cakniluki. Kiimeng wani ukut wani Phillip Moses-ankut atallrat Angalgarmek pilallruat. Angataaramnek angakngamku, angataaramek pitullruaput wangkuta.

Tua-i-llu cali ing'um cali ilu'urma, cali uum wani Nurataam alqaan, ukuk wani, ing'um wani ilungama yaa-i qanlaryaaqeng'ermi, taugaam ciunganicetun qanyuirutellria apertuutnanrianga makunek canek tua-i nallungluki.

Waniwa ukuk wani Kangrilnguum ukut irniarugai wii tutgarqanka tayima ukut wani Mark John-ankuk ingkut-llu Jobe-am cali irniari. Tua-i-llu ukut Jobe-am irniarin tuqluraqlua wiinga Quqiimeggnek. Tua-i waten ilungarma ing'um pillruyaaqaanga, tuqluutepuk-gguq mumigusngauk. Ingna-llu ukut Nurataankut alqaat pillruyaaqluni elliin-gguq tutgarain Quqiiqsaaqaat, wiinga-llu-gguq Maacungaulua. Mumigusngaukuk-gguq taugaam. Maurluirutpuk-gguq imum wani Angalngaam, angataarama aanallra tutgarain, quqiimeggnek pituyaqaat, wiinga-llu-gguq aanallma aanii maacungameggnek piaqluku. Taugaam wii cangalkessuitaqa wii quyakaqluku taugaam tuqluuteka.

Cali imkut Nuralrinkut ilu'uqsaaqanka, ukut Nurataankut. Imna anngallrat Aluvirullugamnek pitullruaput. Tua-i tuqluutekluku tua-i Aluvirullugaq-gguq imna Nuyarralgem Atii.

Tua-i-llu ukunek cali waniwa mikelngurnek yaani Cevv'arnermi caliqallruunga allrakugni malrugni. Ukut wani *school*-arat tuqlungellruatnga, *"Hi Grandma,"* Itraqama-llu, *"Good morning Grandma," school*-artaita-llu *grandma*-qlua tua-i. Ing'um-llu cali atanrata cali *grandma*-qsagullua. Tua-i-llu wiinga umyuanglua akinaurluku akinauqernaluku maurluuyuumiini, Kass'amek tutgarangqerssuumiirutelqa umyuaqluku. [*engelartut*] Waten pillruaqa caqerlua, *"Good morning Grandpa."* Cunawa taqluni, tua-i taqluni tuqlunermek. Tuakenirnek tua-i tuqlunqigtevkenii.

And these people up in [Akiak], the descendants of Taawaq, Assiyaq's mother, using the same term used by my late grandfather for the boys, I also call my *ilurat yagullua.*

Agnes Alexie: It has been a long time since I became a resident of Chefornak. I became a resident of Chefornak in 1953. When I was small and becoming aware of my surroundings, we lived in Nightmute. I actually did have my own children, but I have raised children I have adopted.

Also, I have my children whom I raised call others by their *tuqluutet* that I know of, telling them that they are related to them in that specific way. They used to call Phillip Moses's late father *angalgaq.* I used to call him my *angataaq,* because he is my *angak.* We, the siblings, used to call him our *angataaq.*

And also my *iluraq* out there, and also Nutaraaq's older sister, those two, my *ilungaq* over there, though she talks to me, since she doesn't talk to me about my relatives like she used to in the past, I'm forgetting who they are.

Paul John's many children are my grandchildren, Mark John and his siblings and also Jobe's children. And Jobe's children call me *quqiiq.* But my *ilungaq* over there said the terms used for her and me are switched. And she said that Nurataaq's older sister had said that [my *ilungaq*] should actually be called *quqiiq* by the grandchildren, and they should call me *maacungaq.* However, she said that [our names] are switched. She said our grandmothers, the late mother of Angalgaq [who is my] *angataaraq,* her grandchildren called her *quqiiq,* and they called my late mother's mother *maacungaq.* I don't mind and am grateful for the *tuqluun* they use for me.

Nuralriq and Nurataaq and their siblings are actually my cousins. We used to call their older brother *aluvirullugaq. Aruvirullugaq* was the *tuqluun* of the Father of Nuyarralek.

I also worked for two years with children at Chefornak. These school students started saying this to me: "Hi Grandma." When I would come into the school they'd say, "Good morning, Grandma," and I was also a grandma to their schoolteachers. And I became a grandma to the principal, also. And then I had an idea to repay him, because I did not want to be his grandma, keeping in mind the fact that I did not want a white person for a grandchild anymore. [*laughter*] I said to him one day, "Good morning, Grandpa." He quit after that, he quit calling me [Grandma].

Phillip Moses: Yaa ava-i augna tuqluun qanrutkeqernaluku. Wiinga tuq-luuteka makunun ayuqaituq. Naken-llu ayuqiinek niiteksaunii tuqluu-tekegcilaryaaqelriit cameggnek. Waniwa makut wani apa'urluqestema Apamcimeggnek piuratuatnga. Kumegnaqluni man'a tuqluuteka piuq [*engelartut*]. Angakestema-llu Angamcimeggnek. Tua-i kumkerrlainar-lua tua-i [*engelartut*]. Maani-llu kia yuut amlleret tanglaryaaqekenka tuq-luutmeggnek pilaryaaqelriit, niicuitaqa tuqluuteka wii ilamteni yugnek. Tua-i pimcirrlainarmeggnek taugaam tuqluraatnga tua-i [*engelartut*].

Cevv'arnermiut ingkut yaa-i engellekluki Niugtarmiut, Tununermiut-llu tua-i cakaqamegtenga pimcimeggnek pinauraatnga [*engelartut*]. Tua-ten tua-i ayuqua. Tuar ilaita ataatakestema-llu ataatameggnek piaqatnga quyanrilaama. Tuaten tua-i ayuquq.

Tua-i aug'umek una tuqluun, iluraq una arcaqerluni amllerrluni, pika-ken iluraminek. Imucetun alngaulriacetun ayuquq. Naruyaqluku ilurani, iluriurutnguluni Naruyaq, Qanervik, Qatngun. Tamaa-i tamakut Na-ruyam uum iluraam tuqluutai peksagtellriacetun ayuqluteng. Imumek *number*-aacetun ayuqelriaruluni tuaten umyuartequtellemni. Caminek una qat'ngutminek-llu pikan, tuaggun tua-i elitaqa'artarkauluku tauna pis-tii. Augna-llu ava-i Piunriim Atii qanrutkekiit—iluqaacugmek pivkalall-ruat. Tua-i tamaa-i ayuqevkenani iluriurun. Tuaten ayuquq. Waten augna amllertaqerluku qanrutkaqa.

Phillip Moses: I want to speak a little bit about a *tuqluun*. My *tuqluun* is one of a kind. And I have not heard a similar one anywhere, even though some people have wonderful terms that their relatives call them. My grandchildren always call me their *apamcik*. The term they use suggests that I'm cute and lovable. And my maternal nieces and nephews call me their *angamcik*. They are always fond of me. [*laughter*] And though I've heard many terms used for various people around there, I never hear a *tuqluun* that is similar to mine among us Yupiit. The terms they use for me suggest that I'm cute and lovable.

My relations from Chefornak to Newtok and Tununak, when they address me by my *tuqluun*, the terms they use suggest that I'm cute and lovable. It is because I get unhappy when my paternal nieces and nephews call me *ataata*. That is how it is.

Starting from an *iluraq*, the terms used for close cousins and distant cousins become numerous. The terms are used like signatures or indicators. One's *iluraq* can be called *naruyaq* [sea gull], *qanervik*, or *qat'ngun*. The term *naruyaq* for an *iluraq* can be known by people near and far. As I was thinking about it, it works like an identification number. If someone addresses someone as his *qat'ngun*, they would instantly know who he is. And they just spoke about the Father of Piunriq — they used to have me call him *iluqaacuk*. All the names for cousins are different. That is what it is like. This is all I will say about that subject.

CHAPTER 8

Eyagyarat

Atuqengaput tamalkumta nunami maani eyagkun
taugaam nepaunateng piarkaullinilriit

(135) Frank Andrew, October 2001:5

Makut tang atuqengaput tamalkumta nunami maani eyagkun taugaam elluarrluteng, nepaunateng piarkaullinilriit, yuuyaraput, akluput, makut-llu aulukaaput tamalkuita akluput, nerangnaqsarat piciatun, ataucikun eyagyarakun. Atuqengarput tamalkurmi tua-i inerquusngaluni, tuaten atuusqevkenaku, tuaten-llu yuusqevkenata. Yuuyaraq-llu neryaraq-llu ca tamarmi man'a atuqengarput inerquucetarluni. Inerquatii navgur-pek'naku yuulria tua-i-gguq eyanqegtuq. Eyagyaram-llu piningqercetar-kauluku.

Eyagyarat

(136) Frank Andrew and Alice Rearden, September 2000:32

Frank Andrew: Uuggun-llu waniwa inerquutaq'laraput. *Hospital*-aani-llu maa-i mat'um nalliini yurvirluta yuungcaristem temvut cuqluku inerqularaakut, neqem-llu ilii atunriisqelluku, wall'u cuq'lirluku tauten pitalriamek taumek aturtelluta pisqelluta iralut taukut aturluki. Wall'u temvut una inerquulluta tuaten pitalriamek pilagtullemta kinguani ui-tasqelluta caksaunata, taukut taugaam naakata nutaan piyugngarisqe-lluta. Tauna tua-i eyagyaraq. Lent. Eyagyaramek yugni qanlartukut. Ca tamarmi eyagkun taugaam aturyaraullinilria. Eyallni aturluku yuum pi-

Abstinence Practices

Everything we use here on earth can only be done harmoniously through following *eyagyarat*

(135) Frank Andrew, October 2001:5

Everything we use here on earth can only be done harmoniously through following *eyagyarat* [abstinence rules], our way of life, our clothes and belongings, tools and equipment we use in our daily living and the various subsistence activities. We are admonished about everything we do, not to use it a certain way, not to live a certain way. Our way of life and the way we eat, everything that we do has an admonishment. It is said that one who lives strictly following abstinence rules is referred to as *eyanqellria*. And a person can be strong and healthy by following and living by *eyagyarat*.

Traditional abstinence practices following birth, death, illness, and first menstruation

(136) Frank Andrew and Alice Rearden, September 2000:32

Frank Andrew: They even give us specific instructions to follow in the hospitals these days. The doctor prescribes and gives us restrictions after examining our bodies and tells us not to eat certain foods, or they limit it and ask us to eat only a certain amount within those months, or they tell us to rest and stay inactive after surgery, only to work after a certain amount of time. That is *eyagyarat*. It is like Lent. We Yupiit say *eyagyarat*. It appears that restrictions and limitations must be followed for everything we do. If a person follows *eyagyarat*, he will follow the proper rules

kuni qanruyutmek navguingaunani eyagluni. "Waten pikuma waten pici-
qelliunga, inerquuteka atunrilkumku." Pinritengnaqsaraq waniwa carrlugmun, mat'umun-llu yuuyaramun, wall'u naulluutmun camun mat'umun,
assinrilngurmun. Eyanqellria-gguq yuk apqucim agtuyuitaa. Cangariyuu-
nani tua-i iquklisviminun temii. Imna-gguq taugken eyailnguq, taqtaqan
temni . . . una wani ayagyuallermini-gguq naulartuq kangllicamiu-llu taqluni; acitmun-llu eglercami temii pinialiyarturluni acitmun. Tuaten-gguq
eyailnguq tamaavet atratmuallminun tekitaqami apqucirkarturituuq
temii eyayuilnguq, qanruyutminek navguivakalria canek, kiituan enri-llu
navgungut. Tuaten tamana nalqigutengqertuq.

Alice Rearden: Niitelartua ilait-llu-qaa yuunriraqata eyagyaranek malig-
taqutarkaugut, wall'u ilait yuunriraqata, wall'u-q arnat wani cali angutet-
llu allakarmeng eyagyarangqerrniluki.

Frank Andrew: Arnaq eyagyarangqertuq angun-llu pitatekevkenateng,
aglenrrar, irnicuar. Waniwa ilakelriit ukut ilaseng anelguteteng-llu pikan
eyagarkaugut, mat'umek nunamiutarmek. Caranglluut makut, napat-llu,
ingrit-llu makut ungungsit-llu, yaqulget-llu, imarpiim-llu ungungssii, pill-
gucirluki yuusciigatuten. Ellaicetun nuniitnun mermun upagluten ellaicetun yuusciigatuten. Nalluarput yuuyaraat. Makunek-llu piinateng kass'artarnek. Ellangqerrluteng; unguvaluteng.

Tuamtellu nunam mat'um naunrai carangllui tamarmeng unguvaluteng, ellaluteng taugaam allrakum iluani piutuluteng; aturyugngiimeng
allrakum iluani wangkutnun, aturvikngamceteng. Ungungssit-llu allakarmeng-gguq ellangqertut. Wangkuta pillgucirciiganaki, carangllluurr-
luta-llu carangllutun yuuyaraat aturciiganaku. Wall'u ungungssiurrluta
—angyayagaurrluta, avelngaurrluta, imarmiutaurrluta, wall'u tuntuurr-
luta yuusciiganata. Nalluluku yuuyaraat. Allakarmeng-gguq ellangqertut.
Eyagnarqelria-gguq alikaat pikenrilamegteggu.

Imarpigmi inerquutangqertukut, nunam-llu qaikengraaku, allrakum
kassullranun yaavet cuqerluteng, pitungermi ciungani ilagautevkenani
pillerkaminun. Meq-llu un'a taryuq imarpiim mer'a—eyagnaq atuquniu,
irnicuaq, aglenrraq, wall'u aanani tuqullrukan, wall'u atani tuqullrukan,

for living by abstaining. [He might think and say,] "This will probably happen to me if I do not follow my admonishment." It is a way of avoiding things that are bad for us in life or sickness, things that are not good. It is said that a person who faithfully practices *eyagyarat* is not afflicted by illness and physical ailments. His body does not change up until old age. However, one who does not faithfully follow abstinence rules, when his body gets to the end of the developing stage. . . . they say from a young age a person grows, and when he reaches the top, he stops growing and he begins to descend, and as he comes down his body gets weaker and weaker. It is said that the body of an *eyailnguq* [one who does not follow traditional abstinence restrictions and has broken many rules] is more prone to illness while he is descending from his peak of development, to the point where his bones break. That is how that is explained.

Alice Rearden: I also hear that people are supposed to follow *eyagyarat* when their relatives die and that men and women should follow specific rules.

Frank Andrew: A woman and man have different restrictions to follow. There are rules to follow by those who just menstruated or certain restrictions one must adhere to for babies that are miscarried. If one's relative or sibling [dies], the family members must abstain from doing certain activities on land. You cannot be out on the land with plants, trees, mountains, land animals, birds, and sea mammals. You cannot move to the water with them and live like them. We do not know how they live. They do not go to the store and buy foods like us. They are alive and aware of their own surroundings and environment.

And plants that grow on earth are all alive and aware, but they only live during a certain time of year, because we can use them only during that time. They also say animals have their own sense of awareness. We cannot live with them, and we cannot transform ourselves into plants and live with them. And we cannot become land animals like shrews, mice, mink, or caribou and live like them. We don't know how they live. They say that they have their own sense of awareness. They are afraid of a person who has to follow traditional abstinence practices, because it is not their way.

We are admonished about the ocean and even the land, that we are not to participate [in subsistence and harvesting activities] out in the ocean or even on land for one whole year, even though we have participated in those activities in the past. And saltwater down in the ocean, when one

wall'u anelgutni tuqullrukan, taryumi waten temni tungairluku ivrarngaunani. Qikertat-llu unkut qaugyat, kemni tungaunaku tutmarngaunaki. Tamana-gguq navkuniu yuk ipigglugiarkauguq.

Tua-i-llu tangvallrulua Kakianermek-gguq uumek angutmek, piyuanginanermini uyungqertaqluni tua-i iquluni maavet angutngurcami tua-i. Taum arcaqerluku inerquutaq'lallrua takumtenun wangkutnun, pitsaqutmek pinritellruyaaqniluni, nanikuangami taugaam pistekailami imarpiim mer'anun iverluni angyani tamana nunamun tagutengnaqellruniluku, iverluni tengteqatiini unavet et'ulriamun. Tamatumun irugni tuaten ellirnilukek. Angu pisqevkenata tuaten ellmitun. Wangnun arcaqerluku taum cali inerquutaqlallrua. Ungungssit-llu igtait tuatnakumta qinertaaresqevkenaki. Pull'uta-llu tungaunaku meq mer'esqevkenata. Tamaa-i tamakut inerquutet piuyaaqut, piugut. Temvut una aturluku pitekluku pimaut-gguq.

Alice Rearden: Ciin-gguq tauten pisqessuitatki, igtenun-llu? Apqucingyuartut?

Frank Andrew: Igtenun-gguq qinertaatulit wall' met'ulit pull'uteng takvialituut-gguq envanek ayagyuarluteng, kiituan ilait cikmirtut. Tamaa-i tamakut inerquutat ilait. Makut-llu taperrnat, imarpiim ceniini naumatulit, arnanun arcaqerluteng aglenrarauluki pisqevkenaki. Pania aglellrukan tamakunek angutngungraan-llu pisqevkenaku angayuqrulria, irniani-llu makut tamarmeng allrakum kassullranun. Nunami naumallratnek qecuktaqcesqevkenaku. Naunraat-llu makut acsat pisqevkenaki. Qemini-llu qeminun mayuravkenaku pisqelluku. Tuaten inerquarraarluta pinauraitkut, "Ayagyuarluten tamatumek navguikuvet taqmigpailgan temen alairngaituq tamana, taqmigeskan taugaam temen nutaan temevkun alairarkauguq assirpek'nani nangteqnaqluni."

Tua-i-llu tangvallrulua arnamek ataucimek milurtuuciqellriamek-gguq. Arnaurrluni, arnassagallerkani tua-i nuringaurluku. Arcarillermini qalrirturluni. Acia carringermiu taperrnat imkut *needle*-aaritnek cukiit-

is experiencing a situation such as a miscarriage, first menses, or when his or her mother dies or father [dies], or his or her sibling has died, one is warned not to wade in saltwater with his bare skin whatsoever. And one should not expose his skin and step on the sand on the islands down there. They say a person will develop arthritis in his limbs if he breaks that rule.

And I saw a man called Kakianeq whose knees would suddenly give in as he walked, and he would fall down when he became elderly. That person especially warned us [against exposing our skin to the ocean] and told us that he did not do it on purpose, but he waded in the sea water when in desperation he tried to bring his boat on land when the wind almost blew it into deep water and there was no one there to help him. He said his legs became like that because of what he did that time. He told us not to do what he had done. That was his most adamant warning to us. They also told us not to peer into the dens of land animals or to bend over and drink water whatsoever. Those admonitions still exist, they do exist. These rules are to help ensure good health.

Alice Rearden: Why did they ask them not to peer into dens? Would they develop ailments?

Frank Andrew: They say those who peer into dens or those who drink by bending over develop bad eyesight at a young age, and eventually some of them become blind. Those are some of their admonitions. And they also admonished us against pulling and gathering coarse seashore grass that grows on the beach. They especially told girls who had their first menstrual periods not to [pick grass]. The whole family, even the father, was told not to pick those if his daughter had her first menstrual period, and also his other children [were restricted] until a year passed. They were told not to pull them out of the ground. They also told them not to pick salmonberries and climb bluffs and cliffs. After admonishing us about that they would say, "If you break those rules, you will become sickly and handicapped as a consequence, and those ailments will not show when you are young, before your body is fully grown, but they will start to show when your body is fully grown. It will not be good and will cause you pain and suffering."

And I saw one woman who they said *milurtuuciqellria* [suffered from the wound the *ircenrraat* (extraordinary persons) had made when they threw rocks at her]. She had become elderly but had not become an old

nek unuaquaqan acia-gguq carrirturluku. Temiinek anluteng tamakut taperrnat cukiit.

Tuamtellu cali tamakut qaugyami unani imarpigmi tutmatulit-gguq
arivnerit makut imumek engiuringluteng, assiirulluteng tua-i cingillrit-
llu kankut makut-llu qiaryiggluteng tua-i. Tamaa-i tamakut pitekluki inerquatnguuq. Tamana eyagyaraq atullratni piyugngallerkaat amllerniluki
allrakut amlleret — allrakumi ataucimi uitaqaasqelluki pingraata. Yuk iv-
rucirturluni ivrang'ermi cangaicaaquq, cangaituq imarpigmi, qaugyam-
llu qaingani piyuangermi, kemni taugaam tungairluku inerquutnguut
tamaa-i tamaani pisqevkenaki.

Alice Rearden: Ciin-gguq kangiplugnek nerevkalartatki nervailegmeng
[nutaranek].

Frank Andrew: Tamakut tamaa-i aglenrrarnun pituut. Qemiliuqerraa-
qata'arqata-llu milqaquluki camek, milqaquluki-llu camek urr'armek-llu
pinaurait pisqelluki. Cikmirtetuut-gguq tuaten piaqata. Everrluki-gguq ii-
ngit. Imarpik-llu-gguq call' kan'a, angutet atrarngaitut tua-i. Tua-i-llu imkut qaleqcuuget nayiit-llu tekiskata, up'nerkami qalrialangareskata unani
nutaan camek pivkenateng atraryugngaluteng. Anaranga'artaqata-gguq,
nayiit-llu tamakut augata meciraqaku un'a, augun pitaita, makuara-gguq
merem cikmirtetuuq. Atrang'ermi qaill' pingairulluni, apqucirkaminek-
llu pingairulluni.

Tamakut-wa tua-i cuqait tekiskata qaleqcuuget. Tamakut tamaa-i imar-
pigmun piqarraatuut nunamun pivailegmeng. Tamakut-gguq tamaa-i
anaranga'artaqata unani mer'em imkut makuari cikmirtetuut-gguq. Cali-
llu imkut nayiit kameksautulit, imkut tamakut augit, aunranga'artaqata
pitait, aunranricuilameng unani, tamakut-gguq tua-i pinga'artaqatni eyag-
nairutetuuq imarpik tamakunun aglenrarnun. Cali-llu atani pikan ilani-
llu wall'u aanani ayuqluteng tua-i. Makut inerquutaq'lalput allaurtevkenaki nalqigtelaranka. Taugaam ayuqeqapiaranritut taugaam Kusquqviim
yuini. Kangitmun nunamiuqliit cali allakanek ilangqertut pavani nuna-
miut-llu.

woman yet. When her condition became worse, she would cry out in pain. Even though she swept the area underneath her, there would be sharp points of coarse seashore grass underneath her every day. Sharp points of coarse seashore grass would come out of her body.

And the joints of those who stepped on sandbars in the ocean would become stiff, and their ankles down there and other parts of their bodies would start to make cracking noises. That is an admonishment for that reason. When they had to follow rules associated with abstinence customs, they were told that there were many years when they could be active—that they should abstain for one year. Nothing will happen to one who wears waterproof skin boots when wading in water down in the ocean or walking on sandbars, but they were told not to expose their bare skin.

Alice Rearden: Why did they let them eat charcoal before letting them eat [fresh food following first menstruation]?

Frank Andrew: Those are rules prescribed for those who started their menstrual periods. And when they were going to climb bluffs and cliffs for the first time [after menstruating], they told them to throw even fine ash at them first. They say it blinds [the eyes of the *ircenrraat*]. The ash would get in their eyes and blur their vision. And they told men not to go down to the ocean until *qaleqcuuget* [grebes] and ringed seals arrived during the spring and started making noise down there. They say it blinds the *makuat* [tiny particles] of the ocean. When [grebes] start to defecate and when the blood of the ringed seals they caught soaks the ocean down there, the *makuat* that rise from the water [that act as eyes of the ocean and can see and do harm] get blinded. Even though he went down to the ocean, he won't be affected by bad health or injury in the future.

The arrival of the *qaleqcuuget* was their indication [that they could go down to the ocean]. Those [birds] come through the ocean first before going on land. They say the *makuat* down on the ocean are blinded when *qaleqcuuget* start to defecate. And when ringed seals that are made into boot soles, when their catch started to bleed, for they definitely bleed when they are killed, when those signs begin to appear, those who have had their first menstrual period are no longer restricted. And this will also apply to those who are practicing these restrictions due to their father's death or [the death of their] mother or immediate family members. I explain the rules we had to follow no differently than I heard them.

Yuum iliin taringutkaqaa man'a eyagyaraq. Nallua amllerem. Unguva-llermini eyagarkauguq piciungnaqelria iquklisviminun.

Augkut ava-i eyagyarat nalqigtellrenka tememtenun uumun pimaut, nangtequtekiurluta wangkuta navguq'ngamtenek uumek. Taugken man'a aipaa eyagyaraq, yuullemteni yuuyaram uumun yuucimtenun, qaner-yaram caliaqekiinun, qaneryarakun unguvaarkamun, unguvayugngal-riamun. Tua-i cali tamana tamaa-i eyagkun atu'urkarput. Inerquraakut qanruyutem assirpek'nata yuusqevkenata taugaam assirluta canun tamal-kuitnun yuullgutemtenun qanruyuteput-llu navguavkenaki. Eyagkun taugaam aturyugngaluki. Piluaqerarkauluta navenrilkumteki. Augkucice-tun cangallruvkenata aglenraraam tuqulriim-llu eyagyaraatun.

Alice Rearden: Niitelartua-llu temni-llu-gguq pinrilengraaku, makut-llu neqet wani piyugngai, iciw' neqa amlleq taivkarpek'naku wall'u-q' naunra-nek atsalugpianek pillrukuni atsaq wani amlleq wani im'urluku.

Frank Andrew: Tamakut-llu tamaa-i pimaut. Waten iqvaasqevkenaki inerquumalartut. Cataircetuut nunani tuani, avaqliitni taugaam catairtev-kenateng. Ella-llu una cali augna iqaicetengnaluku tamaani tamakutgun tuaten yuullemteggun, eyagyaratgun. Man'a atuqengarput tua-i eyagkun taugaam aturyarauguq tamalkurmi. Makut-llu taqellrat aipaimta tua-i. Eyagyarakun piyarailkuni alerquutaunani. Maa-i ca tegumaaqamteggu, aturaungermi-llu tauten puqlakun-llu iqairesqevkenaku pimanaurtuq. *Machine*-aq-llu tauten atuusqelluku tamakunek ayuqenrilngurnek. Ca ta-marmi tua-i eyagkun taugaam, inerquutekun. Inerquutem navgunritell-rakun tua-i yuum akluq'luaqerluku akluqsugngaluku, assirluni-llu ak'a-nun atuugarkauluni. Tua-i temvut una tauten ayuquq, yuullerput-llu una. Taumek waniw' yuullemteni una kangautarkaqenritarput temvut assinril-ngurteggun. Umyuamta piyullra maligtaquvkenaku, taugaam pisqutvut taugaam aturluku. Tuaten ayuqsugngauq. Tamaa-i ca tamalkuan takaq-luku. Waniwauguq una. Ca tamalkuan takaqluku, qigcikluku. Tua-i piluaqallerkauguq waniwa una takaqiyaraq, qigcikiyaraq.

But [the rules] are not exactly the same as the ones the Kuskokwim River people follow, and those who live farther inland. They have more rules to follow.

Knowledge and practice of *eyagyaraq* will help some people understand [life, nature, and the world we live in]. Many people don't know them. A person who wants to live faithfully and sincerely while alive must live following abstinence rules until he dies.

Those *eyagyarat* that I just explained are followed for the health of our bodies, and we will cause our bodies to suffer in the future if we break them. But this other kind of *eyagyaraq* has to do with how instructions work on and shape our lives, how we can achieve this [good] life by following the *eyagyarat*. We must live that way through *eyagyarat*. The instructions that we are taught admonish us not to live immorally but to lead good lives and treat everything and everyone around us with kindness and not to break the instructions we are taught. We can live that way only by following abstinence rules. We will be fortunate if we do not break them. [That type of *eyagyaraq*] is no different than the rules one has to follow after one's first menstrual period and after a death in the family.

Alice Rearden: I also hear that [breaking *eyagyarat*] not only affects their body, but also the fish. You know, the availability of fish will be affected, or if they had picked salmonberries, that they would not be plentiful.

Frank Andrew: Those can also be affected. They are told not to pick berries. [Berries] disappear from the area around their village but not from the surrounding villages. They also tried not to pollute the land by following *eyagyarat*. We must follow restrictions in everything we do. This applies even to the things that our non-Native counterparts have made. There is no teaching for it if there are no restrictions and directions attached to it. Even a piece of clothing has instructions against washing it in hot water when we are caring for it. And there are directions on how to use the machine. Everything [has instructions] through admonishments. A person can own that thing for a long time by trying not to break the directions attached to it. And it can be used for a long time. Our body is like that as well as our life. That is why we should not abuse our bodies as we live. We should not follow our minds but only do what is expected of us. That is what life can be like. We should respect everything. This is what it is. Being respectful of everything, honoring everything. Being respectful and honoring others is the way to lead a good life.

Nasaurluq inugualleq uksumi

(137) John Phillip Sr., Alice Rearden, and Theresa Moses, November 2001:157

John Phillip: Taum-am wani aug'um wani quyanaqvaa-ll' apluten aug'u-mek allauguullermek, inuguallermek. Aug'um wani arnassaagaam Jessie-m Arnaan, makumiunguluni, taugaam wani uitatullrulliniuq Luu-marvigmiuni tauna arnassaagaq. Payugquratullruaqa nallunriamku ar-nassaagaullra kanani canek unegkumiutarnek uqurrarmek-llu piaqluku. Naterkanek-llu piyugaqan itrautaqluku. Tua-i taum wani uucetun na-llungermia nallunrirlua quyaaqluni. Caqerluni tua-i taumek aug'umek qanemcitaanga apyutevnek. Elliin-gguq nasaurlullraullrani uanet'lall-ruuq-gguq Luumarvigmiuni. Tua-i piqerluni waten up'nerkami ella assii-rutlinilria. Cunawa-gguq-am tua-i iliita ava-i qanellruciatun inuguaq, irniaruaq ellamun anutellrullinikiit. Tua-i pircirturangelliniluni taqsuu-nani pircirturluni. Kiituan-gguq pirciinanrani pirtuum akuliikun makut yaqulget pilangut.

Atam ukut tua-i qaillukuangellinilriit. Qasgitarluni-llu-gguq tauna. Amllellrunritut-gguq. Qanemcitellruanga taum wani arnassagaam alla-neqlerminia tua-i agutellemni neqkainek. Taukut tua-i mikelnguut inu-guatulit itrutliniluki qasgimun nasaurluut nallaitgun. Itrucamegteki aqumevkalliniluki tua-i waten caniqliqu'urluki. Tua-i tamana picirkiun aturluku ellaita picirkiuteng ak'a aturluku yuaqatarluku tauna wani inu-gualleq. Ellii-gguq tua-i uaqlikacagauluni kiatiini uitallruuq.

Imumek tua-i unrapigarmek cakicillinilriit muragmek taktuamek. Tua-i assinricaaqvaa-ll' tamatumi. Qasgimun agulluki tua-i umyualku-teksagulluteng tamakut paniteng wani. Qasgimun tagulluki ciuqliq una tua-i amelgakun kapluku mayurtaqluku. Tua-i piunrirluni. Pakemna-gguq qanernaurtuq, "Allaugu-u-uq." Anuqa taigaqluni tuaten qanerluni, "Allauguq." Taum tua-i qanemcikellrua. Taukut tua-i ayagturalliniluteng, una tua-i yaaqlia tekiteqerluku, tungliurrluni taum pillerkaa, tauna yaaq-lia mayureskiitni nepaiteqalliniuq. Nepaiteqalliniluni ataucimek yaaq-lingqerluni. Pingayurraat uitaluteng. Assinricaaqengraan waniw' tamana tua-i tamatum allauguullrata. Taum elliin qanemcitellruanga ilagautellru-niluni taukunun. Nutaan tua-i tauna pellaluni, anlliniut ellakegtaar. Ella-kegtaar, akervagluni.

The girl who played with a doll in winter

(137) John Phillip Sr., Alice Rearden, and Theresa Moses, November 2001:157

John Phillip: Thank you for asking about the story of a girl who played with dolls. There was an elderly woman, the mother of Jesse, who was from [Bethel] but had resided at Lumarvik originally. I used to bring her coastal food and seal oil once I knew that she was an elderly woman. I used to go upriver to bring her sealskin for boot soles when she wanted some, too. Even though she didn't really know me, she got to know me and would be very thankful. One day she told me a story about what you are asking. She said that once when she was just a little girl, they stayed out there at Lumarvik. The weather started to get bad in the springtime. Apparently, one of the girls had taken out a doll during winter [breaking the rule prohibiting girls from playing with dolls in winter]. The snowstorm kept on going. And during the snowstorm geese arrived and began to fly around.

The residents got concerned and started to discuss what to do. There was a *qasgi* in the village. She said the village wasn't heavily populated. The elderly woman told me this story when I was a guest, when I brought her food. She said they brought the girls who owned dolls into the *qasgi*, just the girls. After bringing them in they seated them side by side. Following the age-old custom, they were going to look for the one who had played with dolls. That old woman said that she was sitting closest to the exit near the girls.

They sharpened the end of a long piece of straight-grained wood. What happened is terrible. Being in agreement, the parents all brought their daughters to the *qasgi*. They brought them to the *qasgi*, and then they poked the first one through the crotch and pushed her up [through the skylight]. Then she died. They would hear a voice from out there saying, *"Allauguuq* [It's not the one I'm looking for]." The wind would come, they'd hear someone saying, "It's not the girl I'm looking for." That person told the story. They continued on down the line, and when they got to the one who sat near her, when they got to her and lifted her, the voice stopped. The voice stopped when there was one girl left next to [my hostess]. There were three girls left. It's not a good story to tell. She told me the story and told me she had participated in what they did. The girl disappeared, and when they went outside, the weather was so good. The weather was beautiful. The sun was shining.

Alice Rearden: Amtallu-qaa iliini tang niitelalrianga pirciraqan ella-gguq yugmek yuartuq.

Theresa Moses: Pitangyugtuq. Ella-gguq yugmek pitangyugtuq.

John Phillip: Ici-w' tua-i ellangllunga'arrluni, tua-i ellarrlugluni, tua-i iliini-gguq pitangyugaqami tua-i tuaten, imarpik-llu ayuquq anuqvagluni. Picimariami-ll' tua-i ella qakemna piqerluni anuqlirraarluni quunqerluni kayukunani. Tua-i pinaurtut quunkacagarluni cakneq imna anuqlilleq ella. Tua-i-gguq qanercilaraat-am waten. Tua-i-gguq cirimciluni. Cirimciluni ellakeggaar anuqaunani. Tuaten tua-i niitela'arqa augna cirimciyaraq. Cirimciluni-gguq tua-i.

Tuamtallu iliini ella-gguq pitangyugaqami iliini errnaurtuq unganaqluni. Tua-i taumek murilkesqelaqait-llu tan'gaurluut. Iliini tua-i pirtunglartuq uksumi wall'u kiagmi anuqvagluni. Tamani tua-i tamakut iliini qanrucunaitelaameng ilait tamakut nall'arluki pilartut. Nall'arrnganaki qanrucunailnguut ilait pirciulluki ilait tua-ll' qerruluteng. Piciatun pivkenani murilkurallemni wii tamana tuacetun ayuquq.

Aglelriim eyagyarai

(138) Cecelia Foxie, May 30, 1993:5

Stebbin-aami arnaurrlua. Aanaka tua qanruskilaku tamakucimek pinilua. Tua-llu waten pelit'aam tunuanun kangiramun yaavet necuaralikilitnga. Necuaralikilia aanama, aqumesqellua tuavet. Tuani tua necuarmi uitaurlua neqkamnek taitaqlua, qang'a-llu merkamnek. Cetamani tang ernerni pillrungatua tallimiitni-llu tua-i tuaken aug'arlua tauna nayunrirluku. Tauna tua-i atullruaqa. Naquguterrlainarlua cali. Ankuma-llu nacarlua. Nacairesqevkenii. Yaaqvanun-llu kiartaaresqevkenii. Tua-i aturluki tamakut aanama qanellri niicuite'urlung'erma. Tua-llu cali waten. Up'nerkangluni-llu. Up'nerkaurrluni. Atratullrulriakut Qikertarpagmun. Tuall' aanairutma pianga nacairnarinilua maligtesqelluni. Qaillun pillrusia? Wallu-q' ararrarmek pillruunga? Uunguciiruskeka tang tauna. Nangertev-

Alice Rearden: Sometimes I hear when the weather is bad, it is looking for a human.

Theresa Moses: It is hunting with fervor. They say that the weather is going after a person with fervor.

John Phillip: Sometimes when the weather is hunting for a person, it turns bad or the ocean would get stormy and windy. And after the person had been captured and killed the weather would suddenly change, and everything would be calm again. The weather would suddenly be calm and quiet after the raging storm. When it does that, they'd say that the weather was feeling rich and possessed enough to sustain itself. That's what I've heard about *cirimciyaraq* [the way the weather suddenly calms after it captures a person]. The weather would be nice and calm without any worries about anything. . . .

And sometimes when the weather is hunting for a person, they'd wake up to a beautiful day. That was why they taught the boys to always be aware and attentive to weather. Sometimes it gets stormy in the winter or windy in the summer. Sometimes it seems to be targeting the ones who were mischievous and ignored instructions. Sometimes in the winter it would seem to be targeting such individuals, and when they were out it would get stormy, and they would get caught in the blizzard and freeze to death. As I've been observing, I've seen that happen. That's what I've heard about *cirimciyaraq.*

Abstinence practices surrounding first menstruation
(138) Cecelia Foxie, May 30, 1993:5

We were in Stebbins when I had my first menstruation. I informed my mother that I had started. Then they made me a little house in the corner behind the stove. My mother made me a little place and told me to sit there. So I stayed there in the little dwelling, and they'd bring me food to eat. And sometimes they would bring me water. I think I stayed in there for four days, and on the fifth day they removed me from there. I left that place. I was allowed to practice that custom. And I would always use a belt around my waist. When I went outside, I would always put on my hat. She would tell me not to remove my hood. And she would tell me not to look far into the distance. I followed every instruction my mother gave me, even though I was mischievous. And I did this also. It was begin-

kaqilia tua-i. Pianga iqelqugka nuagglukek anuqa una kanakneq atrarr-nguarluku tut'aqluku. Una cauluku tuaten piurturqilii. Cetamaulriit ukut anuqet. Tuaten piurarraarluki nutaan nacairlua taugaam naqugutertuar-lua. Tamana tua-i atullruaqa aanama qanerturallra.

Kanakneq. Negeq. Keluvaq. Ungalaq-llu. Taukut tua-i. Wangni tua-i ce-tamauluki taukut nallunritanka.

Ella maliggluku tua-i piurteskiinga tuaten. Ukatmun uivnaqlalria ella. Tuaten piurcetellrukiinga. Iqelqugka waten nuagarrlukek cayuguarluku wavet tus'artaqluku. Tuaten piurturluku. Nutaan-llu nacairlua.

Camek-wa negacungalleruarmek naquguterlua.

Tuani tua-i arnaurteqarraallemni aanama uumek taitaanga allgiaraam amianek. Taumek tungliisqellua. Tungekluku tua-i aturluku. Tuani-ll' imat'anem waniw' tuaken anngama, nangercama, erurcetaanga teq'umek. Teq'umek qaika erurluku. Tamaani cangalkessuitellruamteki teq'ucugniq-ll' man'a cangalkevkenaku nalluluku. Erurtellua tua-i tamatumek.

Imarpik qenqertetuuq

(139) David Martin, January 2002:131

Imarpiim qenqercaraa. *Meaning*-aara Eskimo-ryarakun imarpiim-gguq qenqercaraa, qingaryugluni-gguq. Tua-i tuaten aprumauq tauna. Ava-i ilailliqelrianek qanemcilriakut. Tamakucim-gguq taugaam navgaqani imarpik tauna qenqertetuuq, ella-ll' tapqulluku.

Nengaqerrluku, anuqvagluni, qairek-llu tamakuk imarpiim anguyag-tek tull'utek. Mer'em anguyagtek taukuk qairek qairvagluni aterpagcimal-riik. Taringaci? Qingaryugyaraq, imarpiim qenqercaraa tua-i ava-i. Ava-i

ning to be spring. It was springtime. We used to go down to Qikertarpak. Then my late, dear mother told me that it was time to remove my hood, and she asked me to go with her. What did I do? Was it a bit of ash they gave me? Now I'm confused about what they did. She asked me to stand up. Then she told me to wet my little fingers in my mouth and lift them up to the west and pull the wind from that direction down to the bottom of my feet and stomp the ground. Facing each direction, I did that. There are four winds. Then after I did that to all the winds, I removed my hood, but I continued to wear my belt. I have practiced that custom, following my mother's instructions.

Kanakneq [west wind]. Negeq [north wind]. Keluvaq [east wind]. Ungalaq [south wind]. They are the winds. I know those four winds.

She had me do that *ella maliggluku* [following the direction of *ella*, clockwise from east to west]. The universe naturally goes in this direction. She told me to pull the energy and step on it after I wet my little fingers with my saliva. I repeated that all the way around. Then at the end I removed my hood.

I was tied around the waist with some string.

At that time when I began menstruating for the first time, my mother gave me the skin of an old-squaw duck. She told me to put that between my legs. I put it there and used it. And I remember also when I came out of my little house there. When I stood up at the end of my seclusion, she let me wash myself with urine. I sponged my whole body with urine. At that time urine scent was natural to us, and we didn't think it was repulsive. She let me bathe myself with urine.

The ocean gets angry

(139) David Martin, January 2002:131

This is how the ocean gets angry. In Yup'ik *qingaryugyaraq* [feeling angry or displeased] is the word we used to describe that the ocean is angry. We just talked about people who are experiencing the loss of family members, *ilailliqelriit*. When one [in that situation] breaks the rules, the ocean gets angry and the weather would also get bad.

The weather would suddenly drop all of its restraints and become enraged and stormy, and the two waves, the warriors of the ocean, would plunge forward and hit. Do you understand? *Qingaryugyaraq* is the way

tuaten ayuqelliniuq. Qingaryugluni-gguq. Qenqercaraa imarpiim, ella-ll'
tapqulluku. Imkunek augkunek ilailliqelrianek tamakunek navegtengqell-
ria.

Mer'em anguyagtek qairvaak, navguilriik cikumek mamtungraan uksumi waten. Navguilriik, mamtungraan ciku navgurluku.

the ocean gets angry. The ocean would go into a rage, and the weather would also get bad. Those who break the rules after the death of family members would cause this to happen.

The two big waves, the warriors of the sea. In the winter they break up the ice, even though it is thick. The two break up the ice, even though it is thick.

Tuarpiaq Yuuyaraat Yupiit Teguq'aqsi

Elpeci-gguq ngelnguuci
(140) Elsie Mather, April 2001:186

Aug'um wiinga qanellranek cali paqnayugyaaqua, pim wani Qulic'am. Yuunrillrulria-wa qangvaq ak'arraurtell' Kuigilngurmiungullruluni. Qanellrulria tape-amni camani uitauq — ellii maa-i *eighty*-q tekitellruyaryugnarqaa. Tauna-ll' *nineteen eighty-four*-aami *tape*-ami uitaluni. Waten qanerluni, waten-gguq tang qanrut'lallrukait, waten elpeciirluci Qulic'atun, "Elpeci-gguq waniwa ngelnguuci."Tua-ll' alerqualuki qaill' pillerkaitnek. Paqnayulartua alerquataitnek tamakunek. Iciw' yuucirkaq man'a, yuucimta cimillerkaa tangerrluki ngelnguniluki. Ngelnguluteng tua-i pitatai.

Nirturluki-gguq tegganrita tamakut pillruit, ellait tua-i ngelnguniluki, aarcirturluki-llu cali, taugaam aarcirtuutait alerquutait niitellrunritanka. Tekiskata makut maa-i Kass'at cat-llu tekiskata qaill' piluki yuusqelluki, ngelnguniluki.

Tuarpiaq yuuyaraat Yupiit teguq'aqsi
(141) Paul John, April 2002:8, 11

Tua-i-ll' maa-i wiinga quyakeqapqapiarala'arqa elpeci waten man'a ciuliat caciryarallrat kangiitulangavciu, wii tamana quyatekqapqapiararqa cakneq. Maa-i ciuliaput wangkuta iquggiqaumastaini aug'um nangqapigteksailamta. Imutun tuarpiaq waniwa teguviirutqatakacagarluku, ca ig-

CHAPTER 9

Catching the Yup'ik Way of Life

They say you are the last generation
(140) Elsie Mather, April 2001:186

I'm also curious about what Qulic'aq [Adolf Jimmie] said. He passed away some time ago, and he was from Kwigillingok. He said, and it is in my tapes over there — he probably would have reached the age of eighty today. That is in a tape from 1984. He said that in the past they used to tell them, and I am going to say it like Qulic'aq did, "*Elpeci-gguq waniwa ngelnguuci* [You are the last generation (after which change will occur)]." Then [their elders] would instruct them about how to live. I am curious about what he was instructed. They told them that they were the last generation, after realizing that our way of life was going to change. Those his age were the last generation.

He said that their elders pointed to them and said that they were the last generation and warned them and told them what they should do, but I didn't hear their warnings and teachings. When the white people and people from other lands came, they instructed them on how they should live and said that they were the last generation.

It seems as though you have caught the Yup'ik way of life
(141) Paul John, April 2002:8, 11

And today I am extremely grateful that you are starting to ask about our ancestors' way of life. Those few of us who experienced the lives of the last generation are still here. It seems as though you have caught the Yup'ik way of life that was almost impossible to catch and about to fall, as you

teqatarluku teguq'aqsi tuarpiaq, yuuyaraat Yupiit, apqaungarrluci mat'u-mek nutem ciuliat qaill' yuucillratnek. Tuarpiaq waniw' ilumun teguq'aqsi cip'ngivailegpeciu. Elitnauyunaqluci cat'airutengramta ciuliat caciryarall-ratnek elitnauyunaqluci. Tuqungramta elpeci kinguqlirpecenun aturar-karpecenek elitnauyunaqluci.

Wiinga qunukenritqapiararqa yuuyararput man'a nutemllarput kalikar-mun eklerkaa qunukenritqapiararqa *tape recorder*-aanun-llu call' eklerkaa qunukenritqapiarluku unguvaurngailamta, kingumteni tamakut igautelci qanelput-llu kingumteni *tape*-anelkuneng kinguliamtenun meqsulrianun, yuucirkamek meqsulrianun mer'utkelarciqngatki, yuucirkamek meqsul-riit. Wii ava-i umyuaqa kiugaqa. Qanelqa *tape*-anun igaulluki-llu qanel-put pimallerkaa wii qunukenritkacagarniluki ukut qanrutanka.

started to ask about the traditional way of life of our ancestors. Indeed, it seems as though you just grabbed onto it before it fell out of reach. It is possible to instruct you, and even though we may be gone soon, we can teach about our ancestors' way of life. We still can teach you our ancestors' values and traditions, which you can pass onto your descendants.

I am not stingy about putting our traditional way of life in books what-soever, and I am not stingy about putting it in tape recorders, because we will not always be alive, because if they are in tapes they can give the things that you wrote and the things that we said to our young people who are thirsty to learn our way of life. This is my opinion. I am telling these people here that I am not stingy about our words being recorded onto tapes and being written down whatsoever.

Glossary

A number of Yup'ik words — those that have no concise English equivalent or are being used in a special sense directly related to oral instruction — have been carried over into translations and are included in this glossary. Adages and verb and noun phrases as well as nouns appearing only once and immediately followed by full translations in the text are not included. Generally, unpossessed nouns ending in *q* are singular, *k* dual, and *t* plural. The *Yup'ik Eskimo Dictionary* (Jacobson 1984) is the source of many of the definitions and etymologies that follow.

aarcirtuutet. Warnings.

aatailnguq. One without a father.

acuniaqengat. Illegitimate children.

agamyak. One who is unsettled or restless, yearning to be elsewhere.

aipaiput. Our counterparts, partners, used to refer to Kass'at (white people).

akusrarutekiyaraq. Act of fooling around, making a commotion, and engaging in physical activity without purpose, especially illicit sexual relations.

alerquun/alerquutet. Law/laws, instruction/instructions, prescription/ prescriptions, from *alerqur-,* "to tell to do something, to advise, to regulate."

allaniuryaraq. Way of treating *allanret* (guests, strangers).

allanret. Guests, strangers.

ancurturyaraq. Way of being cautious and reserved.

angalkuq/angalkut. Shaman/shamans.

anirtaqulluk. "It serves him right," an expression used to declare a good or bad outcome to someone's actions.

apervikuayaraq. To confess or confide in someone about what is troubling one.

aqlii. Woman's scent or emanation, particularly from the lower body area.

arilluut. Waterproof mittens.

atellgun. Person having both name and namesake in common with another, from *ateq,* "name," plus *-llgun,* "fellow."

atellgutet/atellgutkellriit. Ones with the same name.

ateq/atret. Name/names, name-soul/souls.

aurneq. Vapor, particularly something thick and fog-like, sometimes associated with the presence of a ghost.

ayaruq. Walking stick.

ayuqucirtuun/ayuqucirtuutet. Instruction/instructions, direction/directions, from *ayuqucirtur-,* "to instruct."

caarrluk/caarrluut. Piece/pieces of dirt, refuse, debris, or contamination, with negative conotations.

cingumailria. One who gives others positive encouragement.

cirimciyaraq. The way the weather suddenly calms after it captures a person.

ella. Awareness, sense, world, outdoors, weather, universe.

Ellam Yua. The Person of the Universe.

elucirtuutet. Directions or instructions, from *elucirtur-,* "to give direction, to instruct."

evcuun/evcuutet. Tool/tools to remove snow from garments.

eyagyaraq/eyagyarat. Traditional abstinence practice/practices following birth, death, illness, and first menstruation.

eyailnguq. One who does not follow traditional abstinence practices.

iluq. Vocative form of *iluraq,* a man's male cross-cousin, friend, or intimate.

imarnitet. Seal-gut raincoats.

inerquun/inerquutet. Admonishment/admonishments, prohibition/prohibitions, from *inerqur-,* "to admonish, to tell or warn not to do something."

iqailnguut. Ones who are neat and clean, from *iqair-,* "to wash, to clean."

ircenrraq/ircenrraat. Extraordinary person/persons encountered in the wilderness in both human and animal form, sometimes referred to as little people.

issran/issratet. Loose-twined grass storage bag/bags.

ivrucit. Waterproof boots.

kalngaggaq. Small, simple *kalngaq* (storage bag), knapsack.

kangiliriyaraq. Giving someone the name of a deceased person, literally, "to provide with a beginning," from *kangiq,* "beginning, meaning, source."

Kass'aq/Kass'at. Caucasian, white person / white people, from Russian *kázak,* which becomes "cossack" in English; non-Native (adj.).

keggukarangelriit. Very elderly people who, after losing their teeth, grow a set that looks like animal teeth.

kelguqengyaraq. Telling another what someone else has said about him behind his back.

makuat. Tiny particles such as dust or ice crystals glittering in the sun, sometimes referred to as "eyes of the ocean."

milurtuuciqellria. One suffering from the wound the *ircenrraat* (extraordinary persons) made when they threw rocks at that person.

nallunairteqsiyaagyaraq. Being uninhibited, overly sociable.

negcik. Hooked gaff.

niisngayaraq/niisngayarat. Way/ways of listening, with the implication of understanding and obeying, from *niite-,* "to hear."

niiteqainalria/niiteqainalriit. One/ones who just hear things superficially, literally, "those who merely listen."

nukalpiaq/nukalpiat. Good provider/providers, successful hunter/hunters.

nulirruaryaraq. Condition in which a man constantly has sexual fantasies about a woman, causing his health to deteriorate; literally, "having a *nulirruaq* (pretend wife)."

piciryaraq/piciryarat. Manner/manners, custom/customs, tradition/ traditions.

piiyuumiutailnguq. One with no desire to live according to instructions or with no positive aspirations, someone not in need of anything.

piluguq/piluguuk/piluguut. Sealskin boot/boots.

pisqumatet. Sayings, ways of doing things, from *pi-*, "to say, to do."

qacuniaryaraq. Engaging in sexual intercourse.

qalaruyutet. Instructions, from *qalarte-*, "to talk, to speak."

qaleqcuuget. Grebes.

qalugnera. Its odor.

qanak. Roof board, small log from the frame of the *qasgi.*

qaneryaraq/qaneryarat. Word/words of advice, saying/sayings, literally, "that which is spoken."

qanruyun/qanruyutet. Word/words of wisdom, teaching/teachings, oral instruction/instructions, from *qaner-*, "to speak."

qasgi/qasgit. Communal men's house/houses.

qaspeq/qasperet. Hooded garment/garments usually made of cloth.

qigcikiyaraq. Honoring or respecting others.

qingaryugyaraq. Feeling angry or displeased.

qipumalria. One who is twisted.

qunguturat. Wild animals kept as pets.

qutegngalria. One who is arrogant and proud, acting on his own mind and desires.

takartaryaraq. Being respectful of others.

tatailnguq. One who is easy to ask things of, one who is quick to respond to requests.

tatervak. One who is stubborn and doesn't respond quickly to requests, responding only when yelled at.

tekitaq. One who arrives or moves from another village.

tuqluryaraq. Way of knowing one's relatives.

tuqluucaraq. Way to call each other using *tuqluutet* (relational terms), including variations on kinship terms, that community members use to refer to and address one another, from *tuqlur-*, "to call out."

tuqluun/tuqluutet. Kinship and relational term/terms.

tuvqataryaraq. Generosity.

uilgaq/uilgaat. Husbandless woman/women.

uinguaryaraq. Condition in which a woman has sexual fantasies about a man constantly, causing her health to deteriorate; literally, "having a *uinguaq* (pretend husband)."

ulevlalria. One who is talkative, literally, "one who is bubbling out," from
  ulevla-, "to bubble and overflow."

umyuallguteksagutellriik. Two in consensus, literally, "two who have become
  like minded."

umyuangqellria. One with good wishes toward others, one who is thoughtful
  and unselfish, one who uses his mind wisely.

umyuaqeggilriit. Those who have become wise, with strong minds, referring
  to elders.

umyuarrliqelria. One without good wishes toward others, shaman with
  negative thoughts.

umyugiuryaraq. Following one's own mind, both thoughts and desires; living
  without restraint.

umyuiqsaraq. To be depressed, have a troubled mind.

ung'aqercecingnaqellriit. Those who are trying to get affection from others.

uqicetaaryaraq. Sharing freshly caught *uquq* (seal blubber) and seal meat.

usviilriit. Ones with no reasoning, ones who lose their ability to think clearly
  or function normally.

Yup'ik/Yupiit. Real or genuine person/people, from *yuk,* "person," plus *-pik,*
  "real, genuine."

Tuqluutet: Yup'ik Kinship and Relational Terms

uruvak/amauqigtaq. Great-great-grandparent.

amauq. Great-grandparent.

apa'urluq/ap'a. Father's father, mother's father.

maurluq. Father's mother, mother's mother.

aata. Father.

aana. Mother.

caqun. Mother (literally, "container," from being contained in the womb).

ataata. Father's brother.

acak. Father's sister.

angak. Mother's brother.

anaana. Mother's sister.

anngaq. Older brother, mother's sister's older son, father's brother's older son.

amaqliq. Older brother (from *amani,* "over there," literally, "one on the other side of an area but not across a barrier").

uyuraq. Younger brother, mother's sister's younger son, father's brother's younger son.

alqaq/al'aq. Older sister, mother's sister's older daughter, father's brother's older daughter.

nayagaq. Younger sister, mother's sister's younger daughter, father's brother's younger daughter.

iluraq/iluq. General term for cross-cousin, that is, father's sister's son, mother's brother's son, parent's cross-cousin's child, parent's cross-cousin's child's son (male speaker).

ilungaq. Father's sister's daughter, mother's brother's daughter, parent's parent's cross-cousin's child's daughter (female speaker).

nuliacungaq. Father's sister's daughter, mother's brother's daughter, parent's parent's cross-cousin's child's daughter (male speaker).

uicungaq. Father's sister's son, mother's brother's son, parent's parent's cross-cousin's child's son (female speaker).

usruq. Man's sister's child.

qangiar. Man's brother's child.

nurr'aq. Woman's sister's child.

an'garaq/an'gar. Woman's brother's child.

ui. Husband.

nuliaq. Wife.

anngaruaq/cakiraq. Wife's brother, husband's brother.

alqaruaq/cakiraq. Wife's sister, husband's sister.

cakiq. Spouse's parent.

qetunraq. Son.

avaqutaq. Son, term used on Nunivak Island and in stories.

panik. Daughter.

tutgar(aq). Grandchild, parallel cousin's child.

iluperaq. Great-grandchild, parallel cousin's child's child.

maqamyuarun/maqanqaun. Great-great-grandchild.

neruvailitaq. Great-great-great-grandchild.

ukurraq. Son's wife, parallel cousin's son's wife, brother's wife.

nengauk. Daughter's husband, parallel cousin's daughter's husband, sister's husband, father's sister's husband.

amllerutaq. Relationship through one's parents, where one is related to someone in multiple ways.

ilu'urqellriit. Those who are cross-cousins, including *ilungat, ilurat, uicungaat, nuliacungaat.*

piarkaq. Cross-cousin.

qat'ngun. Cross-cousin, originally a reciprocal term used by those whose parents had engaged in spouse exchange.

ilakutat. Relatives.